The Success of India's Democracy

How has democracy taken root in India in the face of a low-income economy, widespread poverty, illiteracy, and immense ethnic diversity? Atul Kohli brings together some of the world's leading scholars of Indian politics to consider this intriguing anomaly. They do so by focusing not so much on socioeconomic factors, but rather on the ways in which power is distributed in India. Two processes have guided the negotiation of power conflicts. First, a delicate balance has been struck between the forces of centralization and decentralization and, second, the interests of the powerful in society have been served without fully excluding those on the margins. These and related themes are addressed by the editor in his introduction, which is followed by an essay on the historical origins of Indian democracy, and two further sections, one on the consolidation of democratic institutions, and the other on the forces which motivate or inhibit democratic growth. While the book offers a clear and coherent approach to the subject, individual authors have their particular take on the subject. It is this combination that will entice a wide variety of readers, from students on the one hand, as a guide to one of the world's largest democracies, to scholars on the other, who are looking for a new approach to this controversial and much debated subject.

This book has been written under the auspices of the Center of International Studies, Princeton University.

ATUL KOHLI is Professor of Politics and International Affairs at Princeton University. His publications include *Democracy and Discontent: India's Growing Crisis of Governability* (1991) and (with Joel Migdal and Vivienne Shue) *State Power and Social Forces: Domination and Transformation in the Third World* (1994).

*Contemporary South Asia 6*

Contemporary South Asia has been established to publish books on the politics, society and culture of South Asia since 1946. In accessible and comprehensive studies, authors who are already engaged in researching specific aspects of South Asian society explore a wide variety of broad-ranging and topical themes. The series will be of interest to anyone who is concerned with the study of South Asia and with the legacy of its colonial past.

# THE SUCCESS OF INDIA'S DEMOCRACY

*Edited by*

Atul Kohli

*Princeton University*

CAMBRIDGE
UNIVERSITY PRESS

CAMBRIDGE UNIVERSITY PRESS
Cambridge, New York, Melbourne, Madrid, Cape Town, Singapore, São Paulo

Cambridge University Press
The Edinburgh Building, Cambridge CB2 2RU, UK

Published in the United States of America by Cambridge University Press, New York

www.cambridge.org
Information on this title: www.cambridge.org/9780521801447

First published 2001

*A catalogue record for this publication is available from the British Library*

*Library of Congress Cataloguing in Publication data*

The Success of India's Democracy / edited by Atul Kohli
   p.   cm. – (Contemporary South Asia; 6)
Includes bibliographical references and index.
ISBN 0 521 80144 3 – ISBN 0 521 80530 9 (pb.)
1. Democracy – India. 2. India – Politics and government – 1947–
3. Central–local government relations – India. I. Kohli, Atul. II. Contemporary
South Asia (Cambridge, England); 6.
JQ281.S84   2001
320.954–dc21   00–067439

ISBN-13  978-0-521-80144-7 hardback
ISBN-10  0-521-80144-3 hardback

ISBN-13  978-0-521-80530-8 paperback
ISBN-10  0-521-80530-9 paperback

Transferred to digital printing 2006

In memory of Myron Weiner (1931–1999)
who led the way

# Contents

x   Contents

# Contributors

PRANAB BARDHAN is Professor of Economics, University of California at Berkeley. He is currently working on the political economy of governance and decentralization in the delivery of public goods and services, the effects of inequality on cooperation in the management of local commons, and the limits to redistribution posed by globalization. His recent books include *The Role of Governance in Economic Development* (OECD Development Center, Paris, 1997), *Development Microeconomics* (Oxford University Press, 1999) and *Readings in Development Economics* (MIT Press, 2000), the latter two books written jointly with Christopher Udry.

AMRITA BASU is Professor of Political Science and Women's and Gender Studies at Amherst College. Her publications include *Appropriating Gender: Women's Activism and Politicized Religion in South Asia* (Routledge, 1998), and "The Transformation of Hindu Nationalism: Towards a Reappraisal," in Francine R. Frankel, Zoya Hasan, Rajeev Bhargava, and Balveer Arora, eds., *Transforming India: Social and Political Dynamics of Democracy* (Oxford University Press, 2000).

JYOTIRINDRA DASGUPTA is a Professor of Political Science Emeritus at the University of California at Berkeley. He is the author of *Authority, Priority, and Human Development* (Oxford University Press, 1981) and *Language Conflict and National Development: Group Politics and National Language Policy in India* (University of California Press, 1970).

MARY KATZENSTEIN is a Professor of Government and a member of the faculty of the Women's Studies Program at Cornell University. She is the author of *Ethnicity and Equality: The Shiv Sena Party and Preferential Policies in Bombay* (Cornell University Press, 1979) and *Faithful and Fearless: Moving Feminist Protest inside the Church and Military* (Princeton University Press, 1998).

ATUL KOHLI is Professor of Politics and International Affairs and Director of the Program in Comparative and Regional Studies at

Princeton University. His publications include *Democracy and Discontent: India's Growing Crisis of Governability* (Cambridge University Press, 1990) and *State Power and Social Forces: Domination and Transformation in the Third World* (Cambridge University Press, 1994). He is currently completing a book on the state's role in late industrialization.

SMITU KOTHARI is one of the founders of Lokayan ("Dialogue of the People"), a center in India promoting active exchange between non-party political formations and concerned scholars and other citizens from India and the rest of the world. He has recently been a visiting professor at Cornell and Princeton universities. He has published extensively on critiques of contemporary economic and cultural development, the relationship of nature, culture and democracy, developmental displacement and social movements.

JAMES MANOR is Professorial Fellow at the Institute of Development Studies, Sussex, England. His recent interests include Indian slum dwellers' relations to state agencies, politicians' survival strategies and democratic decentralization in Asia and Africa. He is the author of *The Political Economy of Democratic Decentralization* (World Bank, 1999) and *Democratic Decentralization in South Asia and West Africa: Participation and Performance in Comparative Perspective* (Cambridge University Press, 1998).

UDAY METHA is a Professor of Political Science at Amherst College. His publications include two important books in political theory, *The Anxiety of Freedom* (Cornell University Press, 1992), and *Liberalism and Empire* (University of Chicago Press, 1999).

SUBRATA K. MITRA is currently Professor and Head, Department of Political Science, South Asia Institute, University of Heidelberg and Visiting Fellow at the Center for the Study of Developing Societies, New Delhi. He has written extensively on Indian politics including *Culture and Rationality: The Politics of Social Change in Post-Colonial India* (Sage Publications, 1999).

LLOYD I. RUDOLPH AND SUSANNE HOEBER RUDOLPH'S most recent book is *Reversing the Gaze: The Amar Singh Diary, a Colonial Subject's Narrative of Imperial India* (Westview Press, 2000). Their current projects are: the politics of multiculturalism in India; the effects of economic reform on the Indian federal system; and a book of essays on Gandhi.

SUMIT SARKAR is a Professor of History at Delhi University in India.

He is the author of *Writing Social History* (Oxford University Press, 1997) and *Modern India: 1885–1947* (Macmillan, 1989).

MYRON WEINER was the Ford Professor of Political Science at the Massachusetts Institute of Technology at the time of his death in 1999. He has written extensively on India and other comparative issues including his well-known book *The Child and the State in India: Child Labor and Education Policy in Comparative Perspective* (Princeton University Press, 1991).

# Acknowledgments

Research and conferences leading up to this volume were financially supported by the Liechtenstein Research Program in Self-Determination (LRPSD) at Princeton University. I owe a profound gratitude to LRPSD's Director, Wolfgang Danspeckgruber, for the financial support as well as for enthusiasm, good cheer, and friendship. The two conferences – one in Vaduz, Liechtenstein and the other at Princeton University – during which the essays in this volume were crafted, would certainly not have been possible without Wolfgang's full support. Thanks are also due to Michael Doyle, the Director of Princeton's Center of International Studies that houses LRPSD. From behind the scenes, Mike provided the quiet encouragement that academic leaders need to provide. The intellectual role of a sizable number of conference participants – who cannot all be listed here – also needs to be acknowledged; not only did they make the Princeton conference lively, but their comments helped paper writers refine their arguments. Karthick Ramakrishan, P.S. Srikanth, and Maia Davis provided research assistance and Edna Lloyd performed the heroic task of creating a unified manuscript out of disparate contributions. Finally, thanks to Marigold Acland, editor at Cambridge University Press, for her encouragment, and to Jeffrey Hawthorn, an academic editor of the Contemporary South Asia book series, for his suggestions and support.

# 1  Introduction

*Atul Kohli*

As India held a general election in late 1999, the *New York Times* (October 8, 1999) editorialized about India's democracy in glowing terms:

As 360 million Indians voted over the last month, the world's largest and most fractious democracy once again set a stirring example for all nations . . . India's rich diversity sometimes looks like an obstacle to unity. But the latest election has proved that a commitment to resolving differences peacefully and democratically can transform diversity into a source of strength.

Even discounting journalistic overstatement and oversimplification, the editorial pointed to a significant phenomenon: for more than five decades India's democracy has succeeded against considerable odds. This volume seeks to explain how democracy has taken root in India amidst a low-income economy, widespread poverty and illiteracy, and immense ethnic diversity. How did India do it? What general lessons are drawn from this singular but significant experience?

The success of democracy in India defies many prevailing theories that stipulate preconditions for democracy: India is not an industrialized, developed economy; Indian businessmen and middle classes do not fully control the country's politics; India is anything but ethnically homogeneous; and India would probably rank low on a number of attributes of "civic culture." Indian democracy is thus best understood by focusing, not mainly on its socioeconomic determinants, but on how power distribution in that society is negotiated and renegotiated. A concern with the process of power negotiation, in turn, draws attention to such factors as leadership strategies, the design of political institutions, and the political role of diverse social groups, or, in short, to the interaction of the state and society. A central theme of this volume is how the central state in India deals with a variety of politicized social groups – ethnic, class, caste, or regional – that periodically demand a greater share of resources, autonomy, and self-government.

India's democratic record suggests that two related sets of political processes have guided the management of power conflicts in that country. First, a delicate balance has been struck and restruck between forces of centralization and decentralization. And, second, the interests of the powerful in society have been served without fully excluding the weaker groups. The record on both of these fronts is far from perfect; the failures have actually put a great strain on Indian democracy. Nevertheless, accommodation of those who mount powerful challenges by granting them greater autonomy and/or a share of resources has been central to a strengthening of democracy.

As federal democracies go, India is a relatively centralized state. While many critics have made this observation, the fact is that demands for decentralization only make sense within the context of centralized authority; authority and power, like wealth, have to exist before they can be distributed. Over the years, as democracy has spread, numerous mobilized groups in India have demanded further redistribution of power. These demands were often resisted, sometimes wisely and at other times unwisely and at a great cost. Overall, however, enough concessions were made so that the Indian political system by now possesses significant decentralized traits. Notable features of these are to be found in the practice of federalism, in the changing character of local governments, and in the evolving constitutional design.

No electoral democracy can long survive without protecting the interests of the powerful, whether these be propertied groups, groups with high status or groups with effective political organization. Long-term exclusion of weaker groups is also not healthy for a democracy. How has this balance been managed in India? While the rhetoric of the Indian state has often been redistributive – socialism, abolition of traditional privileges, reform of the caste system, and populism – political practice has been considerably more conservative, eschewing any decisive redistribution. The Indian state has thus been criticized both for its excessive socialist commitments and for its failure at substantial redistribution. However, the political impact of these twin tendencies – radical in tone, conservative in practice – may well have been benign, strengthening democracy: the powerful in society feel well served by the system but weaker groups do not feel totally excluded or hopeless, at least not so far.

This volume, then, analyzes India's democratic record by focusing on the interaction of the central state with politicized social groups, especially around demands for a greater share of resources and autonomy. The organizing proposition of the volume is that India's democracy has been strengthened by a political process that has facilitated a modest degree of redistribution of power and of other valued resources such as status and dignity, even if not of wealth.

## India's "successful" democracy

After more than five decades of periodic elections in which all political offices are contested, and in which all adults are qualified to vote, there is little doubt that democracy in India has taken root. Moreover, India enjoys free and lively media, freedom of assembly and association, and considerable scope to express political dissent and protest. Even India's founding national party, the Congress – which increasingly came to resemble a dynasty – has by now been voted out of power, replaced by other challengers. It is in these procedural or political senses of the term that India's democracy has succeeded, and that this volume mainly seeks to explore.

A more demanding assessment of the substantial accomplishments of India's democracy would clearly be more qualified and would require a different volume. For example, one could focus – though this volume does not – on how well India's democratic governments have fared in promoting economic growth. India's economic growth has generally been slow to modest, averaging 3–4 percent between 1950 and 1980 and 5–7 percent over the last two decades. Some analysts have suggested that this sluggishness is a result of ideologically motivated, excessive state intervention in the economy (Bhagwati 1993), whereas others have argued that this outcome is best understood with reference to the fractious nature of interest group politics in India (Bardhan 1984; also see his chapter below). Similarly, one could criticize – as other volumes have (Kohli 1987; Dreze and Sen 1995) – the feeble capacity of India's democratic state to alleviate mass poverty. The performance of India's democracy can also be faulted in other specific policy areas – for example, provision of primary education (Weiner 1991), or more broadly for governing poorly (Kohli 1990).

The success of India's democracy that this volume both celebrates and analyzes is less about its substantial accomplishments and more about its institutionalization. Critics may well ask: why focus "merely" on procedural issues? Several answers can be offered. First, a scholastic response of sorts is that no one volume can do everything. Second, some of the essays below indeed explore how "deeply" India's democracy has or has not taken root, and thus touch on questions of substantial outcomes. Finally, and most importantly, however, is a positive response: democracy is a valued end in its own right, and thus worthy of serious study in its own right. Whether democracy facilitates prosperity, or peace, or other "good things" are propositions worthy of a serious debate but far from settled. If citizens across the world clamor for democracy, it is not necessarily because of what democracy may bring them, but because they share a widespread contemporary urge towards self-government. Among poor countries of the world, India stands out as the most significant country that has successfully harnessed this urge into a functioning democracy. How and why India has succeeded is thus an issue of considerable scholarly and general interest.

Finally, this broad question of how and why democracy has taken root in India can be usefully subdivided into at least three interrelated but analytically distinguishable questions: how did democracy originate in India?; what factors helped democratic institutions consolidate?; and what forces propel or inhibit the process of democratic deepening in India? The question of democratic origins in India focuses attention on the role of political elites, and forces us to study earlier periods, especially political processes in the first half of the twentieth century. The issue of democratic consolidation, by contrast, concerns more recent develop-ments and is a broader one; it involves understanding why and how democratic institutions came to be embraced by the political public, including the opposition elites and organized groups. And, finally, the struggle for democratic deepening is an ongoing one. Here one wants to analyze the processes whereby India's unkempt masses are actually incorporated into the democratic system, that is, come to feel some loyalty to it, participate in it, and hope to benefit from it. This volume addresses these issues of democratic origins, consolidation, and deepening in turn.

## The origins of Indian democracy

India's "transition" to democracy in the 1940s is understudied and ought to be further researched. Historians have often left such issues to political scientists, and the latter often do not concern themselves with the "past," the domain of historians. Based on limited study, one argument in the relevant literature suggests that India's democracy is mainly a legacy of British colonialism (for example, Weiner 1989: chs. 5 and 7). This argument immediately runs into the problem of why democracy has not fared as well in so many other former British colonies, including in Pakistan. Nevertheless, the argument is a serious one and merits some attention, especially because the impact of British colonialism varied across its colonies. India inherited a number of political traits from British rule that can be argued to be significant for India's future democratic evolution: a relatively centralized state,[1]

---

[1] While some scholars may have trouble visualizing a ready connection between central-ized authority and democracy, it is useful to recall the important argument of Samuel Huntington (1968) that political order precedes and is often necessary for the subsequent emergence of democracy.

including a well-functioning civil service; early introduction of elections; and socialization of the highest political elite in values of liberal democracy.

As a contrast to this emphasis on the colonial legacy, other scholars emphasize the role of the Indian nationalist elite and nationalist movements in the birth of Indian democracy. Such an approach may focus more on the social origins of the nationalist movements or on their political characteristics. Barrington Moore (1966), for example, interpreted India's nationalist movement as a "bourgeois revolution" of sorts that helped clear the path for democracy. This Marxism-inspired hypothesis also requires further study, especially because it may help explain the India–Pakistan contrast; after all, the Muslim League that spearheaded the movement for Pakistan in the first half of the twentieth century was led by landed aristocrats who often had trouble mobilizing popular support. A more political argument may well focus on the important role of the nationalists in creating a "nation" in India (Varshney 1998), and/or on the practice of inclusive democracy within the nationalist movement.

The first essay in this volume by Sumit Sarkar contributes to this debate involving the respective roles of British colonialism and of Indian nationalists in the origins of Indian democracy. While acknowledging some British role, Sarkar instead emphasizes the role Indians played in shaping their own version of democracy, especially the combination of full adult franchise, secularism, and federalism. The British may have introduced some electoral politics but they also resisted mass adult suffrage. Adult franchise was eventually pushed forward by Indian nationalist leaders working closely with politicized Indian masses. Given India's diversity, crafting a unified nationalist movement also forced Indian leaders to develop conceptions of "unity in diversity" that eventually led to a federal structure – a structure that was quite distinct from what the British had in mind. And finally, the same diversity, but especially the Hindu–Muslim divide of the subcontinent, pushed nationalist leaders to counter the colonial divide-and-rule politics by crafting a pragmatic, political secularism that offered symmetrical treatment to various religious communities.

In addition to emphasizing the indigenous roots of Indian democracy, Sarkar develops a second important theme: Indians were not of one mind. Observing both long-term political trends over the first half of the twentieth century and analyzing the more specific political debates that preceded the formation of the Indian constitution in the 1940s, he analyzes two broad political tendencies. On the one hand, he notices that some Indian leaders argued simultaneously for full adult franchise, real political equality for a variety of religious communities, and genuine federalism with some decentralization of power. This was the political position of real democracy with the emphasis on suffrage, secularism, and federalism; a modified version of this position prevailed at the foundation of the sovereign Indian republic. On the other hand, however, Sarkar also notices that there was a significant dissent from this position, marked by silences on issues of adult suffrage, overtones of pro-Hindu religious politics, and a preference for a unitary, centralized state. This tendency can be characterized as one that preferred a more limited democracy. These early divisions among Indian elites lead Sarkar to suggest that there may be an elective affinity in India for democracy, secularism, and federalism. The contemporary implications of this significant historical observation are worthy of reflection: does the recent shift in India towards a more pro-Hindu politics threaten Indian democracy and federalism?

## Political institutions and the consolidation of democracy

While many former colonies in Asia and Africa started their sovereign journey as democracies, open and competitive politics took root in only a handful. India is the most significant example of democratic consolidation in a postcolonial setting and begs the question: how and why did India succeed? As one may imagine, there is no simple answer, only a large complex one made up of many parts, some of which are analyzed in detail in this volume.

When trying to understand how and why Indian democracy has taken root, it helps to think of India's recent political evolution in three distinct phases. Institutions and practices of democracy found considerable acceptance during the first phase, which was dominated by Nehru and which lasted from, say, about 1950 to the mid to late 1960s. Aside from Nehru's own commitment to democracy, India benefited in this phase from the presence of two very important institutions: a well-functioning civil service and a popular ruling party, the Indian National Congress (or Congress). The civil service constituted the heart of the state that India inherited from the colonial period, and India's "new" civil service was essentially built on this colonial base (Potter 1986). This civil service contributed to effective government and imparted political stability.

The Congress, by contrast, had spearheaded a successful national movement and, as a result, enjoyed considerable popularity and legitimacy. These new rulers of India, especially Nehru, utilized this inherited political capital wisely, accommodating rival elites within the larger political umbrella that was Congress (Kothari 1970b). Moreover, while Nehru and others employed the rhetoric of socialism, political practice was considerably more conservative (Frankel 1978: chs. 1 and 2). The Congress Party, for example, built its political networks on the back of the powerful members of society – often the landowning, upper castes – exchanging state patronage for electoral mobilization (Weiner 1967). This strategy enabled the Congress Party to succeed for a while, at least long enough for practices of democracy to take root.

Indian democracy was also helped by the fact that Indian political society in this early phase was not all that mobilized, certainly far less than in the subsequent decades. Political conflict mainly took the form of claims and counterclaims by rival elites, especially regional elites demanding a greater share of power and resources vis-à-vis the central government. These conflicts could have proven difficult but were successfully accommodated by creating a federal system that recognized linguistic communities as legitimate political components (see the chapters by Dasgupta and Manor below). Elite versus mass conflict in India in these decades was, however, minimal. What class conflict existed was limited to a few regions. Given India's political heterogeneity, such conflicts seldom spread from one region to another. Mobilization of lower castes was also in its infancy and was limited to a few southern states (see Myron Weiner's essay below). Most of India's poor were lower-caste, landless peasants. These groups were generally dependent for their livelihood on those above them, the landowning upper-caste elites. These vertical ties of patronage and dependency, in turn, constrained the political behavior of poor, illiterate Indians.

Democracy has often had undemocratic roots. India's case has been no different, as least not on this score. An effective civil service and relatively low levels of political mobilization meant that, unlike numerous other postcolonial experiments, Indian democracy was not seriously debilitated at the outset by poor governance and multiple political conflicts. The Congress Party further provided the key governing institution that not only transformed nationalist legitimacy into a ruling force, but also incorporated rival elites into a loosely knit organization and promised future incorporation to India's unkempt masses. While the Congress repeatedly won elections during this first phase and dominated India's political landscape, a broader political change was also underway: institutions and practices of democracy took root.

The second major phase during the 1970s and 1980s was dominated mainly by Nehru's daughter, Indira Gandhi. Indian politics during this phase became considerably more turbulent, even temporarily threatening democracy. As the memory of anticolonial nationalism declined, numerous new elites entered the political arena, challenging Congress's hold on power. A rapidly growing population also produced a new generation of potentially mobilizable citizens. The spread of commerce and democracy started undermining the vertical ties of clientelism that had constrained the political choices of the lower strata in the past. India's economic development was also relatively sluggish and elitist, leaving a majority without any significant improvement in living conditions. The political situation was by now ripe for dramatic changes.

After Congress's popularity declined in the second half of the 1960s, Indira Gandhi recreated the Congress during the 1970s and the 1980s as a much more populist and personalistic organ. The old Congress Party, with its modest organizational base, was destroyed in this transformation, creating a significant institutional vacuum in the Indian polity (Kohli 1990). Indira Gandhi instead promised "alleviation of poverty" to India's poor masses, generating considerable popular support. She used this popularity to concentrate power in her person, further undermining existing institutional constraints on the use of power. Indira Gandhi appointed loyal minions to significant political offices across the country, squeezed whomsoever challenged her, and when the opposition itself became strident – as it did in the mid-1970s – imposed a "national Emergency" for two years (1975–7), limiting democratic practices and bringing India's democracy to the brink (Brass 1991).

Indira Gandhi's personalistic and populistic politics definitely weakened some of India's democratic institutions. The old Congress Party was transformed into a personal tool that went into a slow but steady decline following her death. The civil service was politicized. Centralization of power also weakened the federal system, evoking strong opposition in some regions that did not readily accept loss of autonomy (Kohli 1997; also see the chapters by Dasgupta and Manor below). As in many other democracies, personalistic power simultaneously created a viable political center but weakened institutional politics.

The balance sheet of political developments during this phase, however, was not only towards the weakening of Indian democracy. Contrary trends also deserve to be underlined. First, elections were held regularly throughout the period, and political power remained a function of securing popular majority support. Even Indira Gandhi's personal power was a function of her widespread electoral appeal to India's poor masses. It was a need to reconfirm this legitimacy that pressured her to call elections after a brief authoritarian interlude (1975–7). The fact that she was voted out of power following the Emergency only confirmed the efficacy of Indian democracy: those who tamper with the basic system will lose popular support. Second, and related to the first

point, following the Emergency, a number of India's political groups –
for example, some of India's communists, who had hitherto held an
ambivalent attitude towards democracy – realized how much there was
to lose without liberal political freedoms, and became recommitted to
democracy. And, finally, Indira Gandhi sharply politicized the issue of
widespread poverty in India. Even while she failed to deliver on her
promises to the poor, Indira Gandhi thus broadened the scope of Indian
democracy towards a greater inclusion of the lower strata.

Indira Gandhi's assassination in the mid-1980s, and that of her son
Rajiv Gandhi a few years thereafter, brought to an end the era of
Congress's dominance via family rule. While democracy had taken by
now a firm foothold in India – note that even the assassination of the
highest leaders was "dealt with" by yet another round of elections to
select alternative leaders – the quality of government that this democracy
was capable of delivering remained rather uncertain. The critical issue
was the absence of cohering institutions amidst a rapidly politicizing
society. The third and current phase that began around 1990 has thus
been characterized by a variety of national-level political experiments to
find a substitute for the old Congress Party rule, especially by the
emergence of the Bharatiya Janata Party (BJP).

The decline of Congress's hegemony has been met by two important
political developments: the rise of the BJP, especially in India's Hindi-
speaking "heartland" that comprises states in north-central and western
India; and the growing significance of regional parties, especially in
southern India, but also in such other "peripheral" states as West
Bengal, Punjab, and Kashmir. The BJP is a right-leaning, religious–
nationalist party that has successfully mobilized support by simultaneously demonizing India's religious minorities, especially Muslims,
and championing causes that appeal to the majority Hindus. Over time,
however, the BJP has had to moderate its strident religious nationalism,
both to broaden its electoral support and to seek coalition allies. These
and related issues are analyzed below by Amrita Basu.

Regional nationalism has greater appeal than Hindu nationalism in
many of India's "peripheral" regions. A variety of regional parties have
thus become quite significant over the last decade or two. Since many of
these parties arose in opposition to the Congress, they often built their
power base around intermediate castes – the so-called "backward
castes" in India – that the Congress had failed to incorporate.
Championing the cause of their respective regions, and especially of the
middling groups within the region, these parties often tend to be
ideologically fickle. When it comes to participating in national politics,
they can swing more to the left, or to the right, depending on the

political opportunities available, and on the ambitions and convenience of their respective leaders.

This third and most recent phase of Indian politics has thus been characterized by considerable governmental instability. Whereas India's first eight general elections were spread out between 1950 and 1990, India held five general elections in the 1990s alone. The efforts to discover a viable substitute for Congress's dominant role are clearly proving to be difficult. Underlying this instability are two sets of forces. First, regional parties face the problem of collective action: they find it difficult to cooperate to form national governments on their own; and, second, the BJP has so far failed to garner sufficient support to form a national government. The BJP's religious extremism – while popular with some – was also an obstacle for the party in gaining coalitional allies. It was only when the BJP moderated its position towards the end of the 1990s that a number of regional parties joined it as allies, forming a national government that is currently in power as this volume goes to press.

Once again, however, it is important to juxtapose other recent institutional trends that can be viewed as supportive of democratic consolidation in India. First, as difficult as efforts to find a substitute for Congress rule are proving, it is healthy for Indian democracy that the hegemony of a single party, especially via family rule, has come to an end. Second, the BJP has been forced to moderate its ruling strategy. This is a singular victory for Indian democracy, underlining the fact that the logic of democratic institutions is by now clearly stronger than that of extremist forces. While there can be no certainty that the BJP will remain moderate in the future – extremism does happen, even in democracies – the odds set by India's current institutional matrix are against it. And, third, the new ruling arrangement in India represents a combination of centralization – represented by a relatively well-organized and hierarchical political party, the BJP – and decentralization – represented by a variety of regional allies. This arrangement is considerably more accommodating than the centralized system of Indira Gandhi; it may also prove to be less conflict-generating.

Against this general background of political developments in India, five essays in this volume provide more detailed analysis concerning how a variety of political institutions have helped Indian democracy take root. The first two essays are on the Indian federal system. How India has created a successful federal polity in a multicultural setting is a subject of considerable importance. Dasgupta probes the subject deeply in his paper, focusing on the underlying political processes of negotiation and collaboration between national and regional elites. Among the themes that he develops, three are worth underlining. First, evoking a theme from Sarkar's essay, Dasgupta suggests that the original design of Indian federalism was helped by the nature of the Indian nationalist movement. National unity was built while incorporating India's considerable multicultural diversity. As a result, India's Congress Party, even though a hegemonic party in the early decades, balanced centralizing and regional forces within its fold. This institutional development provided long-term "political capital" for crafting a successful federal system. Second, India's constitutional design – though mainly centralist – was also flexible enough to accommodate regional ambitions over time. Initially these constitutional balances reflected the real political balances manifest in India's national politics; over time, however, constitutional provisions became a force in their own right, molding the political process itself. And, third, the evolution of Indian federalism has been helped by the spread of democratic politics. Within the framework of a centralized but accommodating state, democracy has enabled regional forces to successfully press their demands. These successes were manifest early in the area of identity politics, namely, in the reorganization of India along linguistic lines, and over the last three decades in the struggle to share economic resources between the national and state governments.

Manor also analyzes Indian federalism in this volume, but more from the standpoint of Indian states. Manor's paper seeks to answer two main questions. First, why have relations between New Delhi and India's various state governments usually remained manageable? Second, why in some cases have things gone spectacularly wrong, so that violent separatist movements have developed and center–state relations have broken down?

To answer these questions, Manor's paper considers the various "management" strategies used by Indian governments in different times and places. He first focuses on two "reasonably typical" Indian states – Andhra Pradesh and Tamil Nadu. They are analyzed to show that center–state relations have never become wholly unmanageable in such "mainstream" states, even when national leaders abandoned accommodation and bargaining for commandist approaches. He argues that, in addition to politics of accommodation, sociocultural and other conditions within states help greatly to keep relations manageable. Indeed, he goes further, suggesting that no genuine separatist movement has ever arisen in a sizable Indian state (with a population of over 25 million).

His analysis then turns to three regions where breakdowns have occurred – Punjab, Jammu and Kashmir, and India's Northeast. The disasters which engulfed the first two of these regions were avoidable. These were the result of ill-advised, illiberal, commandant interventions from New Delhi. Conditions in those states differed from "mainstream" India in ways that made breakdowns, separatism, and ghastly violence possible – though not inevitable. In the Northeast, however, recurrent breakdowns, violence, and separatism were and remain inevitable. Even the most enlightened and accommodating "management" strategies from New Delhi could not have avoided such episodes – much of the time in nearly all of the Northeast. Manor concludes with a discussion of the realization – among many senior political figures in New Delhi over the last decade – that accommodative approaches are essential in dealing with all regions – troubled and untroubled.

Moving down the government hierarchy, what role does local government play in Indian democracy? Subrata Mitra investigates this question. The answers he provides in his paper are supported by an original and detailed survey of political attitudes within India. Mitra argues that, over the years, local governments have become more and more significant in India's governance. This process has enabled the political incorporation of village-level elites and masses. Not only have the links between the "center" and the "periphery" thus been strengthened, but new political resources have also been infused into the Indian political system. As a result the legitimacy of India's democratic institutions has deepened.

Within this broad picture, Mitra further documents that the effectiveness of local governments varies across India's diverse regions. Surveyed respondents evaluated local governments more positively in some states such as Maharashtra and West Bengal than in, say, Bihar. Mitra suggests that local governments are most effective when local institutions enjoy the trust and confidence of local elites on the one hand, and where local elites remain accountable to the local electorate on the other hand.

The last two institutional essays focus on emerging trends. Given the institutional vacuum created by Indira Gandhi's personalistic and centralized rule, what institutions or processes have filled the gap? Lloyd and Susanne Rudolph focus on the role of the Indian constitution or, more appropriately, on the role of some constitutionally provided institutions. They take as their backdrop a view that both the Indian polity and the economy have experienced significant decentralization in recent years. These deeper changes, combined with less deep ones such as unsavory leadership practices, have weakened some of India's central political institutions, especially a strong and stable executive. One of the reasons why this weakening has not been highly debilitating is because India has a reservoir of other constitutionally approved institutions. The

Rudolphs discuss the important new political roles of the judiciary, the presidency, and the Electoral Commission. Under conditions of a strong executive, the political significance of these institutions in India is generally dwarfed. In recent years, however, especially in the 1990s, these institutions have mitigated and moderated the potential damage that coalitional instability within national governments may have caused.

Finally, based on extensive fieldwork, Amrita Basu provides an analysis of the BJP as a political force in India. She argues that it helps to think of the BJP both as a social movement and as a political party. Whereas the BJP as a movement tends to be more radical – i.e., more extreme in its Hindu nationalist commitments – the BJP as a political party often moves towards the political "center." The paper both documents the BJP's back and forth movement from a more to a less extreme right-wing force within Indian politics, and seeks to explain these swings.

Basu suggests that the BJP chooses to be more or less radical strategically, especially calculating that, given specific political circumstances, one political stance is likely to yield greater electoral dividends than the other. Thus, for example, the BJP and its affiliates mobilized India's Hindus in the early 1990s as a movement that culminated in the destruction of a mosque; the BJP gained considerable electoral benefits as a result. However, when party leaders perceived that returns on extremist politics were declining, they engineered a centrist shift. More recently, therefore, the BJP has offered itself as a party of stability and good governance, a political position that has catapulted it to the position of India's ruling party.

While the BJP in the last few years of power has acted moderately, Basu's analysis implies that this moderation is by no means irreversible. For now the BJP is hemmed in by its coalitional partners. However, the movement versus the party dialectic, which is deeply rooted in the BJP, can readily swing back, away from the logic of a ruling party to more of an extreme religious–nationalist movement, pushed in part by "true believers" and, for the rest, by a need to further bolster its electoral prospects.

## Social demands and democratic deepening

Democracy ensures formal–legal and not socioeconomic equality. A growing embrace of citizenship rights by common Indians has, over time, given rise to numerous demands for more power and resources. Democratic institutions both facilitate such demands and are challenged by them. The balancing act that may facilitate the slow but steady deepening of democracy is never easy, and India is no exception. How has this process of democratic deepening evolved in India?

Over the last five decades, democracy in India has not only taken root but it has spread wide and deep. Before providing a thumbnail sketch of how this process has evolved, it is important to underline both its incomplete and complex nature, as well as its normative ambiguity. The spread of democracy has implied that norms and practices of democracy – not only independent voting, but also expressing dissent, and forming associations to press demands – have been embraced by more and more people, including those at the bottom of India's social structure. The resulting "million mutinies," however, have not always been well coordinated or organized; so far, they have not facilitated any significant redistribution of wealth or income. Nevertheless – to add yet another complexity – it may well be the case that this spread of democracy has prevented further skewing of India's distributional patterns. The political impact of democracy's spread has also been ambiguous. Democratization has weakened India's rigid social inequalities and thus made India's democracy more meaningful for the lowly masses. At the same time, however, the "million mutinies" have also stoked hundreds of political fires and provided ready material for populists and demagogues to exploit.

During the 1950s, a majority of India's citizens did not fully exercise their political rights. The idea of political equality and of democratic rights was rather alien amidst the age-old inequalities of a hierarchical rural society. Congress's early dominance of Indian politics rested heavily on the deference that Congress's allies, India's rural elites, were able to command from their social "inferiors." Over time, however, the spread of commerce and the repeated practice of democracy has eroded the dependencies of social "inferiors" on their "superiors," releasing numerous new actors for political mobilization. The political impact of this shift was already evident in the second half of the 1960s, when a variety of opposition parties mobilized these newly available political actors to challenge Congress's dominance.

Within Congress, Indira Gandhi was among the first to grasp all this; her populist sloganeering was aimed directly at new groups emerging from under the influence of traditional rural elites. Such appeals in effect closed the circle by stimulating further mobilization among the rural lower classes whose new activism it was meant to exploit. Her failure to reduce poverty in the 1970s and early 1980s made it difficult for her to consolidate her position with her new supporters among the rural poor, who then became susceptible to new forms of political mobilization. Their dissatisfaction has found diverse expressions over the last two decades that often vary from region to region.

For example, in the southern states of Tamil Nadu and Andhra Pradesh, the mobilized but unincorporated poor provided ready support to movie-stars-turned-politicians who combined personal and populist appeals to garner popular support (Subramanian 1999). In other states, such as West Bengal and Kerala, the poor have been more systematically incorporated by reform-oriented communist parties (Nossiter 1988; Heller 1999). Where caste inequalities were deeply rooted – as in the Hindi heartland states – the political emergence of the lowest groups has brought forth new forms of lower-caste politics (Varshney 2000; also see Weiner's essay below), either spawning new caste-oriented political parties that cater exclusively to such groups (as in Uttar Pradesh), or precipitating violent reactions from threatened higher castes (as in Bihar).

Along with the poor, the middling groups of rural Indian society have also become more politically active over the last two decades. These groups – especially the so-called backward castes – are the mainstay of the nationwide "reservation" movement, which demands that certain shares of government-controlled jobs and educational opportunities be "reserved" for applicants from certain castes (see Weiner's essay below). Demands of this sort often began with a "top–down" quality: leaders voiced them in the hopes of gaining votes from among the large membership of the backward castes. Over time, of course, backward caste members have become politicized, pressing their own case. Not surprisingly, such an upsurge has provoked a backlash from the higher castes. Some of the political turmoil of the 1980s in states like Gujarat and Bihar could be traced to such caste conflict. The issue took on national significance in 1990 when the then prime minister, V.P. Singh, announced a major shift in national policy designed to favor the backward castes. Protest riots led by high-caste students broke out all over northern India, seriously weakening the government, and paving the way for the emergence of the BJP.

Another movement among middle-level rural groups has demanded higher prices for agricultural products and lower prices for production inputs like fertilizer, electricity, and credit. Such initiatives appeal to peasants who have prospered under the government's "Green Revolution" policies and now wish to transform their new riches into political clout. Fueling their activism is the conviction that the state has favored the urban upper classes while neglecting the farmer.

Finally, note should be made of a variety of nonelite urban groups and movements that Indian democracy has spawned and that are politically active in India (Rudolph and Rudolph 1987: chs. 10, 11). Labor in India is relatively well organized, especially in the public sector. Labor unions, however, are often politically fragmented along party lines and are not as effective as they might be if they acted in unison. Students, especially university students, are similarly quite active politically but are fragmented along party lines. A variety of lumpen groups, especially unemployed youth in northern India, have joined right-wing proto-fascist movements in recent years – such as the Rashtriya Swayamsevak Sangh or RSS (see Basu's essay below) – that in turn have provided support for the BJP, India's current ruling party. A number of movements that seek to promote a specific cause – e.g., women's movements, environmental movements, tribal movements, Dalit movements (or the movements of the untouchable castes) – also dot India's political landscape (see the essay by Katzenstein et al. below).

The last three essays in the volume provide more detailed analysis of a few key themes concerning such growing social activism and democratic deepening in India.

Myron Weiner provides an overview of how India's caste system has interacted with democratic politics. Two of his arguments especially need to be underlined. First, India's democracy has proven to be inclusive, accommodating members of lower and middle castes into the political system. At the same time, however, and this is a second key argument, inclusiveness has not always facilitated public policies that may benefit large numbers of the lower and middle castes. How is this apparent tension to be explained and what may be its long-term implications?

Myron Weiner identifies several long- and short-term trends that help explain why India's lower castes have been successfully incorporated into the democratic system: the long-term spread of anticaste ideologies; the competitive political mobilization of middle and lower castes, first by the Congress Party itself and, over time, by numerous other parties; and an extensive use of "reservation policies" – India's version of affirmative action policies – that have created quotas for middle and lower castes in politics, bureaucracy, and educational institutions. The resulting inclusiveness, however, has ironical limits that were also noted above: the presence of underprivileged castes in positions of power has not resulted in the pursuit of broadly egalitarian public policies. Weiner explains this outcome by underlining that the politics of caste is often the politics of dignity; goals sought are less broad-based education or health, but more respect, equality of treatment, and symbolic gains. As a result, inclusion of caste leaders into visible positions of power has often satisfied – at least so far – the demands of lower-caste groups. Over time, however, further "class"-like divisions within castes, the growing assertiveness of various castes, and the failure of the Indian state to provide such public goods as primary education and health could become future sources of political conflict.

Pranab Bardhan, in his essay below, discusses the issues of "poverty" and "equity" within the context of Indian democracy. He underlines some of the detrimental consequences for development and democracy of equity politics, or what he describes as a "passion for group equity that rages among the common people in India."

Equity politics hurts both development and democracy through a variety of mechanisms. According to Bardhan, numerous economic interest groups within India clamor for a share of public resources. The more the government satisfies these groups, the less it has available to undertake crucial investments that require public money. The resulting bottlenecks hurt economic growth. The political accommodation of various castes, mainly via granting them reserved quotas in public services and in the public sector, has also impaired India's development; excessive "reservations" have diminished the efficiency of governmental performance. And, finally, demands for group equity have hurt the democratic process itself by constantly exposing government decision-making to particularistic pressures.

From these observations, Bardhan does not conclude that "equity politics" always has negative consequences for development and democracy. His suggestions are instead limited to the specific manner – top-down, aimed at symbolic politics, and often unorganized – in which the "rage for equality" is playing itself out in India. He goes further: he suggests that if equity politics focuses on asset redistribution (such as land reforms) within the context of accountable and well-organized local governments, it could be combined with both efficiency and a stronger democracy.

Beyond the politics of caste and class, as noted above, numerous social movements also inhabit India's political landscape. Mary Katzen-stein and her co-authors help interpret this phenomenon, suggesting that, on balance, social movements strengthen India's democracy. More specifically, their essay proposes three important arguments that are worth underlining. First, social movements in India can be usefully categorized as movements that have mobilized primarily around identity issues – caste, language, religion – and those that mainly pursue specific issues and/or interests, e.g., women's, environmental, and/or economic-ally oriented movements. These two broadly distinguishable sets of movements represent their concerns in India within different institu-tional arenas: whereas identity politics is often expressed via electoral politics, interest-oriented movements have operated mainly within the bureaucracy and the judiciary. Second, and related to the first argument, interest- and issue-oriented movements have often remained local and regional movements. By contrast, given the salience of identity politics in India's diverse social setting, movements that mobilize identities have on occasion established themselves as national movements, often through electoral mobilization. And, third, there are yet other movements that do not engage the state directly. These movements often work at the grassroots and aim mainly to change local realities, often by changing the consciousness of one group or another. Taken together, these myriad movements deepen India's democracy and ensure that slippages away from democracy will remain temporary and minimal.

### In sum

The essays in this volume raise numerous important themes that cannot be readily summarized in a brief space. Nevertheless, three main themes can be underlined as "conclusions."

First, this volume is no blind celebration of India's democracy: all the warts and blemishes of the country's democratic record are on display. Among India's problems, analysts point to sluggish economic growth, continuing and massive poverty, growing coalitional instability, regional problems, and the prevalence of a variety of social conflicts, including violence against lower castes and religious minorities. However, none of the analysts consider these problems to be serious enough to require nondemocratic solutions. India's democratic political system is an established fact and the efforts of the analysts in this volume are focused both on how to explain this outcome, and on how the performance of India's democracy may be improved.

How and why India's democracy has become such a well-established fact is, of course, the central theme of this volume. Like all complex outcomes, more than one factor has contributed to the establishment of India's democracy. Some of these factors are of long-term duration and do not readily suggest any "policy" implications for those wishing to learn from India's record. Other factors, however, indeed lead to meaningful lessons.

It is hard to imagine that if India's multicultural diversity was to be organized as an enduring single state, it could be organized as anything else but a federal, democratic polity. It was helpful for India that, early in its modern history, British colonialism established a relatively centralized state and, within that frame, introduced proto-democratic institutions and practices. Indian nationalists further played a critical role, first by crafting the "unity in diversity" that was India's nationalist movement and, second, by pushing for full democracy by instituting mass adult suffrage and tolerance for religious and cultural diversity. These historical preconditions of India's democracy may not be easy to reproduce.

The fifty-year history of the sovereign Indian republic, however, is replete with instances of power negotiations that indeed lend themselves to lessons for others. Most significantly, within the framework of a centralized state, accommodation of group demands has repeatedly strengthened India's democracy. And, conversely, excessive centralization, especially at the expense of the rights and demands of one group or another, has just as often backfired. Some examples, discussed in detail in the chapters below, will suffice. India's democracy was strengthened by crafting a federal structure that gave political power to Indians who speak different languages. Federal structure was further strengthened when the demands of one region or another were partially accommodated rather than flagrantly resisted: the examples of the Punjab and Kashmir provide the most dramatic instances. The creation of local governments and the accommodation of lower castes and of a variety of grassroots movements similarly point towards the deepening and strengthening of democracy.

It is also important to qualify the thrust of this argument. Excessive accommodation of a variety of demands can at times backfire. What one analyst called the "passion for equity" in India has also hurt India's economic development and contributed to the deinstitutionalization of its polity. Successful accommodation of demands often presupposes an effective central state. When accommodation itself leads to fragmentation and threatens the viability of a centralized state, then other problematic political responses may follow; the rise of right-wing religious nationalism in India is at least in part a response to such perceived fragmentation.

These qualifications aside, an important lesson from India's successful democratic record is this: within the framework of a centralized state, moderate accommodation of group demands, especially demands based on ethnicity, and some decentralization of power strengthens a democracy.

*Part I*

# Historical origins

# 2    Indian democracy: the historical inheritance

*Sumit Sarkar*

## I

The survival of Indian democracy "against the odds" has been generally discussed in terms of the tackling of actual or potential challenges after 1950. There has been much less thinking or research as to why India became a democracy at all. Here an element of defamiliarization is required, an effort at getting beyond an implicit assumption that what is so well-known to have happened was bound to happen. The experience of other parts of the South Asian subcontinent provides a reminder that a reasonably stable, democratic, federal, and secular resolution of the colonial legacy was hardly inevitable. It is precisely here, I feel, that a glance at the historical inheritance, both conjunctural and long-term, may prove helpful. In particular, such a retrospective could serve to highlight the interconnections – maybe even the inseparability – in the Indian context, of democracy, secularism, and federalism.

It might be interesting to begin by asking why this question – concerning not the survival, but the constituting of democratic structures amidst the turmoil of the late 1940s – has been so rarely posed. One reason might be the *de facto* division of labor that has developed between Indian political scientists and historians. The former investigate postindependence development; the latter, with a remarkable timidity which they claim to be justified by difficulties of access to official archives, very seldom go beyond 1947. The transitions across the 1947 divide consequently get neglected, feeding into implicit assumptions of "naturalness" and/or continuity. Thus there is no lack of detailed analysis of the legal implications of specific clauses of the constitution, but a notable absence of sociopolitical studies in depth of the Constituent Assembly debates of 1946–9.

The late 1940s, in the second place, had been replete with traumatic events: tragic and embarrassing in ways that have probably inhibited historical reconstruction. These were years, above all, of communal genocide and enforced mass migration, the retelling of which might well

23

have re-ignited barely suppressed recent passions.[1] They were years, also, of fairly sordid negotiations amidst unparalleled human suffering, in which the heroic patriots of yesterday suddenly appeared metamorphosed for many into power-hungry politicians. While these understandably have not been favorite themes for mainstream nationalist historiography, it has been difficult for the latter to dwell over much also on the moments of popular anticolonial and/or socially radical upsurge, that did overcome communal divisions at times. For such upsurges – notably, the Indian National Army (INA) trial protests and the RIN mutiny in the winter of 1945–6, and, a little later, Tebhaga, Telengana, Punnapra-Vayalar – had taken place against Congress leadership desires, and were perceived as potential left-leaning threats (Sarkar, S. 1983: ch. 8).

More directly related to my present argument, however, are the ways in which unstated premises of continuity have been buttressed by two, otherwise sharply conflicting, historiographical frameworks. There is the well-established liberal–imperialist narrative of "constitutional development" broadening through step-by-step reform to ultimate achievement of Westminster-style parliamentary democracy. The many continuities, indeed often reproductions, of sections of colonial enactments (notably the Government of India Act of 1935) in the provisions and language of the constitution of free India are certainly quite undeniable. And then, through a paradoxical continuity-through-inversion, there is today's colonial discourse analysis, where the postcolonial state is seen as fundamentally an outgrowth of the colonial regime, since both are bound up with the post-Enlightenment modern "nation-state project" (Chatterjee 1986a; for an alternative view, Sarkar, S. 1997).

In the outline for the paper on historical inheritance that Professor Atul Kohli formulated in his project proposal, the language used is that of "interaction" or "juxtaposition" of "colonialism and nationalism" in creating "a framework for a democratic state." I intend to problematize this language in two ways. Neither "colonialism," nor, perhaps even more, "nationalism," can obviously be assumed to have been homogeneous blocs. More crucially, "nationalism," and even a broader term like "anticolonial trends," do insufficient justice to the variety of often contradictory impulses which helped to shape the democratic–federal–secular resolution of 1946–9 (Sarkar, S. 1997: ch. 9).

I would like to focus on five key features of postcolonial Indian state

---

[1] Fears of this kind, by no means always unworthy, probably help to explain the relative historiographical silence about Partition violence much more than any ineluctable thrust towards reducing all history to glorificatory narratives of the modern Indian nation-state – as suggested by Gyanendra Pandey (1991).

structure: a framework of basic "bourgeois–liberal" civil rights; parliamentary democracy grounded in universal suffrage; safeguards for "backward" or "depressed" groups through a balancing of "freedom" and "equality" with "justice"; federalism (though eventually with an unusually strong center); and secularism (in one, or perhaps several, of its many possible meanings). My intention is to try to situate these in terms of both longer-term "inheritances" or "origins" and short-term conjunctures. The second will demand a look at some aspects of the making of the constitution through the Constituent Assembly of December 1946–November 1949. For reasons which I hope will become clear in the course of my essay, I want to concentrate there primarily on the aims and objectives resolution moved by Nehru in the first session of the Constituent Assembly, on December 13, 1946 (the direct ancestor of the preamble), and the subsequent debates on it and on drafts of fundamental rights and on safeguards for minorities, in the assembly itself and in its subcommittees.

## II

A "liberal" reading of the problem of historical inheritance or antecedents is likely to emphasize the British "contributions" towards representative government and notions of legal equality and civil rights, buttressed by a judiciary in some degree independent of the executive. It would also refer to late-colonial experiments with federalism, the reservation of seats and jobs for minorities or underprivileged groups, and perhaps to occasional similarities between postcolonial secularism and the colonial handling of Indian religious conflicts. Where such interpretations become problematic is in their tendency to concentrate on originary moments, presented usually in terms of colonial initiatives and formal decisions: the Macaulay minute on English education, Ripon's reforms, the series of Indian Council and Government of India Acts, to cite some of the more obvious examples. The stress persists in recent Saidian critiques of colonial discourse, only the values have been inverted. Thus the introduction of "English" or "Western" education remains crucial, but instead of being hailed as the fountain-head of "awakening," it is nowadays more commonly denounced as an instrument of cultural domination, productive of derivative discourses alone. Such critiques, further, appear at times dangerously open to appropriation by currently ascendant extreme right-wing tendencies that seek to "revise" the secular and democratic bases of the Indian polity. K.S. Sudarshan, the new chief of the Rashtriya Swayamsevak Sangh, has just denounced (March 2000) the entire constitution as no more than a continuation of the colonial 1935 Act. The political implications are wildly varied, but the underlying assumptions remain of an impact-response, acculturative, kind (Sarkar, S. 1997: ch. 6).

What we need are interpretative frames that allow greater scope to possible patterns of excess that go beyond origins, of varied, sometimes mutually contradictory, Indian appropriations. Perhaps the roots of the "liberal," civil-rights aspects of the constitution could be more fruitfully explored through a qualified and nuanced deployment of Habermas's notion of "public spheres," where private people could come together to constitute publics, developing, on the basis of new kinds of communication networks, sites "for the production and circulation of discourses that can in principle be critical of the state" (Habermas 1989; Fraser 1992: 110–111). For colonial India, the focus would then broaden a bit beyond the debates on "English" education to that other, in many ways perhaps more crucial, nineteenth-century innovation of print culture, along with what quickly became its most vital component: imaginative and discursive prose in the various Indian "vernacular" languages. One can, in other words, talk in terms of "literary public spheres," predating and laying some of the bases for "political" ones.[2]

Of course, the differences are as striking. Unlike the West European prototype, the public spheres here were not primarily grounded in the autonomous development of an indigenous bourgeois civil society. The extent of individuation as a mass phenomenon (Habermas's category of "private people")[3] can be questioned, while the origins clearly lay in colonial administrative-cum-hegemonic intentions and initiatives. Thus Western education was instituted with the dual aims of providing cheaper administration through Indian subordinates and breeding a group of brown sahibs. The printing press was needed in the interests of more efficient colonial governance, propaganda, and missionary prose-lytization, while the early history of press freedom and certain judicial rights in colonial India was bound up with pressures from European nonofficial residents. All such developments were associated therefore with a strong element of what Partha Chatterjee has termed "colonial difference," through which promises were simultaneously held out and

---

[2] A recent pioneering study (Bayly 1996; particularly ch. 5) has tried to apply Habermasian notions to a precolonial "ecumene" even prior to the coming of print on a significant scale in South Asia from the early nineteenth century. I think there is here a certain overstress on continuities and an underestimation of the potentially transforma-tive and democratic implications of print culture.

[3] For Habermas, the subjectivity of the private individuals constituting the bourgeois public was bound up with the "degree to which commodity exchange burst out of the confines of the household economy [and] the sphere of the conjugal family became differentiated from the sphere of social reproduction" (Habermas 1989: 28).

withheld, and theoretical equality before the law was repeatedly interrupted by racist privilege. But the point, to repeat, lies in multiple appropriations, in trajectories that go beyond, sometimes confound, their points of origin.

Two specific examples from education in colonial Bengal can illustrate my argument. Its principal beneficiaries, initially and indeed throughout, were middle-class, high-caste males coming in the main from literati groups that had already specialized in higher education and related careers in precolonial times. There was a significant expansion here through the effects of the transition from manuscript to print and the rapid development of vernacular publication, but not any great sense of doing things that were unconventional or subversive. Rather, as nationalist sentiments grew, such groups often developed critiques of British-instituted education as inculcating alienation and servility. Much recent writing in the Saidian mold on the "fruits of Macauley's poison tree" (Chatterjee 1986a) in fact represents a revival of these earlier condemnations. But things start looking rather different when we think of the way Rashundari Debi, an otherwise utterly obscure nineteenth-century Bengali housewife, mastered her (vernacular) letters in total secrecy and fear, defying deeply ingrained superstitions that an educated wife was bound to become a widow soon – and then went ahead to compose and publish the very first printed autobiography in Bengali. The "literary public sphere" that emerged in colonial India thus came to have, fairly soon, a partly autonomous, and very new, feminine component (Sarkar, T. 1999).

Even more revealing perhaps is the *Guruchand-Carit*, the biography in verse of a lower-caste, Namasudra, religious-cum-political leader located in the East Bengal district of Faridpur. In 1908, Guruchand was able to start an English high school in his home village of Orakandi with the help of an Australian missionary, Mead, who also helped him to develop contacts with British officials, get jobs for some of his relatives and caste brethren, and develop a subordinate-caste politics that was loyalist and opposed to nationalism. They certainly collaborated but the biography makes clear that Mead's help was used pretty pragmatically, as a resource without any quid pro quo of the conversion that the missionaries had hoped for. The help had been needed because of bitter opposition from local high-caste men to any idea of a high school being started in a Namasudra village. The biography justified the Namasudra desire for education in terms of a meticulous description of the everyday behavior of landlords and moneylenders, who deceived illiterate low-caste cultivators into putting their thumb impressions on documents that alienated their meager holdings. The Brahmins and Kayasthas of a neighboring high-caste settlement, further, had managed to persuade a benevolent landlord who had initially offered to start a school at Orakandi into reneging on his promise: for, the biography tells us, if Namasudras got education, who would till the lands of gentlemen as share-croppers? Education, at least rhetorically, thus becomes directly related to claims to equality, while to the gentry in contrast is imputed a belief in *adhikari-bheda*, hierarchized order – which the *Ramayana*, we are told, had affirmed through Ram's execution of Shudrak. In effect, of course, only a small minority of Namasudras actually benefited from the drive for education – one of them, Guruchand's grandson Pramatharanjan Thakur, actually became a member of the Constituent Assembly – but the rhetoric is still worthy of some attention (Haldar 1943: 100–110, 136–203).

There was not one, but several "publics", then,[4] which through conflict as well as occasional united effort came to constitute key pressures for democracy. For it must be emphasized that democracy based on universal franchise, totally rejecting qualifications of property, education, or gender, constituted the sharpest possible break with colonial Indian theory and practice. The British consistently rejected universal franchise till the very end: even the legislatures elected in 1946 (and therefore, through indirect election by these bodies, the Constituent Assembly itself) rested on an electorate of around thirty million, less than a tenth of the population. Here the plunge into country-wide mass anticolonial politics after the First World War was evidently crucial. Public spheres now expanded rapidly, well beyond the limits of formal education or literacy. At the same time, tensions should not be ignored through any assumption of automatic, unambiguous connections. There is the by now much explored theme of leadership restraints, accommodating, but only up to a point, pressures "from below." In terms of ideals, the potentially elitist elements in Nehruvian-left models (e.g. the preservation and/or extension of bureaucratic centralization through a "socialism" assimilated into modernizing technocracy) appear important and obvious to many today. But perhaps one needs to recognize also a degree of incongruity between Gandhian ideals of Ram-Rajya (political utopia) and village self-rule (modifying, but without ruptures, existing class–caste–patriarchal structures of hierarchical domination) and democratic egalitarianism. Nor should the limits be seen as set solely by "elite" restraints: "subaltern" protests have often appealed

---

[4] Recent discussions of Habermas have pointed out that in the West, too, there had developed not one but several, often mutually conflicting, publics, and that Habermas's tendency to use the singular in his study of the "public sphere" is quite unhelpful. See Calhoun (1992), containing essays by Nancy Fraser, Mary Ryan, and Geoff Eley.

to higher as against immediate oppressors, and could be associated with dreams of just rule by good kings or leaders rather than democratic self-governance.

Yet the decisive linkage between anticolonial mass nationalism and the coming of democracy remains indisputable. Early specific political demands by Congress had not gone beyond some degree of control over executives and very limited extensions of voting rights, and even one of the initial protests against the partition of Bengal, which marked the beginning of a more militant era, described educated groups as the "natural leaders" of the people. It cited with great approval Edmund Burke's *Regicide Peace*, which had defined public opinion as the views of men with leisure, means of information, and a position "above menial dependence."[5] The twofold expansion that followed – in aims, towards progressively more definitive notions of Swaraj, culminating with the Lahore demand for complete independence in 1929; in methods, particularly with Gandhi, towards enormously widened mass participation – was accompanied by a sharpening of notions of democracy. The Nehru Report of 1928, the nationalist response to the all-white Simon Commission, suggested adult franchise (as against the latter's proposal for an electorate of 10 percent), and from the Faizpur session of 1936 onwards the Congress made a Constituent Assembly elected by universal suffrage one of its central demands. Both nationalist women leaders like Sarojini Naidu and Sarala Devi, and a number of women's groups independent of and sometimes opposed to the Congress, began claiming voting rights for women from around 1918 onwards, and this demand encountered remarkably little open opposition from politically aware male Indians (Forbes 1996: ch. 4). Meanwhile demands for reservations in jobs and assembly seats were being repeatedly voiced on behalf of Muslims and low-castes, with undoubted British encouragement out of divide-and-rule motives but also varying but considerable degrees of autonomy. "Mainstream" nationalism on the whole was able to come to terms with such demands, though with much heart-searching – the key landmarks being the Lucknow Pact of 1916, accepting separate electorates for Muslims, and the Poona Pact of 1932, which laid the basis for the subsequent constitutional provision of joint electorates but reserved seats for scheduled castes.

The democratic content of Indian nationalism in fact stands out quite remarkably in a global perspective too, though this has often been lost sight of through overemphasis on British or Western models. The Nehru Report demand for adult franchise preceded by a year its full

---

[5] "One of the People," *An Open Letter to Curzon* (Dacca, April 1904; enclosed in Government of India Home Public Proceedings Deposit, April 1904 n. 39).

achievement in Britain, where more than a century of struggle had been required to eradicate property and/or education limits, and women had got the vote only after some twenty years of extremely bitter suffrage campaigning in the early twentieth century. Women got voting rights in France and Italy only after the Second World War, and accounts of elections in the southern states of the USA down to very recent times rival the most lurid of tales about Bihar electoral corruption and violence.[6]

Democracy, one could argue, was to some extent forced on the nationalist leadership to counter persistent British claims of being paternalist, impartial benefactors who were better guardians of the "real" Indian masses, and in particular of minorities, underprivileged groups, and women, against a "microscopic minority" of privileged Hindu politicians. The decisive factor, however, was the sheer sweep of mass movements in post-1919 India, leading to quite exceptional degrees of politicization, the vestiges of which have not yet entirely died out. Despite so much disillusionment and cynicism, India still retains a capacity to surprise external observers: the enthusiastic participation in elections even (and often particularly) by many of the poorest, for instance, or the quality of roadside conversations about politics. And once again there is a need to emphasize diversity and conflict. Due weight must be given, in any pursuit of the roots of the drives for equality and socioeconomic justice, to pressures and movements quite often condemned in conventional mainstream nationalist discourses (and histories) as "divisive": autonomous tribal peasant labor and left challenges, of course, but also the contributions of lower-caste move-ments, women's pressure groups, and the resistance to centralizing drives in the name of regional and minority religious identities.

The connections between imperatives of united mass anticolonial struggle and the specific, federal, and secular form of Indian democracy in fact need to be explored much more than they have been so far. Indian federalism is often grounded, in rather over-formal ways, in late-colonial British constitutional experiments: notably, dyarchy, followed by the 1935 Act. Colonial rule, which in the interests of more effective domination and exploitation had integrated the subcontinent far more tightly than ever before, had also begun to feel the need for a measure of decentralization for financial and administrative efficiency from the late nineteenth century. "Provincial autonomy," further, could combine necessary conciliation of nationalists with retention of effective overall control. The "federal" aspects of the Government of India Act of 1935

---

[6] For one vivid account by a civil rights activist of the 1960s who has subsequently become a well-known anthropologist, see Sider (1993: ch. 3).

had as their principal aim the deployment of loyal Indian princes to offset the rising tide of nationalist pressures for responsible government in the center. It should be obvious that the connections between such imperialist "federalism" and the postcolonial structures were not only indirect, but operated mainly through reaction. Thus the evidently divisive nature of the colonial schemes in fact strengthened the centralizing, as distinct from the more "federal," tendencies within "mainstream" nationalism, by evoking fears of Balkanization.

But already in May 1905, long before British federal schemes, Bepinchandra Pal was arguing that "autonomy for India . . . Presupposes the autonomy of every race and community in India itself" – a "federation" the constituent units of which would apparently be the different religious communities (Pal 1905, 1954). A discourse of "unity in diversity" became standard in mature Indian nationalism, particularly in the context of deepening Hindu–Muslim conflicts. This was often vague, platitudinous, and open to diverse interpretations, yet it did involve a recognition of plurality of religions, languages, and cultures that logically favored federalism rather than any totally centralized polity. It needs to be emphasized also that despite the many verbal similarities between the 1935 Act and the constitution of independent India, in one key respect a major rupture had taken place. The federation envisaged in 1935 had been a combination of responsibly governed British Indian provinces with still-autocratic princely states, their borders and political regimes unchanged. That which had emerged by 1950 was based on a destruction of most of these borders through the integration of princely states and the uniform application of democratic principles of governance. A decisive change had been brought about, through varying combinations of pressures from above and popular movements (the most militant among them the armed struggle of Telengana peasants which helped to put paid to the Nizam of Hyderabad's dreams of autocratic independence). The subsequent linguistic reorganization, once again through popular pressure, represented a part-fulfillment of aspirations based on linguistic–cultural affinities: tendencies which, when sought to be suppressed, have repeatedly fueled "separatist" movements. Contrary to the fears expressed by Nehru and many others, linguistic states, and the consequent stimulus to the federal aspects of the polity through consolidation of regional elites, have on the whole strengthened, rather than weakened, Indian unity.[7] Tendencies towards a tighter central-

---

[7] For a brief but helpful elaboration of this point, see Manor (1990). I am grateful to Jim Manor for sending me a copy of this article.

ization have had a contrary effect: the experience of Tamil Nadu stands in significant contrast to Kashmir.[8]

As rulers of a multireligious subcontinent, professing moreover a creed shared by only a small minority of their subjects, it was both expedient and necessary for the British (as indeed it had been for most of their predecessors) to claim to be nondiscriminatory in matters of patronage, administration, and state-funded education: practices which by the early twentieth century were coming to be loosely termed "secular." For many Indians, however, such claims were fairly often belied by signs of tacit support for Christian missionary proselytization, and, increasingly with the growth of anticolonial movements, by what were widely believed to be divide-and-rule strategies seeking to set or keep apart Muslims from Hindus. As with democracy and federation, the roots of modern Indian "secularism" have been substantially indigenous, in the sense of developing from the imperatives of united anticolonial struggle and acquiring its specific meanings in that context. For it needs to be emphasized that, contrary to much recent "antisecularist" polemic,[9] functioning is a necessary (though not sufficient) condition for the coexistence of different religious communities within a single state. This requires also a (varying, and usually partial rather than total) distancing of some public spaces from particular religious affiliations and practices (e.g., nondiscriminatory state employment, civic rights, state-funded education).

Secularism in these precise senses emerged as a response to deepening intra-religious violence, endemic and fairly continuous from the mid-1920s, and at its height precisely during the years the constitution was being worked out.[10] Already in its early, "moderate" phase, the Congress had implicitly recognized the need for a degree of public-space

---

[8]  It is seldom remembered today that in the 1950s the Dravidian movement had seemed to pose the most obvious "secessionist" threat. The initial accession of Kashmir, in contrast, had taken place at the initiative of the popular movement led by Sheikh Abdulla and the National Conference. The subsequent erosion of elements of autonomy, largely through Hindu–chauvinist pressures, has been the decisive factor in the subsequent alienation of the Kashmir Valley.

[9]  Key texts in this polemic include Madan (1987 and 1993); Nandy (1990); and Chatterjee (1994). I have argued elsewhere (1996) that such arguments often proceed by simultaneously narrowing and widening the concept of secularism in quite arbitrary ways. Secularism is narrowed into antireligious skepticism, virtually atheism; alternately, or in combination, it is enormously widened to make it responsible for all the many undoubted misdeeds of the "modern nation-state." The logical hiatus should be obvious: Hitler and Stalin were secular, but was secularism the key ground for Nazi or Stalinist terror?

[10]  Despite the constant identification today of secularism with Enlightenment rationalism, its historical origins in the West had actually not been all that different. The basic contexts there were the sixteenth- to seventeenth-century Wars of Religion, in the wake of the Reformation, and the first group to demand toleration and separation of state

neutrality by stipulating that no issue would be taken up if objected to strongly by the majority of delegates coming from any religious community. By the 1930s, a more specific urgency had also developed for the greater deployment of secularism in the language and programs of the Congress (though this remained much less evident in quite a lot of ground-level practice, as the working of the 1937–9 Congress ministries sometimes revealed). A very sharp decline had taken place in the level of Muslim participation after the collapse of the Non-Cooperation–Khilafat movement and the growth of both Hindu and Muslim communalism. This created the real possibilities of a Hindu majoritarian–nationalist takeover of a movement which, it could be plausibly argued, was largely "Hindu" in its composition anyway. As Nehru would warn in 1958, the communalism of the majority community was particularly dangerous because it could project itself as "national," denouncing all minority opposition as "separatist" and uniquely "communal"[11] – thereby in practice enforcing policies that markedly weakened national unity.

The close association in the Indian context of secularism with anti-colonial nationalist, "nation-building" projects (rather than with any marked spread of rationalistic or free-thinking values), has had contradictory consequences. It has certainly extended the appeal of "secularism" to very many who would not be "secularist" in the sense of unbelief or religious indifference,[12] but also kept open strong possibilities of assimilation or identification with merely statist endeavors. The main arguments denouncing secularism today for being statist, authoritarian, and centralist thus do have a certain point: the problem remains, however, of a conflation of one possibility with something inevitable. There is considerable historical evidence that secularism is not necessarily homogenizing or authoritarian: it can also take on more democratic, decentralizing, or "federal" forms.[13]

from church as matters of principle were not rationalist free thinkers, but the passionately religious Anabaptists of sixteenth-century Germany.

[11] Nehru's speech at the AICC, 11 May, 1958, quoted in Noorani (1991).

[12] It is noteworthy that Gandhi had little difficulty with the notion. He had asserted in September 1946 that "If I were a dictator, religion and state would be separate. I swear by my religion, I will die for it. But it is my personal affair. The state has nothing to do with it . . . [it] is everybody's personal affair." Cited in Madan (1993). The extract consorts oddly with the central argument of Madan's essay that privatization of religion is impossible in non-Protestant cultures.

[13] In post-Reformation France, for instance, the Edict of Nantes (1598) which ended a long spell of religious wars by granting toleration for the Huguenot minority (thus in effect breaching the tight association of the French state with Catholicism) had sought to achieve its objectives by introducing elements of regional autonomy within a unitary state. In 1685, in significant contrast, Louis XIV revoked this edict in an effort to make his Grand Monarchy more centralized and absolute. For an elaboration of these arguments, see Sarkar (forthcoming).

Perhaps one could make this point even more sharply. In conditions of marked religious–cultural heterogeneity, secularism can hope to remain effective only through such forms. A telling example would be the deeply counterproductive consequences of the centralizing assumptions of the Congress leadership, as manifested in the Nehru Report in 1928. The fairly moderate Muslim League proposals for greater provincial autonomy were then rejected, and this became for Jinnah the decisive "parting of the ways," in retrospect a major landmark on the road to Partition.

I turn now to the debates around constitution-making in 1946–9, for these provide a helpful but underexplored site for studying alternative articulations of the interrelationships of democracy, federalism, and secularism.

### III

The conjunctures of 1946–9 were quite exceptionally complex and contradictory. The defeat of fascism had evoked worldwide moods of popular radicalism and anti-imperialism that were democratic and often socialist in aspiration. In India, too, the winter of 1945–6 had witnessed remarkable Hindu–Muslim unity on the barricades, demanding the release of INA prisoners, the withdrawal of the British Indian army from counter-insurgency work in Vietnam and Indonesia, and expressing solidarity with the RIN mutiny. Labor militancy remained high throughout 1946, and peasants, too, were on the move in some parts of the country, through the Tebhaga agitation in Bengal in winter 1946–7 and the beginning of the Telengana armed struggle. Echoes of such moods occasionally entered the precincts of the Constituent Assembly, as when Nehru proclaimed his faith in socialism while moving the aims and objectives resolution at its first session on December 13, 1946,[14] Ambedkar demanded explicit references to the "nationalization of industry and the nationalization of land," and Somnath Lahiri, the lone Communist member, wanted Nehru's "bold words, noble words" to be followed up by real action: "you have to go forward to the seizure of power, revolutionary seizure of power."[15] By December 1946, however, much of this must have sounded merely rhetorical, for after August 1946 in Calcutta, followed by Noakhali and Bihar, the more evident and

---

[14] "Well, I stand for Socialism and, I hope, India will stand for Socialism and that India will go towards the Constitution of a Socialist State and I do believe that the whole world will have to go that way" (Government of India 1947–1948 (henceforth CAD), vol. I: 60).

[15] Speeches of B.R. Ambedkar, December 17, 1946, and Somnath Lahiri, December 19, 1946, (CAD, vol. I: 98, 131).

immediate reality was that of unprecedented fratricidal violence, which increasingly made Partition appear to many the only solution. The Congress leadership had already scuttled the possibility of alternative, more radical solutions by rejecting another round of mass struggle in the winter of 1945-6. I have argued elsewhere that if popular action had been decisive in making the continuance of British rule untenable, it may have been the fear of popular "excesses" that made Congress leaders cling to the path of negotiation and compromise, and eventually accept Partition as its necessary price (Sarkar, S. 1983: ch. 8)

There is little point in indulging in what might have been, but there is at least one bit of specific detail which can help to buttress this argument. The prospect of achieving early power through negotiation made the Congress agree to the Cabinet Mission argument that new elections based on adult franchise, theoretically the most satisfactory way of forming a constituent assembly, would lead to "unacceptable delay" (Shiva Rao 1968: ch. 15). The constitution-making body (which also became the Indian Central Assembly after 15 August) was therefore formed through indirect elections, chosen by provincial legislatures that had been elected in early 1946 on the basis of the 1935 Act franchise of around 10 percent. The Congress thus tacitly withdrew what had been a central programmatic objective since 1936. The one political group that categorically demanded universal franchise in discussions with the Cabinet Mission was the Communist Party of India (CPI). The Muslim League had won an overwhelming majority of reserved Muslim seats in the 1946 polls, and the compromise made by the Congress in effect meant that the League's claim to represent the bulk of Muslims, and in particular its demand for Pakistan, was never really democratically tested. Counterfactual arguments do not lead us very far, but it remains important to note that while the Congress won majorities in democratic elections without a break from 1952 till 1977, the League was routed in East Pakistan in the very first polls conducted on universal franchise, and signally failed to provide stable governments even in the western parts of Pakistan.

Constitution-making began, with the Muslim League staying away, and with the eight-point resolution and aims and objectives moved by Nehru on December 13, 1946, the foundation of which eventually became the preamble (CAD, vol. 1: 55–62; Shiva Rao 1964 (henceforth SD), vol. 1: 3–4). The resolution defined India as an "independent sovereign republic," to be formed through a "union" of British India and Indian states, in which all power would be "derived from the people" (clauses i, iii, iv). Then came clause v, which would be reproduced, though in somewhat abbreviated form, in the subsequent preamble, guaranteeing to "all the people of India justice, social, economic and political; equality of status, of opportunity, and before the law; freedom of thought, expression, belief, faith, worship, vocation, association and action, subject to law and public morality." Clause vi made explicit the prioritization of "justice" in a "social" sense, already suggested by the order of terms in the previous clause: "adequate safeguards" would be worked out "for minorities, backward and tribal areas, and depressed and other backward classes."

The resolution was thus categorical and fairly comprehensive in its catalog of standard liberal equal rights, and simultaneously went beyond standard bourgeois liberalism in its emphasis on social justice. As an interesting, fairly easy attempt to balance equality with justice sought to be ensured through affirmative action or reverse discrimination on behalf of underprivileged communities, it may serve as a reminder that, contrary to much recent argument, discourses of equal rights are not necessarily always "homogenizing," or impossible to combine with some recognition of difference.

Somewhat curiously, however, the aims and objectives resolution did not explicitly mention democracy or universal franchise. How exactly power was to be "derived from the people" was not spelled out. In his speech while moving the resolution, Nehru tried to defend this exclusion by arguing that the notion was included in the term "republic" – which of course was both etymologically and historically unconvincing. He went on to assert that the content, not only of political, but of "economic democracy" was implicit in the resolution. The speech ended with the passage I have already cited: a characteristic Nehruvian combination of passionate statement of personal faith in socialism with a justification for the exclusion of that word on the ground that "we wanted this resolution not to be controversial." One is left to speculate whether specific references to democracy and universal suffrage were not still a bit controversial, too, within Nehru's own party (which of course totally dominated the Constituent Assembly, since the Muslim League was boycotting it).

Where the resolution did differ sharply from the subsequent constitutional structure, however, was in the precise content of its "federal" dimension. Clause iii explicitly stated that the Indian "union" would be one where the constituents "shall possess and retain the status of autonomous Units, together with residual powers . . . save and except such powers and functions as are vested in or assigned to the Union."[16] In the course of the next six months or so, this residual powers provision

[16] Ibid.: 55.

would be progressively whittled down, till on July 5, 1947 the sub-committee on union powers decided "that the constitution should be a federal structure with a strong center," where there would be three "exhaustive" legislative lists, "Union, State, and Concurrent," with "residuary powers for the center" (Shiva Rao 1968: 607–610).

The promises held out by the aims and objectives resolution of popular sovereignty and liberal freedoms were not incorporated into specific constitutional laws without some revealing hesitations. While the unexplained omission of the term "democratic" was remedied in the February 1948 draft preamble (which substituted "sovereign democratic republic" for the repetitive "independent sovereign") (Shiva Rao 1968: 128), the coming of universal franchise, though not opposed openly by any member of the Constituent Assembly, did not happen without a few hiccups. Ambedkar's draft on fundamental rights (March 24, 1947) had wanted a categorical statement that there would be no denial or abridge-ment of any citizen's right to vote "on any account other than imma-turity, imprisonment and insanity": which would have been a neat and effective way of ensuring universality. The draft prepared by K.M. Munshi (March 17, 1947), which the subcommittee on fundamental rights preferred to Ambedkar's as the basis for its deliberations, used a much vaguer formula of equal opportunity "in the exercise of franchise according to the law of the Union." The subcommittee did in the end recommend universal franchise, secret voting, and an independent Election Commission, but there followed a sharp disagreement as to whether these should be given the stature of fundamental rights at the advisory committee meeting of April 21–24, 1947. Ambedkar, sup-ported by Jagjivan Ram and Hansa Mehta – interestingly, two Dalits and a woman Socialist – tried to insist on such inclusion, for he feared that otherwise "it may be later on argued that this particular right [universal suffrage] either was condemned or was not approved of by this com-mittee." He was very strongly opposed by Rajagopalachari, who, while not questioning the principle, did not want electoral laws to be "pre-judged." The chairman of the committee, Vallabhbhai Patel, was clearly inclined to back Rajagopalachari: both leaders, as is well known, had come to be associated with the Congress right. Eventually, at the suggestion of Govindaballabh Pant, the three recommendations of the subcommittee were excluded from the fundamental rights chapter, for inclusion "in some other part of the constitution." Universal franchise eventually found a place way down in the constitution, as article 326 – moved, once again, by Ambedkar – and adopted unanimously on June 16, 1949 (SD, vol. II: 87, 247–252; Shiva Rao 1968: 460–462, 471).

One might also note in passing certain nuances in the debates in the

Constituent Assembly around the civil rights provisions of fundamental rights. The most forthright affirmations here came from the Communist Somnath Lahiri, who was excluded from the crucial subcommittees and usually had to speak amidst constant hostile interjections. Already during the discussion of the aims and objectives resolution, Lahiri had drawn attention to the free use of colonial powers of repression (like externment orders) by Congress ministries. On January 25 he protested against a police search of his own house, with seizure from there of Constituent Assembly proceedings and notes of his speeches: a bizarre infringement which, however, obtained no sympathy from his fellow members and no serious intervention by the Assembly president, Rajendra Prasad. On April 29, 1947, the Communist member criticized the interim report on fundamental rights as being often formulated "from the point of view of a police constable." Even the rather minimum schedule of rights, he felt, was being restricted in every case by provisos for executive abridgement in situations of emergency. There was no clear-cut assertion of freedom of the press, and no repudiation of detention without trial: prophetic remarks, one must admit, keeping in mind the loopholes for preventive detention and emergency powers which were eventually included in the constitution, and their notorious subsequent applications. And indeed Patel, while presenting the "rights to freedom" before the assembly on April 30, 1947 left out the clauses about citizen rights of peaceful assembly and formation of "associations and unions" that had been part of the subcommittee draft, and confined the content of liberty to freedom of speech, expression, and residence ("subject to public order and morality or to the existence of grave emergency" threatening "security" of the union or constituent unit) (CAD, vol. I: 132; vol. II: 340–341; vol. III: 384, 446).

The anger, amounting almost to fear, invoked by a single Communist member might appear puzzling till we recall the wider context of those years, national and indeed international. The CPI was emerging rapidly as the principal challenge to the Congress, a position it would retain for a decade and a half after independence. There was no way really, prior to the first elections held on the basis of universal suffrage in 1952, of estimating how much mass support it commanded. And before that there were the years of militancy, the "Ranadive line" of urban revolution, and armed peasant insurrection in Telengana which at one point is said to have required more troops to brutally repress than were deployed in Kashmir. The real, or perceived, threat from the left perhaps had two, rather contradictory, consequences. It provided the occasion, and/or the excuse, for tightening up repressive state powers, in a pattern that has repeated itself intermittently down to the present, leaving civil rights a crucial, contentious issue. The CPI was banned in several parts of the country in early 1948, immediately after its Calcutta congress and before any violent initiatives on its part, and powers of preventive detention were freely used to round up its leaders and members. At the same time, the danger from the left probably helped to block any basic backsliding on questions of general democratic principle (as distinct from emergency administrative powers).

It was not really possible, for instance, to go back on commitments of universal franchise. And there was further the international dimension, of the apparently sweeping advance of Communist-led democratic and socialist revolutions in the wake of the defeat of Nazism, in Eastern Europe and much of Asia. It may not be irrelevant to highlight a little a coincidence of dates: India's democratic constitution was promulgated on November 26, 1949, less than two months after the formation of the People's Republic of China on October 1. The Communist danger was perhaps seen to demand an at least partially democratic response, even from the point of view of groups that otherwise would have been more conservative. India could then be projected as the democratic alternative to "totalitarian," if socially transformatory, Red China.

The interconnections, in Indian conditions, between democracy, secularism, and federalism now demand closer attention. They can be illuminated through a glance at the specific provisions pertaining to secularism in the fundamental rights, along with some debates in the Constituent Assembly on the extent and nature of rights to religious freedom,[17] and about residual powers. Once again, the contexts need to be remembered: deepening communal riots and Partition, followed by the unprecedented, forced migration of millions. The responses could not but have taken contradictory directions, and many tensions lurk as subtexts within the speeches of Constituent Assembly members despite the fact that nearly all of them were members of the same party, the Congress. There were strong Hindu–communal tendencies, typified for all time by the murder of the Mahatma by a Hindu Mahasabha activist who had been trained by the RSS – but also a strengthening of the recognition that free India could survive and rebuild unity only on the basis of toleration and secularism. There were differences also as regards what could be the most effective political structures for achieving these objectives. Given the immediate background of political chaos and an infant, weak state, leanings toward relatively centralist solutions were not unnatural, and these could also seem to be more appropriate for realizing independent economic growth, radical social change, perhaps

[17] I must acknowledge a major debt here to a paper by Shefali Jha (forthcoming).

ultimately even socialism.[18] Centralism, however, sometimes led to overlaps between secular language and Hindu–nationalist undertones, and we need to pay particular attention to the occasional dissident, alternative voices and try to locate their sources.

The term "secularism" did not figure in the resolution and the preamble, till its highly paradoxical, indeed ironic, inclusion, along with "socialist," through the forty-second amendment during the worst phase of the Emergency.[19] Its precise content and meanings in the Indian context – far removed from the allegedly anti- (or even aggressively non-)religious stereotype often imputed to it – were spelled out, however, with fairly exemplary precision in the fundamental rights to "freedom of religion" (articles 25–28), "cultural and educational rights" (articles 29–30), and "rights to equality" (articles 14, 16, 17). These basic legal provisions in fact approximate quite closely to Amartya Sen's formulation of the minimum prerequisites for being "secular in the political sense." The Indian constitution can be read as having concretized the two key principles of symmetrical treatment and partial distancing of public spaces. It guaranteed equal rights "to profess, practice, and propagate religion" and maintain religio-charitable institutions (articles 25i, 26) and simultaneously provided for certain separation: nondiscrimination before the law and in state employment (articles 14, 16), no obligatory taxes for any religion, and no compulsory religious instruction in state-run or aided educational institutions (articles 27, 28). The third cardinal feature, bound up with the prioritization of social justice, balanced religious freedom with a proviso for state intervention in pursuit of "social welfare and reform" (article 25ii) – thus enabling the abolition of untouchability (article 17). A similar balance was struck between equality of opportunity and affirmative action (reservations "in favour of any backward class of citizens" – article 16).

In March–April 1947 a controversy erupted within the fundamental rights subcommittee about whether religious freedom should involve primarily "worship" or extend more broadly to cover religious "practices." In a significant combination of two women members and the principal Dalit leader, Rajkumari Amrit Kaur, Hansa Mehta, and Ambedkar argued, against K.M. Munshi and the majority in the subcommittee, that the wider definition might block action against un-

---

[18] It should be remembered that the prestige of the Stalinist–Soviet model was still extremely high in countries like India, particularly just after the triumph over Hitler. Admiration for planning, in particular, extended far beyond convinced communists or socialists.

[19] Ironic, because this was precisely the time when planning started to be whittled down, and overtures began to be made towards the Hindu right.

touchability. Munshi's formula of "profess, practice and propagate religion" was eventually accepted, and the final version of the fundamental rights did not include Ambedkar's suggestions regarding a categorical rejection of any state religion, or a clause ruling out compulsion to become a "member of any religious association, submit to any religious instruction, or perform any act of religion."[20] The scope of liberal–individualist rights was restricted in the interests of maintaining the solidarity and discipline of religious communities, in a move initiated by a Gandhian with strong Hindu–right leanings.

So far the difference of opinion could have been read as one between relatively secularist views, in effect restricting through state enactment the "normal" functioning of religious communities, and a more "tolerant" approach. Members like K.M. Panikkar had argued that restricting religious freedom to "worship" alone involved misunderstanding the significance of religion for a believer, to whom it could mean an entire way of life, not just the performance of rituals or going to places of worship (Shfali forthcoming). But the storm that followed in the Assembly on May 1, 1947 over the admissibility of conversion of minors suddenly revealed that for some religious freedom could imply the greater freedom of one religion over the others. It was K.M. Munshi who now suggested what in effect was a restriction on the right of propagating religion, by banning conversion of all minors under eighteen, and soon Hindu–majoritarian notions and language were clearly on display, voiced particularly by a number of members from UP, Bihar and CP. Ostensibly the debate referred to Christian missionary activity, but from the tone and line-up of options we might well suspect that this relatively minor issue contained a subtext about Muslims that was unsayable in the context of devastating riots and impending (but not yet finished) Partition. And the Christian conversions issue, too, evokes powerful resonances today, in the context of the burning alive of Staines and his children and atrocities against Christians in BJP-dominated Gujarat.

Munshi was supported aggressively by Purushottamdas Tandon, champion of Sanskritized Hindi as the national language and, a few years later, a bitter opponent of the Hindu Code Bill. Tandon actually suggested that if parents converted, their minor children should be taken away from them and placed under state guardianship: a striking instance where state action was being proposed to defend one kind of

---

[20] Ambedkar had made these suggestions in the draft of fundamental rights which he presented to the subcommittee on March 24, 1947. The subcommittee, however, decided to proceed on the basis of K.M. Munshi's draft of March 17 (SD, vol. II, part II: passim).

religious solidarity, even at the cost of family integrity. Most violent of all was Algurai Shastri, also from UP, who argued that the conversion of children with their parents was an "evil practice [that] has a very bad effect on the strength of our population," and went on to denounce the many "unfair means [that] have been adopted to trample the majority community under foot." "People of other faiths have intensified and exploited our differences to increase their own numbers" – and Shastri referred in this context to the British-instituted "illusory web of the census." He also brought in a caste–class dimension: "disputes between members of such castes as the sweepers or the *chamars* on the one side and the landlords or some other influential members on the other have been exploited to create bitterness between them." Very interestingly, Algurai Shastri in effect was conflating minors and people he repeatedly referred to as "*bhangis* and *chamars*." And even a left-leaning, apparently radically secular argument was brought into play by Jagatnarayan Lal of Bihar who backed up his threat that "undue advantage should not be taken of the generosity of the majority" with a reference to the Soviet constitution of 1936, in which freedom of religion and of antireligious propaganda had been guaranteed, but not the right, explicitly, to propagate religion.

Opposition to Munshi's amendment came from Christian members (Frank Antony from Bengal, Rev. Nichols-Roy from Assam, Rev. Jerome D'Souza from Madras), a few delegates from the south, Dhirendranath Datta from Bengal (who on an earlier occasion had wanted to extend the condemnation of untouchability to the entire caste system) – and, most powerfully, from Ambedkar. "I would like to ask whether it would be possible for this House to accept that a child of five, for instance, ought to be separated from his parents merely because the parents have adopted Christianity or some religion which was not originally theirs." In the end, clause 17 of the draft fundamental rights giving a restricted right of conversion, which had caused all this controversy, was referred back for further discussion, and eventually dropped (CAD, vol. III: 480–496).

What makes this debate important for my argument is that, a few months earlier, a very similar dividing line had emerged over the question of residual powers to units. Clause iii of the objectives resolution had as its obvious context the provisions to interfere in the Cabinet Mission Plan of May 1946, which set the formal legal parameters of the Constituent Assembly till the Mountbatten Plan. There was also a desire, in the winter of 1946–7, to persuade Muslim League members to rejoin the assembly (their boycott had reduced the Muslim component to just four members), while the whole question of a centralized vs. a more federal polity had of course been vastly complicated by the British deployment of federalism to block anticolonial aspirations, in tandem with princes and the League.

The debate on the aims and objectives resolution still revealed very interesting differences of emphasis and attitude. Nehru, while moving the resolution (as well as when ending the debate on January 22, 1947) kept discreetly quiet over the residual powers issue. But Purushottamdas Tandon, seconding the resolution, immediately made clear his reservations: "For the sake of securing Muslim League's cooperation, we have been accepting many things against our ideal. We should now put a stop to that. Personally, I would oppose the grant of residuary powers to the provinces in the best interests of the country" (CAD, vol. 1: 63–66). This became the dominant note in many speeches: residual powers as a grudging, ultimate concession, plus veiled threats directed at the League of more centralized alternatives if it still refused to cooperate. Thus Srikrishna Singha (Bihar) noticed the emphasis on "centralized republic trends" (ibid.: 86). Seth Govinda Das (Central Provinces and Berar) adopted an openly threatening tone: "if the British Government wishes to fight with us making Muslims their Shikhandi, we will not do what Bhisma Pitamaha did. We will not lay down our arms because a Shikhandi is made to stand against us" (ibid.: 105). Predictably, Shamaparasad Mukherji (Bengal), Hindu Mahasabha leader who would later found the Jan Sangh, strongly opposed giving residual power to the provinces, for a "stronger center" was needed in India's paramount interest (ibid.: 96). But these doughty champions of the Hindu right were joined by at least one leftist, Minoo Masani (still a socialist then), who combined an emphasis on the "social or long-term aspects of the Revolution," and the ways in which it could be interpreted as implicitly rejecting the "social status quo," with a perspective of "one corporate nation, a homogenous nation." "The conception of a nation does not permit the existence of perpetual or permanent minorities, or, in the course of time, it must break up." Curiously, for Mansi this went along with a preference for "democratic socialism" grounded in Gandhian notions of "village-based decentralization," which he sharply contrasted to "Russian totalitarianism" (ibid., 89–92).

But there were also some who defended a more decentralized polity on principle, and even suggested going a bit beyond residual powers for provinces. In a very impressive rebuttal of Masani, Rev. Jerome D'Souza warned of the danger of "love of country" and "desire for rapid improvement and progress" leading to excessive expansion of the "authority and power of the Central State"; of the "desire for unanimity and homogeneity harming minorities or special groups." "Absorption in the sense of cultural or religious or any other absorption is something against which it is necessary for us to guard." Holding out Canada and Switzerland as possible models, D'Souza argued that "cultural autonomy" could be quite consistent with "national unity" (CAD, vol. II: 278–279). Rev. Nichols-Roy strongly supported residual powers for provinces and suggested that in a region like Assam "self-governing units" might be advisable within the "autonomous Province" (CAD, vol. II: 110–112). And once again Ambedkar's intervention was particularly interesting, for he brought out into the open, and explicitly rejected, the hidden, Hindu–communalist agenda of many of the advocates of centralization. Citing approvingly Burke's speech on conciliation with America, he argued that while personally an advocate of a "strong united Centre" (at least one stronger than in the 1935 Act), in the present circumstances "it would not be prudent, it would not be wise." The problem was "how to make the heterogeneous mass we have today take a decision in common." Ambedkar deplored the tone adopted by members like Srikrishna Sinha, Shyamaprasad Mukherji, and some others, who were using a language of "war," which "appalled" him. For this in the present circumstances "will not be a war on the British" (to which he said he had "not much objection"), but "a war on the Muslims." "If there is anybody who has in his mind the project of solving the Hindu–Muslim problem by force, which is another name of solving it by war, in the Constitution that might be prepared without their consent, this country would be involved in perpetually conquering them" (ibid.: 98–101).

And finally there was Somnath Lahiri, once again adopting a tone different from all others amidst repeated interruptions. He called for a renewal of concrete anti-British struggle, through which the divisive shackles of British constitutional devices could be shattered, and the "present fratricidal impasse" overcome: much too optimistic a reading, probably, for December 1946. But, quite strikingly, on the specific issue of residual powers there was an obviously uncoordinated, never developed, concordance between Lahiri, the Communist spokesman, and Ambedkar. Like Ambedkar, the Communist member deplored the tendency among many of implicitly threatening the League that "we are going to evolve out a unitary constitution for India and there is no scope in it for secession." Just giving residual powers to provinces was insufficient, Lahiri argued: the real basis for stable unity could be laid only through acknowledgment of the right of self-determination (ibid.: 130–131).

During the early months of 1947, the subcommittee on union powers (which did not include Ambedkar, nor of course Lahiri) quietly ex-

tended central authority through a notion of "powers implied or in-
herent in or resultant from the express powers of the Union." Defense
and communications thus were held to imply concentration of most
sources of revenue at the center. The process then attained a quantum
leap with the announcement of Partition by Mountbatten on June 3,
1947. Immediately afterwards, the Constituent Assembly with almost
unseemly haste decided to go ahead building a federation with an
unusually strong center. One can almost notice a tone of relief in the
words of K.M. Munshi, now that Partition had ended the possibility of a
decentralized polity. "Strong Central Government" had been sacrificed
by the May 16 Plan (of the Cabinet Mission) "at the altar of preserving
. . . an attenuated unity which would not have lasted longer than the
making of it" (Shiva Rao 1968: 113).

The affinities implicit in some of the early Constituent Assembly
debates were neither general nor consciously built upon. Several Dalit
spokesmen took up sharply communalist positions, utilizing the argument of autochthonous racial origin of untouchables to brand Muslims
as immigrants who had come even later than caste Hindus.[21] Ambedkar
has something of a "centralist" reputation, for he was interested in
having a strong center as protection against regional or local oppression
of underprivileged groups. Except briefly in Bombay in the late 1930s,
he made few efforts to build bridges with the Marxist left (Omvedt 1994:
ch. 6). Conversely, Communists so far as I know took no notice at all of
the rather remarkable socialist elaborations of the notion of fundamental
rights that Ambedkar had attempted in his draft of March 24, 1947 (SD,
vol. II: 87–113), and their relative neglect of caste questions notoriously
persisted till recent developments associated with the Mandal issue.
Lahiri's espousal of self-determination, again, was a legacy of the
Adhikari thesis about a multinational India built like the Soviet Union
on a theoretical recognition of the right to secede. The CPI was already
moving away from that position by 1946–7, in the context of the danger
of this being construed as tacit advocacy of Pakistan. Over the longer
term, both CPI and later the CPI-M have often tried to move closer to
the "mainstream" by affirming more "national-integrationist" positions
that in effect can become rather unsympathetic towards regional aspira-

---

[21] See, for instance, the speech of S. Nagappa (Madras) on January 20, 1947, claiming
that only "we, the Harijans and Adivasis, are the real sons of the soil – we have a right
to ask the Mohammedan, the invader, to go out of the county." "The Aryan, the
migrator could also be asked to leave" – only "the Caste Hindus of this country do not
have any other place to go" (CAD, vol. II: 267). Interestingly, Ambedkar (1948)
launched a sharply-worded attack on the theory of high castes and untouchables being
racially different.

tions. Once again, it is only very recent developments that seem to have produced a significant change.

Let me conclude with two tentative generalizations.

First, the democratic–federal–secular combination, or its absence, has a tendency to change the specifics of all three terms that figure within it. Thus, "federation" as planned by the British in the 1930s, with its basically antidemocratic and divisive thrust, would have had a very different quality if it had ever got off the ground, for it was geared towards retention of ultimate imperialist control, in alliance with princely autocracy and grounded in divide-and-rule strategies. Universal franchise and majority rule across a subcontinent with vast diversities and fairly clearly defined majority and minority religious formations, again, can slide towards majoritarian domination if secular principles are absent or have been whittled down. A purely unitary structure, without some measure of "federal" decentralization, would almost certainly enhance such dangers. The Constituent Assembly debates indicate also that secularism can take on both more centralist and more federal-oriented forms, with the former tending at times towards an overlap with majoritarian Hindu communalism. Consistently anti-communal secularism, conversely, does seem to have some leaning towards federalism, if only because the regional–linguistic solidarities that have constituted the sociopolitical bases of decentralizing tendencies normally cut across notions of religious blocs. Communal ideologies, in partial contrast, seem more or less incapable of being anything but putatively centralist and statist. This applies, notoriously, to Hindu Rashtra aspirations which have always insisted upon the Akhand nature of Bharat – but also to the communalism of a minority of significant size, as indicated by the ways in which the Muslim League after the late 1930s marginalized regional formations like the Punjab Unionists and the Bengal Krishak-Praja Party through its propaganda about Pakistan.

Second, and in today's circumstances most crucial perhaps, there is a need to emphasize that the combination as realized through the 1946–9 Constituent Assembly debates was in no way inevitable or somehow in the nature of things. Born amidst unprecedented communal strife, violence, and misery – which it did help to allay for several decades – with many inadequacies, it was recognized as a major political and human achievement: this achievement, however, can no longer be taken for granted and left underanalyzed, for it is very seriously threatened today.

*Part II*

Political institutions and democratic
consolidation

# 3    India's federal design and multicultural national construction

*Jyotirindra Dasgupta*

There may be something strikingly novel and promising about the durability of federal institutions in India during the last five decades. It was not difficult to proclaim, even at the moment of federal inception, that profound social divisions in the country would destroy political cohesion and lead to a "collapse of the Indian state" (Harrison 1960: 339). The grip of the conventional frames of reference was so strong that most scholars were unprepared to recognize that the established frames were negatively affecting their understanding of an obviously unfamiliar context. Thus, even in the 1990s, the best estimate of the federal experiment in India offered in a study of comparative federalism could not go beyond the dismissive description of an "ethnofederation" caught in a growing crisis (Smith 1995: 4–25). It does not easily occur to these observers that the growing crisis actually may be associated with the fact that the novelty of multicultural federalism and nationalism may not be intelligible within the established frames (Rorty 1998: 29) that dread cultural differences and group-differentiated democratic competition (Kymlicka 1995; Bhabha 1994; Taylor 1999).

This paper begins with the assumption that India's bold experiment of combining democratic responsiveness to cultural differences with a federal conciliation of regional community, identity, and autonomy claims and a nationally concerted promotion of regional capability, has tended to ensure a novel mode of multicultural national development. We have tried to trace the narrative from the preparatory moments of the formation of conciliar political culture aided by the nationalist movement, the founding moments of constitutional crafting, the working of the constitution through many anxious moments over five decades, and the auxiliary layers of support from what one may call societal modes of federalization emerging in discernible ways. Of course, we have to be selective. The emphasis is on the linkages of the elements and their mutually augmenting effects to strengthen the developing institutional process of federalization and national coherence. The focus is on the pattern and why it is sustainable. It is from this perspective that the

49

issues of the formulation, working, revisions, resilience, and political resources of the constitutional design of federalization, rather than just federal government, offer the anchor point of our analysis. We suggest that the political prudence, legal flexibility, institutional inclusion, and interactive opportunities incorporated in the federal design can account for an important measure of the durability of Indian federalism.

Some points of clarification may be in order. We concede an important formative function to the constitution (Murphy 1993: 8–17). Interactive opportunities encoded in a democratic constitution tend to evoke legitimacy sentiments (Linder and Guy Peters 1995; Dryzek 1996). While these opportunities, including the impact of popular movements, have enabled the Indian constitution to adapt to dynamic needs, they have also led to a "reasonable degree of predictability" (Austin 1999: 635). The constitution's readiness to respond to changing patterns of regional identification, allegiance, and alienation may call for more significant reviews and revisions (Venkatesan 2000; Austin 2000). Hence, more than the constitutional document, it is the process of constitutionalism that may be more important for our purpose. However, our view of constitutionalism is not limited to the normal legal concerns for allocation and distributive aspects of power. Our concern extends to the developmental issues of the collective production of power. This marks an important point of departure from the conventional analysis of federalism. Also, the time orientation of our analysis is a long-term one.

### Federal culture and preparation: legacy as political capital

Federal ideas generally oscillate between the polar models of uneasy political union by compact and deliberate national consolidation. Even in the classic case of American federalism, the issue of whether federalism can play a role in making the nation is still being debated (Beer 1993: 1–25). In the Indian case the connection between mainstream nationalism and federalism was always intimate. Long before independence, the largest organization of the nationalist movement opted for a mode of federal sensitivity and culture that was largely dictated by the need to coordinate nationalist sentiments emerging from different cultural regions that were separated by distressing physical and communicative distances. Given the vast size of the country, the formation of political associations in the nineteenth century in relatively isolated regions like Bengal, Bombay, Madras, and other areas posed a major problem for the leaders. They perceived a basic disadvantage in relation to the colonial authorities who could obviously command more centralized power and effective communication. Building a coalition or modes of coordination across regions was then crucially important for the advancement of the nationalist movement. By the last quarter of the nineteenth century, a number of important regionally based nationalist associations came together to build one unifying organization. The Indian National Congress, created in 1885, initially served as an inter-regional coalition engaged in carefully generating a composite sense of national becoming (McLane 1977).

It was not surprising that a federal political culture (Duchachek 1991: 26–30) implying a collective orientation toward combining regional autonomy with national coordination was deliberately cultivated to fashion a strong platform of unity and action. During the early years of the Congress, organizational resources at the national level were understandably weak and thinly spread in different regions and depended heavily on the better-organized regional associations which had a longer history and stronger base. In fact, the very first session of the Congress in Bombay held in 1885 affirmed that the resolutions passed by it "be communicated to Political Associations in each province and that these Associations be requested with the help of similar bodies . . . within their respective provinces to adopt such measures as they consider calculated to advance the settlement of the various questions dealt with in these resolutions" (Majumdar and Majumdar 1967: 5). More than a decade later, when some of the most important Congress leaders were visiting England on a political mission to promote a nationalist demand for a greater share in the Indian administration, not surprisingly they chose clearly to identify themselves in a public statement as the leaders of their respective regional associations based in different parts of India (ibid.: 44–45).[1]

Their eagerness to publicize interregional collaboration as the basis of nationalism in India reflected a federal organizational orientation that was widely shared in the nationalist movement. From the founding years of the Indian National Congress, as one observer has put it, a clear enunciation of "a commitment both to representative institutions and to an accommodation of India's pluralism in a future Indian constitution was made . . . and it remained central in Congress thinking through the drafting of India's constitution after independence in 1947" (McLane 1977: 94–95). The implementation of this commitment during the long and eventful anticolonial movement was, of course, affected by the forces it encountered on its way.

---

[1] The reference is to G.K. Gokhale, S.N. Banerjee, D.E. Wacha, and Subramania Iyer who identified themselves as officials of regional organizations based in Poona, Calcutta, Bombay, and Madras.

The multicultural sensitivity and an inclusionary sense of combining autonomy with a nationalist mission obviously proved to be more demanding as the organization grew larger and the colonial ploys to curb it became more cruel and consummate. It required "special efforts unknown to other parts of the world" to pursue a strategy of federalized nationalism (Chandra 1989: 75). While participating in the national organization, the members, and especially the leaders, increasingly appreciated the rules of generating collaborative authority and power by respecting the autonomy of regions and the dignity of cultural space. The national sessions of the organization were rotated between different regions. The fourth session held in 1888 adopted a rule that no resolution was to be allowed to which the Hindu or Muslim "delegates as a body object, unanimously or nearly unanimously" (Zaidi 1987: 40). Language divisions in India increasingly demanded attention as the organization and the movement expanded their popular base. By the third session of 1887, held in Madras, there were many delegates as well as several speakers who were unable to communicate in English. The idea that the Congress organization was merely a platform of English-educated persons was already difficult to sustain. Nearly a third of the Provincial Standing Congress Committee members at that time were not educated in English and it was reported that in the lower levels of the organization "the English-educated are the exception" (Majumdar and Majumdar 1967: 15).

Gradually, the Congress organization proceeded to institutionally inscribe the importance of regional autonomy based on language by endorsing the language principle for reorganizing its provincial units in 1920. The reorganization was realized in 1921. In a series of steps taken by the Congress in 1927, 1928, 1938, and again in 1946 it encouraged the reorganization of provinces along language lines in the entire country (Chitnis 1990: 370).[2] However, autonomy in a multicultural context like India also poses a plural problem. An appropriate initiative in one domain involving speech communities needs to be seen in the context of autonomy demands involving religion or other markers of identity. The increasing salience of Muslim separatism during this period and the failure of the Congress leaders' negotiations negatively affected the general enthusiasm for autonomy on the part of at least some leaders. It is possible that these leaders, including Pandit Nehru and Sardar Patel, were always more committed to a centralist than to a federal political culture.

[2] At the same time, the important role of the regional languages in national and provincial communication was recognized by the Congress Party. See, for example, Rajkumar (1949: 85), for a relevant article in the party constitution of 1934.

### Disquieting dawn: formative challenges

The framers of the constitution of newly independent India were placed in a distressingly confusing situation. Within a few months of the beginning of the working of the Constituent Assembly of India the issue of Partition was decided in favor of the formation of Pakistan (Hasan 1994). The country was already trapped in a situation of unprecedented violence, destruction, and uncertainty. A few months before independence, in December 1946, the nationalist leaders including Nehru were still hoping that the Constituent Assembly would have the authority to construct a constitutional design for the undivided country. The objectives resolution, moved by Nehru in the same month, stating the aims of the Constituent Assembly, clearly reiterated that the constitution of the undivided country would be based on a system that would allow the regional units to "retain the status of autonomous units" in a substantial manner (Shiva Rao 1968: 79ff). However, the Muslim League was in no mood to accept any arrangement for a system to serve a united India. When the objectives resolution was passed in January 1947 the Muslim League opposition to unity became stronger and louder. By July 1947, the colonial decision to divide the country dramatically transformed the context of constructing a constitutional design for India.

Most accounts of Indian independence extol the legacy of the administrative order that was supposed to have been a benign colonial gift to a developing country. What was this order really like? According to the Government of India Act 1935, the reference to India actually indicated three distinct territorial categories. The first category included Governors' Provinces and Chief Commissioners' Provinces. The second comprised more than 500 princely states. Nearly 60 percent of the subcontinent was included in the first while the second commanded close to the rest except for a third category known as "tribal areas" in the northwest and northeast including relatively small parcels of territory. The actual patterns of authority exercised over the latter were various and in some cases quite tenuous. It was only in the areas covered by the first category of British India that the idea of federalism had some currency, particularly in the 1930s.[3] The territories covered by the other categories actually represented hundreds of different administrative systems. No wonder the units of British India turned out to be arbitrary

---

[3] A nationalist evaluation of this colonial plan for federalism without an assurance of independence can be found in the "Congress Resolution on Federalism" of February 1938 (Shiva Rao 1964: 102–103). The problem of the princely states' fear of federalism, even of the limited kind enunciated in the colonial constitution of 1935, and a more positive attitude revealed by the leaders of the states' people's movement is discussed in Shiva Rao (1968: 19–20) and Patil (1981: 107ff).

entities with no necessary social basis of unity or community. This is the kind of liability that set the context of federal construction in independent India.

The dilemma of the new constitution's designers was also perplexing in another way. What examples of federalism based on democracy and difference in world history could aid their novel reconstructive mission? They obviously did not have the option of going for a voluntary union of well-formed units of prior autonomous or sovereign standing. They could see that the American system, for example, was not expressly designed to reconcile different ethnic or cultural demands (Forsyth 1989: 3). The absence of the rights of the southern black people, to cite one instance, to have a voice in the federal design was inconsistent with the kind of democratic federalism that the Indian framers were interested in. The American framers' presumption of this federalism being associated with a homogeneous people – "a people descended from the same ancestors"[4] – was unlikely to be of service for designing multicultural federalism in a diverse continental country. Could the Indian leaders then learn something substantial about multicultural design from the Swiss historical experience? But there too was a case of nearly 500 years of authoritarian domination of Germanic people and the German language before the turn of the nineteenth century when the Swiss union actually became multilingual.[5] However, the Canadian federal design appeared to be more promising and relevant. In fact, the perception that even today multicultural federalism as theory remains an "abiding preoccupation" of the Canadian people and that the problems of "excess of federalism" continue to cause concern, appear to be reassuring even to the contemporary Indian participants in the federal process (Milne 1993: 203).

## Federal construction: institutional design and elaboration

India's federal design was envisaged as a project to ensure reasonable national agreement across regions and communities to support and develop durable political order. The Partition of the subcontinent, while

---

[4] This is the way the notion of American people was presented by John Jay in Hamilton et al. (1941). A fuller version is: "I have as often taken notice, that providence has been pleased to give this one connected country to one united people – a people descended from the same ancestors, speaking the same language, professing the same religion, attached to the same principles of government" (Hamilton et al. 1941: 9).

[5] As Murray Forsyth puts it: "Even the federal system of 1815 was not instituted or supported primarily because it was a means of uniting different linguistic communities" (Forsyth 1989: 3).

not solving the problem of communalism, fortunately facilitated the fashioning of a consensus that made for the smooth sailing of the basic federal design in the Constituent Assembly. There were, of course, many debates and arguments but little that could be described as profound conflict of interest.[6] Neither the committee drafts nor the members' debates suggested anything like what one would expect from the negative references to ethnofederalism in the comparative literature of our time. The overwhelming majority enjoyed by the Congress Party did, of course, facilitate the amicable dialogue. At the same time, it is interesting that the confident Congress leadership also actively encouraged non-Congress leaders of various persuasions to be elected with Congress nomination. Also, it was the Congress initiative that ensured the presence of minority groups other than Muslims and Sikhs. The latter were, of course, allowed guaranteed seats in the Assembly by the original plan.[7] Within the Congress, a cohesive group of leaders including Nehru, Patel, Prasad, and Azad dominated most of the important business of the Assembly. They did so either directly through their crucial committee roles or in association with a larger group of about fifteen supporting leaders including some who either had never been close to Congress or had been its active opponents. The latter category included B.R. Ambedkar, the leader of the Scheduled Castes Federation who became the chairman of the Drafting Committee of the Constituent Assembly (Shiva Rao 1966: 295–297; Austin 1966: 18ff).

The deliberate attempt of the party enjoying an overwhelming majority to resist the temptation of exclusively taking charge of the business of the Assembly facilitated the future legitimation of the constitutional design. If the sense of sharing did not apply equally to all the political groups, it was difficult to deny that most of the prominent political forces and sources of professional expertise were carefully included.[8] Mahatma Gandhi's advice to Congress to incorporate the largest measure of nonpartisan support and knowledge was also probably

[6] The idea of "amicable union" is documented by Granville Austin (1966: 186–234). According to him: "The Proceedings of the Assembly revealed none of the deep seated conflicts of interest evident in Philadelphia in 1787 or like that between Ontario and Quebec" (186).

[7] "Of the 205 members elected to the Assembly from the Governors' Provinces on the Congress vote, as many as thirty were from outside the party. From the minorities other than Muslims or Sikhs, the Scheduled Castes accounted for 29, Indian Christians had 6, Anglo-Indians had 3, Parsis 3, and Tribals 4" (Shiva Rao 1968: 96).

[8] Non-Congress experts like N. Gopalaswami Ayyangar, Hriday Nath Kunzru, and Alladi Krishnaswami Ayyar had open access to the Congress Assembly party meetings. The representation of the left was thin. There was one Communist member for a brief period and the Socialists decided not to join. Officially, the religion-based right was also absent though some leading Hindu Mahasabha leaders like Shyama Prasad Mookherjee were inducted in other ways (Austin 1966: 14ff).

informed by a strategic concern for evoking a sense of trust and accept-ability that could offer a valuable political resource for the constitutional process during the founding moment (Shiva Rao 1968: 96–97).

The importance of such a strategic concern for cultivating consensus was particularly appropriate for gaining regional assent for the federal provisions. Even the usage of terms like "federal" or "union" to describe the federal arrangements apparently required careful calculation from the perspectives of initial as well as future evocative appeal and prospects of generating centripetal sentiments. The earlier deliberations in the Assembly used the term "the Federation of India." But the Drafting Committee settled for the term "Union" instead of "Federation." The reason for avoiding the term "Federation" in the draft constitution, as explained by Ambedkar, was to "make it clear that though India was to be a federation, the federation was not the result of an agreement by the states to join in a federation, and that the federation not being the result of an agreement no State has the right to secede from it" (CAD, vol. VII: 43). He strongly reiterated that this was going to be a federation by division for convenience of administration while the country continued to be one integral whole.[9] He wanted to make sure that inadvertent ambiguities did not leave any room for catastrophic possibilities like the American civil war that cost more than 600,000 lives. His concerns were widely shared by members, including leftist leaders like H.V. Kamath (ibid.: 31–44; Shiva Rao 1968: 14). The new constitution of 1950 was designed to permit a national political system to rationally reorganize the colonial inheritance of more than 500 units including the provinces, princely states, and special territories in the frontier areas. Gradually, a series of reorganizations created twenty-eight states, six union terri-tories, and the National Capital Territory of Delhi. These steps involved a number of pieces of legislation and amendments over five decades (Basu 1999: 429–430).

A close look at the reason, pattern, and sequences of the reorganiza-tion of regional entities, and even at times the significant alteration of subregional arrangements, should convince one that the idea of regional autonomy can admit of at least as many interpretations as there are regions. Consequently, if the people or organizations outside a region fail to be persuaded by a particular definition of a region or state, or claims of identity articulated by some regional leaders or groups, it can be reasonably subjected to legitimate interrogation. If, however, the

[9] He also said: "The Americans had to wage a civil war to establish that the States have no right of secession. The Drafting Committee thought that it was better to make it clear at the outset rather than to leave it to speculation or to dispute" (ibid.: 43). This was included in his speech moving the draft constitution on November 4, 1948.

questioning authority at any time happens to be the central government, it may be unfair necessarily to identify that skepticism with hostility or denial of autonomy. There are, of course, a number of reasons for the popular presumption of central hegemony. The system of sharing power as encoded in the design, clearly and deliberately, allows for a decisive advantage on the part of the central government. Whether in the matter of constitutional amendment or the division of powers or even with respect to the issue of altering the boundaries of the states, the formal advantages of the center appear to be formidable. But then the design of federal distribution of authority and power needs to be read in the context of the actual exercise of the relative powers of the units and the dynamic struggles and collaborations in a multicultural country like India. Regrettably, the scholarly evaluative focus has been largely innocent of that interactive connection and its implications for long-term national development.[10]

### Region, nation, and institutional promotion of autonomy

The issue of autonomy in a federation is usually more celebrated than scrutinized in the discourses on federalism. What does the term imply in terms of regional and individual rights? Does it need a more sensitive and complex specification particularly in rapidly changing multicultural contexts (Kymlicka 1995: 76ff; 1999: 131–140; Walker 1999: 141–165; Dryzek 1996: 57–75)? Does the issue of autonomy in a developing country also call for a necessary concern for those material and human resources and conditions without which the promise of making appropriate choices in order to dynamically pursue human competence and capabilities may remain largely unrealized (Sen 1997: 3–10)? Given the uneven distribution of resources and conditions across regions in India, is there a special need for a crucial institutional role to promote and materially coordinate the possibilities of exercising prudent choices and to clarify the alternatives that may be attainable by such choices? These are some of the questions that deserve close attention in order to

---

[10] A long tradition of literature originating in the West and India has concentrated on the mechanical balance issues of federal government, without much concern for the broader aspects of federalism. K.C. Wheare's early use of the term quasi-federal to describe India has been repeatedly used since the very second year of Indian federalism (Wheare 1952: 28). Later editions of this work or later works by many other authors may convey different nuances of this notion but negative or near-negative assessments have persisted through fifty years. Semantic problems associated with the usage of the terms of federal analysis also stand in the way of fair assessments. See, for example, Arora and Verney (1995: 19–70) for the views of Verney and Watts.

evaluate the quality of autonomy that is contributed by the federalizing design and processes in India. What scope for reorganization was actually left in the constitutional design? How did the constitutional design work? What did it accomplish for the regions? What did the regions do in their turn to sustain the national system of federalism? Only a few illustrative points can be discussed here.

It was obvious at the founding moment that regional reorganization would involve a careful processing over a long time. Given India's cultural complexity, interlinkages, and the prospects of changing priorities of identity and representations on the part of individuals and collectives due to the shifting agenda of interests induced by developmental processes over time (Dasgupta 1995: 287–294), any course of reorganization was likely to leave room for several revisions. Changing perceptions of cultural differences and political preferences as projected in the future did not make the choice of regional boundaries either easy or enduring. The most reasonable course at the moment of founding was to generally anticipate these problems and to leave the course of successive phases of specific negotiation open and institutionally secure for democratic participation. It is easy to observe that articles 2, 3, and 4 of the constitution offer extensive formal powers to the national parliament to reorganize states. These provisions "enable Parliament by law to admit a new state, increase, diminish the area of any State or alter the boundaries or name of any State" (Government of India 1988, vol. 1: 9). They may help amend the specification of the states included in the first schedule of the constitution and also the fourth schedule (allocation of the seats in the council of states) without encountering the difficulties of the constitutional procedure for amendment as specified by article 368. The exercise of these powers requires that the president's recommendation would be necessary and that the president shall ascertain the views of the legislature of the state affected by the proposal in the bill.[11] The role of the president in doing this would not seem substantially to affect the power of parliament since there is no provision for him to be bound by those views expressed by the respective states. Normally, in a parliamentary system as it pertains to India, the rules guiding "recommendation" or "ascertaining" by the president appear to be a formality, particularly so long as common political affiliation builds a bridge between him and the parliamentary leadership. This would apply even more (as it did in the era of Congress Party dominance) if that bridge extended to link the central ruling party with its counterparts in most of the states.

---

[11] A much stronger provision was made in the case of the applicability of article 3 to the state of Jammu and Kashmir. In this case a prior consent of the state legislature is required to introduce such a bill in parliament.

Increasingly, however, those bridges have eroded and the countervailing influence of the president may now turn out to be a genuinely reassuring possibility for the aggrieved regional forces in particular states or their national clusters. The bold action of President K.R. Narayanan (a Congress leader) to return the union cabinet's recommendation for imposing president's rule in Uttar Pradesh in October 1997 and the subsequent retreat of the cabinet leadership (United Front) may clearly suggest that counting on the countervailing possibilities in a context of party pluralization may not be that unrealistic after all. The coalitional turn in Indian politics, the ability of the president to rise above partisan politics, and the strong case made by the supreme court in its S.R. Bommai judgment against arbitrary central action may generate a new sense of federal balance with respect to the autonomy of states (Ghose 1997: 11, 21). This assurance was considerably strengthened when in September 1998 the same president refused to support a union cabinet recommendation for the imposition of president's rule in Bihar. Faced with this rebuff, the then Bharatiya Janata Party (BJP) retreated and simply settled for a new debate on the issue (Swami and Mahalingam 1998: 4–14). Even aside from the new assurances, the history of the formidable formal powers of the center need not be interpreted as necessarily implying a gross negation of regional interest or federal objectives. It is interesting that nearly five decades of such imbalance have not induced a sufficiently strong feeling to substantially alter the provisions of article 3. According to the report of the Sarkaria Commission of 1988, only one state government had asked for the removal of those provisions. Two states were in favor of prior consent of the states affected by intended changes while a few modifications were proposed by two other states (Government of India 1988, vol. 1: 73). This would hardly signal a general sense of outrage.

The history of the processes of the reorganization of states suggests that there was generally a strong sense of caution about hasty moves. Most of the national leaders were also regional leaders. They could anticipate the waves of demands that would follow once the case for redrawing the regional boundaries was rushed. The Linguistic Provinces Committee of the Constituent Assembly advised against such a move. The JVP Report of the Congress Party agreed with that view but conceded that democratic opportunities would be likely to make the language-based demands difficult to resist in future. The constitution, as a result, while postponing reorganization, actually inscribed generous opportunities in article 3 for responding to strong expressions of popular claims.

The notes of excessive caution, ironically, appeared to provide an incentive for the development of strong popular sentiments cutting across party loyalties in favor of the reorganization of regions along language lines. By 1951, the movement for a separate Andhra state succeeded in gaining wide popular support. The failure of the union-level Congress leaders to anticipate the intensity of popular affection for a regional community based on the Telugu language created a new problem (Bondurant 1958: 32–42). In an important sense, the regional movement became a reconstructive moment of a federalizing process. The prominent part played by the Communist and Socialist parties of national persuasion in successfully carrying the movement forward clearly indicated that the Andhra case for reorganization was not just a narrow expression of regional particularism. Rather it signified some interesting socially integrative dimensions that were often missed by the political observers. For example, this was also a movement to bring together the Telugu speakers of all social levels of Madras and Hyderabad into a large community of cultural and administrative unity. The resulting unity of the Telugu community and its sense of solidarity was expected to make it a more constructive partner in a multicultural nation. Was this expectation misplaced?

When in 1952 the popular reaction to the death of Sriramulu helped intensify the mass movement and pushed it to a point of violent agitation that finally made the union leaders concede the separation of Andhra, an interesting political development followed. By 1953, when the new Andhra state was created, there was a feeling that the Communist Party would win the forthcoming elections. However, both in the 1955 mid-term elections for Andhra and in the 1957 elections in Andhra Pradesh (following the inclusion of Telangana in 1956) it was the Congress Party that unexpectedly scored a decisive victory (Reddy 1989: 280–281). A strategic policy of accommodation with the smaller parties enabled it to offer a strong base of *regional* support to the *national* Congress organization. The deep suspicion about the disintegrative impact of regionalism thus proved to be grossly unfounded in just less than two years. Another integrative dimension was illustrated by the fact that there was an expanding process of incorporation of support of the cultivating peasant castes in the Congress organization. Though the political activation of these groups began earlier, largely as a result of communist mobilization, the new consolidation of the Congress Party appeared to gain more regional and national dividends out of it than the radical parties (ibid.: 281).

Thus the Andhra transition demonstrates that the formal provisions of the hegemonic authority of the center actually turned out to release forces of regional autonomization in a manner that contributed to the durability of federalism. Later, when a frankly regionalist party became prominent, it was quickly transformed into a constructive partner, and frequently a leader, of the ruling national coalition. Thus the role of the Telugu Desam Party (TDP) (formed in 1982) and of N.T. Rama Rao in providing crucial aid to the maintenance of the National Front as an alternative to Congress dominance cannot be overestimated. Even his successor's crucial role in securing a new lease of life for the United Front government in 1997 must have surprised those who refuse to admit the national role that the regional communities and leaders could play.[12] When the parliamentary elections of 1998 for the twelfth Lok Sabha failed to return a comfortable majority for any political party, it was again the TDP that played a crucial role in making the BJP and its allies win the vote of confidence. Along with the support of Farooq Abdullah's regional party, the National Conference (Jammu and Kashmir), the TDP leaders made it possible to continue stability in governance. The 1999 elections for the thirteenth Lok Sabha returned a stronger BJP coalition with the TDP as its largest ally, lending the strongest regional base of support for national stability (Dasgupta, S. 1999: 14–16). The generous support that the DMK and the AIADMK parties (despite the reversal of 1999) have historically contributed to the federal government beginning, in the case of the former, from the late 1960s would be another interesting example. In fact, the continued informal cooperation between the ruling parties in the non-Congress-ruled states paved the ground for the type of multiparty coalitional rule that offered a viable national alternative to Congress rule in 1989 and 1996. The ruling BJP alliances of 1998 and 1999 also crucially depended on the participation and support of more than fourteen regional parties.[13]

But democratic participation and competition can also undermine the strength of the established regional movements. This refers to the incentive that democratic competition offers to *subregional* movements and leaders to challenge the politically dominant groups who claim to speak for the regional community with an authoritative voice. The subregional movements for a separate Telangana in the 1960s or for the separation of the Andhra region from Andhra Pradesh in the 1970s indicated how the claims of collective solidarity could also induce

[12] The reference here is to the chief minister of Andhra Pradesh, Chandrababu Naidu, who played a key role in installing I.K. Gujral as India's prime minister. His national role became more important later.

[13] The National Democratic Alliance (NDA) led by the BJP registered a majority composed of 302 members (out of 538 elected) in the 1999 elections. The BJP had 182 seats and the regional partners secured the rest of the NDA tally. The Congress and its allies got 134, of which 22 were accounted for by regional parties (Iyer 1999: 1).

significant fragments of regional communities to go their own way to seek autonomy (Reddy 1989: 283ff). This is a story that has been repeated in almost all the regions of India. Most of these subregional claims for autonomy (Chandra et al. 1999) have been accompanied by serious charges of denial of autonomy against the regional governments. Whether in Assam or West Bengal or elsewhere, such claims, ironically by deflating the privileged regionalists, offer an unearned dividend to the federal authorities. If, again, the claims of the subregional groups lead to the building of autonomous administrative institutions within regions with federal support and constitutional assurance, then a new and deeper process of federalization may be encouraged. This kind of extension of federalization at substate levels, for example in India's Northeast, Bihar, and elsewhere, deserves serious attention. It tells us a story that offers an interesting insight into subregional innovation in multitier federalization (Dasgupta 1997: 345–370). We should also recognize that an autonomous council for the Jharkhand area of Bihar, for instance, included a territory and population that were much larger than those of many states in India or countries elsewhere. The movement in this area had originally equated autonomy with statehood within the federation. The wider movement for Jharkhand has a support base in a number of districts in West Bengal, Orissa, and Madhya Pradesh, in addition to the districts originally covered by the autonomous council in Bihar (Basu 1994: 2–18). These areas of Bihar gained statehood when the Jharkhand state was created by the end of 2000.

## Centralism and fairness: formal authority and political reality

A focus on political autonomy, however, offers only a partial account of the problems of federalism in a developing multicultural country. Autonomy involves a complex series of issues and processes. It calls for a public life that is supposed to value basic rights and liberties. The pursuit of political autonomy, in this sense, whether applied to individuals or communities, would require a delicate cultivation of reflective capacity to define goals with a keen sensitivity for the rules of social cooperation so that the prospect of institutional support of autonomy for others is not impaired (Rawls 1993: 77–78). At the same time, the issue of institutional facilitation would imply that rather than presuming that people and groups are always naturally endowed with the necessary faculties to set and pursue their goals, it is important to create conditions to assist their choices or, if necessary, to help revise them (Dryzek 1996: 72).

It is this notion of institutional promotion of autonomy that sets the proper context of the role of centralism in the design and practice of Indian federalism. A major assumption of the nationalist movement was that a concerted drive for development of material, human, and political resources was necessary to overcome poverty, exploitation, injustice, and a general sense of lack of power and collective dynamism. Such a drive was supposed to be led by a national set of leaders who would be mainly associated with the central government. Brave sentiments were expressed in favor of a national authority during the Constituent Assembly debates (CAD, vol. v: 80).[14] But the extent to which the central government was to be equated with national authority was not made very clear. The reports drafted by the Union Constitution Committee treated issues such as the distribution of powers, union executive powers, the distribution of revenue, and amendment in ways that steadily contributed to conspicuously superior central power (Austin 1966: 19ff). The members of the assembly were understandably apprehensive of the dangers of the territorial vulnerability of the new state. Basic issues of food availability, rationing, price control to serve the poor, nationally uniform standards for training, technology, and production, and coordination of higher education were discussed with a sense of urgency that would be difficult to appreciate more than fifty years later. The case for regional allocation of power was also considerably weakened by the fact that the nature of the regional units and their boundaries were as yet uncertain and that the exact transformation and integration of the princely states was not yet determined (CAD, vol. v: 80).

The formal share of power allocated to the union government, even for normal times of constitutional operation, obviously suggests a high degree of centralization.[15] The emergency provisions of the constitution, however, push the catalog of central powers to an alarming extent, supposedly in order to enable the national state to meet extraordinary moments of crisis.[16] Emergency powers used during cases of external aggression in 1962 and 1971 appeared to accord with the original

---

[14] As one member (G.L. Mehta) stated: "Unless there is a national authority, unless there is an authority to allocate the resources and determine the priorities and coordinate these different plans, we cannot really have the development of these less developed . . . areas in our country."

[15] Only a few indicative points will be mentioned here. The union list of legislative powers include ninety-nine subjects and the state list sixty-one, and concurrent powers belonging to the union and the states extend to fifty-two items. The first list includes defense, external affairs, major taxes, etc.; the second covers public order, agriculture, etc.; the third includes economic and social planning and education. In cases of overlap, the union wins.

[16] Articles 352–360 and the forty-second (1976) and forty-fourth (1978) Amendment Acts would offer the relevant provisions. The fifty-ninth amendment of 1988 is also important for one regional application.

expectations of legitimation of special powers for responding to grave threats to the nation. On the other hand, frequent abuses of the emergency provisions for internal requirements have generated strong popular reactions leading to several important changes in the constitutional system to discourage future abuses.

The worst abuse of emergency powers at the *national level* took place in 1975 and continued until March 1977. The flimsy grounds of "internal disturbance" (article 352) were used by Prime Minister Indira Gandhi who had a hard time distinguishing between the rule of law and rule by law (Dasgupta 1978: 315–349). The authoritarian abuse of the system clearly exposed the hollowness of some of the centralist arguments that had been repeatedly used to equate centralism with the national authority that was presumably required for disciplined development.[17] Popular reaction fortunately led to a decisive verdict against the ruling Congress Party in the dramatic elections of March 1977. The new coalition government, consisting mainly of the organizers of popular movements in different regions against the Congress Party, used the forty-fourth amendment of 1978 to make sure that "internal disturbance" would no longer be sufficient grounds for proclaiming an emergency (Austin 1999: 417–430). Participative politics as ensured by the democratic system thus proved to be a significant instrument of correction, revision, and adaptation of the constitutional design of the federal system.

However, there is also another problematic emergency provision which refers to situations of breakdown of the constitutional machinery in a state, popularly known as the president's rule, whereby the president, in association with parliament, can assume the normal powers of a state, remove a state ministry, dissolve the state legislature, and empower the union legislature to exercise the respective state's power for a temporary period. The overriding central authority is supposed to serve the national purpose of disciplining particular state governments straying from the expected norm of constitutional practice or to cope with the cases of political breakdown in specific units of the federation. This special power under article 356 has been used more than 100 times since 1950, frequently in political contexts that rarely resembled major crisis events. It has been used in all the states and with a relatively high frequency in Kerala, Punjab, and Uttar Pradesh. The Sarkaria Commis-

---

[17] The most damaging abuse of the constitutional system and extension of the authority of parliament and the ruling leadership at the central level was exemplified in the forty-second amendment (1976) that affected nearly sixty clauses of the constitution. Following the electoral defeat of the Congress Party, the Janata Party government succeeded in correcting the damages by the forty-third and forty-fourth Amendment Acts of 1977 and 1978 respectively.

sion, after a careful examination of seventy-five cases, found that only twenty-six cases of the use of article 356 were "inevitable" (Government of India 1988). It is interesting that all major political parties have used or supported such intervention when it served their purpose, just as when viewing from the other side of the fence they often resented it. Popular opinion, however, supported intervention in situations of terrorism and violence in the 1980s in Punjab, and during the first half of the 1990s in Jammu and Kashmir, as well as in four states in 1992 following the demolition of the Babri mosque (Chandra et al. 1999: 323, 338, 442). The Sarkaria Commission also suggests that this type of overriding special power can be a positive resource for the federal system. In fact, it "firmly" believes "that Article 356 should remain as ultimate constitutional weapon to cope with" extreme situations that may signal "secessionist" foreboding (Government of India 1988: 177).

The major issue then is how to prevent the "ultimate" weapon from being a daily instrument of expedient politics by central leaders, especially in a growing situation of lack of organizational linkage between the ruling parties at the central and state levels. Fortunately, the supreme court's decision in the S.R. Bommai case delivered in 1994 promises to reduce the risk of arbitrary central intervention and restrain the central leaders from recklessly using exceptional powers for partisan purposes. The court held that a proclamation under article 356 can be judicially reviewed.[18] The central government has to reveal to the court the relevant material on the basis of which the proclamation was made. The court viewed the president's rule as an exceptional power. It made use of the Sarkaria Commission Report to specify the situations in which the use of such power would be inappropriate. It would be unconstitutional, for example, to use article 356 to remove a duly constituted ministry merely because the party in state power had been defeated in the Lok Sabha elections or on the grounds of bad administration or instability (Mozoomdar 1995: 160–168). Proper occasions for using the president's rule were identified by the court mainly in terms of a situation where it was impossible to proceed with constitutional government. It is interesting that the *federal structure* was unanimously recognized by the court as a basic feature of India's constitution. The status of the states as constitutional entities was clearly affirmed. The supreme court, as a common resource of the states and the center as per the original design of federalism, thus offered a timely voice of authority to restore federal balance. Both the report of the Sarkaria Commission and the court decision and close reading of the Constituent Assembly debates con-

---

[18] See *S.R. Bommai* v. *Union of India, All India Reporter,* 1994: September (SC 1918ff).

siderably helped President K.R. Narayanan to refuse assent to a cabinet decision to use article 356 to impose president's rule in Uttar Pradesh in 1997 and again in Bihar in 1998.

A realistic possibility of a more chastened center learning to engage in a fair partnership with states of different sizes, resource bases, cultural claims, and party alignments is likely to be strengthened by the expanding legitimation of regional political expressions and the pluralization of parties occurring since the 1990s. At the same time it is important to note that the reality of central powers has always depended on the real regional support recruited by the parties dominating the center. Even during the days of Nehru dominance, resistance to the center conducted from the regional bases of the Congress or non-Congress parties and popular movements was highly effective, especially when the issues were concerned with regional boundaries or interstate cooperation for large development projects such as river valley projects (Franda 1968: 35–128). We have already examined how the states' reorganization movements extracted responsiveness from the reluctant central leaders. The entire history of such movements in Andhra, Punjab, Maharashtra, Gujarat, and elsewhere would show the difference between the appearance of central authority and the regional reality of power in matters of important federal business (Kumar 1988: 38ff). Besides, the politics of official language policy of the union in the 1960s indicated not merely the informal strength of regional leaders within and outside the ruling party at the center but also the institutional strength of the Chief Ministers' Conference representing the states to generate negotiated compromise to ensure federal balance (Dasgupta 1970: 245ff). Some of the most interesting institutional interactive processes involving the center and the states can be observed in the processes involved in the sharing of the economic and political resources of the nation.

### Federal resource-sharing and national development

The idea of shared national development based on democratic planning was popularized by many nationalist leaders long before independence. This concept was, for Nehru and his supporters, national in scale with a general emphasis on the freedom and equality of citizens regardless of their group affiliations or membership.[19] The idea of explicitly group-

---

[19] For Nehru especially, communities and classes were markers of divisiveness that went against the grain of disciplined national development. As one of his biographers commented, what Nehru with his national project hoped to do "was to lead his party and the Indian middle classes generally to socialism without their knowledge" (Gopal 1976: 246).

differentiated rights to complement individual rights was not favored by them.[20] Planned action for developing the nation as a whole was conceptualized by them as a matter of scientific problem-solving where the problems of group endorsement involving classes, cultural communities or regional formations were not relevant. Nehru and his supporters' sense of scientism and rationalist adventure in making a modern egalitarian nation based on large-scale industrialization was resented by Gandhi and his followers.[21] But Nehru was appointed as the chairman of the Congress Party's National Planning Committee in 1938 by the then party president Subhas Chandra Bose whose fascination for the collectivist notion of national development was well known. It is interesting that the decision to set up the committee was taken at a meeting of ministers of industry from the provinces that were then ruled by the Congress Party. This committee included scientists, economists, and industrialists. Scientism and statism ruled equally after independence when, as the first prime minister, Nehru initiated the Planning Commission and became its first chairman.

It was actually a resolution of the central government that brought into existence the organization of the Planning Commission in 1950. By 1993 it commanded a total staff of more than 5,000 persons including a research staff of experts recruited from virtually all fields of development (Dandekar 1994: 1459). When the number of the experts is added to those who are employed by various union ministries, the potential dominating effect of knowledge, used as power, on the states may not be hard to guess. Even during the Eighth Plan (1992–7), despite public statements of support for liberalization, the commission appeared to control 50 percent of capital expenditure and nearly a third of the total expenditure of the union government (ibid.: 1457–1458). The historically crucial role of the commission during the last five decades, both at the central and also indirectly at the state levels, suggests a continuity of central dominance that was problematic for federalism. If the Planning Commission was an executive product of the union government, the Finance Commission was set up as a "quasi-judicial" body by the constitution. It was supposed to be an independent body mainly to recommend the distribution of sharable taxes between the union and the states and also among the states. The Finance Commission deals with the shares of personal income tax and union excise duties. It also allocates grants under article 275 to meet certain non-plan needs of

[20] For one way of differentiating these rights, see Kymlicka (1995: 34–35, 80). Liberal theories are not usually sensitive to group rights.
[21] Mahatma Gandhi advised "his followers to stay away from the Planning Committee" (Gopal 1976: 247).

deficit states. The commission is supposed to safeguard the financial autonomy of the states in accordance with the federal principle of the constitution. It accounts for nearly the same proportion of the total central transfers as that determined by the Planning Commission. For example, the respective share of each in 1993–4 was approximately 45 percent. Total net transfers for the year amounted to about 44 percent of the expenditure of all the states and union territories taken together.[22] Unfortunately the plan transfers have been historically marked by a patronizing pattern of central discretion which impairs a shared sense of national collaboration. The element of discretion was reduced after 1969 when a consensual formula for the allocation of plan transfers on the basis of population, relative backwardness, and fiscal competence of the states was adopted (Wallich 1982: 6–7). This method, better known as the Gadgil formula, despite some modifications over time, proved to be relatively reassuring for the states in a context of political development that was moving in a new direction.

The political scene in the country in the late 1960s was marked by an unprecedented confidence of regional leaders. Their eagerness to affirm the autonomy of their regional communities and to claim a more reasonable share of national resources was facilitated by a rapid decline of Congress dominance in the late 1960s. Extensive setbacks in the 1967 general elections and again in 1969 in selected states rudely reminded the new Congress leaders of the post-Nehru period that their right to dictate the terms of national development was rejected by the national electorate. Leaders like Indira Gandhi discovered new grounds for cultivation of support from the poorer people in disadvantaged areas and regions. The Fourth Five-Year Plan (1969–74) accorded special attention to the problems of development in backward areas. Gradually, a sense of location-specific treatment for accelerated development in such areas was avidly pursued through the Fourth and the Fifth (1974–9) plans (Sarker 1994: 623–625). Special attention was given to area and group-differentiated needs. Specific programs aimed at the development of drought-prone areas, tribal areas, hill areas, poorer farmers, and agricultural workers proliferated in the 1970s and continued later (Dasgupta 1981: 51–100). Since these activities, obviously demanding more decentralized attention, were to be conducted in the states, the case for a more concerted action with them became much stronger.

The great diversity of the resource base of the states implied that the severely depressed states were likely to be keenly interested in working

---

[22] This was lower than the average annual figure registered during 1987–90 which was about 46 percent.

closely with the central planners for collaborative development of their basic resources. A glance at the complexity of disparity may be necessary for our purpose. A quick comparative estimate of per capita net state domestic product at current prices for 1994–5, for example, may offer an indication of the severe disparity between the relatively larger states. Thus, for that reference period, the states at the low end remained near the level of Bihar (Rs. 3,816), while the states at the high end enjoyed a level close to that of Punjab (14,188) or Maharashtra (13,112) (GOI 1997: PS-12). However, the domestic product or income figures do not adequately convey the actual resource standing of the states. The composite index of infrastructure employed by the Tenth Finance Commission shows, for example, that while Kerala's income rank was quite low, its infrastructural development rank was close to that of Punjab and significantly higher than that of Maharashtra (GOI 1994: 24, 132). Similarly, some "capability poverty measures" based on nutrition, health, and female literacy levels would appear to place Kerala at the top, with Punjab at 3 and Maharashtra at rank 7 among fifteen major states (Dev and Ranade 1997: 71). The small northeastern states which receive favorable treatment from the center because of their low infrastructural resource base, nevertheless, when judged by the "capability poverty measures," remained close to Punjab with a rank score of 4. In fact, disparity at the district level within and across states tends to be more severe. While the rural female literacy rate in one district of Rajasthan was only 4 percent in the early 1990s, it reached 98 percent in another district of Kerala (ibid.: 7). Simple aggregate interstate comparisons thus may be highly misleading for evaluating the proper logic of the fair sharing of resources for national development.

The problems of interdependence have been highlighted by a growing importance of regional authority in Indian politics (Hasan 1999: 179). However, the capacity of the states to raise their own resources has been quite low compared to that of other federations (Rao 1999: 279). The states in Canada or Brazil mobilize resources that take care of nearly 80 percent of their expenditure but in India the corresponding figure would be about 45 percent (World Bank 1995: 32). While the revenue receipts of state governments from 1992 to 1996, for example, showed a very modest increase, the revenue expenditure figures indicated a rapid rise. In particular, the persistent increases in nondevelopmental expenditure during this period, despite increases in tax revenue and current central transfers, created a disturbing imbalance in the revenue situation. This was, understandably, accompanied by a concomitant reduction of development expenditure. The share of nondevelopment expenditure in the total expenditure of the states has steadfastly increased from about 19 percent in 1980–1 to 32 percent in 1996–7. On the other hand, the corresponding figure for development expenditure declined from about 70 percent in 1980–1 to 63 percent in 1996–7 (Reserve Bank of India 1996, vol. I: VIII 9; vol. II: 187–188, 210). At the same time, since the 1980s or even earlier, vast resources have been invested in the development of infrastructure without making reasonable provisions for cost recovery. The subsidies provided by the State Electricity Boards and the losses incurred by the State Transport Boards together accounted for nearly 1.5 percent of GDP in recent years (World Bank 1995: 32). The poorest states depended heavily on the center for their fiscal support. Central transfer of resources accounted for nearly 62 percent of their spending in 1992–3. The comparable figure for the richest states was 46 percent. No wonder that between 1998 and 2000 the revenue deficit has more than doubled (Saran 2000: 18). Both the poor and the rich states have come to depend extensively on central resources. It is the states that carry the major responsibility for conducting the social and economic services. However, the design of the federation left most of the resources to the center. But the increasing prominence of regional politics, both in the form of strong regional parties governing important states or working through coalitions winning national power in 1989, 1996, and later, made the issues of financial power balance more salient. The National Development Council, created in 1952 to serve as an advisory body to prescribe guidelines and review plans in a forum including the chief ministers of states and the central planners, assumed greater importance only after the non-Congress and regional parties gained power in important states. After 1977, when the Janata Party assumed national power, the chief ministers of sixteen states proposed a strong case for the reform of the resource-sharing system. The strength of the regional voices helped register important changes in the formulas for resource-sharing used by the Finance Commissions and the Planning Commission by the 1980s and later. However, the logic of fair sharing and collaborative fiscal relations for national development call for a more radical restructuring of federal finance.

The states have consistently asked for a share of a wider range of central taxes. They have resented the limited range of taxes that have been shareable under the terms of the constitution. A report of the Tax Reforms Committee suggested that "in the light of experience, it is necessary to re-examine the constitutional provisions regarding tax sharing" (GOI 1991: 45). The Tenth Finance Commission boldly recommended an alternative system that envisaged a mandated sharing of gross proceeds of *all* central taxes in a manner that will leave an assured share of 29 percent with the states (GOI 1991: 60–61). It has been suggested that this reform would "increase the center's interest in collecting income tax and give the states greater transfer payment stability" (World Bank 1996: 65). The idea of a single divisible pool as suggested above was accepted by the United Front government in the 1997 budget session.[23] The regional parties of this coalition government were not the only ones that considered it as "a major step towards federalization."[24] Many other parties including some Congress Party leaders also welcomed this move for restructuring finance for inducing collaborative national development. A clear case for the devolution of financial and administrative power was also reiterated in the national agenda for governance affirmed by the BJP-led ruling alliance of parties in March 1998. The decision to review the constitution, as announced in February 2000 by the BJP-led government, also gave prominence to this concern (Mitra and Ahmed 2000: 14–17).

If the growing strength of regional leaders made these reforms possible it must be difficult for them to evade the issue of reforming finance within the states. The states whose performance in internal resource mobilization remains poor obviously impose a burden on all other states. A state like Tamil Nadu which has a better record (in the 1990s) of tax effort (12 percent of the state national product) may reasonably raise questions about the claims of states with low tax efforts like Bihar (5 percent of the state national product) on national resources (World Bank 1996: 36). Empirical indicators of fiscal performance indicate a consistently low score for states like Bihar, Orissa, Uttar Pradesh, West Bengal, and Punjab, for example.[25] Their autonomy and resource claims have been made less persuasive by their failure to generate the kind of overall fiscal competence and reform that some of the better performers like Tamil Nadu or Karnataka have pursued. The states lagging behind, despite huge agricultural endowment, did not even try to generate any substantial resources from either agricultural income or land revenue. The share of land revenue as a proportion of tax revenue for all states in India declined from 2.7 percent in 1981–2 to 1.91 percent in 1993–4 (Bagchi 1994: 2813). By 1995–6, the share of land revenue collected by a large state like Uttar Pradesh as a proportion of its total expenditure was a mere 0.16 percent. Whom should the

---

[23] Jha (1997: 47).
[24] Ibid. This statement was made by M. Karunanidhi, the DMK chief minister of Tamil Nadu. Supporting statements were also made by the chief minister of Maharashtra (Shiv Sena), and deputy chief minister of Orissa (Congress).
[25] For a relevant analysis and elaborate data (including reference periods 1980–7 and 1987–94 for the performance index) see Pattnaik et al. (1994: 315–367). Recent reports are worse (Saran 2000: 19–23).

states which are lagging behind blame when they themselves are becoming more involved in central rule?

## Collaborative production of power: capability for autonomy

The post-Partition reconstruction in a precariously poised international situation understandably put a premium on centripetal sentiments. At that founding moment, constructive constitutionalism was not a simple question of the division of preexisting power or a rigid separation of domains of authority. There was, rather, a general aspiration for urgently attending to the question of collective power (Ball 1988: 80–105) to serve a new nation. The issue of power was translated as one of deliberate creation of capabilities in the economy, competence in organization, effectiveness in communication, and efficacy in participatory citizenship. Issues of autonomy were envisaged more in terms of the promotion of capabilities in groups or individuals, to expand the range of choices to be accomplished by strenuous cultivation, rather than simply expecting them to be matters of the natural endowment of individuals or communities. This is the context of constructive constitutionalism to creatively build a multicultural nation based on democratic foundations and federalizing institutions that makes Indian federalism instructive.[26] The Congress Party dominance connecting the center with most of the states during the formative decades positively aided the collaborative production of resources. Unfortunately, the benefits of political capital and party inheritance often encouraged leaders like Nehru to act as national preacher and political instructor. His letters to state chief ministers, for example, were possibly designed to keep lesser leaders in line.[27] How seriously the state-level leaders took his instructions is of course another story. The entire history of agrarian reform in India would have been very different if the Congress top leaders' or even the Planning Commission's sermons were always taken seriously (Kumar 1988: 48–50). The central government and the central Congress leadership officially advocated a comprehensive implementation of laws limiting land ownership from the early 1950s. But only a partial implementation of these in the following decades clearly shows how the state leaders, including those belonging to the central ruling party, were able to have their way.

[26] Witness one recent assessment: "In contrast to the fate of the Soviet federation, the Indian republic has endured acid tests to emerge as a highly instructive case of successful federation" (Ratnapala 1999: 131).
[27] See Morris-Jones (1992: 225ff).

However, the state governments have always been eager to cooperate with the national planning organizations in the policy areas which call for central financial support in the form of plan assistance. The Planning Commission prepares a national plan that includes both central and state plans. As we have noted before, the incredible diversity of the country and the complexity of determining the differential needs of regions, subregions, and specially defined disadvantaged categories of population make it difficult for planners to devise an appropriate allocation of resources. But the centrally coordinated system has continued to work irrespective of party labels, ideologies, or advocacy of regional interests (as in the case of coalition governments) associated with central leadership in different phases of Indian politics. Even in the Eighth Five-Year Plan (1992–7), despite the presumed change of policy in favor of liberalization, total central public-sector outlay was of the order of 59 percent (Dandekar 1994: 1463–1464). This allowed the center to make large investments even in areas that should normally have been the domain of regional governance. In addition, the "centrally sponsored schemes" brought attractive central assistance to states, though not without strings. The discretionary elements and the strings offended the states but did not necessarily reduce their temptation. When the same state leaders ascend the steps of national power, they rarely seek radically to change the system. They want to participate in the huge national pool of divisible developmental resources, the vast national market, the structure of support for the specially needy regions, and the national assurance system for regional contingencies.[28]

Even a limited area of economic collaboration would show that plan resource allocation has had a positive impact on the state of development, though not all the states have benefited equally. Using a system of combined component scores, considered as the composite index of development, one study found that at the end of the 1984–5 plan period (Sixth Plan), per capita cumulative plan outlay helped explain approximately 82 percent of the development index (Sarker 1994: 621–633). A cursory observation of the ranking of major states (fifteen) based on the component scores suggested many interesting changes between 1960 and 1987. West Bengal slid from rank 3 in 1960 to 9 in 1987 while Gujarat moved from 7 to 3. All southern states improved their ranks. Despite all talks of Hindi heartland and dominance, Bihar was locked at 15 and Uttar Pradesh scrambled from 13 to 12. Punjab and Haryana steadily maintained their ranks of 1 and 2 respectively. The study,

[28] The special case of federal transfers needed by states affected by calamities and the burden of relief expenditures requiring national effort rarely receive a fair deal in the literature on equity in transfer. See Govinda Rao and Chelliah, (1996: 40–41).

however, points out that Bihar had received about a third of what Punjab and Haryana received as per capita cumulative plan outlays and West Bengal's share was about half of Punjab's.

## Concluding observations

However, there is more to the regions' attraction to federal collaboration than just material assurance, advancement, or equalization. A cumulative fund of centripetal sentiments has gradually grown across communities through the engagement in a national political culture, a nationally coordinated and emulated educational system, nationally sponsored modes of communication, and the sheer habits of the heart[29] that have been nurtured by nationwide systems of patriotism, literary ideas, music, the arts, the press, cinema, movies, and competitive sports. There is also the growing tradition, and a long one at that, of intertranslated literature, theater, and popular music and lyrics ranging widely across languages and regions. Through these processes, the experience and emotions of one region consciously or imperceptibly move to others to intimate both surprising similarities and interesting differences. The interlearning initiative has been increasingly facilitated by the expanding exposure to the visual media including competing television programs of national, regional, or global origin. The movie industry in India, irrespective of language affinity or regional location, represents an incredible linkage of diverse personnel and markets in the nation and abroad (Rajadhyaksha and Willemen 1999).

The importance of cultural interactions and transmissions for generating national sentiments across communities and regions has been recognized in the works of eminent authors and cultural leaders in different parts of India from at least the early phases of the nationalist movement.[30] Their systematic promotion through nationally sponsored formal institutions for interregional collaboration generally began after independence. The role of the Sahitya Academy, the Lalitkala Academy, the Sangeet Natak Academy, the National Film and Television Institute, and the Press Council of India in mobilizing and coordinating contribu-

---

[29] I am using this notion in the wider sense of the term "manners of the people" employed by Tocqueville. My purpose is to indicate its role in the maintenance of an institutional system. For Tocqueville's notion see Tocqueville (1990: 299).

[30] A good example from the early history of nationalist discourse would be Ramesh Chandra Dutt (President, Indian National Congress, 1899) who was also a famous novelist in Bengali literature. He was the author of major Bengali historical novels dealing with Maharashtrian and Rajput history. Among his many works in English, perhaps *The Economic History of India* (1902) is best known. A complete list of his works is in Dutt (1982: 24ff).

tions across regions should be recognized as deliberate ways of promoting societal processes of federalization.[31] Witness, for example, the history of Swiss federalism. The crucial role of cultural associations in the nineteenth century in promoting federal unity, mutual solidarity, and common identity when neither the cantonal nor the supra-cantonal authorities were able to collaborate for the sake of common national bonds of cohesion is not easily forgotten by Swiss historians. In particular the role of the association to promote Swiss music (La Société Helvétique de Musique) in strengthening the national bond in different regions forms an important part of the history of federal development in that country (Eschet-Schwarz 1991: 174–175). If any observer of India doubts the role of music in contributing to the centripetal process she should at least examine the impact of the versions of "Vande Matram," a nationalist song offered by a Tamil composer and a Maharashtrian singer to the Indian audience on the occasion of the fiftieth anniversary of freedom, if not the wider spectrum of cooperation across regions in Indian classical, popular, and movie music.[32] An important aspect of societal federalization may be recognized in the institutional processes associated with many nationally popular groups and social movements. These organizations strive to maintain a fair representation of regional members and leaders. The culturally diverse composition of the national working class or professional organizations, for example, may indicate how systems of recruiting and maintaining the support of regional components have become compelling conditions of national organizational success. Learning to work with the multicultural sharing of authority through institutional systems of society and culture is, to be sure, most likely to reinforce the citizens' habituation to federalism. Federalizing habits in societal transactions tend to offer auxiliary layers

[31] The first was for literature, the second was for fine arts and the third was for promoting music and drama. Various sports authorities for the national coordination of soccer, field hockey, athletics, and especially cricket, also need special attention. An effusive account of the success of the Indian cricket team in international competition in 1998 was instructive. It explained regional balance as the reason for success: "the West [Sachin], South [Rahul] and East [Saurav] holding up the hopes and aspiration of a nation with the North [Sidhu] and Center [Azhar] as axis." For details see Prasad and Bahal (1998: 69–70). The "axis" moved from the center to the west in 1999 and to the east in early 2000.

[32] See "A. R. Rahman," a note in *India Today*, international edition, January 5, 1998. The title is also written as "Vande Mataram." This song (officially a national song) was written by Bankimchandra Chatterji for a Bengali novel. It was sung on the occasion of the 1896 session of the Indian National Congress. An English translation was rendered by Sri Aurobindo. Many new recordings have been released in recent years in northern and southern India. Rahman is also a leading composer of film songs in Hindi. The Maharashtrian singer is Lata Mangeshkar, a national legend who sings in many regional languages, commanding incredible interregional popularity.

of potential support (Habermas 1999: 160) for political federalization. They may also compensate for the limitations of political leadership and organizations, as we have seen, for example, in the Swiss case cited above.

We began this study with the suggestion that the reconstructive opportunities incorporated in the constitutional design of federalism in India when treated in the context of the operation of democratic participation can reasonably account for the durability of Indian federal institutions. We have explored the interactive processes in multicultural politics to examine how the federal system learned over time to cope with pressing demands at critical moments of the formative decades of political development. During the early moments of transition, democratic political movements constructively aided the *system* whenever the formal authorities faltered. The combined development of democratization and federalization, though rare in world history (Stepan 1999: 228–231), crucially contributed to India's systemic coherence. Our exploration of the role of this system in actively promoting the capacity to pursue substantive autonomy rather than simply to wait for and passively respond to autonomy demands has indicated how the collaborative development of complementary resources can help evoke and maintain legitimating sentiments and strategic political support for the multicultural federal system. The emphasis in our study has been on the gradual attainment of resilience of the system (Habermas 1993: 166) rather than on the governments of the moment or specific parties and coalitions. If, someday, the dependence of the national political parties on coalition politics gives way to a new phase of party dominance, the resilience of the system may be tested anew but not necessarily gravely threatened. Any unfederal attempt will have to face the same kind of corrective movements conducted in and across regions as the public space has offered in the past.

Our focus on the developmental dimensions of federalism has also implied that the changing perceptions and representations of cultural or regional differences cannot be captured by some simplistic notions of primordial ethnic or community demands (Chandra 1999: 299ff). The equation between ethnic allure, affinity, and uncompromising demands can be grossly mistaken. It may be as misleading as the alleged opposition between ethnic nationalism and civic nationalism – read non-Western for ethnic and Western origin for civic. As can be easily seen in our Indian case and elsewhere (Brubaker 1998; Fearon and Laitin 1996), ethnic ties are perfectly compatible with the simple logic of gain from intergroup cooperation and avoidance of the unnecessary cost of conflict. In fact, the multiplicity and malleability of identity in India's context offers a constructive opportunity to the democratic system (Dasgupta 1995: 288–289; Stepan 1999: 232). Common interest can be constructed either by conscious craft or inadvertent convergence in institutional space. Also, institutions can "create identities and preferences at the same time as they respond to them" (March 1997: 695). Even the apparently cold constitutional designs of the federal system can promote, support, and sustain multicultural and transregional cohesion based on inclusionary political culture. Whether this should be conceptualized as an instance of "constitutional patriotism" (Habermas 1998: 500) or, as in the case of India, the constitutional consolidation of emerging forms of wider identification across communities predating modern nationalism by centuries (Bayly 1998: 23ff), is beside the point. It is more important for us to indicate the profoundly generative role that prudent constitutional designs can play to construct a federalized nation in a multicultural society.

# 4    Center–state relations

*James Manor*

A central aim of this book is to understand how the demands of groups in Indian society for greater power, resources, autonomy, and – let us not forget – respect are dealt with in this complex, culturally heterogeneous democracy. How and to what extent do politicians, parties, and governments accommodate these demands? In so far as they fail to do so, what sort of frustrations develop, and what impact does that have on the democratic process?

Within this broad context, the present chapter examines center–state relations. It differs from Jyotirindra Dasgupta's closely related study of the federal system in two ways. The first is its angle of vision – this chapter looks at things mainly from the state level upward, while Dasgupta examines the federal system mainly from the apex downward. The second is its preoccupation with informal rather than with formal political institutions which are Dasgupta's main concern, although each of these two chapters necessarily intrudes somewhat into the other's territory.

"Formal" institutions are entities of state created by India's laws and constitution – legislatures, the federal system including the instrument known as president's rule, the bureaucracy, the courts, etc. The category of "informal" institutions includes, most importantly, political parties, but also movements, factions, patronage networks, and the vast army of political activists and fixers which drives and sometimes disrupts the democratic process. But that category also embraces nonofficial institutions which are both actors and arenas of contestation – cooperative societies, the boards of private trusts, schools, colleges, temples, plus other institutions devoted to the furtherance of religion, social welfare, and the influence of organized interests such as caste associations, unions of farmers, workers, and other voluntary associations.

Informal institutions stand between and integrate the state and civil society, but they also intermingle very substantially with civil society (defined here as "associations of a voluntary nature, standing between the household and the state, with at least some autonomy from the state").

Two main questions are addressed here. First, why have relations between New Delhi and the various state governments usually remained manageable? Second, why in some cases have things gone spectacularly wrong, so that violent separatist movements have developed and center–state relations have broken down?

In part, the answers provided here cover the same ground as an analysis offered by Atul Kohli which focused on two "proximate variables" – "the level of institutionalization of the central state, and . . . the degree to which the ruling strategy of leaders accommodates demands for self-determination" (Kohli 1997: 329). In part, however, this discussion goes beyond that very state-centered approach and considers social, cultural, geographical, historical, political and economic elements that are (in varying degrees) external to the state in several Indian regions. (It does so not to attack Kohli, but at his request.) We shall see first that these latter elements exercise a potent influence over events, and second that economic conditions have had less importance than the other elements noted above.

The answers to our two questions change somewhat over time. During the first twenty years or so after independence in 1947, society in most of India (especially in rural areas) was sufficiently self-regulating that it posed few serious problems for political institutions – formal or informal. And in that early period one informal institution – the Congress Party's cluster of regional political "machines" – possessed the substance and the reach to manage most of the social tensions that arose.

Since the late 1960s, things have become more difficult on both the sociocultural and the political fronts. Interest groups have crystallized and have become increasingly well organized and aware of their political concerns. They have pressed harder for resources, power, and respect, and have exhibited growing impatience with mere tokenism. This has made India a more genuine democracy and a more difficult country to govern.

At the same time, political decay has afflicted most formal and informal political institutions. This has partly resulted from ossification, but its main cause has been attempts by politicians to erode the substance and autonomy of institutions in the interests of personal rule. Decay has damaged the instruments which politicians need to manage such a lively polity. This has sown frustration among organized interests and has produced far more strife of a destructive sort than occurred in the first two decades after independence.

In very recent years – since the passing from power in 1989 of the Gandhi "dynasty" which was the main source of attempts at deinstitutionalization – an important counter-tendency to decay has become particularly evident. Numerous damaged institutions – informal and especially formal – have been rebuilt, at least to some degree, and have begun to function in more autonomous and nonpartisan ways. The federal system is one example – thanks in part to a 1994 supreme court ruling setting down guidelines for the imposition of president's rule (Mozoomdar 1995) and to the disinclination (and perhaps the inability) of most national governments in the hung parliaments which existed between 1989 and 1999 to be as commandist as their predecessors. The courts have become far more assertive, as has the Election Commission. We have also seen the creation of new formal institutions which hold considerable promise – most notably the *panchayats* and municipal bodies which have emerged after the seventy-third and seventy-fourth amendments to the constitution came into force in 1993 (Crook and Manor 1998). These and other tendencies make it possible to speak not only of decay but of political regeneration in India (Manor 1996).

This does not mean that India's institutional difficulties are at an end. But they continue to be eased by elements of the political sociology and the political culture to be found in most (though not all) Indian regions which lend themselves to the functioning of open, liberal politics generally and to a federal system in particular. There are, none the less, vivid (indeed hair-raising) exceptions to this generalization. Both the generalization and the exceptions will be explored here.

This chapter tackles these issues mainly by examining events in a number of specific Indian states. The first two, "mainstream" states – Andhra Pradesh and Tamil Nadu – illustrate the generalization that center–state relations have been reasonably manageable. We then turn to three "troubled" states or areas – Punjab, Jammu and Kashmir, and the Northeast – which represent exceptions. More attention will be devoted to the exceptions than to the generalization. This might seem somewhat misleading, since states where center–state relations have never degenerated into severe crisis greatly outnumber those where breakdowns have occurred. So let us note here at the outset that the exceptions are just that – unusual cases which help to inform us about the more general tendency.

The exceptional, "troubled" cases assessed here fall into two categories. The first two – Punjab, and Jammu and Kashmir – are states where center–state relations were bound to be difficult, but where creative "management" from New Delhi could have prevented the breakdowns which occurred. In the other case – the Northeast – break-

downs were and remain unavoidable. New Delhi's "management" there
has sometimes left much to be desired, but even if it had been
impeccable, it would have been impossible to prevent breakdowns from
occurring.

### Explaining "manageable" center–state relations – sociocultural conditions and the politics of bargaining

Center–state relations have tended strongly to remain "manageable,"
though not trouble-free, for four main reasons. First, powerful group
demands seldom take the form of states' (or state*wide* elites') demands
which impinge mainly on New Delhi and which – if frustrated – might
generate secessionist sentiments. Demands tend far more often to arise
out of *intra*-state conflicts, so that the resulting pressure is felt mainly or
exclusively at the state level. This supplements Myron Weiner's insight
that the formal structures of the federal system tend to quarantine
conflicts within regional arenas (Weiner 1989: 36).

The second reason provides the main explanation for the first. The
social and cultural complexity and heterogeneity – indeed, heterogeneities within heterogeneities – that we encounter within most states are so
formidable that they make it exceedingly difficult to develop the kind of
statewide solidarity which secessionism requires.

Third, this sociocultural complexity and heterogeneity have contributed to a strong tendency among Indian citizens to shift their preoccupations from one to another of the many identities which they have
available to them – often and with great fluidity. Depending upon
circumstances and recent events, they may fix for a time on their *jati*,
*jati*-cluster, *varna*, or other caste identities, on their local, subregional or
national identities, on their class, linguistic, communal identities, or on
sectarian identities which fragment Hindu, Muslim, and other communal identities, etc. But they seldom fix ferociously and tenaciously on
any one of these, as people in, for example, Sri Lanka have done.

This is discouraging for those on the Indian left who would like
people to cleave to their class identities, and to those on the Hindu right
who seek to make communal identities preeminent. (The BJP's show-
ings at the 1998 and 1999 general elections have done nothing to alter
this point.) This penchant for fluidity and fickleness is not diminishing
in the face of the complex trends noted in Yogendra Yadav's important
recent research at the Centre for the Study of Developing Societies.[1]

---

[1] Interview with Yogendra Yadav, Delhi, August 7, 1996.

The tendency towards fluidity reduces the severity and longevity of most conflicts within most states (and undermines the threat of secessionism which requires sustained solidarity round regional identities) *because it prevents tension and conflict from building up along a single fault line in society* (Manor 1996b).

Finally, despite the decay which formal and informal political institutions have suffered in recent decades, they often remain capable of making the politics of bargaining work. This comment refers mainly to political parties (and occasionally to factions within them) and to the organized interests with which they interact. All of these informal institutions still tend to contain enough people with appropriate skills and attitudes to sustain the bargaining process, imperfectly but at least adequately. Indeed, this small army of political activists and "fixers" constitutes a major national resource which is unavailable to most other countries in Asia, Africa, and Latin America. This capacity to practice the politics of bargaining prevents the sociocultural heterogeneities noted above from creating such political chaos that accommodations – within states, and between center and states – unravel. (We will see that this generalization cannot be applied to India's Northeast, but it is valid in most of the rest of the country.)

One further comment is in order here. Rob Jenkins' recent research (Jenkins 2000) has stressed the importance of the number and diversity of arenas in which political conflict occurs within individual Indian states. Contests take place frequently for seats in the national parliament and in state assemblies, for seats on councils in the multiple tiers in the *panchayati raj* system (since 1993), and for positions of influence in a number of quasi-official and nonofficial boards, cooperatives, associations, etc. The existence of so many opportunities to capture at least some power tends to persuade parties and politicians to remain engaged with the politics of elections and bargaining, even when they suffer defeats in some contests.

On those rare occasions when separatism is contemplated by powerful regional interests, the coercive power of the Indian state tends to discourage such thinking. But separatism seldom comes into play, for the reasons set out above and because those interests tend to the view that the politics of bargaining – mainly within individual states, but also between those states and the central government – offers them sufficient incentives to make open revolt unpalatable.

What constitutes a creative "management" approach by the government of India to center–state relations, and in particular to disenchanted regional groups which have turned or might turn to separatism and/or violence?

It contains several strands. It entails a very visible willingness to listen to the grievances and discontents of regional groups, and to change some policies in response to them. Policy changes are sometimes accompanied by political enticements, such as promises to include such groups in ruling coalitions if they moderate their more extreme demands. At the very least, groups which have been disinclined to take part in "normal" electoral politics are commonly encouraged to abandon their reluctance. They are told that if they succeed in such elections, the central authorities will welcome them as the new government of their state. Packages of economic assistance and new development programs are often offered at the same time – indeed, they often precede negotiations on the lines set out above, as a sign of the government's good intentions.

Such initiatives sometimes have to be pursued at the same time as Indian security forces are engaged in conflict with members of such disenchanted groups, when disorder has reached serious levels. That can cause problems for attempts aimed at accommodation, but the central government has succeeded often enough at such attempts to make this kind of twin-track approach worth trying – as many people in New Delhi understand.

Finally, it needs to be said that, on occasion, the creative "management" of center–state relations entails the imposition of president's rule – direct rule from New Delhi, after the suspension or dissolution of a state assembly. This comment will raise hackles, because this constitutional provision has often (indeed, usually) been abused by commandist national leaders to uproot legitimate state governments headed by their opponents.

But we need to consider the reasoning that led the framers of India's constitution to arm the central government with these powers. They concluded that occasions would arise when state governments would prove incapable or unwilling to cope with severe conflict. They thought that, in such circumstances, New Delhi might justly conclude that to quell disorder, or to prevent it from reaching ever more dangerous levels, president's rule needed to be invoked.

In this writer's view, they were correct. Such occasions have indeed arisen in postindependence India. It would be very surprising if they had not, since the stresses that attend an adventurous experiment with democracy in a society like India's are bound to overwhelm liberal institutions – not often, but now and again. (Doubters should consider the hair-raising array of problems faced by the authorities in India's Northeast, which are surveyed below.) The extravagant abuse of these powers by both the Congress and Janata governments of the 1970s and

1980s, and any future abuse which may occur, should not blind us to this patent fact.

D.A. Low, who knows both India and Africa well, has rightly noted how much destruction might have been avoided if the Organization of African Unity had possessed such powers to snuff out strife in member nations before it reached grotesque levels. This would have made it possible to revive "normal," minimally civilized politics and relations between warring social groups, using just the kind of creative management approaches outlined above. A decision of India's Supreme Court in 1994, requiring the central government to justify more systematically its use of these powers, establishes some welcome safeguards against their misuse. More safeguards are needed, but the legitimate use of these provisions should not be excluded from a menu of creative approaches to extreme (if unusual) problems.

## Case studies of individual states

### Mainstream states

To examine these themes in more detail, let us consider two "mainstream" – that is, reasonably typical – states. We begin with Andhra Pradesh, a state which has been swept by various movements – including regional movements that might be termed "nationalist" or "subnationalist." But it is also a sufficiently typical state to provide an approximation of a national "norm."

Note that we turn for our "norm" not to New Delhi and the Lok Sabha (the lower house of India's parliament), but to a *state*. The reason for this is that politics at the national level and in the Lok Sabha are abnormal, in that they differ from most states and their state assemblies in several respects, most crucially in one.

Caste has far less importance at the national level than in the politics of any single state. This is because India has not one caste system but many. Speaking very roughly, each linguistic region has its own distinctive caste system. And since most state borders (the Hindi belt excluded) conform, again roughly, to the boundaries of linguistic regions, politicians in each major state share not only a common language but a common traditional social system which differs (slightly or radically) from those of other states.

Being a Brahmin in, say, Bihar or Uttar Pradesh, where these groups have considerable numerical strength and economic power, means something very different from being a Brahmin in the four southern states where Brahmins comprise only 3 or 4 per cent of the population and are far less prosperous. And there are no indigenous Kshatriyas or Vaishyas in South India. So when members drawn from the four *varnas* meet in the Lok Sabha, they find their common caste status to be of little relevance. The only caste bloc which constitutes an approximately similar proportion of the total population in nearly all of India's major states (Gujarat excepted) are the scheduled castes. So national-level politics cannot provide us with the kind of "norm" that a state like Andhra Pradesh can.

This is true despite the fact that the social composition of this and all other southern states differs strikingly from that found in the rest of mainstream India. That means that there is considerable sociocultural distance between the southern states and the rest. But despite this, all four South Indian states have exhibited the kind of sociocultural heterogeneity which prevails in other mainstream states, and which helps to prevent tension and conflict from developing along a single fault line in society. They have also (partly as a result of this heterogeneity) managed to sustain the politics of bargaining. (We return to this theme in the section on the Northeast below.) Taken together, these two elements constitute the "norm" upon which we must fix.

### Andhra Pradesh

Andhra Pradesh has witnessed a variety of political excitements since the 1940s. Before 1952, two sizable and somewhat interrelated agitations occurred there – one for the democratization of the former princely state of Hyderabad and its inclusion in the new Indian union, and the other a radical movement among disadvantaged groups in the Telengana sub-region. In each case, the ultimate outcome was determined by "managerial" interventions from New Delhi. The first agitation succeeded, thanks in large measure to the intervention of India's security forces. The second failed because those forces suppressed it.

The early 1950s also saw a passionate campaign for the unification of the Telugu-speaking areas of South India – those which had been in princely Hyderabad, plus those which had been directly administered by the British in the multilingual Madras Presidency – within a new state to be called Andhra Pradesh. In 1953, after a "fast unto death" by a leader of this movement raised the agitation to a dangerously high pitch, New Delhi agreed to create such a state.

This hastened a more generalized, nationwide revision of state boundaries along linguistic lines in 1956 which was the most creative "managerial" decision ever undertaken by the government of India in the field of center–state relations. Nehru was extremely hesitant about it, because he feared that it might lead to secessionism. But he soon realized that his fears had been baseless. When Telugus, Tamils, Gujaratis, and others were thrown together within single political arenas, they soon discovered all of the things that divided them – caste, class, subregional, urban/ rural and other divisions. This undermined the solidarity which is essential to any secessionist movement. The heterogeneity *within* each linguistic region has been the main bulwark that sustains the unity of this linguistically heterogeneous country. (This theme crops up again in the discussion of Tamil Nadu below.)

In the late 1960s, another movement in the Telengana subregion acquired genuine ferocity – this time for secession from Andhra Pradesh (but not from India) on the basis of unjust treatment by the state government. A party representing these sentiments swept the board at the 1971 parliamentary election, capturing ten Telengana seats. But soon thereafter the problem was resolved when the ruling Congress Party provided a package of concessions and – not incidentally – offered the movement's leaders prominent roles in its leadership. From then until 1980 the voters of Andhra Pradesh gave enthusiastic support to Indira Gandhi and identified strongly with the all-India party that she led. This was true despite the Emergency, which took an extremely mild form in the state, thanks mainly to a sensible Congress chief minister (Manor 1978).

During the early 1980s, however, bullying interventions in the state's affairs by central Congress leaders and frequent changes of chief ministers – some of whom were incompetents chosen for their slavish loyalty to Indira Gandhi – alienated voters in Andhra Pradesh. The upshot, in 1983, was the election of the first non-Congress government in the state. The new ruling party, the Telugu Desam, had been founded only one year before that election. But it evoked widespread enthusiasm thanks both to the popularity of its film star leader, N.T. Rama Rao (NTR), and to his complaints about insults from New Delhi to the honor of the Telugu people.

NTR scrupulously avoided secessionist rhetoric, but the national leaders of the Congress sought to depict him as "antinational" and arranged his ousting by inducing a number of his legislators to defect. This backfired by reviving resentments against New Delhi which enabled him to return to power for longer than he might otherwise have done.

By the late 1980s, however, poor performance by his government had generated sufficient disillusionment to enable the Congress to defeat him at a state assembly election. This was followed, at the next time of asking, by NTR's return to power after a period of incompetent Congress rule and eventually – after further insensitive behavior by the chief minister – to his ousting at the hands of elements in his own party. At the time of writing, the Telugu Desam is firmly in control of affairs. But some Congress Party leaders, searching desperately for an issue on which to revive their fortunes, are seeking to develop subregional separatism in Telengana on issues which differ from those that arose in the early 1970s.

There are two things to emphasize about this all-too-brief survey of the recent history of Andhra Pradesh. The first is the frequency with which people there have shifted their preoccupations from one to another (and then another) of the many political identities available to them. The agitation to make the princely state of Hyderabad part of democratic India was based on an enthusiasm for *Indian nationalism*, although it was undercut somewhat by class and other identifications of the disadvantaged groups involved in the initial, radical Telengana struggle. By 1970, a different but quite heated campaign for Telengana separatism was rooted in a *subregional* identity. But within a few years of that, the state's voters (including those of Telengana) were exhibiting enthusiasm for Congress leaders at the *national* level. By 1983, they had turned to NTR out of anger at national leaders' affronts to their *regional* identity – and so it goes on.

This habit of shifting identities – despite the passion generated at any single moment – often and with great fluidity, persists in most Indian states throughout the postindependence period. It constitutes a national norm at the level of political behavior among ordinary folk, and makes the task of "managing" center–state relations comparatively easy. Things can still go wrong because aggressively commandist, manipulative modes of "management" tend to create problems – as we saw in Andhra Pradesh in the early 1980s. Accommodative approaches, however, tend to ease such problems. They constitute another norm at the level of central management of center–state ties.

### Tamil Nadu

Tamil Nadu is the only large Indian state (that is, a state with a population of over twenty-five million) where separatism has *appeared* to acquire real force. But when what is sometimes called a separatist "movement" is subjected to careful examination, major doubts arise about whether it amounted to much.

There are three fundamental problems here, all of which have been underemphasized. First, it was never clear quite who was supposed to do the seceding. So nationalists in the state were confused about what the actual "nation" was. Second, there were always doubts about how much popular support this "nationalism" commanded. Finally, the alacrity with which the leaders of the Dravidian party abandoned separatism, and their disinclination to revive it at the moment of greatest conflict with New Delhi (the anti-Hindi riots of 1965), inspire skepticism about whether they had ever been firmly wedded to the idea at all. Let us briefly consider these issues.

What "nation" was supposed to be served by this "nationalism"? At first – in 1914 – an organization called "the Dravidian Association" sought "a Dravidian state under the British Raj" which would "safeguard the political, social, and economic interests of the Dravidian people." But this "people" was defined entirely in *caste* terms. The association was seeking "a government of, by, and for the non-Brahmin" (Hardgrave 1965: 12) – on the assumption that South Indian Brahmins were outsiders. The "movement" at this point did not desire separation from India or any other entity, but rather the destruction of Brahmin influence within South India – or, more precisely, within that portion of South India covered by Madras Presidency.

It is difficult to regard this as "nationalism," and that difficulty persisted into the next phase – the 1920s and 1930s, the era of the Justice Party – and beyond. The Justice Party was, like its Dravidian party successors, so "riddled with factionalism" (ibid.: 24) that it lacked the solidarity that is often associated with nationalist movements. And its overwhelming emphasis was not on "nationalism," but on anti-Brahmin grievances (ibid.: ch. 3).

In the next phase in the story, E.V. Ramaswami Naicker – who generated something that we can justly describe as a "Dravidian movement" – confused things further. He came to prominence in 1937–8 by organizing protests against the Congress government's introduction of Hindi as a compulsory school subject in Madras Presidency. As Robert Hardgrave accurately reports, he saw this "as a subjugation of Tamil peoples which could only be avoided through the creation of a Dravidian State" (ibid.: 27). But this comment plainly illustrates the confusion. Was it the *Tamils* who needed to be rescued, or the *Dravidians* – that is, the people in the four Dravidian regions: the Tamils, Malayalis, Telugus, and Kannadigas? No one quite knew.

Ramaswami Naicker backed the call for Pakistan because it might assist with "the creation of Dravidisthan" or "Dravida Nadu" – a term that embraced all four linguistic groups. But the party which he eventually formed, the Dravida Kazagham (DK), "brought the message of *Tamil* nationality to the masses" (ibid.: 27 and 31). These are different things.

I have, during twenty-five years of research in South India, sought in vain to identify a single political figure among the Malayalis, Telugus and Kannadigas who ever identified with the notion of a Dravidian "nation." Scarcely any had even heard of the idea. Tamil leaders made next to no effort to carry the message to their Dravidian brethren. Why? Because they were not serious about pursuing this alleged dream; because this was an entirely Tamil affair. And yet – presumably because it was a more grandiose bit of pretence or bluff than talk of an independent Tamil Nadu – these leaders continued to press on with the confusing call for an "independent," a "sovereign" Dravida Nadu (Barnett 1976: 93 and 109).

The high water mark of this campaign came during the mid- to late 1950s. The Dravida Munnetra Kazhagam (DMK) – which by then had taken over from the DK as the main bearer of this theme – made "a separate Dravida Nadu" its central issue during the Tamil Nadu state assembly election of 1957. But, again, there are reasons to doubt their seriousness about this. The theme was seized upon in large part because it was convenient in two ways. First, it enabled them to appropriate an idiom which had developed during the struggle for independence – the belief that the change demanded would be a panacea for all ills. Congress freedom fighters all over South India had earlier presented *swaraj* (self-rule) as their panacea.[2] The DMK now couched its appeal for Dravida Nadu in similar terms – "All good things would come with Dravida Nadu" (ibid.: 93) – and numerous supporters slipped easily into this familiar mode of thinking.

More crucially, the demand for Dravida Nadu offered "a *convenient* focal point for elaborating DMK ideas about social reform" which enabled the party to "appear to stand for something concrete." Had they fought the election on their main concerns – "that caste prejudices and religious 'superstition' should be eliminated" – they would have run up against efforts by the ruling Congress in Tamil Nadu to promote both justice within the caste system and secularism (ibid.: 93–94).

The view that Dravida Nadu was stressed more out of convenience than conviction gains credence when we see how swiftly the demand was abandoned soon thereafter. It became inconvenient for several reasons. No support for the idea had emerged from the other three southern states. Tamil Nadu might still have sought independence on its own, but DMK leaders feared that "it might not be economically and militarily viable." And if the government of India banned separatist parties – which at the time seemed "likely" – it could have been disastrous for a party which, after the 1957 election, only had 15 of the 205 seats in the state assembly (ibid.: 94 and 109).

[2] This is based on numerous interviews with South Indian congressmen in the 1970s.

By late 1960, these thoughts persuaded DMK leaders to drop the demand. A slight delay ensued to enable them to prepare party activists – who, unlike the public at large, had some enthusiasm for the notion. But it was informally abandoned in 1961, and the decision was formalized in 1963 (ibid.: 89 and 110). It is worth stressing that the idea was *not* revived during the anti-Hindi riots of 1965 in Tamil Nadu, even though that marked the low point in New Delhi's relations with the state. It cropped up again among some DMK activists in 1968, one year after that party took power in Tamil Nadu. But party leaders ignored it, relegating it to the status of an "undercurrent" in Tamil politics that was "vitiated but not eradicated" (ibid.: 114). Little has been heard of it since.

Separatism was more a helpful device for advancing the DMK's serious concerns than a genuine demand. It was always undermined by the confusion over the composition of the so-called Dravidian "nation" – was it all South Indians, all non-Brahmin South Indians, all Tamils or all non-Brahmin Tamils? No clear answer ever emerged. DMK leaders were intimidated by the coercive potential of the Indian state – but it must be stressed that this never had to be brought into play. Most crucially, separatism's mass appeal was nonexistent beyond Tamil Nadu and weak within it.

This meant that it did not pose a serious "management" problem for India's central authorities. Relatively little in the way of a "management" approach to Tamil Nadu emerged in the period up to the late 1960s – but then little was actually needed. Instead of a coherent "approach," what we see in those years is a rather haphazard mixture of neglect, accommodation, and occasional acts of insensitivity. The most notable such act was the attempt to impose Hindi, but when it triggered rioting, New Delhi soon backed off and accommodated Tamil sensibilities.

New Delhi's most important initiative, which was not a response to separatist demands, was (as we noted above) the decision to redraw state boundaries roughly along linguistic lines. By bringing nearly all Tamils together in a single state, this compelled Tamils to confront all of the things which divided them. Given the heterogeneities within heterogeneities that existed within this and other regional societies, these were immensely formidable. In most Indian states – and in all of the large states – they undermined the kind of solidarity which is necessary to mount a credible separatist movement. This provides most of the answer to the question posed by Amrita Basu and Atul Kohli: "why have regional movements apparently supplanted linguistic movements?" (Basu and Kohli 1997: 323). It also largely explains why no regional movement in any large Indian state except Tamil Nadu has ever become avowedly separatist, and why in Tamil Nadu separatism never became a serious threat.[3]

It is fortunate for India as a whole and for Tamil Nadu in particular that the system of monolinguistic states had taken firm root long before the early 1980s when Indira Gandhi adopted a new, deeply destructive "management" approach. This entailed efforts to foment suspicion between "ethnic," especially religious, groups and then to deploy coercive force in response to the very ructions which she had catalyzed – on the dubious assumption that this would yield short-term partisan advantages. Had the central authorities adopted this posture towards the likes of Tamil Nadu in the 1950s and 1960s, it might have produced disastrous outcomes. But by the 1980s, most "mainstream" states had evolved to the point where such initiatives would not have wrought havoc. Perhaps sensing this, Mrs. Gandhi targeted other more susceptible states – mainly but not only Punjab – with ghastly results. It is to Punjab and two other troubled regions, outside the "mainstream," that we now turn.

### Troubled states

We need to consider three areas in which severe conflict between the central government and groups in various states has led to breakdowns in relations. We examine in turn the cases of Punjab, Jammu and Kashmir (or, more precisely, the Kashmir Valley) and India's Northeast.

It was never going to be easy to maintain congenial relations with any of these areas – for reasons set out below. But there are important differences between these cases. Creative "management" could probably have avoided breakdowns in relations with Punjab and Kashmir. But at least occasional breakdowns in relations with most states in the Northeast were and remain unavoidable, no matter what approaches New Delhi might have tried.

---

[3] Two further questions which Kohli and Basu pose (ibid.: 323) appear to me at least to be less well grounded in empirical reality. These are: why have movements that made regional demands often found expression through religious idioms?; and why have movements that started out as caste movements often ended up persecuting religious minorities?

The word "often" in both questions is inaccurate. Both of these things are true of the Shiv Sena in Maharashtra, but what other cases can we cite? The only answer I can think of is N.T. Rama Rao's habit of posing in saffron clothes or allowing cut-outs to be erected showing him playing divine roles in films. But this is at most a mild version of the trend noted in their first question above.

*Punjab*

The ghastly crisis that gripped Punjab for more than a decade from the early 1980s was plainly avoidable. It would not have occurred if leaders in New Delhi had restrained themselves from meddling in potentially explosive disputes within the Sikh community there, and from exploiting anti-Sikh feelings among Hindus once the explosion occurred. This episode demonstrates what should have been obvious – that social diversity within religious minorities (along caste and class lines in the case of the Sikhs) will not suffice to prevent them from reacting ferociously and in numbers to perceived affronts to their faith.

In the late 1970s, Indira Gandhi's son Sanjay and her senior political lieutenant from Punjab, Zail Singh, sought to undermine the strength of their main opposition in the state – the Akali Dal (an overwhelmingly Sikh party) – by encouraging the emergence of the Sikh extremist Sant Jarnail Singh Bindranwale. When lethal violence broke out in 1978 between Bindranwale's group and a heretical Sikh sect, the Nirankaris, the Congress-I publicity machine backed Bindranwale. Zail Singh lent financial support to Bindranwale's newly formed political party, even though – as a government White Paper declared – it was "established with the avowed intention of demanding an independent sovereign Sikh state" (Tully and Jacob 1985: 58–60).

In 1979, Bindranwale's candidates failed miserably (despite support from the Congress-I) in elections to the committee which oversees Sikh shrines. But Congress-I support continued and, in return, Bindranwale campaigned actively for that party's candidates at the parliamentary election of 1980 which brought Mrs. Gandhi back to power.

She made Zail Singh India's home minister, but – to keep him from establishing a dominant position in Punjab's politics – she named his arch rival, a more secular-minded Sikh, Darbara Singh, as the state's chief minister. The latter adopted a hard line against Sikh and Hindu extremists in Punjab, while Zail Singh continued to promote and defend Bindranwale from New Delhi. Mrs. Gandhi oscillated between support for these two leaders – a policy which alienated Sikh extremists even as one section of her party encouraged them (ibid.: 60–66; Nayar and Singh 1984: 36–39). It is difficult to imagine a more dangerous approach to the problem.

When mounting violence from Bindranwale's group persuaded the Punjab government to seek his arrest, Zail Singh (whose job included oversight of law and order in India) arranged for a police car from neighboring Haryana state to ferry him safely to his *gurudwara* (temple) in Punjab. Soon thereafter, an outraged chief minister Darbara Singh had Bindranwale arrested, an act which triggered massive violence including murders, train derailments, and an airline hijack. Zail Singh – acting on Indira Gandhi's order – then had Bindranwale released from jail, telling parliament that there was no evidence that he had been behind the crimes for which he had been detained.

This decision had appalling results. The Punjab police – who were now targeted for retribution by Bindranwale's assassins – were deeply demoralized. Bindranwale seemed a hero who had successfully challenged the might of the Indian state, and he was free to plot further atrocities. When one of his close allies was killed by a rival Sikh politician, Zail Singh and Rajiv Gandhi attended the memorial service and allowed themselves to be photographed in Bindranwale's company, despite insulting remarks which the latter made about Zail Singh (Tully and Jacob 1985: 67–72 and facing 117).

There followed (from 1982 onward) a series of negotiations with Sikh extremists, first directly involving Mrs. Gandhi, and then through intermediaries. She again oscillated between accommodation and obduracy – an inconsistent approach which solved nothing. In mid-1982, amid continuing violence, Bindranwale took refuge in the Golden Temple in Amritsar, the Sikhs' holiest shrine from which he never again emerged alive. By late 1983, his forces escalated their campaign of mayhem – slaughtering Hindus at random and committing outrages at Hindu temples. This led to the imposition of direct rule from New Delhi in the Punjab. And yet Congress-I opponents of Zail Singh – whom Mrs. Gandhi had by then made president of India (head of state) – have claimed that he remained in daily contact with Bindranwale thereafter. So, on frequent occasions, did Mrs. Gandhi through an emissary, until less than a month before she sent the army into the Golden Temple in June 1984 (ibid.: 73–105 and 121; Nayar and Singh 1984: ch. 2).

That military action is sufficiently well known to require little retelling here, but two depressing points are worth stressing. First, the incursion by the army might not have been necessary had the will existed in New Delhi to let the Punjab police do their job properly much earlier. Second, the timing of the army's attack on a holy day – marking the martyrdom of Guru Arjun – ensured that many innocent pilgrims were killed in the firing. This was an act of colossal insensitivity.

The attack caused severe damage to the shrine, deeply offended even moderate Sikhs, and provoked mutinies in several Sikh army units. It touched off years of terrorist activity by Sikh militants and led, on October 31, 1984, to the murder of Indira Gandhi by two Sikh bodyguards.

The severity of the crisis deepened as a result of vengeful responses to the assassination. Over 3,000 Sikhs were massacred during the days which followed, in Delhi and elsewhere. Much of the slaughter was carried out by groups of Congress-I supporters, often led by prominent party leaders. The police were restrained by senior Congressmen from intervening to stop the carnage.

In the weeks that followed, senior officials actively sought to thwart efforts to identify and apprehend the murderers. For example, a bureaucrat atop the Ministry of External Affairs sought to bully a European diplomat into suppressing photographic evidence of an attempt by a mob including prominent Congressmen to torch the Sikh-owned house where he resided. An official of his seniority could only have been acting on orders from politicians at the apex of the system. The government refused to establish a commission to inquire into the massacres, so groups of eminent citizens – one including a retired state governor – felt compelled to do so independently.

During the parliamentary election campaign soon after the assassination, the Congress-I took out a full-page advertisement in national newspapers which offered a coded appeal to the fears of Sikhs. I attended an election rally in Delhi at which Rajiv Gandhi did nothing to prevent the crowd from shouting down the Sikh mayor of the city (a Congressman) and then spoke of taking revenge (*badla*) when discussing his approach to the crisis. Actions such as this only deepened the dangerous gulf between Sikhs and others, despite the fact that the country now faced its worst postindependence crisis – which, among other things, had compromised the defense of India.

There followed nearly a decade of Sikh terrorism and severe counter-insurgency campaigns by India's security forces. The government adopted a time-honored model for dealing with such breakdowns – coercive force to impose minimal order, coupled with accommodative initiatives to ease discontents and to persuade moderates to resume "normal" representative politics. But the grotesque events of 1984 had so severely ruptured relations between New Delhi and the Sikh majority in the state that this required much longer than ever before, roughly a decade, to yield something resembling the preferred outcome. And terrible scars, many of them left by the draconian actions of the security forces over that decade, remain among the Sikhs of Punjab.[4]

The misguided actions of national leaders in this episode were based on a strange mixture of naiveté and cynicism. These may seem to be opposites, but they go together far more often than many suppose. And they tend to produce very similar, deeply damaging results.

The horrors of Punjab's recent history have yielded one positive

---

[4]  I am grateful to Gurharpal Singh for stressing this.

result. Many senior figures in New Delhi now firmly avow what was obvious to most of their counterparts early on – but not to the erstwhile leaders of the Congress-I – that it is dangerous folly to play politics with religious sentiments. It is politically insane to encourage extremism among religious minorities. The upheaval in Kashmir has, as we shall see presently, reinforced the message. We must hope that the coalition led by the Hindu nationalist BJP which now holds power in New Delhi will heed these lessons.

### Jammu and Kashmir

The story of Jammu and Kashmir (or, mainly, of the Kashmir Valley where the state's Muslim majority is concentrated) differs dramatically from that of all other states. It pains a friend of India to say it, but New Delhi's approach to Kashmir has – by India's own democratic standards – been excessively manipulative and destructive. This was true not just in the Gandhis' commandist and manipulative phase, but during the entire period from independence until very recent years. (An encouraging change of view, as we shall see, began to emerge in the 1990s.) Coercion, electoral fraud, and much else have marked central governments' "management" of Kashmir. This often happened because the central authorities were ill informed or maladroit, rather than because of a malevolent conspiracy in New Delhi.[5] But it happened none the less.

The first major departure from India's democratic norms and the then Indian government's accommodative approach to most regional problems came in 1953. One year after Nehru and Sheikh Abdullah had worked out an agreement that might have provided a basis for something approaching "normal" representative politics, New Delhi – tiring of Abdullah's autocratic behavior and his references to the possibility of complete independence for the state – arranged a split in the ruling National Conference there. Abdullah was jailed and one of his lieutenants, Bakshi Ghulam Mohammed, was inserted in his place at the head of the regional government. The widespread protests in the Valley which ensued were quelled by the security forces (Bose 1997: 32).

The following year, the Indian government issued a constitutional order which effectively negated both article 370 of the constitution (which made special provisions for the state) and the 1952 agreement with Abdullah. It gave New Delhi unlimited powers to legislate on all matters – including those that had been granted to Kashmir under article 370 – and severely curtailed basic liberties. The Bakshi govern-

---

[5] Two recent studies provide correctives to Bose (1997), on which this chapter draws heavily for its narrative, and in which Bose overstresses malevolent intent. They are Schofield (1996), and Hewitt (1995).

ment in Kashmir proved corrupt during its ten years in power (1953–63), but its willingness to accept these impositions ensured its survival. At "elections" in 1957 and 1962, it won between 95 and 97 percent of the seats in the state assembly. This was sufficiently unsubtle to persuade Nehru to ask Bakshi to lose "a few seats" in subsequent "elections," for appearances' sake (ibid.: 33–34; Akbar 1985: 258).

Bakshi was ousted on New Delhi's initiative in 1963, in defiance of the wishes of a majority in the state assembly, and replaced by G.M. Sadiq. An effort to pass a no confidence motion foundered after the arrest of Bakshi. Protests from people in the Valley – which *still* centered on democratic demands rather than separatism or a desire to join Pakistan – again received a coercive response.

In 1965, Sadiq transformed his National Conference into the state unit of the Congress Party and two years later won another dubious state "election." In 1972, however, Sheikh Abdullah's followers proposed to take part in the next assembly election. The then Congress chief minister, Mir Qasim – believing that they would win (Qasim 1992: 106 and 132; Bose 1997: 36) – banned their participation in the poll and arrested large numbers of their leaders. Congress then won the ensuing "election" (Bose 1997: 34–37).

Three years later, Sheikh Abdullah abandoned his demand for self-determination in order to be permitted – late in life – a further chance to take power. In 1977, his National Conference won well at the first genuinely competitive election to occur in Kashmir. The Congress Party lost every seat in the Valley.

A further free election took place in 1983, a year after Sheikh Abdullah's death. His son and political successor, Farooq Abdullah, led the National Conference to victory again in an aggressively fought contest with the Congress. The Conference then joined other anti-Congress parties in a nationwide opposition front. Mrs. Gandhi's response was to engineer yet another split in his party in 1984, only a year after it was elected. Defectors from the National Conference, with Congress support, formed a new government. Two years later, this government was dismissed and president's rule under Jagmohan was introduced after "carefully organized riots . . . provided the pretext" (ibid.: 41–43).

The next state election in 1987 saw a return to fraudulent practice. Farooq Abdullah, who the previous year had entered an alliance with Rajiv Gandhi, faced a popular backlash in the Valley. To ensure his "election," rigging and muscle power were used. This, plus his government's corrupt and repressive ways and the chief minister's own foolishness, eventually provoked a widespread upsurge of protests. These were put down by force, and that triggered the start of serious armed resistance in the Valley.

One remarkable feature of this story is the great length of time it took for Muslims in the Valley to resort to outright resistance. This strongly suggests that accommodation at many points before the late 1980s would have worked – and may still have some promise. But opportunities for accommodation were repeatedly spurned. If future Indian policymakers want an object lesson in how *not* to manage relations with sensitive regions, Kashmir provides it.

Many senior figures in New Delhi have lately come to understand this. In 1994, it became apparent from discussions that I had with senior officials of the government of India that they recognized that they had gone badly wrong in their handling of the region and that they were determined to seek accommodation.

The various New Delhi governments since 1991 have sought to apply the lessons of the Punjab "solution" to Kashmir – where the story is far from over. They may or may not have been inappropriate, they have certainly been rushed, and the results have been mixed. More generous concessions to the people of the Valley and perhaps of the entire state of Jammu and Kashmir may be required before something approaching political "normality" can be reestablished – if, indeed, that will ever be possible.

### The Northeast

India's Northeast is the one region of the country where center–state relations have been and remain unmanageable much of the time. In most (though not all) of these states – Mizoram in recent years is an important exception – relations are bound to degenerate from time to time into severe conflict. New Delhi's "management" of the region has at times contributed to breakdowns. But even when this has not been true, the states of the Northeast – especially those with higher percentages of tribals in their populations (Dasgupta 1997: 349) – and the center's relations with them are afflicted by so many excruciating problems that even the most effective management strategies were and remain bound to prove insufficient, again, much (though not all) of the time.

To say this is not to deny Dasgupta's observations that we need to pay attention to the positive aspects of community formation, the lineage of communities in wider political institutions as parts of the Northeastern administration and representative systems, and the contributions of these processes to the national systems – and to the long history of peace, social collaboration, and political reconciliation, democratic participation, and innovations in institution-building and sustenance (ibid.: 345).

All of these things are important realities. But they have not yet succeeded in bringing extreme conflicts in most of the Northeast to an end, and it seems unlikely that they will do so anytime soon (ibid.: 347).

Consider the problems that confront those who seek to manage the region through accommodation. When the British ruled India, they did not assert sovereign control over much of the Northeast. They relied instead on a policy of "least interference" and permitted "traditional institutions" to govern many of the more remote areas of the region. When disturbances or actions occurred which the British deemed unacceptable, they resorted to punitive responses which inspired a tradition of bitter resentment among groups in the Northeast toward India's central authorities and toward forces in the region which aided or acquiesced to the British. That resentment survived the transition to Indian independence and posed huge problems for New Delhi thereafter. The British approach to the Northeast also left a legacy of confusion about the borders – formal and informal – between areas in which different tribes and clusters of tribes enjoyed preeminence (Verghese 1997: 103–104 and 137).

After independence, India's new rulers did not have the luxury of sustaining the British approach to the region. It now faced potentially (and often actively) troublesome neighbors – East Pakistan, China, and Burma. This left them no option but to fix and to police international borders, and to develop arrangements for the exercise of sovereign authority over the Northeast. But since the central government's relationship with the Northeast was far less well institutionalized (Kohli 1997: 329) than relations with areas of "mainstream" India, immense difficulties ensued.

To make matters worse, the Partition of the subcontinent had severed traditional trade routes – most crucially down the valleys and rivers leading to the port of Chittagong (then in East Pakistan) – and had cut the Northeast off from most of its former markets. This made the economic development of the region, which might have eased resentments and the threat of turbulence there, exceedingly difficult. The Northeast now stood at the extreme end of poorly developed communication and transport lines which – since they ran through a narrow strip of difficult terrain up over the hostile territory of northern East Pakistan – were vulnerable to disruption. This made and continues to make the commodities which must be brought in from the rest of India extremely expensive – another irritant.

The lack of clarity and consensus over informal demarcation lines between areas occupied by the diverse social groups of the Northeast has continued to bedevil the region – despite, or often because of, Indian efforts to formalize these lines into boundaries between states and union territories there. When a state or union territory is carved out in response to a demand for autonomy – usually from a cluster of tribes which have developed a sense of common "ethnicity," a tricky word in South Asia (Manor 1996) – other groups, that are not part of the cluster but which find themselves within the borders of the new arena, raise objections and sometimes resort to outright resistance. Entire clusters granted a state or union territory often remain unreconciled to the noninclusion of others from their "ethnic" group who stand beyond the state or even the national boundary. And they may resent the presence of other social groups within their new bailiwick, or the migration of "strangers" into the area.

Squabbles and splits within tribal clusters frequently develop which undo political accommodations that were forged in response to what had seemed a cluster's unanimous demands. Individual tribes within such clusters sometimes complain of injustice. Even when such resentments have little force, strife can arise out of rivalries between leaders of different tribes, out of "localism," or out of linguistic and even ideological disputes (Verghese 1997: 115–117). Religion sometimes provides groups in the region with a sense of common identity, but it can also sow division among them. And the list of religions which command devotion is remarkably long – Christianity, Hinduism, Buddhism, Islam, and even Judaism! None of the world's major religions is absent. Generational rivalries often develop between older sets of leaders and younger, better-educated elements – especially when there are large numbers of educated unemployed, but not only then. At times, these have been compounded by conflict over systems of collective ownership of land, to which older leaders cling but which impede the acquisition of institutional finance that is badly needed for development (ibid.: 120–123, 127–129 and 137).

The number, frequency, and complexity of such problems in the region is mind-boggling, even for someone like me who is steeped in the heterogeneities of regional societies in peninsular India. This is vividly apparent from B.G. Verghese's long and bafflingly detailed account of all this (ibid.). Even the most enlightened and sensitive attempts to "manage" such areas by the government of India can all too easily unravel as a result.

Here the states of the Northeast differ crucially from most "mainstream" states – in a way which reminds us of something important about most of the rest of India. We noted earlier that, in most states, internal heterogeneities undermine the state-level solidarity which might otherwise yield secessionist movements. The same can be said of the Northeast, but the heterogeneities that we encounter there tend to go further. They undermine not just state-level solidarity but the politics of bargaining and political stability more generally – so that accommodations, once established, tend not to hold.

When they break down, the door opens again to renewed calls for secession, sometimes from their state and sometimes from India. Groups in the region tend strongly to turn – far more quickly than their counterparts elsewhere in the country – to armed struggle against the central government and/or one another. The proximity of the Northeastern states to neighboring countries which provide a ready source of weapons offers part of the explanation. So does the opportunity to generate funds to purchase arms by smuggling teak, narcotics, etc. But the main root of the problem appears to be the difficulty which most societies in the Northeastern states experience in sustaining the politics of bargaining. (A full explanation of that requires further primary research.)

Enlightened central government efforts to manage relations with states in the Northeast have often, especially in recent years, been admirable (Dasgupta 1997: 362–368). Openness to tribal preferences, offers of elections, and a willingness to revise boundaries have all been apparent much of the time. Generous developmental assistance has raised per capita incomes in most Northeastern states to quite high levels (ibid.: 349). But there have also been mistakes. Early efforts often suffered from ad-hoc-ism. Nehru's own postures on Northeastern questions sometimes shifted unhelpfully, inspiring resentments among groups in the region. New Delhi's failure to deliver on some promises was and continues to be a serious irritant. The responses of the security forces have often been excessive – particularly in the days when people were forcibly herded into "strategic hamlets" on the British Malayan model, but not only then. And Verghese's long catalog of initiatives which might yet be tried suggests that more could have been done (Verghese 1997: chs. 8 and 16–18). And yet – to reiterate – even if much more had been done, severe troubles would still have occurred.

To conclude, let us briefly consider first the sources of the difficulties that have afflicted center–state relations, and then the prospects for a more accommodative central government "management" strategy.

Little has been said here about the role of economic conditions in destabilizing center–state relations. This is no oversight. Such conditions appear to have had far less importance than sociocultural and political factors in generating these problems. It can be argued that the remarkable prosperity which Punjab experienced in the years before the early 1980s, or the economic hardship that has long afflicted Kashmir, contributed to the disasters that struck these two regions. There is something in both arguments. But the irresponsible actions of politicians at both national and state levels appear to me to have loomed much larger in both cases. So, surely, did sociocultural realities like the majority status within each state of religious groups which were minorities in the country at large. In other states where such sociocultural factors were absent, we find levels of prosperity or deprivation which match those in these two states – and yet they have not faced the kinds of grotesque breakdowns which have occurred in Punjab and Kashmir.

In Punjab, Kashmir, and especially in the Northeast, geography also matters greatly. All three regions share borders with troublesome neighbors who have often done their best to compound problems which the government of India faced and, to varying degrees in the various regions, created. The geographical isolation of the Northeast from the rest of India, and its separation from most of its traditional trading partners and markets as a result of Partition, have generated immense difficulties.

The mention of Partition reminds us of the negative impact of certain historical legacies – especially in Kashmir and the Northeast. When a Hindu maharaja in Kashmir decided to take his Muslim majority state into the Indian union in the 1940s, this was bound to generate long-term problems for New Delhi. The troubles in the Northeast have intensified as a result not just of Partition, but also of the British disinclination to exercise sovereign power over much of this region. The Indian government after 1947 had no option but to assume the sovereign's role, and that has led inevitably to excruciating dilemmas. The historical legacy in "mainstream" India has posed far fewer problems.

So historical, geographical, and sociocultural elements – together with political achievements and miscalculations – have counted for much more in these varied stories than have economic factors.

To say this is not to rule out a link between continued economic growth and the survival of the politics of bargaining in India. P.V. Narasimha Rao clearly perceived a connection between these things. He recognized that the decay of political institutions and excessively confrontational political postures were major factors, during the 1980s, in the intensification of social conflict across India and in the mounting difficulties that confronted both center–state relations and the politics of bargaining more generally. But he also believed that sustained, and indeed accelerated, economic growth was required if the politics of bargaining was to survive amid rising demands from organized interests. This was an important consideration in his decision to liberalize the Indian economy.[6] The point here is not to deny that his views were justified, but to argue that noneconomic factors appear to have had greater importance in the cases that we have examined.

The severe troubles that arose during the 1980s, especially in Punjab and Kashmir, have persuaded many (though not all) key figures in New Delhi that they need to pursue more accommodative approaches to center–state relations. Those inclinations resonate with more generalized changes in security policy – a phrase which covers responses to internal disturbances and to external threats. As one specialist wrote in 1997:

While New Delhi has not – scarcely could – ignore military preparedness and deterrence, it has lately changed tack. A greater emphasis on negotiated settlements and in particular a more economistic vision of security policy have gained ground. Put differently, India is still carrying a big stick, but it is talking more softly and is increasingly using the language of economic ends and means (Bajpai 1997: 1).

Despite grave developments over Kashmir since early 1999, long experience in coping with a diversity of crises, great and small, in a wide array of states, equip the Indian authorities with the skills and attitudes that will help to make the politics of bargaining work – not perfectly, but tolerably well. They will also be assisted by a major, seldom recognized national resource – the vast army of political fixers at all levels of the system who share those skills and attitudes. The constitution rightly arms New Delhi with adequate powers to cope with breakdowns. And a supreme court decision in 1994, which requires the government of India to provide detailed justifications for the imposition of president's rule, will help to curb overly aggressive actions that were once routine. All of this suggests that accommodative inclinations at the apex of the system might yield substantial benefits.

---

[6] This is based on discussions with the then prime minister during the second week of February 1992.

# 5 Making local government work: local elites, *panchayati raj* and governance in India

*Subrata K. Mitra*

## Introduction

No description of India's political landscape will be complete without her local elites. The ubiquitous presence of these influential men, and increasingly women, in *panchayat* and *gramsabha* meetings, cooperative societies, election campaigns, *morchas*, *loan melas* and the inevitable road-side tea shop is a fact of life that civil servants, politicians or media persons can ignore only at their peril. However, while their influence is widely recognized, local elites remain elusive as a political and social category. Consequently, the evaluation of their contribution to the functioning of local government, or in a general sense to India's democracy, remains inconclusive (Brass 1997; Mitra 1991). Just as it is commonplace to see the local *netas* cast as despicable parasites, manipulators of local society, exploiters, usurers, and *pyraveekars*, one is also likely to come up with field reports that present the very same category as culture brokers, but for whose liminal presence and mediating skills the hiatus between the modern state and traditional society would render the institutions of formal democracy unworkable in the postcolonial context (Bhattacharyya 1999; Mitra 1990, 1999a). The overall picture, split between these contradictory images, tends to be schizophrenic.

The main argument of this chapter is that the judicious use of local government has infused new political resources into the political system of India, and enhanced the resilience and legitimacy of the state. This is of course only a very general picture of India which conceals great diversity of democracy and governance at the local level. On the whole, the complex nexus of the national, the regional, and the local has been possible through a number of national legal and political initiatives, and has been more successful in those parts of India where a competitive party system has successfully integrated the local with the national. By extension of the same argument, the experimentation in local democracy has been the least successful in those regions where no autonomous empowerment of subaltern social groups has taken place. The essay examines this argument by drawing on survey data relating to popular attitudes towards local government and the analysis of case-study and interview material from secondary sources.[1]

## Local government and the relative autonomy of the state

The ambivalence towards local government which one notices in India actually has an older, European genealogy. The ambiguity about the role of the local in the making of the national, or the contribution of the traditional to the shaping of the modern, is also visible in the role of local politics in the making of modern nation-states and industrial societies (Rudolph and Rudolph 1967). Whether it is seen in terms of its spatial location at the lowest level of the political system, or in class terms as the voices of the *petites gens*, politics from below has been seen as that of hapless victims (Moore 1966), of dysfunctional supplication (Huntington 1968), of the angry rebel fighting for what he considers justly his (Gurr 1971), or of effete resistance to the relentless march of central power (Scott 1985). But the debate is far from closed. The recent publication of Putnam's *Making Democracy Work* (1993) and the controversy around it have revived the debate about local community and civil society as the basic building blocks of modern, democratic nation-states (Tarrow 1996; Blomkvist 1996).

India's achievements in drawing strength from the local for the making of the national are in this sense of general interest. One should notice at the outset, however, that though India as a whole is an important example of successful democratic transition, there is considerable variation in the effectiveness of local government. Besides, as a whole, there has not been one blueprint from which the institutions, processes, and policies of local government are drawn. Rather, it is a case of continuous experimentation and transfer of knowledge from one region to another. Analysis of the variation in the performance of the Indian "model" in time and space is crucial to the understanding of its strengths and limitations.

## The evolution of local government in India

Local government, like many other postindependence institutions, is of preindependence vintage and shows the same differences of opinion

---

[1] The national survey was undertaken by the Center for the Study of Developing Societies, Delhi. A national representative sample of about 10,000 men and women was interviewed in 104 parliamentary constituencies in face-to-face interviews. See Mitra and Singh (1999).

among the leaders of the freedom movement as in the matter of the confessional or the economic character of the state. Just as Gandhi held the role of the village republic as the necessary building block of nation, state, and society in India, Nehru famously espoused the opposite view.[2] This conflict between the modern and the traditional, the scientific as opposed to the vernacular, the view from above as opposed to the meso and micro perspectives from below, has made its routine appearance on the Indian political scene. One finds traces of these ideological debates among the leaders of the freedom movement, in preindependence icons like Savarkar and Bose and post-independence celebrity dissidents like Ram Manohar Lohia and Jaiprakash Narain.

The same debate surfaces in the mainstream theories of politics in India with reference to the autonomy of the state from society. The Rudolphs' characterization of the manifold character of the Indian state (Rudolph and Rudolph 1987: 400–401) was the subject of sharp criticism by the Indian left at its first appearance.[3] On the basis of the analysis of a broad spectrum of India's regions, Kohli (1987) has shown that the state is at its most effective when it is reinforced by a regime at the regional level also committed to the same objectives as the national state, and has the support of a well-organized political party with its own links to the peasantry. The negotiating stance of the state could be a crucial variable on its own. When the state sends mixed signals, such as its readiness to negotiate on transactional issues like redistribution but its resistance to such transcendental considerations as the territorial integrity of the state, or the secular basis of the nation, its legitimacy is considerably enhanced (Mitra 1990, 1999c). Many of these considerations have been recently brought together by Arendt Lijphart (1996) in a general interpretation of Indian democracy drawing on consociational theory.

[2] "I do not understand why a village should necessarily embody truth and non-violence. A village, normally speaking, is backward intellectually and culturally and no progress can be made from a backward environment. Narrow-minded people are much more likely to be untruthful and violent": Nehru (1960: 508). Equally dismissive of the current reality and future potential of the village as a political unit for the building of the new India was Ambedkar: "That they [the villages] have survived through all vicissitudes may be a fact. But mere survival has no value. The question is on what plane they have survived. Surely, on a low, selfish level. I hold that these village republics have been the ruination of India. I am therefore surprised that those who condemn provincialism and communalism should come forward as champions of the village. What is the village but a stink of localism, a den of ignorance, narrow-mindedness and communalism? I am glad that the Draft Constitution has discarded the village and adopted the individual as its unit" (CAD, vol. VII, no. 1: 39).

[3] Byres (1988: 246–269). Scholars of the Indian left see the relative autonomy of the state as a measure of their relative softness or hardness.

Generally speaking, the efficacy of local government in quickening the pace of democracy and adding a deeper layer of legitimacy to the state is crucially contingent on the relative autonomy of the state in the first place. Local leaders, competing for power and influence in the local arena, in the context of institutions and processes that are relatively transparent and a participatory local political culture, can be effective only in the context of a national policy and regional government that anticipate sufficient room to maneuver on the part of local government. India's success in institutionalizing an effective role for local government, as we shall see below, therefore begs a host of further questions: how did the Indian state acquire the necessary relative autonomy, to provide the requisite room to maneuver to local elites and inspire among them trust for the various levels of government?[4]

The contrast of the Indian case with stable Western democracies could not be more striking. In the West, the local, the minority, and the poor were violently cleansed prior to the introduction of modern, democratic institutions (Moore 1966; Tilly 1975; Gilmour 1992). India at independence faced a different and difficult scenario. The constitutional guarantee of the right to participation, the judiciary and other watchdog institutions protecting citizens' rights, and competitive politics enjoined upon the national leadership to induct the local and marginal as partners in governance. Unlike their tragic European counterparts during the period of the transition to industrial society, these vulnerable social groups and the local level of politics acquired a new lease of life. Looking five decades back, comparing the resilience of India's democracy to the dire predictions of imminent collapse (Harrison 1960), one is entitled to ask: how could these "undemocratic roots" ensconced within the traditional world of local politics sustain a democratic system based on radically different values?[5]

The success of local government depends to a large extent on the type of leadership that obtains at the local level. The latter, in turn, is greatly influenced by two crucial dimensions: namely, the awareness of the given set of leaders of local democracy, and the extent of social closure that keeps those not born to power and privilege from entering the arena. Using combinations of both, one can construct a fourfold typology (figure 5.1).

In the first type, the local leaders are not aware of the existence of modern political institutions or simply do not consider it worthwhile to

---

[4] For a theoretical analysis of the role of trust for democracy and governance, see Sztompka (1999) and Braithwaite and Levi (1998).

[5] I have made the point more fully in Mitra (1999b).

*Social closure*

|  |  | high | low |
|---|---|---|---|
| *Awareness and power of local institutions* | *low* | (type 1) feudal | (type 2) anomie, fragmented |
|  | *high* | (type 3) paternalistic, managerial | (type 4) democratic |

Figure 5.1 *A typology of local leadership.*

take an interest in them. Next are two different scenarios. The second type is one where local-level politics is polarized on the lines of caste and class. Local government, caught in the cross-fire, has lost its autonomy and real power has slipped into the hands of mafia dons, warlords, and armed gangs. The third type represents a situation where the leaders are aware of the institutions of local government and have taken charge of them but positions of power remain closed to the poor and lower social classes. The fourth type is one where the avenues to power lie through democratic competition and the leadership is aware of local democracy. In this case, local government would be both effective and legitimate.

The situation depicted in type 1 of figure 5.1 describes the baseline which legislation and social policy in India uses as a point of departure. From its rudimentary beginning in the 1880s until its formal appearance as part of a national policy after independence, the objective of the state has been to move local government in the direction of type 4. The idea was formally enshrined in the constitution (article 40). But the path from the first to the fourth type has occasionally led to type 2, as in Bihar, where local government lies paralyzed in the midst of vicious caste wars, or type 3 as in Maharashtra where the evolution of local government has run into a wall of opposition from paternalist and managerial upper social classes.

Following the report of the Balawant Rai Mehta Committee, and its incorporation into the recommendations of the Planning Commission, a three-tier structure was expected to become the institutional basis for local self-government for the whole of India.[6] Maharashtra took a lead with the report of the V.P. Naik Committee which recommended the devolution of the power of taxation and disbursement of development funds to the Zilla Parishad, the majority of whose members were to be

[6] See Khanna (1994) for a detailed account of the growth of local self-government in Indian states.

directly elected. However, a period of decline set in soon afterwards, which lasted from Nehru's death up to the revival of the idea of *panchayats* as the basic units of the political system by Rajiv Gandhi in 1985. Khanna (1994) lists a number of factors as responsible for this decline, among them the food grains crisis of the early 1960s, followed by the introduction of the cluster of policies known as the Green Revolution which transferred the initiative for production and distribution of vital agrarian resources to the state government departments. The subsequent programs of poverty alleviation and agrarian reform such as the Small and Marginal Farmers, Food for Work, Drought Prone Areas, and Minimum Needs programs etc. were often conceived, financed, and administered by central agencies. Besides, under the dominant central government of Indira Gandhi, many state governments turned on local democracy with the same authoritarian measures as the center, namely, postponement of elections, which cut off the periodic infusion of new blood into these institutions. The Janata Party, upon taking office in 1977, set up the Ashoka Mehta Committee in order to revive local autonomy and participation. However, in spite of its recommendations, very little changed in terms of reality on the ground.[7] Internal conflict greatly paralyzed central initiative during the brief Janata rule of 1977–80. Except in West Bengal where the Left Front government seized the initiative, the central administration and coordination of all development activity in the district under the auspices of the District Rural Development Agency (DRDA) became the rule. The next radical change in policy came from Rajiv Gandhi who initiated the move to institutionalize *panchayati raj* in terms of a distinct tier of the federal system with constitutionally guaranteed power.[8] Though the initiative failed to get through the parliament the idea was not entirely lost. It resurfaced in 1992 in the form of the seventy-third amendment to the constitution which gives constitutional recognition to *panchayati raj* as a tier of the federation. Elections to *panchayats* have been mandatory, to be supervised by an independent State Election Commission. Similarly, the *panchayati raj* bodies are to be endowed with independent taxation power and central funds whose disbursement is to be supervised by a State Finance Commission.[9] The *panchayats* today have far more potential power than before and in some parts of India they have become viable political units in their

[7] See Government of India (1978a).

[8] The initiative lost bipartisan support in the parliament when it appeared that Rajiv Gandhi might have been motivated by the prospects of having a more pliable instrument of government in a nationally constituted prefecture of local governments as compared to the more assertive regional Chief Ministers.

[9] For details of the seventy-third amendment, see Khanna (1994: 34–35).

own right.[10] Why and how this came about, what makes it effective
and how it varies from one region to another are issues which will be
taken up below.

## The normative and political basis of local government

With regard to the literature on local government in India, it is certainly
not a case of paucity but rather of an overabundance (Khanna 1994).
Only rarely does one come across works that rise beyond moralistic
undertone and depict the political universe of local government in terms
of real flesh-and-blood political actors, pursuing their interests drawing
on all the resources at their command, their collective impact affecting
the nature and course of local government in predictable manners.
Empirical accounts of local government use their idealistic communi-
tarian objective as their point of departure and end in the abject
admission of the defeat of these noble ideas of simple living and high
thinking as soon as they hit the reality of the Indian village. Not much
effort is invested in treating *panchayati raj* – the institutionalized form of
local government ordained by Indian legislation – as a specific form of
rule, so that its spread can be analyzed in terms of the political perceptions and choices of the people who form the backdrop to these political
processes.

Looking beyond the idealistic rhetoric that accompanied its launch,
one can see a combination of motives that account for the introduction
of democratic decentralization in India. It offered several attractive
features to the postindependence policy community of experts keen on
rural development and resource-hungry politicians happy to gain access
to patronage. Four main factors can be pointed out. Nonviolent and
incremental structural change was a constitutional commitment and
*panchayati raj* offered a middle way between centralized, bureaucratic
planning and revolution from below.[11] The possibility of communal
mobilization of resources in a decentralized context was the developmental planner's hope of inducting resources tied up in the countryside.[12] A micro basis for local initiative crucial for the structure of a

[10] Bhattacharyya (1993) suggests that as much as 50 percent of public funds in West
Bengal pass through the hands of the *gram panchayats*.

[11] This seems to have described the thin consensus that held the Nehru coalition of
1947–51 together. *Panchayats* were used as a contemporary mantra – one of those
periodic slogans like the Green Revolution, *garibi hatao*, or liberalization in the 1990s
that afflict Indian politics every so often, and that are supposed to achieve important
political results without entailing too much politics, at any rate without causing
violence.

[12] The influence of Gandhian thinking is clearly discernible with regard to a future polity
whose "structure [was] composed of innumerable villages [with] . . . ever widening

mixed economy appeared innovative.[13] Finally, *panchayats* appeared as a potential source of unlimited patronage to service the needs of the party machines (Kothari 1970a). These mixed motives also provide insights into the variable fortune that the experiment in democratic decentralization faced in different parts of the country.

## Trust in government: local, regional and national

Not surprisingly, *panchayati raj* drew a lot of criticism from those committed to structural change as a precondition of democracy and development in India. One of the most trenchant criticisms came from Barrington Moore. Writing in the 1960s, shortly after the implementation of the Balawantrai Mehta Commission's recommendations for the introduction of three-tier local self-government at the village, block and district levels, Moore wrote: "if democracy means the opportunity to play a meaningful part as a rational human being in determining one's fate in life, *democracy does not yet exist in the Indian countryside*. The Indian peasant has not yet acquired the material and intellectual prerequisites for democratic society. The *panchayat* 'revival' . . . is mainly romantic rhetoric" (Moore 1966: 408; emphasis added).

We do not have any independent survey evidence to determine the extent to which Moore's rather dismissive comments about the effectiveness of local governments as units of development were true for his time. However, assuming they offer a reasonable benchmark, survey data from 1996 give a picture of the considerable gains that local political arenas have made in the intervening three decades. Working on the basis of the assumption that trust in local institutions is a surrogate for their effectiveness, the results of the question "How much trust/confidence do you have in the central government – a great deal, somewhat or no trust at all?" and repeated for the "state government" and "local government/*panchayat*/municipality," reported in table 5.1, can be used as an indicator of their current standing in a number of regions in India.

never ascending circles. Life will not be a pyramid with the apex sustained by the bottom. But it will be an oceanic circle whose center will be the individual always ready to perish for the village, the latter ready to perish for the circle of villages" (Gandhi, *Harijan*, July 28, 1946).

[13] Local participation was seen as a crucial instrument of capital mobilization. The Balawantrai Mehta Committee argued: "So long as we do not discover or create a representative and democratic institution which will supply the local interest, supervision and care necessary to ensure that expenditure of money upon local objects conforms with the needs and wishes of the locality, invest it with adequate power, and assign it appropriate finances, we will never be able to evoke local initiative in the field of development" (Government of India 1956: 5).

Table 5.1. *Regional variation in trust in central, state, and local government* *(%)*

| High trust in different levels of government | Central | State | Local |
|---|---|---|---|
| All India (N = 9,589) | 35.3 | 37.5 | 39.9 |
| Bihar (880) | 29.9 | 30.0 | 29.9 |
| Maharashtra (860) | 30.8 | 34.0 | 40.7 |
| West Bengal (769) | 35.9 | 40.8 | 50.6 |

Considering India as a whole, the level of trust in local government is actually higher than either regional or central government. The effectiveness of *panchayati raj* in terms of the trust that people have in it varies widely across India. At the lower end is Bihar where trust in all three levels of government tends to be low. At the upper end are West Bengal and Maharashtra where trust in government is higher.

Since trust in government is affected by the visibility and effectiveness of the governmental structure, we need to examine the brief history of the implementation of *panchayati raj* in India in order to explain the variation in the levels of legitimacy accorded to local government. Until the passing of the seventy-third amendment to the constitution, which radically altered the picture and brought about a certain measure of uniformity in the institutional structure of *panchayati raj* all over the country, the states of India had very different practices. They can be divided roughly into three different types: states like Maharashtra where *panchayati raj* became a reality before other regions of India; West Bengal which entered the race for successful *panchayati raj* later but where a combination of circumstances made *panchayats* the focus of state activity, leading to spectacular success; and those like Bihar where a mobilized, politicized, and rural population divided on the lines of class and caste conflict has found in *panchayats* their main arena in the battle for supremacy, reducing the institution to low levels of efficacy and trust. In order to examine the variation in terms of regions and within each region, across social classes we need first to look at the history of the implementation of *panchayati raj* in these regions.

### Elite mobilization from above: Maharashtra

Maharashtra belongs to those states where *panchayati raj* was introduced in the first wave.[14] The *panchayats* became the bastion of local elites,

[14] See Khanna (1994: 210–244); Sirsikar (1995).

then dominated by the landowning, relatively high-status regional castes. Subsequently, as political mobilization brought the lower social classes into the local political arena, the richer, erstwhile social elites fled the *panchayat* for higher-level political arenas, for more lucrative markets abroad, or to take refuge in cooperatives where membership depends on shares. In Maharashtra, the *panchayat* is an administrative outlet of the largesse of the welfare state, the more important political decisions and their implementation being more under the control of the regional government and cooperatives, coalitions of agri-business, NGOs and caste associations. *Panchayat* elections have become less regular than during the heyday of their early prominence. Even "the important subjects pertaining to 'co-operation and industries' which were initially entrusted to the Zilla Parishads have been [subsequently] withdrawn" (Khanna 1994: 213).

### Popular mobilization from below: West Bengal

West Bengal represents the category of regions where *gram panchayats* became the chosen political and legal instrument for the implementation of state policy with regard to land reform, distribution of surplus land, registration of land records, rights of share-croppers, tenancy rights, distribution of state subsidies, welfare and loans. Politics from above (in this case, the CPM-led state government) favored these changes; politics from below (the political machinery of the CPM and their allies) was in a position to take advantage of these new political resources and harness them for its own political purposes, leading to the creation of red *panchayats*. *Panchayats* in this case emerged as the focus of both implementation and legitimization. Though the normative and legislative basis of *panchayati raj* was already present at an all-India scale by the 1970s, a fortuitous set of circumstances led to the *panchayati raj* being adopted as the main focus of the state government. The explanation in this case goes beyond the politics of the state to the partisan preferences of the CPM for reasons that we shall see below.

Towards the late 1970s, the CPM was locked in a battle on two fronts in the Bengal countryside. On the one hand, the party felt that without the countervailing institutional power of the state, the Left Front would not be able to break the dominance of the *jotdar* (the local rich peasants), nor implement its agrarian program because of the apathy of the lower bureaucracy towards land reform and redistribution and in some cases its active collusion with the *jotdar*, who largely constituted the support base of the Congress. On the other hand, making appeals to peasant activism held the potential of getting out of hand and developing into insurrectionary violence, both politically damaging to the electoral prospects of the CPM and a likely harbinger of direct central rule on the grounds of the deterioration of law and order. Out of this double bind was born a consensus that saw the *panchayat* as the optimal strategy to promote the political goals of the party and the empowerment of the poor in the most effective way.

### Stalemated conflict: fragmentation and anomic violence in Bihar

This is a situation where the mobilized poor, taking advantage of their numbers, have often succeeded in capturing *panchayats*. But the local social and economic elite, who see power ebbing away from their control, have not found any alternative arena. As a result, *panchayats* and local politics have become the scene of sporadic violence and caste conflict.

Reports on *panchayati raj* in Bihar suggest that the institution had made its appearance as early as 1949, though the "upper two tiers, the Panchayat Samiti and Zilla Parishad functioned only in some parts of the state continuously from 1964 onwards and all over the state from 1979 onwards till their suppression in 1986" (Khanna 1994: 84). Khanna evaluates the contribution of *panchayati raj* in Bihar to the "politico-administrative system, democratization and development" as limited. Two government-appointed committees, the Bage Subcommittee of 1973 on *gram panchayats* and the Tyagi Subcommittee on Panchayat Samitis and Zilla Parishads, recognized the malaise and made specific recommendations. Little action was taken towards the implementation of these recommendations.

Khanna quotes from another report of 1985 that "caste domination of Panchayati Raj is apparently visible and that the majority caste uses all sorts of means and practices to capture positions within *panchayati raj* institutions. Factionalism based upon caste and personality has affected working of *panchayati raj* institutions at many places." The same report points towards some of the reasons for the poor performance of *panchayati raj*, among which the more important ones are irregular elections and suppression of local democracy by the state government on "extraneous considerations." Yet another report from 1988–9 suggests that *panchayat* institutions in Bihar were malfunctioning due to inadequate finances, insufficient staff, and "self-seeking leadership" (Khanna 1994: 87). As a consequence, Khanna reports the mobilization of the "rural proletariat and poor peasantry in defence of their rights and benefits," leading to an increase in violent and nonviolent conflict. A reaffirmation of these sentiments came from a team of social scientists from the Indian Institute of Public Administration who summed up the situation as follows after a study visit to Bihar in 1989–90. They reported the loss of effectiveness and legitimacy of *panchayati raj* institutions as a result of "inordinate delays in holding elections" and the "suppression of Zilla Parishad." *Gram sabhas,* designed to be an instrument of accountability of the *panchayat* to the village community as a whole, were reported to be largely a "defunct body" (reported in Khanna 1994: 88).

### Political and social dynamics of *panchayat* elites in West Bengal

The survey data reported in table 5.1 and the anecdotal accounts in the section above provide some insights into the circumstances that produce the success stories of *panchayati raj*. A contrasting picture to that of local government in Bihar is provided by West Bengal. The background to the survey evidence of West Bengal's better performance as compared to Bihar can be seen in interviews with officeholders at various levels of Bengal *panchayats*.

One of the main achievements of the Left Front government has been to have successfully persuaded the *jotdars* that their best chance of achieving moderate affluence and security lay in conceding legitimacy to *panchayats* as the intermediary between them and agricultural workers. Once they were in place and effective links between rural society and the state were established, the mediation by local government became an optimal instrument of "parliamentary communism."[15] The instruments through which this has been achieved include the recording of the sharecroppers, distributing land deeds to poor peasants and causing a more accessible and transparent bureaucratic process. Thanks to these initiatives, the *panchayat* assumed a significant role. From arranging credits to the supply of seeds and fertilizers, from rationalization of the available employment opportunities in the village to the determination of a uniform wage rate, everything is channeled though the *panchayat*. Field reports from West Bengal affirm that the *panchayat* has become "the most immediate structure of democratic representation." Rather than confining the meetings to the formal buildings, the *panchayat* has moved to where the people are, meeting in the courtyards of ordinary people.[16]

[15] Kohli (1990). The Congress might have been the first preference of the *jotdar* but the least preferred alternative during the early years of the Left Front government was to face the murderous assault of the Naxalites. Out of this marriage of convenience was born the long cohabitation of the CPM and the middle peasant.

[16] "Suddenly the esoteric rule of the state got partly de-mystified and the villagers themselves became witness to, if not actual participants in, the planning and

The functioning of West Bengal *panchayats* takes place in the context of a *panchayat*-friendly legal environment. The Left Front government has ruthlessly implemented the ceiling laws regarding ownership of agricultural land. It secured legal right of share for about 200,000 of its share-croppers and stopped for good their coercive eviction by the landlords. Finally, it has instituted a three-tier *panchayat* system (at village, block, and district levels) on competitive party lines and held four successive elections to these bodies since 1978, the last (1993) of which sent more than 91,000 elected representatives (a third of them women).

### A case of Bengali exceptionalism?

West Bengal and Bihar are not only neighboring states: there are common administrative features and a history of shared rule under the British. In order to avoid any cultural or idiosyncratic overtones to the significantly better performance of *panchayati raj* in West Bengal, one needs to look at some structural factors that distinguish West Bengal from other parts of India. The political character of rural elites who are the crucial links between local government and the local people is an important factor in this context. Further questions such as the actual role of the rural elite, particularly those directly involved with *panchayats*, their social origins, and the dynamics of the social process in which they are ensconced, require us to look beyond survey data and into an in-depth case study of West Bengal *panchayats*.[17] Roughly three sets of factors, namely the effectiveness of other complementary organizations such as cooperatives, the combination of communist Pradhans (local government leaders) and ordinary non-party members of *panchayats*, and the symbiotic relations of party and *panchayat* can be identified as explanations for the environment in which *panchayats* in Bengal function, and the role played by the rural elites.

prioritization of administrative works. In addition to this, and this is important, the *panchayat* eventually gave the village a common identity by formally unifying the entire village into a single unit and liquidating the divisions based on caste based localities . . . As an arbitrator between individuals and families in disputes, the *panchayat* and the entire population of the village involved and delivered a process of adjudication which is quicker, cheaper and more transparent" (Bhattacharyya 1996: 22–23). Both the nonpartisan character of Bengal *panchayats* and the extent of their efficacy in creating a village community might have been somewhat overstated. See the account of Harihar Bhattacharya below for a critical analysis of the role of the CPM in the running of Bengal *panchayats*.

[17] Except for newspaper reports, the bulk of the field data on which this section is based are drawn from an unpublished study (Bhattacharya 1997). The permission to quote is gratefully acknowledged.

Panchayats in West Bengal are part of a grid of organizations that are engaged in giving loans, supervising the distribution of welfare, and making lists of minor developmental works that should be taken up, and of beneficiaries who would be entitled to different forms of resources once they are available. There is considerable awareness at the level of the ordinary citizen of the existence of such organizations, their functioning, their lapses, and the difference they have made to welfare.[18] Bhattacharya (1997) gives an example of a "poor peasant" who "directly goes to the [co-operative] society to receive loan[s]," "attached to the Kisan Sabha and DYFI," "[who] believes the co-operatives are the only instrument for improving life situation[s], although sadly he often has to take loan[s] from "'mahajans' (moneylenders) to repay co-operative loan[s]" and a "rich peasant" who is "confident about the role of co-operatives."[19]

The political leadership that the Bengal *panchayats* have developed shows the combination of the organizational resources of the CPM at the level of the higher leadership and an openness to induct a wide cross-section of local society as ordinary members. The Prodhan (known as Sarpanch in other parts of India) is the veritable fulcrum of the *panchayat* organization. Usually, the Prodhan is a party man.[20] The average profile of the Bengal Prodhan shows a veritable workhorse, involved in a number of subcommittees specializing in the problems of particular segments of society such as agricultural labor, women,

---

[18] Bhattacharya's interview data are rich with examples. He talks of a literate agricultural laborer, aged forty, landless, belonging to the scheduled castes, who has been receiving loans for quite some time and that too without the help of any middleman. "He takes the help of a co-operative leader who arranges [a] loan quite easily for him. [He is] attached to DYFI and the Agricultural Workers' Union since 1980 and his life condition has not improved much. None the less, he believes the co-operatives are the most important instrument for improvement in life and is quite optimistic about the same" (Bhattacharya 1997: 34, interview conducted on July 4, 1996).

[19] In the words of the rich peasant, "Due to the co-operative, I am able to cultivate land twice, and to produce sufficient quantity of potato. I did not know before that such an organization can be so helpful" (ibid.: 35, interview, July 4, 1996). Bhattacharya concludes from these interviews that: "there was a very striking similarity of the effects of co-operatives on the [*panchayat*] members' lives and hence their views of and confidence in co-operatives. True, co-operatives have not been able to produce the same effects on each member because its members are differently located in the socio-economic scales. But they have helped each member to make a difference to their life-situation. Even the very poorer classes who as members have not been able to improve their lot much thanks to lower levels of loans, still have a fairer impression and a good measure of confidence in the co-operative. We have not come across any member we interviewed who has held a negative view of and is pessimistic about the role of co-operatives."

[20] "The party has seen to it that such strategic posts do not go out to non-party men/women. This shows, among others, that the party lays emphasis on this post. In many cases, the Prodhan is the sole party man in the Panchayat" (Bhattacharya 1997: 81).

literacy, culture, and so on, both at the level of the village and at higher levels of the *panchayat* system. Middle-aged men coming from the middle castes predominate, but there are appreciable numbers of Prodhans who are Muslim, or come from the scheduled castes and scheduled tribes. But these semi-professional organization men are ensconced within a more politically open milieu with substantial representations of non-party men and women. These are housewives, wage workers, rich or poor peasants, and so on who are engaged in myriad committees, neighborhood committees, Roads and Beneficiary Committees. There is little money involved. What stands out from the descriptions of their role perception is an impression of efficacy and the satisfaction of being engaged in public works.[21]

The West Bengal CPM has developed an effective policy with regard to the functioning of *panchayat* institutions. The CPM has developed a specialized party organ – the PPN, Panchayat Parichalona Nirdeshika (Directives on running the *panchayats*), in the form of a newsletter issued directly by the West Bengal State Committee of the CPM and sent to every *panchayat* and municipality through the District Committee in order to coordinate its ideological and political work with that of the *panchayat* institutions. The *panchayati raj* institution is part of the public manifesto of the CPM and the party is keen on defending its record on this score. In an interview, a party spokesman explained the founding of the party's *panchayat* newsletter as part of its efforts to "strengthen democratic method in running the Panchayats, and to encourage more active popular participation in Panchayats."[22] The less visible private face of the party is keener on the political and ideological dividends that this bourgeois democratic initiative might bring.[23] This constant struggle between the public and the private – in an environment that has increasingly become more conscious of democratic rights

---

[21] The following self-portrayal of a middle-class, middle-caste, middle-aged housewife, member of the *panchayat* and the Road Committee, provides some insights into the construction of the office by ordinary members of the rural society: "I attend to all the problems of the villagers, from the construction of roads to family problems, often I tend to defy the party's strictures. I cater to Panchayat needs after looking after my family. The Scheduled Castes predominate in my area and have got me elected as I stand by their problems. The Panchayat should always obey rules though that is not always done" (Bhattacharya 1997: 90).

[22] Interview, Bhattacharya (1997: 41).

[23] Harihar Bhattacharya quotes from an inner party document (Hoogly District Committee) to suggest as much: "That the activities of the *panchayat* will be performed by elected members of Panchayats alone is the outlook which is opposed to the long term political objective of the Party. In order to transform Panchayats into the weapons for struggle, what is necessary is strong party control over *panchayat* units, collective decision and leadership and regular check up of Panchayat activities in party committee meetings" (Bhattacharya 1997: 42).

118     *Subrata K. Mitra*

and the need for transparency – has become the hallmark of CPM politics in contemporary West Bengal.

Top party brass are aware of the pernicious effect of power and patronage and of the opposition parties lurking in the shadows. As a consequence, a self-denying ordinance is very much the rule at lower levels, though here, as elsewhere, exceptions to the rule are not unknown. Thus, the party is ever solicitous of the opinions of those *panchayat* members who are elected on the party symbol without being party members. There is an explicit party directive to the effect that "elected members or their relatives should not be on the top of the list of beneficiaries so that the people must see that the *panchayats* are not meant for the elected members or their relatives." The directives also caution against basing the Beneficiary Committee on the extent of the party's support in an area.[24]

While the main incentive for the CPM in supporting *panchayat* institutions is undoubtedly instrumental – for the *panchayat* is the new fountain-head of resources in the countryside and allegations of irregularities are not unknown[25] – the consequence of the partnership between party and *panchayat* has been the creation of a supportive political environment for the new institution to strike root in the interstices of rural Bengal society. The range of committees such as the Public Health Standing Committee, the Village Education Committee, the Ration Committee, the Afforestation Committee, and the Night School Committee, with their rules and formal procedures, their records, the watchful members creating an environment of transparency and self-policing, create a dynamic of their own. These organizational

[24] Ibid.: 45.
[25] Under a news item entitled "Panchayats told to account for funds," the Panchayati Raj Update (Delhi: Institute of Social Sciences, July 1997), # 43 reports: "The government [of West Bengal] has directed all *panchayats* in the state to account for the money that had been sanctioned to them in fiscal years 1995–96 and 1996–97. District magistrates have been told to personally check the accounts and ensure that no part of the money is misused. In a circular, the Chief Secretary warned *panchayats* of penal action if, despite repeated notices, they defaulted in furnishing detailed accounts of the money they had spent. According to a state government official, the *panchayats* were granted over Rs. 500 crore during the past year and a half for various rural development programmes. This fund was jointly provided by the Union and State governments. Many *panchayats* have not furnished audited reports for the money they have spent" (5). Two further reports also deserve our attention. In the first, "Task Force to Check Panchayat Irregularities," Surjya Kanta Mishra, the *panchayat* minister, had set up a task force consisting of officials from *panchayats* and rural development departments to check into confirmed reports against several *panchayat* units and to check their accounts; and, in the second, "CAG Flays Municipal Bodies," the comptroller and auditor general of West Bengal had made recommendations for investigations into various irregularities, including "idle investments." It is noteworthy that the initiative for these inquiries came from people who are either party men or had the approval of the party.

innovations have succeeded in inducting whole new groups of people into leadership roles with power and responsibility. These indicate long-term gains for Bengal society. One implication arising out of this is a rather optimistic prospect for long-term institution-building, independent of the rule by a specific political party, though the process still has a few obstacles to overcome.[26]

### Trust in local government

We shall go back once again to the survey finding on trust in government which is a product of personal experience, affected in turn by the life situation of the actor as well as the effectiveness of the institutions and processes that constitute his political world. The variation in trust, thus, offers some insights into the performance of local government and its implications for people in different regions and in different social situations. Table 5.2 reports these findings, where, by comparing across columns and rows one can make a comparison across regions and social classes in the three prototype states of India.

Looking at the distribution across urban and rural populations in the three states, one can see the spectacularly low level of trust in local institutions in Bihar's urban residents. Exactly the opposite is the case with the urban population in West Bengal, a possible consequence of the good performance of Bengal *panchayats* and good communication of this performance by the state government. The scenario continues with caste status in Bihar where members of scheduled castes and tribes have a lower level of trust than the upper castes, unlike Bengal where the scheduled tribes actually have a higher level of trust than the rest of the population. On education, Bihar presents an almost linear relationship with level of education and trust in local government, the level going down somewhat for those at the highest level of education, but not

---

[26] This view is shared by those who have examined *panchayati raj* in West Bengal from close quarters. Thus, Mukherjee and Bandopadhyay, in a report submitted to the government of West Bengal, observe that, "In the decade and a half of their existence, the Panchayats have achieved much that is tangible, especially in land reform but also in rural development. More than this, they have also brought about a churning of the submerged humanity in the rural areas and created a high degree of social and political awareness among all sections" (216). "These are encouraging developments, indicating that the *panchayats* have helped in strengthening the roots of democracy. The intangible achievement this represents is of inestimable value" (217). However, on the negative side, they note that "the leaders among the elected functionaries are not clear about the objectives of the *panchayats* . . . The concept of the *panchayats* being institutions of self-government is either missing or only dimly perceived": Mukherjee and Bandopadhyay (1994: 217).

Table 5.2. *Trust in local government across regions and socioeconomic strata (%)*

|  | Bihar | Maharashtra | West Bengal | All India |
|---|---|---|---|---|
| All | 29.9 | 40.7 | 50.6 | 39.3 |
| Rural | 31.2 | 45.3 | 50.0 | 42.5 |
| Urban | 18.2 | 30.0 | 59.3 | 29.3 |
| Men | 35.5 | 39.7 | 52.7 | 42.9 |
| Women | 24.0 | 41.6 | 48.2 | 35.6 |
| Scheduled castes | 27.0 | 41.7 | 52.5 | 39.2 |
| Scheduled tribes | 6.5 | 50.0 | 57.1 | 38.9 |
| OBCs | 33.6 | 44.6 | 48.4 | 40.9 |
| Upper castes | 31.7 | 31.5 | 50.0 | 37.3 |
| Illiterates | 23.5 | 42.2 | 56.5 | 35.8 |
| Up to primary | 37.6 | 43.6 | 47.6 | 43.1 |
| Middle school | 38.6 | 38.3 | 39.4 | 40.6 |
| Higher secondary | 43.9 | 38.8 | 51.5 | 42.4 |
| College + | 36.1 | 34.7 | 58.6 | 38.9 |
| Up to 25 years | 34.5 | 37.3 | 42.9 | 38.2 |
| 26–35 years | 30.2 | 43.1 | 50.0 | 40.4 |
| 36–45 years | 23.9 | 40.9 | 56.1 | 39.2 |
| 46–55 years | 30.7 | 38.5 | 56.1 | 37.6 |
| 56 years or more | 28.1 | 43.2 | 52.1 | 40.6 |

dipping to the level of illiterates and staying way above the average. Bengal presents an interesting curvilinearity, levels being high at the highest and lowest levels of education (possibly active adherents of the Left Front where party ideology compensates for the low trust "normal" in the illiterate caused by personal inefficacy, and lower trust in the most highly educated from an elitist disenchantment with mass democracy). The true surprise of Bihar is the relatively high trust in local government among the youngest – at 34.5 percent not far from the comparable level in the national sample and way above other age groups in Bihar. Bengal, on the other hand, expects the youth possibly to serve their time before they can stand up and be counted, and be in a position to have a relationship based on trust with the local government. The CPM banks heavily on the trusted and loyal middle-aged cadre in key positions and inducts locally influential individuals as candidates for local elections who are allowed to compete under its symbol even if they do not belong to the party. Neither of the two tactics favor the rapid induction of the youth into playing an influential role in the *panchayat* structure, unlike in regions which are relatively less institutionalized and where the younger and the more educated have fewer organizational hurdles to cross. The Maharashtrian data confirm the image one gets from the literature of moderately performing *panchayat* institutions which have lost some of their earlier prominence – and trust from the upper and more educated strata – but continue to be strong, welfare-administering institutions, inspiring more trust in women than men, unlike the national average and unlike our other two regions.

### Elites, nonelites and local government

The typology depicted in figure 5.1 helps to understand the variation in the effectiveness and legitimacy of local governance in India. Which type a specific local government belongs to depends upon a number of factors. But a crucial component is the perception of local government by the local elites and non-elites. In order to analyze the variation of local governance in terms of its typology, the survey sample was stratified into four categories: namely, rural elites, rural nonelites, urban elites and urban nonelites, using membership of parties (present or past), personal sense of efficacy ("vote has effect"), and place of residence (urban or rural) as the constituent variables. Urban elites are normally resident in an area classed by the Indian census as urban, they are or have been members of a political party, and believe that their vote "has effect." Rural elites, like their urban counterparts, are people with a high sense of personal efficacy and party membership except that they reside in areas classified as rural. The national sample, thus stratified, produced four categories: rural nonelites (66.7 percent), rural elites (9.4 percent), urban nonelites (20.3 percent) and urban elites (3.7 percent).

Before we can use the statistical variable of elite status as an empirical surrogate for the conceptual variable, we need to perform a further test to establish its validity. It should be noticed here that elite status is the product of at least two different attributes. On the one hand, those described as the elites of the rural universe must think of themselves as the movers and shakers of their world – an aspect that has already been incorporated into the construction of the variable in terms of their sense of personal efficacy, membership of a political party. But one needs a second attribute, namely, social perception of these people as elites – i.e., those who are better informed, more active in mobilizing opinion, and important enough to be sought out by parties and candidates looking for entry points into the world of mass politics. Some of these data are analyzed in table 5.3.

We learn from table 5.3 that our elites are indeed people who matter, not only in terms of their self-perception, but also in terms of more than average political information, in this case knowing the name of the member of parliament from their constituency, a level of interest in the campaign about three times that of the national average, a similarly high level of participation in the electoral campaign and, finally, a higher than

Table 5.3. *Social construction of elite status (%)*

|  | Rural nonelite | Rural elite | Urban nonelite | Urban elite | All |
|---|---|---|---|---|---|
| Correct naming of local MP | 47.6 | 76.0 | 63.6 | 82.9 | 54.8 |
| Great deal of interest in campaign | 7.6 | 30.5 | 7.4 | 29.3 | 10.5 |
| Campaign meeting attended | 11.8 | 44.7 | 12.9 | 42.4 | 16.2 |
| Participation in campaign | 5.1 | 35.3 | 6.3 | 35.3 | 9.2 |
| Canvasser came to home | 37.4 | 64.4 | 44.6 | 65.0 | 42.4 |

average probability of being contacted by election canvassers. The second important message we get from looking at the data in table 5.3 is that there is practically no difference any more between rural and urban elites in terms of these indicators. Democracy, in this respect, has been a great leveler.

Having thus tested the measurement of elite status in terms of the new variable created for this purpose, we can now compare their perceptions of three levels of government in India. The data, presented in table 5.4, show first of all the high level of trust that rural elites have in local government compared to the national average, as well as compared to their trust in the national government. In this, they are well above urban elites. Interestingly, even rural nonelites have higher trust in local government than urban elites and a level of trust in the central government which is comparable to that of the urban elite.

Finally, we shall turn to the variation in "great deal of trust in local government" across our three regions, analyzed in terms of the perception by different types of respondents according to their status on the elite typology (see table 5.5).

One of the most important features of the findings reported in table 5.5 is the narrowing of the gap between rural elites and rural nonelites in West Bengal and Maharashtra, in both of which the rural elites are above the nonelites in terms of trust in local government, but only barely. In comparison, Bihar stands out dramatically, with the majority (even higher than in Maharashtra and West Bengal) expressing their trust in local government, leaving the rural nonelites a good twenty percentage points below.

The survey findings nicely confirm the anecdotal and interview data we have about the venality, corruption, and nepotism that characterizes *panchayats* in Bihar compared to the relative transparency and propriety one hears about in Bengal and Maharashtra. The other feature of West Bengal is the generally high level of trust in local government across all four categories – showing perhaps the combination of secular gains

Table 5.4. *Trust in different levels of government (%)*

| Great deal of trust in: | Rural nonelite | Rural elite | Urban nonelite | Urban elite | All |
|---|---|---|---|---|---|
| Central government | 35.6 | 47.6 | 28.8 | 35.3 | 35.3 |
| State government | 36.6 | 50.1 | 32.9 | 47.3 | 37.5 |
| Local government | 41.4 | 49.4 | 27.3 | 40.5 | 39.3 |

Table 5.5. *Trust in local government: by region*

| Great deal of trust in local government | Rural nonelite | Rural elite | Urban nonelite | Urban elite | All |
|---|---|---|---|---|---|
| Bihar | 29.0 | 53.6 | 17.9 | 20.0 | 29.9 |
| Maharashtra | 45.2 | 46.4 | 26.1 | 45.3 | 40.7 |
| West Bengal | 49.7 | 51.0 | 58.5 | 61.5 | 50.6 |

through two decades of good administration, but perhaps also the results of sustained propaganda by the left government. The opposite is the case in Bihar, where all except the rural elites show low trust, the rural elites being obviously in the know about where the new fountain-head of resources lies and making good use of this knowledge.

### Conclusion

This chapter suggests that local government is at its most effective when local institutions enjoy the trust and confidence of local elites and are simultaneously accountable to the local electorate. However, elite confidence in institutions to the exclusion of electorate involvement produces elite complacency and breeds corruption; electorate involvement alone produces authority without responsibility, leading to chaos and ultimately a decline in governance. Institutionalized political participation at the local level is the crucial link between democracy and development. It is this democratic base that gives the larger structure of the state its resilience. To suggest otherwise, such as the fond hope that divisive party politics should be kept out of the local arena, is indeed to abandon hard political realities in favour of a neo-communitarian utopia.[27]

---

[27] Keeping political parties out of *panchayats* was advocated by the Congress Party in the first years following the introduction of local self-government. There was no doubt a grain of Gandhian communitarianism about it. But the less noble intention of keeping competition out and using *panchayats* as their personal fief could not have been far from the strategic calculations of national political parties. See Weiner (1962b).

That India has put the institutions of local government for democracy and governance to good use is now very much an accepted fact. But why is it that within the context of a roughly comparable constitutional–legal structure instituting local government and democracy there is such regional variation in the breadth and depth of local governance; and what broad implications can we draw from the regional comparison of local democracy for the resilience of the state in India?

Instead of thinking of India's regions in idiosyncratic terms, this essay has concentrated on understanding their experience with regard to local governance as the consequence of a cluster of factors, most of which are general to all regions and in some sense collectively describe the nature of the state and the political process in India. It takes capable and imaginative leadership at the regional level to put many of the legislative, political, and material resources to work in order to produce the required results in local governance. But while the political institutions of local democracy are necessary, they are not, on their own, sufficient. As the West Bengal interviews indicated, the availability of collateral institutions like cooperatives is exceedingly important for the democratic institutions to perform at their best. Thus, the good results of West Bengal do not show the idiosyncrasy of Bengali culture but a particularly fortuitous ensemble of factors. Nor are the Bihar results entirely negative, for the high trust of the young and the rural elites in local government are important resources which, in combination with other democratic and secondary institutions, party competitiveness and political and financial accountability, could also possibly produce good results for local governance in Bihar.

The other states of India could profitably transfer some of the knowledge gained from the West Bengal "experiment" with great profit. Important among these good practices are cooperatives, proper use of local bureaucracy, effective implementation of land reform and minimum wage legislation. The CPM's presence happens to provide a sufficient political condition at the local level to bring all these resources to their optimal use; but it is not a necessary condition. The crucial test cases are regions with non-CPM governments. Karnataka could be one such state.

The main thrust of our findings is to show that since power in the Indian political system has emerged from coalition formation at the lower levels, everyone engaged in it has had a vested interest in keeping the "democratic" game going, though, once again, the stakes are not the same for everyone. Democratic participation can very well coexist with legal and political irregularities, unfair and unequal distribution, corruption and venality. True, general elections often succeed in throwing rascals out, but they also induct some rascals in, and the political process turns some into rascals once they are within the government. General trust in government as a measure of legitimacy could be only a starting point of analysis because one encounters difficulties almost immediately. Do local elites trust local government precisely because they do not fulfill norms of rational public management? Since surveys are typically used to measure behavior and attitudes rather than causal motives, we need to look at the partial evidence that we have from in-depth interviews to develop further conjectures on this score. On the face of it, Bihar rural elites trust "their" local government for reasons that one associates with warlord regimes rather than democratic govern-ance. On the other hand, we have enough evidence to assert that while corruption and nepotism are not entirely unknown in West Bengal *panchayats*, they are usually kept under check. Perhaps nonelite trust in government is a better measure – one where Bengal performs better than Maharashtra (a close second so far as rural nonelites are concerned but not urban nonelites) and Bihar, which performs abysmally among both rural and urban nonelites.

It is of course only an illusion to think that any government, but most of all local government, could be trusted entirely to the safe hands of the expert, or that local governments are a happy family, keeping divisive politics at bay. Similarly, we have to come to terms with the fact that it is not very realistic to devise the structure of local governments without any role for local elites to play in them. The true challenge for the theorist of local government in changing societies lies in devising a scheme where local democracy, elites, and experts can play complemen-tary roles.

The emphasis on the local, also suggested by new communitarians like Putnam, has an important implication for postcolonial societies. It suggests that one should accord legitimacy and the status of full actors to premodern social structures and groups. This sits uncomfortably with the more conventional theories of social and political change, born out of the historical and political context of European nation-states. The incorporation of variables such as social networks, interpersonal trust, and shared norms into conventional theories of social and economic change creates a dilemma for the development planner and the builders of states and nations about how to reconcile the twin task of accumula-tion, extraction, transformation, and rationalization on the one hand and the legitimization of these measures within the framework of representative democracy on the other. Caught in this double bind, politicians – in Yeltsin's Russia, Mandela's South Africa or Laloo Yadav's Bihar – prefer to fudge the issues and muddle through, with the usual combination of rhetoric and inaction. For the same reason, understanding local government, as a key both to legitimacy and democracy, but also in terms of its limitations as seen in the case of Bihar, is an important challenge for the comparative politics of changing societies.

# 6    Redoing the constitutional design: from an interventionist to a regulatory state

*Lloyd I. Rudolph and Susanne Hoeber Rudolph*

On January 27, 2000, President K.R. Narayanan, in an address in the central hall of parliament to mark the golden jubilee of the republic and the constitution, asked whether "it is the constitution that has failed us or we who have failed the constitution."[1] The president was responding critically to the appointment of a commission "to comprehensively review the Constitution of India in the light of the experience of the past 50 years and to make suitable recommendations."[2] Unlike the presidential speech at the opening of parliament, President Narayanan's golden jubilee address was not written for him by the government of the day. It

---

[1] The full text of the President's golden jubilee speech is given in *Seminar*, 487, March 2000: 88–90 and in *Mainstream*, 38 (8), February 12, 2000: 9–11. Accounts of the debate surrounding the speech are given, *inter alia*, in *Asian Age*, January 28, 2000 and *Business Line*, February 1, 2000. See Mitra and Ahmed (2000) for an overview.

[2] This is the language of the BJP's (Bharatiya Janata Party) 1998 manifesto. Although the BJP, like the other twenty-one parties of the National Democratic Alliance (NDA), dropped its manifesto in favor of a common minimum program on which all parties of the coalition contested the thirteenth national election in 1999, the language of the minimum program and of the postelection government announcement closely followed the language of the BJP's 1998 manifesto. The BJP 1998 manifesto is given in Aggarwal and Chowdhry (1998: 43–44).

   The NDA government asked former chief justice and former chair of the National Human Rights Commission, M.N. Venkatachaliah, to chair an eleven-member commission. His acceptance was conditioned on an understanding that he would have a say in choosing the commission's members and that there would be no change in the constitution's "basic features," a term made famous by the landmark *Keshavananda* (1973) case. Justice Venkatachaliah's conditions seemed to exclude the "presidential form of government" favored by BJP ministers of the NDA government who sought "stability." The president obliquely addressed those seeking "stability" in his golden jubilee address by placing accountability above stability "which could slip into an authoritarian exercise of power." *Mainstream*, February 12, 2000: 10.

   On February 23, 2000, when President Narayanan opened the budget session of parliament, he read from a text written for him by the government. Nevertheless, his words seemed to show traces of his own input. "While keeping the basic structure and salient features of the Constitution inviolate," he told parliament, "it has become necessary to examine the experience of the past 50 years to better achieve the ideals enshrined in the Constitution." He assured his listeners that the recommendations of the review commission "will be presented before Parliament." *Hindustan Times*, February 24, 2000.

represented an autonomous presidential perspective. Widely reported and much discussed in print and the electronic media, the speech deepened and accelerated a national debate on the constitution that the NDA government's action had provoked. The speech also signaled that presidents have been able to be more independent of prime ministers and cabinets since 1989 when coalition governments displaced majority party governments.[3] Such basic changes in the party system and electoral outcomes show that a constitution is a living thing, a process, not a blueprint; a work in progress, not a monument.

Because a constitution is a living thing we read the word "constitution" to mean more than its formal aspect, more than a text frequently amended by parliament and interpreted by the supreme court.[4] We also mean the conventional constitution, consisting of widely recognized and commonly accepted rules, practices and institutions, and the symbolic constitution, consisting of collective representations, signifiers, and metaphors that help to define "India" and Indianness. Whether constitutions are formal, conventional, or symbolic, their meaning is continually contested and their legitimacy is subject to renewal.[5]

Attending exclusively to the formal constitution would miss fundamental changes in constitutional ideas and practices that distinguished the Indian state of the 1990s from that of the 1950s. Neither the party system nor the Planning Commission, central forces in creating the constitutional order, are mentioned in the formal constitution. Attention to the conventional constitution directs us to analyze change in the party and federal systems, and the changing balance of power between branches and units of government. It highlights, as no close analysis of formal constitutional provisions can, the erosion of the centralized Nehruvian state and economy that prevailed for four decades after

---

[3] After eight national elections, 1952 through 1984, that yielded eight majority governments, five subsequent national elections, 1989 through 1999, produced four coalition governments and one minority government.

[4] Like the United States, India has a written constitution whose provisions are subject to amendment and to judicial review. In India the doctrine and practice of judicial review was challenged by the claim that a sovereign parliament had unlimited powers of amendment. In particular Prime Minister Indira Gandhi in 1976 tried, by having parliament adopt the forty-second amendment, to override the supreme court's decision in *Keshavananda Bharati* (1973) that parliament's power to amend the constitution was limited by the constitution's basic structure, or "essential features," e.g., holding free and fair elections. The forty-second amendment made parliament's claim to unlimited sovereignty explicit. *Minerva Mills* (1980) invalidated the two clauses of the forty-second amendment meant to reverse *Keshavananda*. For a detailed account see Rudolph and Rudolph (1987: ch. 3) and Basu (1999: 1138–1149).

[5] A longer revised version of this paper is to appear as a chapter in our forthcoming study, "Living with Difference: Economic, Political and Cultural Dimensions of Sharing Sovereignty in India's Federal System."

independence in 1947. Analysis of the conventional constitution reveals that in the 1990s a multiparty system, including strong regional parties, displaced a dominant party system; market ideas and practices displaced central planning and a "permit-license raj"; and the federal system took on a new lease on life with the federal states gaining ground at the expense of the center. With the launching of economic reform in 1991, a centralized, tutelary, interventionist state whose political and administrative elites were committed to the notion that they knew best and could do best was challenged by an increasingly decentralized regulatory state and market economy whose politicians and entrepreneurs turned to voters, consumers, and investors for ideas and actions.

The formal constitution too was not static. The balance of power between central institutions that was provided for in the formal constitution was reshaped by the practice of actors responding to historical challenges. The balance shifted in favor of the supreme court, the Election Commission and the president at the expense of parliament, the prime minister, and the cabinet. Here we address changes in only one aspect of the formal constitutional design, the contribution of enhanced roles for the supreme court, the president, and the Election Commission to the emergence of a regulatory state.[6]

### Renegotiating the balance of power: the judiciary, the presidency and the election commission

We have noted that since the onset of economic reform in 1991 the Indian economy has moved away from central planning by an interventionist state and moved toward market competition fostered by a regulatory state. Something similar happened in the conduct of politics: a dominant party system and majority governments have given way to a multiparty system and coalition governments. In institutional terms, the displacement of an interventionist by a regulatory state has meant a diminished executive and legislature and enhanced regulatory institutions – less scope for cabinet and parliament, more scope for the supreme court, the election commission, and the president.

The role of regulatory institutions is more procedural than substantive, more rule-making and enforcing than law-making and policy-making. Regulatory institutions are needed, not only to create, sustain,

---

[6] We have borrowed the term "regulatory state" in the sense used in this paper from Matthew C.J. Rudolph who is working on a comparative study, "Making Markets: Financial Organization, Economic Transitions, and the Emergence of the Regulatory State in India and China," Ph.D. proposal, Department of Government, Cornell University, 1998.

and perfect markets, but also to ensure procedural fairness in the election and operation of a multiparty system and the formation and conduct of coalition governments in a federal framework. The difficulties and failures of transitions to market economies and to democracy in a variety of settings have revealed their dependence on the rule of law and a viable state (Holmes 1977). The emergence in some Eastern European states and particularly Russia of what Max Weber would have called political capitalism,[7] the accumulation of wealth through power rather than entrepreneurship, has been accompanied by fraud, crime, and violence. The result suggests that transitions to a market economy and to democracy require more than privatization and liberty.

Such considerations apply to India even though the economic and political transitions it has experienced have been less traumatic than those in Eastern Europe and Russia. Three constitutionally mandated institutions, the supreme and high courts, the president, and the Election Commission, became more visible and effective in the 1990s as the reputations and authority of political executives (union and state cabinets) and legislatures (parliament and state assemblies) lost ground. During the Nehru/Gandhi years of Congress dominance, political executives and legislatures benefited from association with the (declining) political capital of the nationalist era's struggle against colonial rule and for independence; the one-party-dominant party system; and the authority and resources of a command economy. As these three predisposing conditions lost their potency, political executives and legislatures receded, opening space and creating opportunities for courts, presidents, and election commissioners to act in ways that emphasized their constitutional roles as the regulatory mechanisms of democratic politics.[8]

The fading of structural conditions that supported the preeminence of executives and legislatures by itself does not account for their fall from grace. Prime and chief ministers, legislators, and the civil servants who served them discredited themselves in the eyes of India's educated

---

[7] For a systematic development of the idea of and practice of political capitalism in Eastern Europe and Russia with Bulgaria given special attention see Ganev (1999).

Thomas L. Friedman (1998) argued that the ultimate test of US policy in China is "how well the US uses its influence to promote a more rule-of-law system in China – one that first constrains the Chinese state and then gradually lays an institutional foundation that can carry Chinese society forward after the inevitable collapse of the Communist Party or its evolution into an electoral body." Chaudhry (1997) shows how the quality and strength of institutions have determined economic viability and market success and failure in Yemen and Saudi Arabia.

[8] For an authoritative overview of the complex 395-article constitution that came into force on January 26, 1950, see Basu (1994).

middle classes[9] who, as producers, consumers, and citizens, cared about the reliability and security that a government of laws promised to deliver. A burgeoning constituency, the middle classes, responded in the mid-1980s to Rajiv Gandhi's promises to provide clean government and a high-tech, reformed, environmentally friendly economy that would take India into the twenty-first century. After Rajiv disappointed them, the symbolic politics and practical measures spawned by the supreme court, the president, and the Election Commission spoke to their attitudes, moods, and interests. The Bofors scandal that drove Rajiv Gandhi from office in 1989 symbolized the pervasiveness of corruption. From *bakshish* for the little guy to bribes for his boss to "commissions" for the governing elite, office was seen to serve as a source of income. Permit-license raj had become "rent raj." Intimidation, violence, and black money were being used to win elections. In the early 1990s an unprecedented number of ministers at state and national levels were indicted for taking bribes.[10] The complexity and fragility of the coalition governments formed after 1989 on the basis of hung parliaments (and of hung state assemblies), their rapid turnover and their dependence on regional parties created complexity and ambiguities that further en- hanced the role of the regulatory branches of government.

As executives and legislature were perceived as increasingly ineffectual,

---

[9] We use "educated middle classes" as a portmanteau phrase to refer to old, raj era as well as new professional and Green Revolution era middle classes in so far as their education, which usually includes some English, enables them to share an information (media) and consumer (market) culture. We are aware that these differences are further cross-cut by the cultural variations that mark India's federal states. A Mumbai wallah is not the same as a Calcutta, New Delhi, or Chennai wallah, although many share enough in the way of attitudes, moods, and interest to speak on occasion of national middle classes – readers of the national weekly magazines and buyers of nationally advertised brands.

[10] The most spectacular cases of the 1990s were associated with illegal transactions which the seized diary of businessman S.K. Jain was said to have documented. According to accounts leaked to the press, nine serving or former ministers were implicated by illegal payments and use of foreign exchange. Subsequently all charges were dropped. In 1993, then Prime Minister Narasimha Rao was accused of having had Rs. 10 million paid to four Jharkhand Mukti Morcha MPs to secure their support in a confidence vote designed to bring down his government. Large sums of cash were found in Telecommunications Minister Sukh Ram's house at the height of decision-making about which firms were to be awarded contracts for providing regional service contracts. The then chief minister of Bihar, Laloo Prasad Yadav, was forced to resign and was temporarily imprisoned over a $280,000,000 cattle fodder scam.

The degradation of the early to mid-1990s came against the background of the Bofors case, the allegation that Prime Minister Rajiv Gandhi and/or those closely associated with him had accepted substantial "commissions" when the GOI placed an order for $1.4 billion worth of artillery pieces with Bofors, a Swedish armaments firm. The charges against Rajiv Gandhi as of 2000 remained unsettled. They haunt his memory and hover like a dark cloud over the Congress Party presidency of his widow and political heir, Sonia Gandhi.

unstable, and corrupt, the supreme and high courts, the presidency, and the Election Commission became the object of a middle class public's hope and aspiration, only partially fulfilled, that someone would defend a government of laws and enforce probity and procedural regularity.

## Judicial activism

India's judiciary, a supreme court created by article 124, and state high courts created by article 214, are important components of India's written constitution. In the era of unstable, short-lived coalition governments in the 1990s,[11] the supreme court's judicial activism helped to repair and correct the Indian state. The court played a critical role in approximating a framework of lawfulness and predictability that has had some success in protecting citizens' rights, limiting malfeasance and safeguarding environmental and other public goods.

The court's judicial activism marks a novel turn in India's constitutional history. For the court's first four decades it was pitted against the Nehru and Gandhi governments' efforts to expand parliamentary sovereignty at the expense of judicial review.[12] The contest arose because the framers of India's constitution created a hybrid that joined the parliamentary sovereignty of the British model[13] with the judicial review of the US model.

[11] Between 1989 and 1999 eight governments held power: V.P. Singh's Janata Dal minority coalition government 1989–91; S. Chandrasekhar's six-month minority government, 1990–1; Atal Behari Vajpayee's minority BJP government, 13 days in June 1991; V.P. Narasimha Rao's mostly minority Congress government, 1991–6; Deve Gowda's minority United Front government succeeded by Inder Kumar Gujral's minority UF government, 1996–8; Atal Behari Vajpayee's two BJP-led coalition governments, 1998–9 and 1999– .

[12] India's written constitution and contested practice of judicial review does not mean that those who framed India's constitution were committed, as the US framers were, to protecting liberty by constructing a system of separation of powers and checks and balances. It is important to remember that even the US constitution did not explicitly provide for judicial review of legislative acts, i.e., laws passed by the two Houses of Congress, the House of Representatives and the Senate, and presented to and signed by the president. It was Chief Justice John Marshall who, in *Marbury* v. *Madison* (1803), established "the principle of judicial review and the Supreme Court's sovereign right to interpret the meaning of the Constitution" by striking down the Judiciary Act of 1789 (Ellis 1998: 267). The next time the court declared a legislative act unconstitutional was fifty-four years later, in 1857, when, in the Dred Scott case, it held the 1820 "Missouri Compromise" law barring slavery in northern territories unconstitutional.

The relative ease with which the contemporary US supreme court declares legislative acts unconstitutional should not obscure Marshall's innovation or judicial review's very tentative beginnings.

For a more detailed analysis in a comparative framework, see Rudolph and Rudolph (1987: 103–126).

[13] The term "parliamentary sovereignty" refers to the preeminence of a hyphenated entity, cabinet-in-parliament. The executive, the prime minister and his or her council of

The first clashes between parliamentary sovereignty and judicial review occurred when the court in *Golak Nath* v. *Punjab* (1967) invoked the constitution's protection of fundamental rights (Basu 1994: 433, table VI), particularly the right to property, to challenge the Nehru government's land reform legislation. The decision restricted parliament's competency to amend fundamental rights.[14] A more momentous round of confrontations surrounded the Emergency regime (1975–77) imposed by Indira Gandhi.[15] Using the Congress Party's parliamentary majority to pass the forty-second amendment (1976), she tried to eliminate the court's use of judicial review to limit parliament's power under article 368 to amend the constitution. She did not succeed. An earlier landmark case, *Keshavananda* v. *State of Kerala* (1973), persisted and was again upheld in the *Minerva Mills* case in 1980.[16] In *Keshavananda* the justices agreed that, using article 368, governments could amend fundamental rights, but held that there were certain *basic features* of the constitution that could not be altered. "If, therefore, a Constitution Amendment Act seeks to alter the basic structure or framework of the Constitution, the Court would be entitled to annul it on the ground of *ultra vires*, because the word 'amend,' in Art. 368, means only changes other than altering the very structure of the Constitution, which would be tantamount to making a new Constitution" (Basu 1994: 151).

The practice of judicial review survived the buffeting of the 1970s, though the court emerged chastened. It showed skill in recapturing its

ministers or cabinet, is elected by the legislature and is dependent on its continuing support. Put another way, the prime minister and his ministerial cabinet colleagues are members of parliament and have the confidence of the lower house. They do not confront the legislature as a contrary force. The Indian supreme court invoked a conventional English characterization when it referred to the relationship as "a hyphen which joins, a buckle which fastens," in *Ram Jawaya* v. *State of Punjab*, 1955, 2 SCR 225.

14 *Golak Nath* v. *State of Punjab*, A 1967 SC 1643. It reversed *Shankari Prasad* v. *Union of India* 1951 AIR (SC) 458 which held that no part of the constitution was unamendable, and *Sajjan Singh* v. *State of Rajasthan* 1964 AIR (SC) 845. The Indira Gandhi government response to *Golak Nath* was the twenty-fourth amendment which modified article 368, the amendment clause, so as to make the fundamental rights provided for by part III of the constitution susceptible to parliamentary amendment.

15 For a discussion of supreme court opinions in relation to the court's internal struggles and to varying political environments, including the Emergency regime, see Baxi (1980). See also Rudolph and Rudolph (1987: 118–120).

16 The cases are *Keshavananda* v. *State of Kerala*, A 1973 SC 1461 (FB) and *Minerva Mills* v. *Union of India*, A 1980 SC 1789. In the *Minerva Mills* case, the court invoked *Keshavananda* to declare invalid, because they attacked the basic structure of the constitution, the two clauses of the forty-second amendment meant to reverse *Keshavananda*. The first prohibited court review of laws that contravened fundamental rights if parliament declared that they gave effect to directive principles of state policy; the second proscribed judicial review of constitutional amendments. See Rudolph and Rudolph (1987: 117). For a thoughtful consideration of the issues in the *Minerva Mills* case, see Noorani (1981: 293–300).

role in the 1980s when, by beginning to entertain public interest legislation (PIL) – similar to class action suits in the US – it laid the basis for the judicial activism of the 1990s. Because the court's PIL version of judicial activism suited Indira Gandhi's (1980–4) and Rajiv Gandhi's (1985–9) populist agendas, the two Congress prime ministers did not perceive PIL as a threat to their governments' claim to parliamentary sovereignty. The court's decisions and actions in the pre-economic reform phase of judicial activism sought to enforce citizens' fundamental rights (Basu 1994: 433, table VI) and, more broadly, to protect the human rights of the poor and powerless. The court sought to safeguard human rights against state abuses, e.g., police brutality and torture, custodial rape, inhuman treatment in jails and "protective" homes.[17] In the late 1980s and early 1990s, the court extended its judicial activism to protecting the viability of public goods, e.g., clean air and water, and uncontaminated blood supplies.

In the mid-1990s the court's judicial activism turned in yet another direction. Coincident with the rise of precariously balanced coalition governments and of a marked increase in ministerial-level corruption, the supreme court moved to restore the independence of the Central Bureau of Investigation (CBI), the union government's principal investigative agency. As far back as January 1988, after Prime Minister Rajiv Gandhi had been implicated in the payment of illegal commissions by the Swedish armament firm, Bofors, for a gun deal with the GOI, the CBI was made subject to "the single directive," i.e., "prior consultation with the Secretary of the Ministry/Department concerned before . . . [the CBI] takes up any enquiry, including ordering search . . . Without this concurrence, no enquiry shall be initiated by the [CBI]."[18] "Prior consultation" and "government concurrence" meant that prime ministers, who also controlled CBI appointments, promotions, and transfers, dominated CBI initiatives and actions. The extent of control was highlighted with the discovery of the "Jain diaries," a record of transfers to

---

[17] The judges, led by Chief Justice P.N. Bhagwati, were initially responding to a case (*Upendra* v. *State of U.P.* [1981] 3 Scale 1137 SC) in which two law professors complained that the fundamental rights of inmates of a protective home were being violated by the government (Basu 1999: 270).

After the initial encouragement given to PIL by Chief Justice Bhagwati in the early 1980s, there was a lull of some years. PIL resumed in 1993 with the twenty-month term of Justice M.N. Venkatachaliah who "set the tone for a new activism." He was soon followed by Justice, later Chief Justice, J.S. Verma and Justice Kuldip Singh (Gupta 1996).

[18] For more details see Rani (1998: 24–26), and Jha and Kang (1996).

The January 1988 order was issued by the then minister of state of the personnel department, P. Chidambaram. The personnel department ministerial portfolio is usually held by the prime minister, often, as in this case, with a minister of state to assist him.

politicians by an influence-peddling commission agent, S.K. Jain.[19] As news of the Jain diary's contents spread, seemingly implicating not only cabinet ministers and leading politicians, but also the then sitting prime minister, Narasimha Rao, the CBI's inability to act without government concurrence seemed to some, including eventually supreme court justices, unconscionable. There was a "common belief," a leading news magazine reported, "that it is the near complete abdication of responsibility by the Government as well as Parliament which has created the conditions for the current bout of judicial activism."[20]

A supreme court division bench headed by then Justice, later Chief Justice, J.S. Verma "felt it was necessary to free the CBI from the Prime Minister's charge to eliminate any impression of bias." The court asked the CBI not to furnish information to Prime Minister Rao on the details of the investigation. This meant that, for all practical purposes, the CBI would report only to the supreme court with respect to investigations and charge sheeting (indictments) arising from information found in the Jain diaries.[21] After issuing directives removing the CBI from direct executive supervision, the court asked it to follow up on evidence found in the diaries. They implicated many leading politicians with respect to illegal foreign exchange violations, bribes, and kickbacks. With court prodding and supervision, twenty-six politicians were indicted including seven of Prime Minister Narasimha Rao's cabinet colleagues.[22]

While most of those implicated by the Jain diaries were found not guilty,[23] the court, supported overwhelmingly by middle-class public opinion, persisted in its role as upholder of norms and agent of good government.[24] On December 18, 1997, after the Rao Congress govern-

---

[19] See note 10 for details.

[20] Jha and Kang (1996: 13).      [21] Ghimire (1996).

[22] Vineet Narain and Kamini Jaiswal, both civil rights lawyers, "persuaded the Supreme Court to get the CBI to hasten its investigations in the multi-crore havala transactions case" (Jha and Kang 1996). Several of those indicted were not prosecuted, e.g., Madhavrao Scindia and Sharad Yadav. "Law Makers or Breakers? 39 MPs have Criminal Cases Pending Against Them," *Outlook*, August 14, 1996: 6 and 9.

Further investigation and court reviews of procedure and evidence led to the dropping of charges, including those against the Jain brothers. *Deccan Chronicle*, February 10, 2000. Already as of December 1997, according to a CBI spokesman, "20-odd charge-sheeted politicians were sitting pretty in their bungalows. All but two charge sheets have been thrown out in the preliminary stages for lack of prima facie evidence . . . The Supreme Court pressurized us [the CBI] into charge-sheeting these politicians" (Rani 1998: 25).

[23] By 1999, observers worried whether, with the retirement of Justice Kuldip Singh and others of the activist generation, the court would resile from its role as anticorruption watchdog. See *India Today*'s comments on the reversal of the Rs. 50 lakh exemplary damage assessed against former petroleum minister Satish Sharma for mishandling his discretionary powers to award petrol pumps (August 16, 1999).

[24] An opinion poll in February 1996 found that 89 percent of urban respondents felt that

ment had been rejected by the electorate, the supreme court in a landmark judgment made its arrangements of March 1996 permanent. It did so by removing the "single directive" (government concurrence) that governed CBI investigations and by giving the CBI director a minimum two-year term of office.[25] These actions left the CBI somewhat freer to investigate on its own cognizance ministerial cases and to follow up on *prima facie* cases it had left unattended because it lacked "government concurrence."

Not surprisingly the court's judicial activism with respect to the CBI and on other matters precipitated countermoves to limit the court initiatives. The careers and political survival of leading politicians were at stake. One countermove was an initiative to remove the constitutional prohibition (article 121) against parliamentary discussions of the conduct of supreme court or high court judges. Another was a conclave called by the then speaker of the Lok Sabha, Purno Sangma, to address the question of judicial activism. It concluded that "the judiciary was exhibiting a dangerous tendency to encroach on legislative and administrative foundations beyond its ambit [and] that the judges were populists playing to the gallery in the recent spate of widely-publicized corruption trials."[26]

The court's activism arose not only as a response to state processes but also from the interplay between state and civil society. The 1980s saw an extraordinary burgeoning of nongovernmental voluntary organi-

---

the judiciary was doing "a commendable job" and 94 percent that "the judiciary should continue to cleanse the system." "Judiciary is doing a great job; An Outlook-MODE opinion poll finds overwhelming support for judicial activism," *Outlook*, March 6, 1996: 18. The sample was made of up 551 respondents in Delhi, Bombay, Calcutta, Madras, and Bangalore. Another urban poll in October, 1996 found that 75 percent of the sample thought politicians were corrupt and 73 percent thought the court was proceeding fairly against them. The results of the poll are reported in *Outlook*, October 23, 1996. A total of 1,234 interviews were conducted on October 9–10 by MODE in five cities – Delhi, Bombay, Madras, Calcutta, and Bangalore. For details of the results see 8 and 9.

According to CPI-M spokesperson H.K.S. Surjeet, "Politicians of all hues – including those who were part of the government in the last five years – unanimously subscribe to the view that the judiciary stepped in to compensate for a weak, listless executive . . . 'a vacuum created by an executive that has stopped functioning.' The judiciary, he says, has 'stepped in largely on behalf of the people and is seen to be doing so in popular perception.'"

Ramakrishna Hegde, former chief minister of Karnataka, spoke of the "'unhealthy camaraderie between legislators and civil servants' [that] has led to the latter abdicating their responsibility to discharge their duties without fear or favor." Sushma Swaraj, BJP spokesperson, believed that "judicial activism has come into play because of the failure of the executive." At the same time, she, like politicians across the party spectrum, thought that judicial activism is "a dangerous trend in itself." *Outlook*, October 23, 1996: 7 and 6.

[25] Rani (1998: 24); *India Today*, December 29, 1997: 30–31.
[26] *Outlook*, October 23, 1996: 6.

zations and social movements dedicated to a wide variety of goals and causes, from opposing environmental degradation and big dams (Narmada, Tehri) to exposures of child and bonded labor, Dalit (ex-untouchable) empowerment, and historical and cultural preservation. In the early 1990s there may have been between 50,000 and 100,000 NGOs at work in India (see Katzenstein et al. below; Kothari 1993; and Omvedt 1993). Together with an array of individual litigators, e.g., Goldman Environmental Prize winner M.C. Mehta and H.D. Shourie of Common Cause, NGOs used public interest litigation to advance their agendas. In the 1980s and even more in the 1990s a growing synergy linked the supreme and high court justices, a resurgent civil society, and reform-minded members of the middle classes.

Public interest litigation could begin and did flourish in India because its supreme court exercises original jurisdiction not only with respect to disputes between different units of the federation (article 131) but also with respect to the enforcement of fundamental rights (article 32). Evolution of the court's original jurisdiction under article 32 led to the so called "epistolary jurisdiction"[27] – recognizing postcards from victims of state impropriety and lawlessness as writ petitions, including postcards from jail inmates. In the early 1980s Chief Justice P.N. Bhagwati and Justice Krishna Iyer took the lead in promoting this novel jurisdiction. The court further modified article 32 by allowing PIL litigators to bring class action suits on behalf of the poor, oppressed, and victimized because, in the court's view, they are often not in a position to represent their own interest.[28]

[27] The term seems to have been coined by Upendra Baxi.

The legal meaning of article 32 was expanded through aggressive litigation by social activist lawyers acting on behalf of social movements and NGOs to override the principle that only the person who has suffered injury by reason of violation of his or her legal rights or interest is entitled to seek judicial redress.

[28] The court enlarged the concept of "persons aggrieved" to include public-spirited individuals or associations, "provided only he . . . is not actuated by political motive or other oblique motive" (Basu 1999: 289).

Basu suggests that these decisions have carved a legal space beyond conventional adversarial law, "involving collaboration and cooperation between the Government and its officers, the Bar and the Bench, for the purpose of making human rights meaningful for the weaker sections of the community" (ibid.: 291).

The enlargement of the concept, together with the invoking of original jurisdiction, has led to a horrendous overload of the courts, with a backlog, in 1995, of 28 million cases in the supreme court and the eighteen high courts; 37,000 of these were accounted for by the supreme court, and 765,426 by the Allahabad high court, in India's largest state, Uttar Pradesh.

For a running discussion of the overload problem by legal professionals sympathetic to public interest legislation, see the annual publication of the Indian Law Institute, *Annual Survey of Indian Law.* See especially the discussion by Parmanand Singh, "Public Interest Litigation," in the *Annual Survey of Indian Law, 1988,* vol. xxiv. For a wider, sympathetic discussion of what he calls social action litigation see Baxi (1985).

Supreme and high court activity on behalf of environmental and other public goods has been as striking as activity on behalf of victims of state lawlessness. Attracting most media coverage were actions to save the Taj Mahal from the effects of pollutants. By 1992, the supreme court had ordered the closure of 212 industries near the Taj Mahal that were in chronic violation of environmental regulations. It took similar action with respect to 190 polluters on the banks of the Ganges river.[29] In 1996 and 1997 it extended its enforcement rulings to industrial violators in the heavily polluted Delhi area. Even more than its PIL actions, its environmental enforcement efforts generated resistance from powerful interests and suffered from civic inertia. In 1999, the Delhi government was requesting two years' grace for noncomplying polluting industries. In February 2000, however, the supreme court ordered the closure of outlets emitting pollutants into the Yamuna river and threatened to jail for contempt state government officials who obeyed Delhi Environment Minister A.K. Walia's and industry minister Dr. Narendra Nath's orders to keep them open.[30] It remains to be seen whether constituencies for human rights and environmental protection will continue to support the court's judicial activism.

In the context of the hung parliaments and coalition governments of the early 1990s, the court acted formally to change the balance of power between the judiciary and the executive. Supreme court judgments in 1991 and 1993 shifted the authority to appoint and transfer supreme court and high court judges from the president of India acting on the advice of his council of ministers (the prime minister and his cabinet) to the president acting on the advice of the chief justice of the supreme court.[31] Until the early 1990s article 124, which establishes and consti-

---

[29] Indian Law Institute, *Annual Survey of Indian Law, 1992*, vol. XXVIII: 251. The actions were in enforcement of the Environmental Protection Act of 1986. In 1999 the supreme court directed Uttar Pradesh to set up a monitoring committee including the PIL petitioner who brought the relevant case to supervise steps to improve Agra drinking water supply and sewage facilities. *Hindu*, November 24, 1999.

[30] *Hindustan Times*, February 27, 2000.

[31] The background to this shift in authority lies in Indira Gandhi's highly political use of the appointment powers. In advising the president about court appointments she overrode the seniority convention that was thought to govern the appointment of the chief justice. She also intimidated judges with the threat and practice of transfers. The seniority rule, which was and is part of the conventional constitution, was designed to protect the autonomy of the court. Transfer rules had a similar aim.

An early Law Commission report recommended that judges not be appointed to the high court of their home state in order to insulate them against parochial and familial influences. But the meaning of this protective device has also been used by the executive as a convenient weapon of harassment. Judges who had served for years in a particular state and who had children in school have been abruptly uprooted and sent to distant states with different cultural traditions and languages on the grounds that they were too close to the public they served. Indira Gandhi's abuse of the appointment

tutes the supreme court, was understood to mean that while the president would consult with (take the advice of) the chief justice and such judges of the supreme court and of the state high courts as he deemed necessary, ultimately he would act on the advice of his council of ministers (the government of the day) in appointing the chief justice and other justices of the supreme and high courts (Basu 1999: 382). Until 1993, there was "a consensus of opinion that 'consultation' does not mean concurrence" (Basu 1999: 381); the president and his council of ministers could have serious conversations with the chief justice or other justices but in the end the council of ministers' advice was to prevail.

All this changed in 1993. The governing case, *S.P. Gupta v. Union of India* (1982)[32] was modified by a decision of October 6, 1993, giving legally binding power to the chief justice's advice to the president. The judgment, *Union Government v. Advocates on Record* (1993), gave primacy to the chief justice's views as against those of the political executives, center and state, in the appointment and transfer of high court and apex court judges.[33] In practice the chief justice acted within a small collegium consisting of the second most senior member of the apex court and, in the case of state high court appointments, the supreme court justice from the relevant state. There were differences between the justices about whether the chief justice could override his brother justices.[34]

The new assertiveness of the court drew a predictable response from the now disenfranchised executive. The 1996 United Front government headed by Prime Minister Deve Gowda charged the law ministry with

and transfer power put the question of the appointment and transfer of judges at the center of the struggle over the constitutional balance of power. For a more detailed discussion of the appointment and transfer struggles, see Rudolph and Rudolph (1987: 112–116).

[32] *Gupta v. Union of India*, A.1982 SC 149, laid down that the president, acting with the council of ministers' advice, has primacy among those consulted. In *Subhash v. Union of India*, 1991, 1 SCJ 521, a three-judge bench asked for a nine-judge bench to modify *Gupta* and declare that the chief justice should have primacy in the appointment of high court judges. See Basu (1999: 551).

[33] See *Data India, A Weekly Digest of India News* (1993: 776). The Bar Council of India, an interest group of lawyers, called for a uniform transfer policy, and specifically recommended the first assignment for judges not be in their home state to check the possibility of their favoring legal practice by their kith and kin. *Ibid*, 1993: 858.

A three-judge bench of the supreme court (the twenty-five justices can meet in partial benches) offered the following reassuring statement to the lawyers and the public: "The Chief Justice of India, as the pater familias of the judiciary, can be safely relied upon in his wisdom to ensure that transfer of a judge is so effected as to cause him minimum inconvenience" *Ibid.*: 116).

[34] *India Today*, October 6, 1997. Chief Justice M.M. Punchhi was said to have favored the override position.

drawing up legislation to reverse the court's expansion of its powers.[35] Its task was made easier when it was alleged that the highly reputed then Chief Justice J.S. Verma might have committed (a minor) malfeasance. Minor malfeasance was also found in the record of M.M. Punchhi, the justice slated to succeed Verma as chief justice.[36]

The fall of the United Front government temporarily ended efforts to transfer the balance of decision back to the political executive. But the unease of the legal profession and the judges with vesting all power in the chief justice led to yet another step. In November 1998 a nine-judge bench mandated a collegium of five, the chief justice and his four most senior colleagues, to make appointments, and implied but did not explicitly provide that the chief justice could not override its recommendations.[37] In January 2000 NDA Prime Minister Atal Behari Vajpayee advanced the idea of a National Judicial Commission to monitor the ethical conduct of the judiciary and to take responsibility for the appointment, removal, and transfer of judges.[38] Somehow such a commission, its proponents argued, would be exempt from the ordinary temptations of power that afflict the judicial and presidential nominating process. "It should not be left in the hands of either government or chief justice assisted by four judges," ventured ex-chief justice P.N. Bhagwati, "because they are all human beings."[39]

The high judiciary promptly took steps to ward off the challenge such a commission would pose. The annual conference of chief justices (state and center) passed a fifteen-point code of conduct and promised to devise "in-house procedures" to implement self-regulation.[40] The promise was, however, met with skepticism. Ex-chief justice J.S. Verma, for example, argued that "neither the impeachment procedure nor internal judicial machinery is workable."[41] The constitutional design in this as in other respects remains a project in the making.

---

[35] *India Post*, Chicago, December 27, 1996.

[36] A group of antiestablishment lawyers, several active in public interest litigation, feared that the prospective future chief justice, M.M. Punchhi, had doubts about *Union Government* v. *Advocates-on-Record* (1993), giving the chief justice the last word on appointments and transfers. Justice Punchhi had joined Justice A.M. Ahmadi in a dissent from the judgment in *Union Government*.

The antiestablishment lawyers also feared that as chief justice Punchhi would put self-imposed restrictions on the flood of PIL cases. *India Today*, October 6, 1997. The lawyers tried but failed to prevent Punchhi's appointment. In the event, Justice Punchhi succeeded Justice Verma as chief justice.

[37] "We have little doubt," the decision said, "that if even two of the judges forming the collegium express strong views, for good reasons, that are adverse to the appointment of a particular person, the chief justice of India would not press for such appointment." *India Today*, November 9, 1998.

[38] *Times of India*, January 21, 2000.    [39] *Hindu*, February 20, 2000.

[40] *Times of India*, December 7, 1999.    [41] *Statesman*, November 4, 1999.

## The president steps forward

The presidency like the judiciary became more visible and influential in the era of hung parliaments and coalition governments that began in 1989. Nehru's claim in the Constituent Assembly on behalf of parliamentary sovereignty that "No Supreme Court and no judiciary can stand in judgment over the sovereign will of Parliament representing the will of the entire community" began to ring hollow when governments, lacking the two-thirds majority in both houses required to pass a constitutional amendment, could no longer try to override supreme court judgements.

Although article 53 vests the "executive power of the Union . . . in the President," as constitutional head of state he is expected to act as an agent of the political executive (the council of ministers or cabinet), not as a principal. But the office has a residual identity separate from cabinet, parliament, and the civilian and military services – an identity beyond government and opposition, beyond partisanship, as representative of the interests of the nation. The rise of coalition governments and the spread of corruption – in the political executive, legislatures, and civil services – has provided a space for presidents as well as for the courts and for the Election Commission to act as guardians of fairness and constitutional balance.

The Constituent Assembly assumed that Indian presidents would conduct themselves like modern British monarchs; as head of state he or she would act on the advice of the council of ministers, that is, the prime minister and cabinet observing the conventions of collective responsibility. Rajendra Prasad, president of the Constituent Assembly and, after 1950, India's first president, articulated the standard this way: "It is hoped that the convention under which in England the King always acted on the advice of his ministers would be established in this country also and the President would become a constitutional President in all matters" (Basu 1994: 184).

This understanding was not, however, made part of the constitution, but left to convention. In 1951, after he had become president of India, Rajendra Prasad saw the matter rather differently. Advised by his council of ministers to assent to a Hindu Code Bill to which he was adamantly opposed, he wrote to Prime Minister Jawaharlal Nehru that he wished to act solely on his own judgment when giving assent to bills, sending messages to parliament, and returning bills to parliament for reconsideration.[42] Prasad put his position even more succinctly in a

---

[42] The act would have erased Hindu personal law. Prasad's tactics led to the bill being twice withdrawn, toned down, rewritten and divided into three separate bills. For details see Austin (1996: 140) and Levy (1973).

speech to the Indian Law Institute in 1960: "There is no provision in the Constitution which in so many words lays down that the President shall be bound to act in accordance with the advice of his Council of Ministers" (Basu 1994: 184).

The president's dual identity, as voice of the government of the day and as guardian of constitutional propriety, formulated by President Rajendra Prasad in the early days of the republic, dramatically reappeared in President K.R. Narayanan's golden jubilee address of January 27, 2000 and his speech opening parliament on February 23. Both speeches dealt with the NDA government's efforts to revise the constitution in the light of fifty years' experience. In the first, speaking on his own as president, he argued that parliamentary government and accountability were more in keeping with the basic structure of the constitution than the "presidential" system and stability favored by the government. By the time he spoke on February 23, what the government had him say reflected the intense national debate launched by his golden jubilee address on January 27. Government was no longer asking that revisions include radical departures from the parliamentary form, a directly elected political executive, or a fixed-term parliament.[43]

Under the Emergency regime which she imposed on June 25, 1975, Indira Gandhi tried, in the forty-second amendment (1976), to put parliamentary sovereignty in an unassailable position by removing any ambiguity with respect to presidential discretion (Rudolph and Rudolph 1987: 107–119). One clause of the amendment provided that "There shall be a Council of Ministers with the Prime Minister at the head to aid and advise the President who shall, in the exercise of his functions, act in accordance with such advice" (Basu 1994: 185).

Even if such a clause had existed in June 1975 when Indira Gandhi as prime minister had the then president, Faqr ud din Ali Ahmed, declare a national emergency (article 352),[44] it would be hard to call her actions constitutional. Her midnight letter "advising" President Ahmed to sign the emergency proclamation had not been discussed by the council of ministers, nor did its members sign the request. When President Ahmed

---

[43] In his golden jubilee address on January 27, 2000 President Narayanan had quoted Dr. B.R. Ambedkar, law minister in the Nehru government that dominated the Constituent Assembly-cum-parliament of 1947–50: "Dr. Ambedkar explained that the Drafting Committee [of the Constitution], in choosing the parliamentary system for India, preferred more responsibility to more stability, a system under which the Government will be on the anvil every day." *Mainstream*, February 12, 2000: 10. See also *Hindustan Times, Hindu,* and *Statesman,* February 24, 2000.

[44] For an account of the three national emergencies declared under article 352, including the third by Prime Minister Indira Gandhi on June 25, 1975, and the forty-second amendment inter alia substituting the phrase "armed rebellion" for the phrase "internal disturbance" used by Mrs. Gandhi, see Basu (1994: ch. 28).

objected that the council of ministers had not agreed collectively or signed her letter to him she told the president that she would have her cabinet colleagues sign "first thing tomorrow morning." The president succumbed;[45] his late-night signature enabled the prime minister to utilize surprise in the midnight arrest of opposition leaders and the closure and/or censorship of newspapers.

After Mrs. Gandhi was turned out of office in 1977, Morarji Desai's Janata government passed another omnibus Amendment Act, the forty-fourth, in 1978. It gave the president some discretion in responding to the advice of his council of ministers. It took the form of a suspensory veto, i.e., the president was allowed to return bills for reconsideration. If he is again advised to sign by the council of ministers, he must do so (Basu 1994: 185).

The request for reconsideration is a more powerful device than it might appear at first sight, providing the president with a lever to call into question and direct public attention to a problematic piece of legislation or act of the executive. President R. Venkataraman used this provision of the forty-fourth amendment in 1987 to express his displeasure with a postal bill that would have authorized the government to open the mail of suspect persons. The bill was withdrawn (Venkataraman 1975: 36). President Shanker Dayal Sharma did not assent to two ordinances sent to him on the eve of the 1996 parliamentary elections by the Narasimha Rao government. Both could be read as efforts to influence the outcome of the impending election. One extended reservations of seats in legislatures, places in educational institutions, and jobs in government to Dalit (scheduled caste) Christians, the other moved up the date of the eleventh parliamentary elections.[46] President Narayanan returned for reconsideration a resolution of the cabinet invoking presidential rule (article 356) against a majority government in Uttar Pradesh.

The transformation of the party system and the rise of coalition government have profoundly affected the president's role in the constitutional design. In the era of Congress Party majorities, presidents had few responsibilities in the making of governments. The constitutional

---

[45] She wrote to the president: "I would have liked to have taken this to Cabinet but unfortunately this is not possible tonight. I am, therefore, condoning or permitting a departure from the Government of India (Transaction of Business Rules, 1961), as amended up-to-date by virtue of my powers under Rule 12 thereof. I shall mention the matter to the Cabinet first thing tomorrow morning." Government of India (1978b: 25).

Such exercise of the prime minister's power was banned after Indira Gandhi's Emergency ended, by Article 352(3) which requires the union ministers of cabinet rank, headed by the prime minister, to recommend the proclamation of an emergency before the fact and in writing.

[46] *Outlook*, April 3, 1996.

design was clear: ask the leader of the majority party to form a government. But when the era of minority and coalition governments began in 1989 with the defeat of the Rajiv Gandhi-led Congress Party by the V.P. Singh-led Janata Dal/National Front, the constitutional design needed to be reworked in practice and precedent. The regulatory role of the presidency expanded as uncertainty and discretion began to characterize the process of selecting a government.

President Ramaswami Venkataraman in 1989 and 1991, President Shankar Dayal Sharma in 1996, and President Kocheril Raman Narayanan in 1998 and (possibly) 1999 were all faced with hung parliaments. No party commanded a majority; several claimed they could form viable coalition governments. Under such circumstances, should a president use his discretion in deciding which of several party leaders to invite to form a government? The leader he invites gains a tremendous advantage over his rivals because he can use offers of ministerial posts and material incentives to win over lesser parties and pliable or wavering members.[47] The track record of state governors suggests that the use of discretion can be more influenced by partisan and personal preferences than by concern for making a viable, stable government. The constitution offers no specific direction for what the president (or governors) should do when a single party or pre-poll alliance fails to gain a majority of seats. Until President R. Venkataraman's tenure as president, precedent too provided little guidance.[48]

When President R. Venkataraman inaugurated the era of coalition governments, he shaped the constitutional design for making governments by creating constructive precedents and making the process transparent. Like Presidents Sharma and Narayana after him, he had a long association with the Congress Party and its governments. Before being sworn in as president on July 25, 1987, midway through Rajiv Gandhi's prime ministership, Venkataraman served as vice president to President Zail Singh. During his two terms as president he dealt with

---

[47] We read the failure of BJP leader Atal Behari Vajpayee to gain the confidence of the Lok Sabha in June 1996 and of NDA leader Nitish Kumar to gain the confidence of the Bihar Vidhan Sabha in March 2000 as exceptions to this generalization due to special circumstances. In June 1996, the BJP was still regarded as a pariah by the non-Congress opposition parties. The Bihar NDA was badly divided by rivalries between coalition parties and their leaders. Governor G.C. Pande's hurried decision to call Nitish Kumar was widely regarded as a poor precedent. The Congress and other opposition parties denounced his decision as unconstitutional and called for his removal. (See "Pande's Haste Baffles Opposition," *Hindu*, March 4, 2000; "Bihar Governor Acted in Haste: Karunanidhi," *Hindustan Times*, March 14, 2000.)

[48] See Jha (1996) for a useful overview of presidential conduct in the making of governments.

the formation of the V.P. Singh, S. Chandrasekhar, and V.P. Narasimha Rao governments.

Venkataraman regarded himself as a "'copybook' President [who] would act strictly according to the rules" (Venkataraman 1975: 405). His most basic rule was first to ask the largest party to form the government and, within two or three weeks, to test its majority on the floor of parliament.[49] If the party with the most seats declined or failed to gain the confidence of the House, he would ask the next largest party to try.

On December 1, 1989, after the ninth parliamentary election had produced India's first hung parliament, President Venkataraman began to turn this rule into a convention. He told a National Front delegation headed by V.P. Singh that "as the largest single party [Congress-I] had not staked a claim to form the government, I invite you [V.P. Singh] as the leader of the second largest party to form the government and take a vote of confidence of the House within 30 days."[50] When the V.P. Singh government fell in November 1990, President Venkataraman asked the Congress-I party leader of the opposition, Rajiv Gandhi, "whether he was able and willing to form a viable government. The Congress [I] did not stake a claim for forming the government but offered unconditional support to Shri Chandra Shekhar."[51] In June 1991, when the Congress-I

[49] This rule eliminated as far as possible the hazardous path of a personal headcount, which, at the state level, had often produced bizarre scenes of coercion and instant horsetrading in the governor's office. All three presidents followed the rule of asking the leader of the largest party (or, if he failed, the next largest party) to establish that they commanded the confidence of the House, not in the president's residence, the Rashtrapati Bhavan, but "publicly" on the floor of the parliament. These days publicly can mean before a national TV audience tuned in to broadcasts of confidence debates and voting.

[50] Venkataraman (1975: 275) and *Outlook*, May 15, 1996: 7.
    Madhu Dandavate, who was chairman of the meeting that elected V.P. Singh leader, handed over a letter to President Venkataraman saying that "the BJP with 85 members and the Left Front with 52 members had pledged their support to the National Front government" (Venkataraman 1975: 275).

[51] "Thereafter, the President sounded the Bharatiya Janata Party and the Left Front whether they would be able and willing to form a viable government. On both parties expressing their inability to undertake the responsibility, the President enquired from Shri Chandra Shekhar if he was in a position to form a viable government. Shri Chandra Shekhar responded to the offer and produced evidence of support to his group from the Congress [I], AIADMK, Bahujan Samaj Party, Muslim League [and other lesser parties and independent members]." The president declared himself satisfied *prima facie* that Chandra Shekhar had the strength to form a viable government.
    Also influencing his judgment about the formation of a minority Chandra Shekhar government was President Venkataraman's "considered opinion" that it was "not in the national interest to plunge the country into general election at this time," a time when the Mandal reservations for other backward castes and building a Ram temple at Ayodhya were convulsing the country. Venkataraman, (1975: 373).
    See Jha (1996: 5) for another gloss on the formation of the Chandra Shekhar

emerged as the single largest but not the majority party in the tenth parliamentary election and V.P. Narasimha Rao had been elected its parliamentary leader, President Venkataraman sent him a letter which read: "As the leader of the Congress [I], the largest party in the Lok Sabha, I appoint you as the Prime Minister of India and invite you to form the council of ministers. I advise you to establish your majority in the Lok Sabha within four weeks."[52]

After the eleventh parliamentary election in May 1996, President Sharma followed Venkataraman's precedents. Sharma, who served from 1992 to 1998, came to the president's office with a reputation for impartiality. In 1984, as governor of Andhra Pradesh, he had reversed Indira Gandhi's controversial use of article 356 (of which more below) to oust the chief minister of Andhra, N.T. Rama Rao, when it became clear that NTR still commanded a majority in the assembly. "His innings as governor alone was enough to endear him to the non-Congress parties and convince them of his sense of fair play." Later after serving as governor of Punjab and Maharashtra, Sharma showed courage and independence as Rajya Sabha chairman.[53] To the discomfort of the Narasimha Rao government, Sharma used the authority of the presidency to tell state governors at a seminar he organized that they should observe constitutional standards before calling for president's rule under article 356. Sharma, himself a legal scholar and teacher, no doubt welcomed President Venkataraman's precedents but also charted his own constitutional path.

His big moment came in May 1996 after the eleventh parliamentary election. Confronted with a hung parliament in which the Hindu nationalist BJP had won the most seats, with the United Front second and the Congress third, he first asked the BJP parliamentary party leader, Atal Behari Vajpayee, to form a government and gave him two

government. "Aware of the 'ugly incident in our parliamentary history' when Indira Gandhi first extended support to Charan Singh in 1979 and then withdrew it within a week, Venkataraman probed the nature of the support and the minimum period it would last." Only when Rajiv Gandhi assured him that his support to Chandra Shekhar was "neither temporary nor conditional," did he agree to allow him to form a government. "I asked Rajiv Gandhi if this support would continue at least one year. He replied, 'Why one year? It may extend to the life of Parliament'" (ibid.: 7).

[52] Ibid.: 464. Rao's government won its vote of confidence with the help of AIADMK, the Jayalalitha-led Tamil Nadu party with which the Congress was allied in the 1996 election.

Rao's Congress government almost lost a vote of confidence in 1993. It was saved by the votes of a small party seeking statehood, the Jharkand Mukti Morcha (JMM), to which Rao seems to have committed himself in exchange for their votes in the confidence motion. He is also accused of making a large sum of money available to the JMM MPs. As of this writing this matter was *sub judice*.

[53] For further details of Sharma's career see Jha (1996: 5-10).

weeks to gain the confidence of the House. When, after thirteen days, Vajpayee failed to convince any other party to cross the aisle to his side, the President turned to the second-largest grouping, the United Front, a fourteen-party coalition. With Congress's outside support it won a vote of confidence. The UF government lasted for nineteen months, until December 1997.

In March 1998, after the twelfth parliamentary election, President Narayanan followed the Venkataraman and Sharma precedents when he asked the BJP, again the largest party in a hung parliament, to form a government and gain the confidence of the house. Having worked hard since its failure in June 1996 to persuade voters and potential coalition partners that it was capable of being centrist and moderate, the BJP succeeded this time where it had failed in 1996.

However, in the era of coalition governments, the Venkataraman rule, that the president should first ask the largest party to try to form a government, is not the sure guide it appears to be. The 1999 parliamentary election could have resulted in an outcome that would have cast the rule into doubt by raising the question whether the proper candidate for government was the "largest party" or the largest pre-poll alliance. The National Democratic Alliance led by the BJP consisted of twenty-two parties. Each party had agreed to give up its manifesto, to adopt a common program and to campaign in support of it. Each party also agreed to recognize Atal Behari Vajpayee as the leader of the NDA and as the NDA's candidate for prime minister. Prior to the result being known, the country debated whether the president, in calling on the single largest party to try to form a government, should turn to the BJP or the Congress, the two principal conventional parties, or the NDA, an alliance made party-like by its pre-poll agreement on a common minimum program and leader. Prior to the election results being known, Congress spokespersons tried to preempt possible claims by the NDA to "single largest party" status by arguing that if, hypothetically, Congress won 180 seats, BJP 175 seats, and the NDA a narrow majority with 275 seats, the president was bound by precedent to call Congress first as the "single largest party" to try to form a government.[54] The election results rendered moot, for the moment, the question whether the president should count a pre-poll coalition such as the NDA as "the single largest party." Congress did badly, winning only 112 seats, 32 less than in the previous parliament. The BJP won about the same number of seats as it held in the previous parliament, 182. The NDA, however,

---

[54] Jairam Ramesh speaking for the Congress Party, Door Darshan, election program, October 7, 1999.

with 296 seats, won a comfortable majority of twenty-five, largely because the BJP's regional party allies did better than anticipated.

The formulation by presidents of nondiscretionary conventions, such as first calling the single largest party, tends to affect the conduct of governors who, at the state level, play an analogous role to the president at the union government level. Like presidents, governors have dual identities, one as a spokesperson and symbol for governments of the day, the second as a nonpartisan public person speaking and acting on behalf of the common good. The second identity is meant to come to the fore when, like the president at the national level, governors choose a party leader to try to form a government and (unlike the president) recommend to the president the removal of a government and the imposing of "president's rule" under article 356 of the constitution.[55]

In the run-up to the twelfth national election in 1998 President Narayanan tried to get state governors to follow presidential precedents in forming governments and to use impartial and transparent procedures. At stake was a five-month effort by the National Front government at the center to topple the government of India's largest state, Uttar Pradesh. Not only did the president reverse an "unconstitutional" use of article 356 in October/November 1997 but also, at the end of February, 1998, on the eve of the twelfth parliamentary election campaign, he, along with the Allahabad high court and the supreme court, prevented UP governor Romesh Bhandari from arbitrarily dismissing Kalyan Singh's BJP government and replacing it with Jagdambika Pal's Congress/Samajwadi government. President Narayanan reprimanded Governor Bhandari for dismissing the Kalyan Singh government "in a partisan manner" designed to help the ruling United Front and Congress in the upcoming election. Bhandari had not allowed a trial of strength in the assembly and had hastily sworn in Jagdambika Pal as chief minister.[56] A "landmark" supreme court verdict reinstated Kalyan Singh and gave him an opportunity to prove his majority. The procedure the court mandated for the notoriously unruly and often violent UP assembly was "unprecedented in constitutional history": a vote of

[55] Article 356 lists provisions in case of failure of the constitutional machinery. The principal provision says that "if the President, on receipt of report from the Governor of a State . . . is satisfied that a situation has arisen in which the government of the State cannot be carried on in accordance with the provisions of this Constitution [e.g., the government has lost its majority and no alternative government can be formed, the government cannot maintain law and order], the President may by Proclamation assume to himself all or any of the functions of the Government of the State." See also below for a discussion of the article.

[56] " 'Why must I resign?' UP Governor Romesh Bhandari justifies his actions," *Sunday*, 8–14 March 1998: 30.

confidence had to be held on the floor of the assembly by signed ballots and was exposed to public gaze by TV coverage.[57]

The steps the court prescribed underline that fairness, transparency, and civility are matters of low as well as of high politics. Knowing the UP legislators too well, the Speaker had got the ballot box chained. The hall was made free of microphones to avoid their misuse as missiles, as witnessed in 1997 and 1995. Entry was restricted to members, personnel on duty, and the media. Mobile phones, pagers, briefcases, and even file covers (which, experience shows, could be used as missiles) were not allowed. Perhaps what prevented the rival groups from getting in on the act was the sword of Damocles hanging over them in the form of the supreme court interim order directing that a floor test between Kalyan Singh and Jagdambika Pal be held and a warning that "Violence in any form would be taken serious note of," and the full gaze of the video cameras.[58]

President Narayanan stayed aloof from the controversy surrounding Bihar governor V.C. Pande's controversial decision in early March 2000 following a state assembly election to ask NDA leader Nitish Kumar rather than Rashtriya Janta Dal (RJD) leader Rabri Devi to form the government. A retired Indian Administrative Service officer appointed by the NDA government at the center, Pande hastily turned to NDA leader Kumar even though Kumar's shaky pre-poll coalition had fewer seats than Devi's RJD and even though Congress leaders in Delhi told him that Congress's Bihar MLAs would support an RJD-led

[57] See *The Hindu*, February 27, 1998, and *India Abroad*, February 27, 1998. On February 25, 1998, the wire services were writing "Mr. Bhandari's [the UP governor's] position became untenable when he chose to ignore the advice of the President [Narayanan] and went ahead with the dismissal of the Kalyan Singh Government instead of giving it an opportunity to test its strength in the State Assembly."

I.K. Gujral, whose UF government was about to lose badly in the twelfth national election, ducked a decision that would have displeased his defense minister, former UP chief minister, Mulayam Singh Yadav, and Congress president, Sitaram Kesri, upon whose support Gujral's government depended. Gujral's dubiously constitutional view was that "the Center didn't come into the picture because . . . right or wrong, the Governor acted at his level, in the exercise of his discretion." Gujral's justification flew in the face of the president's "advice" to Bhandari and the supreme court decision the president's advice reflected, *S.R. Bommai* v. *Union of India*, that made the use of article 356 subject to judicial review. India Server News Briefs for February 25, 1998, brief@Indiaserver.com and Muralidharan (1998c: 4–7).

Atal Behari Vajpayee's BJP coalition government won its vote of confidence on March 29. Bhandari's friends at court had been removed by the results of the twelfth national election which were known by mid-March. In the certainty that Vajpayee would do what Gujral feared to do, Bhandari submitted his resignation on March 16, 1998, thereby justifying President Narayanan's view of the impropriety, not to say unconstitutionality, of his conduct. Pradhan (1998b: 15).

[58] Pradhan (1998a: 28–31) and India Server News Brief, February 27, 1998, brief@Indiaserver.com.

government.[59] After two days, well before his allotted time, Nitish Kumar gave up and resigned. The fact that a Rabri Devi RJD coalition government quickly won a vote of confidence intensified the clamor against the governor's precipitous and apparently partisan action.

Under article 356, governors can recommend the suspension of state governments and the imposition of "president's rule," a critical feature of the constitutional design that the Constitutional Review Commission appointed in February 2000, is certain to examine. Article 356, which allows the president to assume the government of a state in case "the government of a State can not be carried on in accordance with the provisions of [the] Constitution," is liable to partisan use by the party or parties in charge of the central government. Pliant state governors, themselves appointed, transferred, and dismissed by union governments of the day, can report to the council of ministers the failure of the constitutional machinery in particular states. The council of ministers then advises the president to suspend or dismiss the government and to carry on its administration in his name for six months to two years.[60] By comparison with the 1960s and 1970s, the article has been somewhat more protected, since the onset of coalition governments in 1989, from abuse by union governments and state governors.

Article 356 was intended as a measure of last resort in times of severe governmental crisis.[61] Starting in 1957 when Indira Gandhi as Congress

[59] The RJD with 123 seats claimed to be the single largest party. With the votes of its pre-poll ally, the CPI-M it also claimed to be the largest alliance. Before Governor Pande invited Nitish Kumar the NDA leader to form a government, Pande had been informed by phone from New Delhi that the Congress Party would support an RJD government and that a letter to that effect was on its way. With Congress seats, an RJD-led government could credibly claim 161 of the 163 seats needed for a majority, while the most the Kumar-led NDA could muster was 151 members.

The press widely supported the view that the governor's hasty action carried overtones of partisanship. See, for example, the *Hindustan Times* and *The Hindu* for March 4, 2000.

[60] Article 352 allows a presidential proclamation of emergency if there is an imminent danger of war, external aggression, or armed rebellion. It was the vehicle of Indira Gandhi's national Emergency in 1975. The term "armed rebellion" was substituted by the forty-fourth amendment for the weaker "internal disturbance" to raise the criteria by which an emergency might be declared. Indira Gandhi had used the weaker phrase to justify her action. An emergency declaration under article 352 does not result in the suspension of the state government but does allow the national parliament to exercise concurrent powers with state assemblies.

The much more commonly used article 356 allows a proclamation that the state legislature and executive authority of a state are suspended because of failure of the constitutional machinery. In this case the president may delegate the functions of government to his appointees, generally serving civil servants but sometimes retired ones – thus "president's rule."

[61] Dr. B.R. Ambedkar, a principal architect of the constitution, told the Constituent Assembly that "the proper thing we ought to expect is that such articles [as 356] will

Party president arranged for the dismissal of a CPI-M (Communist) government in Kerala, Congress governments began using article 356 routinely to remove troublesome opposition state governments. Article 356 was used 100 times between 1950 and 1994, mostly by Congress governments.[62] Perhaps the most constitutionally problematic use of article 356 was in 1977 by the Janata Party government that took power after Indira Gandhi's Emergency regime. Claiming that the Congress "opposition" governments of nine northern states that had been independently elected in separate state elections had lost their mandate as a result of the Janata party's parliamentary election victory, the Janata government used article 356 to impose president's rule on all nine. When a Congress government was returned to power in 1980, its prime minister, Indira Gandhi, used the Janata government precedent to justify the dismissal of nine independently elected Janata state governments.

Reports on reforming the federal system were commissioned in the 1980s by Karnataka, Tamil Nadu and West Bengal, all states ruled by opposition parties and eager to loosen the hold of the center. As a cooptive measure, Indira Gandhi appointed a central body, the Sarkaria Commission. Sarkaria not surprisingly found that article 356 had been misused and recommended its replacement. One of the reasons that the BJP when it was an opposition party dropped its commitment to a centralized, unitary state and opted for a decentralized, federal state was its response to Congress's abuse of article 356.[63]

As long as union governments commanded secure majorities (1952–89), it was difficult for presidents to resist partisan use of article 356. The rise of coalition governments has changed the rules of engagement. During the era of hung parliaments, from the ninth national election in 1989 through the twelfth in 1998, when no single party commanded a parliamentary majority, central governments have been a little more sparing in their use of article 356. These days a party at the center that manages to use article 356 for partisan advantage against a rival party in a federal state risks finding itself on the receiving end. Even so, the temptation of a short-term gain often weighs strongly.

It was already noted above that in October 1997 Prime Minister

never be called into operation, that they remain a dead letter." CAD, vol. IX: 177, cited in Basu (1994: 311).

[62] Congress governments held power between 1952 and 1977, from 1980 to 1989 and from 1991 to 1994. For further details see Basu (1994: 335, table XXI, and 459–461), which details the use of article 356 by state and date. See also Dua (1979, 1985) and Rudolph and Rudolph (1987: 101–102).

[63] See, for example, Government of Karnataka (1983), Government of Tamil Nadu (1971), Government of West Bengal (1978). For a summary of some of the regional demands for decentralization in the early 1980s, see Saez (1999: ch. II). See also Government of India (1988).

Gujral's National Front government concurred in UP with Governor Bhandari's attempt to supersede Kalyan Singh's BJP government. President Narayanan invoked his prerogative to return the Gujral government's directive for reconsideration, thereby blocking what was widely seen as a partisan act.[64] The BJP, which headed a coalition government at the center in 1998, was itself tempted to make partisan use of article 356. To do so would have contradicted its declared policy position in the manifesto it adopted for the 1998 election[65] and would have risked repudiation by the president. In the event, the BJP resisted the demand of its troublesome key coalition partner, the Tamil Nadu regional AIADMK headed by the scheming Jayaram Jayalalitha, to topple the government of Jayalalitha's arch rival, Tamil Nadu's DMK chief minister, M. Karunanadhi. It paid a heavy price when Jayalalitha withdrew AIADMK support and the BJP-led coalition fell.[66] Earlier, on February 12, 1999, the BJP-led government had initiated the use of article 356 to

---

[64] After the UP Bahujan Samaj Party chief minister Mayawati had withdrawn her party from a BSP–BJP coalition government, a BJP government led by Kalyan Singh had won a confidence vote on the assembly floor. President Narayanan had been so informed by Home Ministry observers. Mulayam Singh Yadav, defense minister in the UF government, UP Samajwadi Party leader, and former UP chief minister, led the faction in the UF cabinet supporting president's rule for UP. In effect he wanted to use his role at the center to his advantage in UP politics. Other regional party leaders in or associated with the UF government, such as West Bengal's CPI-M chief minister Jyoti Basu, Tamil Nadu's DMK chief minister M. Karunanadhi, and Andhra Pradesh's Telugu Desam chief minister Chandrababu Naidu, were opposed in principle and for practical political reasons to the use of article 356 in UP.

The Congress Party was supporting the UF government from the outside. Without its votes the UF government would fall. Sitaram Kesri, the octogenarian Congress president, pressed Prime Minister I.K. Gujral to use article 356 against Kalyan Singh's BJP government in the expectation that under president's rule, with Romesh Bhandari in charge as governor, Congress would be able to restore its fortunes in India's largest state.

For more details on the machinations surrounding this important constitutional event see *Sunday*'s (2–8 November, 1997) cover story, "Enemy or Friend? I.K. Gujral's refusal to toe Mulayam Singh Yadav's line in UP has a ripple effect on ruling relationships": 14–25.

[65] Aggarwal and Chowdhry (1998: 143): "The Party is committed to take necessary steps to prevent misuse of article 356 of the Constitution."

[66] Jayalalitha had been chief minister of Tamil Nadu between 1991 and 1996. She and her party were routed from office in the 1996 state assembly elections, in part because voters perceived her and her government as corrupt and vicious. Two years later she allied her AIADMK Party with the upper-caste BJP in the twelfth parliamentary election of 1998, an event that must have made Periyar (great leader) E.V. Ramaswamy Naicker, the religion- and upper-caste-hating leader and founder of the anti-Brahmin Dravidian movement, turn in his grave.

The BJP, with only 179 parliamentary seats, needed help from almost 100 MPs to form a government and had to keep their support to stay in power. Jayalalitha put on pressure for almost a year, threatening periodically to withdraw.

When two earlier Karunanadhi DMK governments fell victim to the Congress abuse of article 356, the BJP as an opposition party at the center and as an occasional state governing party was outspoken in its condemnation. For details of the BJP coalition's

remove an RJD Rabri Devi government in Bihar after it failed to prevent two major massacres of Dalits by an upper-caste private army. It was widely believed that the Rabri Devi government could not maintain law and order. At the same time, it continued to command a legislative majority. The center's move in this case appeared to have the approval of the president as well as the support of national public opinion. However, this effort to use article 356 aborted when Congress reneged on its commitment to support the move in parliament.[67]

Another arena for a presidential regulatory role was created in the 1990s by the rapid turnover in governments. When a government falls and an election is called, as happened in 1998 and 1999, the president has the authority to designate a caretaker government. The caretaker government will hold office until an election can produce a new parliament and a new government. What actions is it proper for such a government to take, given its limited authority and time in office? In 1999, the BJP government fell on April 26 and a new postelection government was not installed until October. During this six-month period the Vajpayee caretaker government conducted and concluded a limited war in the Kargil sector of Kashmir, carried on intensive negotiations with respect to the Comprehensive Test Ban Treaty and tried to move ahead with economic liberalization.

A caretaker government is no longer responsible to the legislature; it has lost its confidence. If it is responsible to anything or anyone, it is to the president who has authorized its existence. The president has no constitutionally explicit means for holding a caretaker government

efforts to stay in power in the face of coalition partners' threats, see Dasgupta (1998: 12–17).

[67] Not that there were no ambiguities about the disinterested nature of BJP conduct. On the one hand, the RJD government headed by Rabri Devi, wife of RJD leader Laloo Prasad Yadav, had an unenviable record for massive corruption and populist inefficiency. On the other hand, there was strong partisan pressure within the BJP by its coalition partners, the Samata Party leaders Nitish Kumar and George Fernandes, opposed to the Rabri Devi RJD government in Bihar, to oust that government at all costs. The governor, S.S. Bhandari, a longtime RSS *sanchalak*, was generally regarded as a crucial partisan connection for the center. In October 1998 the center attempted to oust the Bihar government without the backing of Dalit massacres, but was invited by the president to reconsider. In the event, the February ousting failed because the Congress Party made it clear that it would not support the ousting in the Rajya Sabha, the upper house, where the BJP-led alliance lacked a majority. It presumably denied support because it feared that if the partisan Governor Bhandari was in charge of president's rule in the state, he would favor the BJP and Samata parties and disfavor Congress and its potential ally, the RJD. *India Today*, February 22, March 1, and March 8, 1999.

In November 1999, when there was another massacre, this time by left terrorists, of Muslims belonging to a competing left faction, Congress called for dismissal of the government. By that time its alliance with the RJD had soured. *Times of India*, November 20, 1999.

responsible. Much depends on what kind of a political issue he is willing to challenge a caretaker government on. During the six months of the Vajpayee caretaker government in 1999, the opposition petitioned the president to require the government to debate the conduct of the Kargil war in the Rajya Sabha. The opposition also petitioned President Narayanan to halt the government's bailout of the telecommunications industry, a major and costly policy initiative.[68] The president placed both demands before the caretaker government. It responded by modifying rather than acceding to the Kargil demand. It would discuss the onset and conduct of the Kargil war at an all-party meeting rather than allow a full-fledged parliamentary debate on the war. It turned down the telecom demand.[69]

In the era of a multiparty system and coalition government, presidents have played a more active role. They have made use of their constitutional powers to influence the formation and dismissal of governments at the state and union level. Presidents have elaborated rules for the government-making process, and made the procedures transparent. At the union level, presidents have adhered to the rules elaborated by President Venkataraman. At the state level, the use of article 356 now seems closer to the position Dr. B.R. Ambedkar intended for it, "*a matter of last resort.*" It has been restored to a matter of last resort in part because state governments and regional parties have gained authority in the operation of the federal system; in part because state governors and the union governments and presidents that appoint them have recognized the political prudence and constitutional desirability of a governor being both independent and impartial; and, most important, because presidents have found constitutional grounds and appropriate occasions to act independently of the union executive in the public interest.

### Election Commission activism

Starting in 1991 with the tenure of T.N. Sheshan as chief election commissioner (CEC), the Election Commission (EC) joined the supreme court in improving the legal conditions that make representative government and democratic participation possible. Not that the EC had not been a bulwark for free and fair elections in India before 1991 (Rudolph and Rudolph 1987: 89–91.) But in the 1990s, with the electoral process threatened by criminalization, violence, and bribery, with gun-toting candidates portrayed in daring television exposés, the EC gained national prominence as a prime force in restoring and

[68] "Chronology of Events," *Mainstream*, 37 (30): 33–34, July 17, 1999.
[69] "Chronology," *Mainstream*, 37 (29): 33, July 10, 1999; (32): 31, July 31, 1999.

maintaining free and fair elections in India. Polls suggested that, more than any other political institution, it was trusted by the public.[70] Like the court and the presidency, the Election Commission attracted support from urban middle classes who welcomed its ability to expose and limit the lawlessness and corruption of politicians, state officials, and police. Together with the court and the presidency, the Election Commission has contributed to the making of a regulatory state in India.

The EC is a constitutional body. Article 324 vests the "superintendence, direction and control of elections . . . in an Election Commission." The EC consists of a chief election commissioner and "such number of other Election Commissioners, if any, as the President may from time to time fix . . . When any other Election Commissioner is so appointed the Chief Election Commissioner shall act as the Chairman of the Election Commission." The commission's independence is assured by clause 5 of article 324 which provides that "the Chief Election Commissioner shall not be removed from his office except in like manner and on like grounds as a Judge of the Supreme Court," i.e., by each house of parliament, by a special majority, and on the grounds of proved misbehavior or incapacity. Other election commissioners may not be removed by the president except on the recommendation of the chief election commissioner.[71] The only path available to the executive to influence the Election Commission is to pack it, a strategy made possible by a constitutional clause that allows multiple members of the commission to be appointed. The flamboyant, arrogant T.N. Seshan, CEC from 1991 to 1996, for a time became a hero of middle-class reform.[72] He fought successfully to keep the commission a one-man show until reined in by the Narasimha Rao government's appointment of two additional commissioners.[73] The 1996, 1998, and 1999 national

[70] In a nationwide poll conducted by the Center for the Study of Developing Societies for the Indian Council of Social Science Research and *India Today* just after the eleventh national election in June and July 1996, 62 percent of 15,030 respondents rated the Election Commission as trustworthy, the highest score, followed by 59 percent for the supreme court. *India Today*, August 31, 1996. For an extended discussion of this survey result see de Souza (1998: 51–2 and endnote 1).

[71] For provisions and practice beyond the language of article 324, see Basu (1994: 365–366).

[72] "More than any politician, sportsperson or film star, it is the Election Commission which has managed to stay consistently in the limelight during the last five years, thanks largely to the consummate knack of its colourful chief, T.N. Seshan, in dramatising issues and non-issues": Mahalingam (1996: 14).

[73] Differences over whether there should be additional election commissioners began just a week before the commencement of the ninth national election when the Rajiv Gandhi Congress government, on October 16, 1989, appointed two more commissioners. The move "created a suspicion that it was an attempt to compromise the independence of the Commission." The incoming National Front returned the commission to a one-person body as of January 2, 1990.

Taking advantage of a provision of article 324 that allowed the appointment of

elections provided no evidence that adding two commissioners had weakened the Election Commission's considerable capabilities.

The commission's task is enormous. It deals with an electorate of 600 million,[74] 57 percent of whom vote.[75] Contrary to Western electoral behavior, participation is higher in state and local elections than in national elections and higher among the poorly educated and lower castes and classes than the better educated and higher castes and classes. "The poor, the underclass, the uneducated, the former untouchables, tend to vote not less but *more* than the others."[76] M.S. Gill, CEC from January 1997,[77] recognizing the imperfections of the electoral

additional election commissioners to act with the chief election commissioner, the Narasimha Rao government, in September 1993, attempted to rein Seshan in by appointing two commissioners, M.S. Gill and G.V.G. Krishnamurthy. Seshan, charging that the appointments were motivated by the Congress Party's desire to prevent his reform of a corrupt electoral system, challenged the appointments before the supreme court, asking the court to block the appointments on constitutional and procedural grounds.

A constitution bench headed by then Chief Justice A.M. Ahmadi and including the next chief justice J.S. Verma and Justice N.P. Singh upheld the constitutionality of the appointments and ruled out all *mala fide* intentions of the ruling party.

The court also remarked on Seshan's "insustainable" decisions, "abrasive public utterances, appearances on commercial television and in newspaper ads." The court opined that "Serious doubts may arise regarding his decisions if it is suspected that he has political ambitions" (in 1997 Seshan stood unsuccessfully for president of India against K.R. Narayanan) and accused him of being "totally oblivious to a sense of decorum and discretion that his high office requires, even if his cause is laudable." Fernandes (1995: 28–35).

Shortly after the thirteenth parliamentary elections the BJP-led coalition was thought to favor a five-person commission in order to get its own appointees in place. Such intent was denied. *Hindu*, November 24, 1999.

[74] The 600-million-strong Indian electorate elect about 5,000 representatives to the national parliament and the state assemblies. Elections have been held at regular intervals since 1952. There have been twelve national or parliamentary elections since 1952. A national election requires 900,000 polling stations scattered from Cape Cormorin at the tip of India to the Himalayas in the north. The electoral process requires 4.5 million persons to administer. They are seconded from state and local government services and temporarily placed under the authority of the Election Commission. By the end of 1999 each of India's 600 million voters was supposed to have a photographic identity card.

[75] Unlike the US where registration is the citizen's responsibility, in India it is that of the state. The 57 percent average turnout across twelve national elections is that much more impressive because it is a proportion of the total eligible electorate. See Gill (1998: 24–27).

[76] Ibid.: 25. There are those that argue that one of the determinants of higher levels of voting among lower castes including in particular Dalits, lower classes, and marginal persons more generally is the improvement of protection and the security environment surrounding voting. Intimidation was, and to an extent still is, practiced by upper over lower castes but it seems to have declined substantially as a result of Election Commission measures, including those taken by T.N. Seshan to bring central security to bear on the voting process.

[77] T.N. Seshan's term as CEC ended in December 1996. He was succeeded as CEC by Commissioner Manohar Singh Gill. J.M. Lyngoh was appointed as election commissioner at this time. G.V.G. Krishnamurthy stayed on as the third commissioner.

process, nevertheless claimed, not implausibly, "that these inadequacies do not affect the overall outcome of elections, either at the state or the national levels . . . Those who govern do so because the voters chose them."[78] The proof lies, he argued, in the defeat of incumbent parties, chief ministers and prime ministers. In 1996, for example, Narasimha Rao's Congress government was badly defeated. It was Congress's third loss at the national level in the last six elections. Between 1993 and 1997 in elections for all of India's twenty-five state assemblies the incumbent party lost in nineteen.[79]

The EC's most visible success has been getting India's parties and candidates in the eleventh (1996), twelfth (1998) and thirteenth (1999) national elections to comply with its code of conduct.[80] The code is divided into seven sections, general conduct; meetings; processions; polling day; polling booths; observers; and party in power. Rules of conduct are specified under each heading. One rule that dramatically changed the feel and spirit of Indian elections and benefited the urban landscape was the ban on pasting posters and notices on walls and buildings and the ban on vehicles with loudspeakers. Under "party in power" the code bars ministers and other authorities from making promises of financial grants for the construction of roads, the provision of drinking water facilities, or the laying of foundation stones for projects of any kind from the time elections are announced. Ministers may not combine official visits with electioneering and/or use official machinery (e.g. helicopters) or personnel during the official campaign period. Parties are prohibited from campaigning from places of worship or making appeals based on caste or communal (religious) feeling.[81] Not

---

[78] Gill (1998: 25).        [79] Ibid.: 26.

[80] The code, under a court ruling, becomes operative with EC notification of the dates for the campaign and the polling dates, usually three spread over about 10 days. (This enables the EC to use a finite number of personnel and facilities in several polling places.) The code is not statutory although its provisions are recognized and enforced by the courts. It originated in 1983 as a voluntary agreement, an "all-party consensus," among all recognized political parties and was renewed by the political parties before the 1996 (eleventh) election in November–December 1995 (Venkatesan 1996: 29–31).

[81] Here are a few of many examples of the application of these rules. After the 1996 election was announced Prime Minister Narasimha Rao was forced to abandon a March 20 foundation-stone-laying ceremony for a Rs. 7,000 crores oil refinery at Azadpur in Rae Bareli, Uttar Pradesh. State governments had to postpone until after the election the tendering process for liquor and tendu leaf concessions.

Section 123 of the Representation of the People Act, 1951 makes promoting "feelings of enmity or hatred between different classes of [citizens] . . . on grounds of race, caste, community [read religion] or language" a corrupt electoral practice warranting disqualification of a victorious candidate from elected office. Section 125 enables the prosecution of "any individual" who uses appeals to the criteria mentioned in section 123. The Indian Penal Code (section 153A) provides for the proscription of political organizations that advocate the views proscribed in section 123.

After the 1989 national election the Bombay high court disqualified Manohar Joshi (later Maharashtra chief minister) and other BJP and Shiv Sena candidates under

all the rules are complied with all the time, but they are taken seriously, in part because it suits incumbent candidates and their opponents to use them to monitor each other.

In 1999 there were some complaints that the EC's enthusiasm for fairness had overreached itself. The Madras high court and the Andhra high court called "arbitrary," "discriminatory," and "unreasonable" the EC's ban, new in 1999, on the dissemination in the media of opinion polls, exit polls, or electoral ads. The commission claimed it was protecting voters from inappropriate influences on their voting decisions. When the commission appealed to the supreme court for support, the court refused and lifted the EC's ban on media use of voting survey results prior to the closure of the polls.[82]

Enforcement of rules, e.g. for polling day and polling places – against "booth capturing," "ballot snatching," intimidation, and violence – was partly in the hands of local officials deputed to serve the EC, partly in the hands of central security forces (a legacy of the Seshan years), and partly in the hands of 1,500 EC observer teams equipped with video cameras. Their footage not only provided evidence of wrongdoing to the EC but could also expose criminal conduct to national audiences.

During the six months of 1999 in which India was ruled by a caretaker government, the president and the Election Commission worked in parallel to keep the rules fair for the opposition. The opposition parties wanted strict prohibition of government acts of patronage that could function as preelection incentives to voters. Both president and election commission supported the opposition's resistance to a major bail-out of telecom operators disadvantaged by an earlier bidding process.[83] The commission barred the government's monopoly broadcast facility from allocating 150 new FM stations to private parties in forty cities and prevented government from issuing an ordinance that would have given the government-controlled television system the exclusive rights for five

sections 123 and 125 which gave legal backing to EC code of conduct rules for campaigning on a "Hindutva" platform. In 1995 the supreme court overturned the Bombay high court's judgment, holding that it was not proved that the candidates had appealed to religion by speaking of Hindutva and that, in any case, candidates did not necessarily consent to the conduct of their election agents who appealed to religion. Sukumar Muralidharan writes that "the decision appalled all those who had watched the growing salience of religion, caste and communal appeals in electioneering with a sense of alarm" (Muralidharan 1998b). In 1999, however, the president accepted a recommendation of the Election Commission to strip Shiv Sena leader Bal Thakeray of his voting rights for violating the Representation of the People Act during the 1987 by-election by invoking religion to promote a candidate. "Chronology," *Mainstream*, 37 (33), August 7, 1999.

[82] "Chronology," *Mainstream*, 37 (39), September 18, 1999.
[83] "Chronology," *Mainstream*, 37 (29), July 10, 1999. The government resisted on the ground that the decision about telecom preceded issuance of the code of conduct.

years to direct home television.[84] On the other hand, the commission did not forbid a 10 percent hike in support prices for ten agricultural commodities – higher than the Agricultural Prices Commission had recommended – or a 5 percent hike in the inflation allowance for central government employees.[85]

The EC continues to have an uphill battle. In the face of what CEC Gill called a "democratic upsurge," a rising tide of democratization that brings with it "social unrest and political instability," the commission, he believed, must "assert its constitutionally guaranteed independence more fiercely than ever" if India is going to continue to hold free and fair elections. In 1999 the upsurge was as usual particularly visible in relatively lawless Bihar, where the commission found itself the target of accusations that it had not adequately controlled partisanship among its army of local officials and observers. The commissioners were particularly disturbed by a lame duck minister's charge, quickly proved false, that the EC had colluded in the printing of extra ballot papers for use in ballot stuffing in key Bihar constituencies.[86]

The EC faces two immediate challenges: criminalization of politics and making the parties internally democratic. In increasing numbers "criminal elements" have taken advantage of "loopholes" in the law to be nominated and elected to parliament and state assemblies. No parties are exempt from the charge of criminalization. The EC has tried to close one loophole by prohibiting criminals convicted in a lower court from contesting elections during the long period when their appeals are being heard by higher courts. Parties that conduct their internal business in "an entirely undemocratic manner" have been directed to conduct organizational elections "in accord with their own constitutions," a directive with which, the EC claimed, it "got all parties to comply," a claim which may have been premature.[87]

---

[84] "Chronology," *Mainstream*, 37 (30), July 17, 1999 and (32), July 31, 1999.

[85] "Chronology," *Mainstream*, 37 (39), September 18, 1999.

[86] The charges were brought by Defense Minister George Fernandes, not famed for conspicuous moderation, who charged that he had the information from the Bihar state intelligence bureau chief. The EC was supported by the secretary to the central government Home Ministry in its assertion that the IB had no such information, and that printing extra papers was a routine back-up precaution. The EC asserted that the papers were intentionally printed out of state, in Calcutta, to assure their security. "Chronology," *Mainstream*, 37 (41), October 2, 1999.

[87] Gill, (1998: 26).

A maladroit effort by Commissioner G.V.G. Krishnamurthy in December 1997 on the eve of the twelfth national election to enforce the internal democracy standard on the Shiv Sena failed. M.S. Gill, with help from President K.R. Narayanan, was able to smooth over the situation.

In 1993 Seshan had "put all parties on notice . . . 'that they should constitute their various governing bodies/committees and elect their office bearers at different levels in

The latest frontier for fair electoral practices is the struggle to insulate a new tier of state-level election commissions, put in place to conduct elections to local bodies, from the political interference of state governments. Enthusiastic about their own autonomy from central government control, most state governments are less enthusiastic about the new third tier of the federal system, mandated in 1992 by the seventy-third and seventy-fourth amendments of the constitution. It further decentralizes political power to local bodies. State governments have been scrambling to control those institutions, such as state-level election commissions, that ensure the autonomy and viability of these grassroots foundations of power.[88]

Tough longer-run problems remain, problems that will not be unfamiliar to US and other Western publics. One is what to do about campaign finance, particularly the role of "illegal" money,[89] both the black money generated in India's vast underground economy that finds its way to parties and candidates, and the often related money that parties and candidates spend above the limits set by EC rules. Another is how much and in what way the state should fund elections. Because the Indian state owns the most widely viewed and heard television and radio stations, the EC is "considering the establishment of a fair mechanism for allotting time to political parties and candidates during

---

accordance with their own party constitutions within a reasonable time'" on pain of derecognition by the EC, i.e., loss of legitimacy with which to contest elections and nonrecognition as a national or state party. Muralidharan (1998a).

[88] The governments of Karnataka and Andhra both promulgated ordinances affecting the parameters and timing of local elections. Andhra sought to appoint special officers for *panchayati raj* bodies. The Andhra election commissioner, K. Madhava Rao, moved the Andhra high court against the Andhra government ordinance. The Karnataka government sought to postpone local government elections by issuing an ordinance redefining *panchayat* boundaries. The Karnataka election commissioner complied with the Karnataka government's ordinance, but a public interest petition moved the high court to block the ordinance. The court declared that the legislative power of the state government in this matter was extinguished by the constitution. When the Karnataka government appealed the Karnataka high court decision to the supreme court, it stayed the high court order. The issue was pending at this writing. *Hindu*, February 19, 2000. For the constitutional basis see Basu (1999: 761–777).

[89] According to Sukumar Muralidharan, Seshan in his later years (1994–6) resurrected long neglected ceilings on election expenses and enforced them despite their obvious inadequacy. He also tells us that "a loophole in the [electoral] law that allowed parties to meet a candidate's expenses with little restraint was plugged by a parallel intervention from the Supreme Court . . . that no party was exempt from the requirements of submitting income tax returns." The Congress-I was the main target of this ruling "but it managed to meet the deadline imposed by the court." "This dual system of vigilance – between the EC and the Income Tax authorities – makes it conceivable that the abuse of money power in elections could be curbed" (Muralidharan 1998b).

election campaigns. Given free, this time will . . . amount to indirect state funding for campaigns."[90]

A review of the role of the constitutionally mandated Election Commission over the past decade suggests that the strengthening of its regulatory role has coincided with the period during which confidence in cabinet and parliament, the instruments of a developmental, interventionist state, has eroded. The EC has played its role as envisioned in the formal constitution by strengthening free and fair elections, the necessary conditions for representative democracy. In the 1990s, under the mixed blessing of T.N. Seshan's leadership, and in the late 1990s under the strong but fair hands of M.S. Gill, the EC improved the conditions under which elections were held in India. High levels of public trust in the EC suggest that Indian electoral processes diverge strikingly from the tainted ones common in other developing and some developed nations.[91]

## Conclusion

We read "constitution" to include symbolic, conventional, and formal dimensions. Our examination here of some aspects of the formal constitution in the 1990s reveals major modifications of India's constitutional design. Our story of an interventionist state giving way to a regulatory state shows how process, agency, and event modified and redirected the effects of structural determination and path dependency. The initial triumph of a developmental, interventionist state was foreshadowed at the symbolic level by Nehru's rejection in 1945 of Gandhi's imagined village as the lodestar of economic development and state formation. After independence and Partition, with Gandhi, Sardar Patel, and Subhas Chandra Bose dead, Jawaharlal Nehru and his supporters in the party and the civil service were free to construct a state suitable for a dominant party system and a planned economy. After 1989 both the planned economy and the centralized state have gradually given way to a regulatory state more suited to coalition governments in a multiparty system, to economic decentralization, and to more independent and competitive federal states. Judicial activism and an indepen-

---

[90] Gill (1998: 26). Gill's claims have to be qualified by the impact of satellite TV. For example, "there are satellite television channels in all the four southern languages . . . The question . . . is what impact these channels will have on the electorate [in the 1996 national election] . . . there are . . . indications that these channels influence the masses far more than the print media" (Panneeselvan 1996).

[91] See note 70 for the 1996 survey results by the Center for the Study of Developing Societies showing the EC with the highest trust rating at 62 percent, ahead of the supreme court.

dent president and Election Commission have filled the space partially vacated by a less ambitious, less capable, and more constrained parliamentary executive. Our analysis of India's emergent constitutional design reveals how a relatively centralized, interventionist, and tutelary state is being replaced by a relatively decentralized regulatory state willing to rely on, but not surrender to, a market economy and self-reliant (and sometimes self-destructive) civil society.

# 7    The dialectics of Hindu nationalism

*Amrita Basu*

Debates about the implications of Hindu nationalism for Indian democracy are highly charged. Some observers claim that, as the most disciplined political party, the Hindu nationalist Bharatiya Janata Party (BJP) provides the greatest hope for political stability, a prime goal in this era of short-lived minority governments. Moreover, they assert, the dynamics of electoral competition and the exigencies of governing have drawn the BJP towards the center. Other observers believe that the BJP will periodically return to a more militant Hindu nationalist posture in keeping with the philosophical commitments of its leadership. This posture threatens secularism, cultural pluralism, and minority rights.

The BJP's stance before and after the 1999 national elections could be interpreted as lending support to both sets of arguments. The BJP projected itself as the party that was best equipped both to provide stable government and to represent the Hindu majority. Although it had moderated its stance, it had not entirely abandoned militant, nationalist appeals. Thus the BJP's unimproved performance in the last elections might be considered a reflection of *either* its growing moderation or its militancy. I will argue that we can best understand the overall character of the BJP if we view it as combining two very different identities: as militant social movement and moderate political party. By emphasizing one identity the BJP has encountered certain problems which it has sought to address by highlighting the other identity. Each of its swings between party and movement has generated a new set of challenges both for the BJP and for the Indian political system as a whole.

The first part of this paper explores the significance of the intertwining of social movements and political parties in postindependence India and suggests why Hindu nationalism should be considered a social

I am grateful to participants in the conference "Against the Odds: Fifty Years of Indian Democracy" and the organizer, Atul Kohli, for lively discussions of early drafts of this paper, both in Vaduz, Liechtenstein in June 1997 and at Princeton University in November 1997. I also received helpful comments on later drafts at the annual meeting of the Asian Studies Association in March 1998 and at the University of Chicago in May 1998. Special thanks to Mary Katzenstein, Mark Kesselman, Lloyd Rudolph, Susanne Hoeber Rudolph, and Elizabeth Wood.

movement. The second part explores the BJP's militant social movement phase (1989–92), which came to an end when the BJP's violent and destructive campaign around Ayodhya antagonized the public and laid the groundwork for it recasting itself as a moderate party (1993 until the present). The concluding section explores why it is useful to view the BJP as combining party and movement identities, in cyclical and sometimes simultaneous fashion.

## Party–movement dialectics

There is a longstanding chasm between scholarship on movements and on parties. In part this reflects the boundedness of disciplinary inquiry, which relegates the study of "social" matters to sociologists and "political" matters to political scientists. It also reflects the different predilections of scholars of movements and parties. Most scholarship on social movements has focused on left-wing movements and ignored ethnic, religious, and right-wing movements. By contrast, students of political parties tend to ignore movements and their relations with parties, relative to their much greater interest in political institutions (important exceptions to this rule include Markovits and Gorski 1993; Keck 1992; Tarrow 1991; Katzenstein 1998). However, to understand some of the most important upheavals taking place in the world today requires dismantling the boundaries that have separated the study of parties from movements and the study of movements from ethnic and religious nationalism (Giugni, McAdam, and Tilly 1998: 17–34).

Before developing my argument further, it might be useful to identify certain broad tendencies of parties and movements. Parties tend to organize on the basis of numbers, movements on the basis of beliefs. Although some parties of the far left and far right are not concerned with electoral success and can thus afford to remain small and ideologically pure, electoral success and therefore numbers matter to most parties. For parties the preoccupation with numbers entails a tendency to be inclusionary and to compromise principles more readily than movements would. By contrast, movements tend to be more committed, more uncompromising, and sometimes more exclusionary. Parties tend to mobilize most intensively just before elections. If elected, mobilization is likely to subside. By contrast, movements tend to view mobilization as an end in itself, a source of creativity, empowerment, and identity-building rather than simply a route to achieving power. Thus their mobilization tends to be more confrontational, spontaneous, and open-ended than that of political parties.

Party agendas tend to be much broader than those of movements. Whereas parties must adopt positions on a whole gamut of issues, the

most effective social movements are often single-issue campaigns.
Indeed the greater movements' commitment to a single issue, the more
confrontational they are likely to be if the state refuses to concede to
their demands. Conversely, the breadth of parties' agendas moderates
their stance, for parties often demonstrate ideological inconsistency
about the various issues they address.

The differences between parties and movements may be mutually
advantageous. Allying with social movements is likely to heighten
parties' aura of being committed, egalitarian, and grassroots-based.
Conversely, through their connections to parties, movements may
achieve longevity, national prominence, and political access. However,
differences between parties and movements can also become the source
of tension. While movements may organize agitations that are more
militant than parties find acceptable, parties may make compromises on
matters that movements consider non-negotiable. The extent to which
party–movement relations are on balance productive or unprofitable is
highly variable.

Parties and movements have long been intertwined in the postcolonial
world. Social movements yielded the major political parties in Mexico,
China, and South Africa, to name just a few cases. Those countries
which experienced protracted nationalist movements, communist revolutions, and national liberation struggles often founded parties which
were characterized by grassroots networks, popular leaders, and programmatic commitments to eradicating injustice and inequality. Conversely, in those parts of the postcolonial world where independence was
not the result of a mass nationalist movement, parties tended to be
weak, illegitimate, and corruptible.

The prime example of a movement spawning a party is the Congress
Party in India. At its origins in 1885, Congress was not a movement but
a small urban elite organization. In the early 1920s it eschewed its elitist
character and became a movement which undertook mass civil disobedience campaigns. But this did not prevent it from functioning effectively as a party in the 1930s, when the British introduced provincial
elections.

While this combination of movement and party identities was a major
source of Congress's strength in the early years, it increasingly became a
source of tension as Jawaharlal Nehru's vision clashed with that of M.K.
Gandhi (Brass 1990: 21; Chatterjee 1986b). Although the Nehruvian
state-building project triumphed in the postindependence period, the
Congress Party periodically revived the Gandhian vision when its
popularity was flagging.

The major challenges to Congress Party dominance from the 1950s
on have come from party–movement combinations at the state level. In

Tamil Nadu, the non-Brahmin movement laid the foundations for the Dravida Munnetra Kazhagam (DMK) party. In Assam, the Punjab and Jammu, and Kashmir, ethnic movements have laid the foundations for the emergence of ethnic parties which have come to play an increasingly important role at the national level. The CPI-M in West Bengal, and to an even greater extent in Kerala, achieved success as a party by providing leadership to mass-based land reform movements (Heller 1999).

This pattern of movements spawning parties also characterizes the national level. The Congress Party was defeated at the polls for the first time in 1977 and 1989 as a result of the challenge it faced from movement–party combinations. In 1977, the Gandhian Socialist leader Jayaprakash Narayan led the movement for total democracy that sought to remove Congress from office. This movement paved the way for the election of the Janata Party. A decade later, V.P. Singh resigned from Congress and formed the Jan Morcha (People's Front), an avowedly "non-political" people's movement. Various social movements responded positively to V.P. Singh's appeals, thereby laying the foundations for the National Front Party, which won the 1989 elections.

Why a party periodically adopts movement tactics is in part situationally determined. As we have seen, the resort to movement tactics initially provided a means for the Congress Party to transform itself from a small elitist organization into a successful opponent of the British colonial government. In the post-independence period, movement tactics similarly enabled opposition parties to rival Congress Party dominance at the state and national levels. However, not all parties are equally equipped to combine party and movement roles. Next to the Congress Party, the BJP has best succeeded in doing so.

## Hindu nationalism as a social movement

The BJP has functioned, since its formation in 1980, as a highly successful political party that is characterized by mass membership, several charismatic, nationally prominent leaders, a high level of ideological commitment, and a tightly knit party structure that has endured without splits since its formation. The fact that the BJP is so well institutionalized means that it can develop links to social movements without losing its own identity.

The BJP has been closely affiliated with the Rashtriya Swayamsevak Sangh (RSS), a militant Hindu nationalist cultural organization that was formed in 1925. The RSS is considered the parent to a number of organizations, the most important of which are the BJP and a religious organization, the Vishva Hindu Parishad (VHP). Since its formation in

1964, the VHP has regularly organized agitational activities; its relationship with the BJP became particularly close in the late 1980s. Together the RSS, VHP, and their affiliates are often described as the Sangh Parivar. While the delineation of party and movement corresponds to the distinction between the BJP and the Sangh Parivar, the BJP contains within itself both movement and party tendencies, corresponding in part to the diverse orientation of its leadership.

The notion that Hindu nationalism constitutes a social movement may be jarring and even offensive to those who associate social movements with struggles of oppressed and exploited groups. It may seem peculiar to use the term social movement to characterize movements that are more orchestrated than spontaneous, more elitist than subaltern, and more hateful than compassionate. To describe the Ayodhya campaign as a social movement is to support BJP's characterization of this campaign as "the greatest mass movement in recent history."

The BJP did not create or organize the Ayodhya movement. From 1983 to 1989, that is before the BJP lent its support, the movement had already begun to stir the people. The commitment of the BJP to the electorate to remove the hurdles in the way of construction of the Temple at the very place where the idols of Rama were . . . were mere consequences of a mass movement that had already taken shape . . . (Bharatiya Janata Party 1993: 8–9).

Calling attention to the movement politics of Hindu nationalism is critical to understanding how a "movement from above," dominated by upper-caste and class elites, comes to acquire the attributes of a "movement from below." Affinities with left-wing social movements are rooted in Hindu nationalists' periodic engagement with street-level politics at the local level, accented by a deep-seated alienation from the formal political process. However, Hindu nationalism has very different implications than most left-wing movements for Indian democracy.

The supporters of most social movements in India tend to be members of subordinate groups who seek to make democracy more inclusive of those who lack resources and political clout. By contrast, the core supporters of Hindu nationalism are dominant caste and class groups whose interests lie in strengthening social hierarchies. Their ability to forge a sense of collective identity among Hindus depends heavily on perpetrating bigotry and violence against Muslims. Even when they have attracted the support of lower-caste groups, OBCs in particular, they have not done so by committing themselves to their economic and social betterment. Thus the more responsive the BJP is to its movement side, the more it has undermined democratic norms. This contradicts many party–movement relationships in which movements sustain the democratic character of parties.

A key feature of social movements is to enlarge the sphere of politics.

This entails politicizing questions that were formerly considered private or social, transforming public discourse, creating new arenas and forms of participation, and bringing new groups into politics. The women's movement best exemplifies each of these traits. Its insistence that violence against women is a political rather than a private question enabled it to demand new forms of state intervention and regulation. Its use of song, dance, and street theater enlarged the forms of political participation. Other social movements have followed suit.

Hindu nationalists have similarly transformed public discourse by making matters that are generally considered private into public concerns. The very premise of Hindu nationalist mobilization around Ayodhya, namely that both the public and the state should take a stand on the question of when and where Ram was born, seeks to blur the boundaries between private and public life. Another instance of this attempt to make the private public concerns Hindu nationalists' voyeuristic interest in Muslim fertility, divorce rates, polygamy, and use of birth control. In all of these instances, Hindu nationalists have sought to politicize Hindus by revealing the supposed injustices that both Muslims and the state perpetrate.

Hindu nationalists have also sought to invest old concepts with new meanings. The best instance concerns their redefinition of secularism and its relationship with democracy. The BJP holds that the Indian conception of secularism is inspired by the notion of "sarva dharma sambhava," or equal respect for all religions, and not the Western notion of separation and often opposition between religion and the state. The BJP criticizes the state for its *unequal* treatment of Hindus and Muslims. All of the examples it then cites concern the state's "appeasement" of Muslims and discrimination against Hindus. Atal Behari Vajpayee, party moderate and prime minister, argues that the state has failed to implement family planning programs and pass a uniform civil code for fear of offending Muslim religious sensibilities. It has unfairly denied majorities the rights that it accords minorities to establish and manage educational institutions of their choice. By opposing safeguards of minority rights, the BJP has in effect redefined democracy as majoritarianism and minority rights as a case for special bargaining.

Hindu nationalism is an identity-based movement. While its most explicit objective is to politicize both Hindu and Muslim identities, it has also heightened caste identities. The major support for Hindu nationalism historically came from upper-caste groups in North India. Their caste backgrounds implicitly informed their support for the BJP but did not constitute the explicit basis for mobilization until 1990 when the Ayodhya movement became the site of caste-based opposition to certain government reforms. It also became the site for women's activism.

## The militant social movement phase (1989–1992)

Tensions within the BJP over whether to function as a militant social movement or a moderate political party were evident as early as 1986. The BJP considered the results of the parliamentary elections in 1984, when it won only 7 percent of the vote, a repudiation of the path of moderation that it had pursued under Atal Behari Vajpayee's leadership. Local-level cadres were pressuring it to assume a more activist, militant posture. However the BJP also recognized that by functioning as a moderate party, it might be able to participate in coalition governments at the state and national levels. Fifteen of the BJP's seventeen candidates were elected to the Haryana legislative assembly as a result of its alliance with Devi Lal in 1987. Two years later the National Front was forming a coalition to contest the national elections and the BJP would only be asked to join if it assumed a more moderate stance.

The BJP's attempt to reconcile divergent objectives is evident from the proceedings of its national executive committee at Palampur (June 9–11, 1989). On the one hand, it committed itself to working with the Janata Dal to defeat Congress by playing the role of a responsible opposition party. On the other hand, it decided to work with the VHP to build a temple at Ayodhya. Its formal resolution stated (Bharatiya Janata Party, June 9–11, 1989: 14):

The National Executive of the Bharatiya Janata Party regards the current debate on the Ram Jamma Bhoomi issue as one which has dramatically highlighted the callous unconcern which the Congress Party in particular, and the other political parties in general, betray towards the sentiments of the overwhelming majority in this country – the Hindus . . . The sentiments of the people must be respected and the Rama Janmasthan handed over to the Hindus.

The BJP effectively combined party and movement-based approaches. Although it refused to compromise some of its hardline positions, the Janata Dal agreed to seat adjustments which enabled the BJP to make significant gains in the 1989 elections. The electoral system of first past the post, which translates a small lead in votes into a much larger lead in parliamentary seats, allowed the BJP, with just 11.9 percent of the national vote, to become the single largest opposition party. It gained further credibility when the Janata Dal invited the BJP to support the central government, retracting along the way the stipulations that the BJP demonstrate its moderate, "noncommunal" character. The February 1990 legislative assembly elections brought the BJP to power on a moderate platform in Rajasthan, Himachal Pradesh, Madhya Pradesh and, in a Janata Dal-led coalition, in Gujarat.

At the same time that the BJP was pursuing a party-based approach that entailed participating in coalitions and electoral arrangements, it was also pursuing a movement-based approach which entailed close collaboration with the VHP. The VHP had been organizing around the Ayodhya issue in a sustained fashion since 1984. It put forward its initial demand, that the government open the locks of the *babri masjid* (mosque) and allow Hindus to worship there, by organizing several massive processions and demonstrations in various parts of the country. After a court conceded to this demand and ordered that the locks be opened in 1986, the VHP demanded that the state permit the construction of a temple devoted to Ram on that site.

As a religious organization rather than a political party, the VHP was freer to assert its commitment to ultimate values and to adopt positions which it refused to negotiate. Thus the VHP claimed that Hindus knew that Ram was born in Ayodhya and required no documentation of this. The VHP was not accountable to a broad constituency, and short of being censured by the state, faced no other constraints upon its activities. However, the Ayodhya campaign only had a cataclysmic effect on Indian political life when the BJP took it up. The BJP ensured that, unlike many social movements, which functioned at the margins of political life, the Ayodhya movement would be at its nerve center.

The BJP's decision to join the Ayodhya movement in 1990 was precipitated by V.P. Singh's announcement that he would implement the Mandal Commission recommendations that provided reserved seats in public education and employment for the so-called other backward classes (OBCs). The BJP was outraged by the decision, ostensibly because the government had not consulted with it in advance, but in fact because reforms would heighten caste identities to the detriment of religious ones. Shortly after the government announced its actions, L.K. Advani launched a procession from Somnath temple in Gujarat, which covered 10,000 kilometers before reaching Ayodhya. The route that the procession took was marked both by scenes of jubilation, as it drew cheering Hindu crowds, and scenes of devastation caused by the riots it provoked in many places along the way. When V.P. Singh ordered the arrest of Advani in Bihar, on October 23, the BJP announced that it was withdrawing support from the Janata Dal government at the center. Meanwhile a group of men and women reached Ayodhya on October 30, climbed atop the mosque and planted a saffron flag on it. Some of them attacked and damaged one of the domes. The national government collapsed and elections were held the following year.

When the BJP was elected to power in 1991 in Uttar Pradesh (UP), it faced a major dilemma over whether to emphasize party or movement tactics. It had been elected to power in the key state of UP for the first time ever, largely as a result of its movement tactics. The VHP, which had contributed handsomely to its success, was putting pressure on it to begin construction of the temple. However, as a governing party, the BJP was under pressure to demonstrate its capacity to respect the law, maintain order and protect the minority population. While the democratic system pulled the BJP towards the center, the VHP drew the BJP away from it. The BJP could not afford to antagonize either its movement or electoral constituencies.

The BJP steered a middle course by pursuing its demand for the construction of a temple in Ayodhya initially through negotiation rather than agitation. It acquired 2.77 acres of land adjoining the *babri masjid* complex, ostensibly to plan a tourist complex there. Ignoring supreme court directives, the VHP began constructing a wall enclosing a large area, including the acquired land around the mosque. A few months later, in July 1992, the VHP undertook a pilgrimage to Ayodhya in order to construct a platform within the mosque complex. It announced that it would undertake a massive procession to Ayodhya that would culminate in the construction of the temple. On December 6, a group of Hindu activists wearing saffron head-bands crossed the police cordons and descended on the mosque. With a variety of tools and implements, they methodically razed it to the ground. While a few BJP and VHP leaders weakly tried to stop them, most remained silent, and some, like Uma Bharati and Sadvi Rithambara, goaded the crowd on. The destruction of the mosque precipitated a major political crisis and riots that claimed thousands of lives.

The BJP's initial response to the destruction of the mosque was apologetic. Kalyan Singh resigned from the post of chief minister of UP and L.K. Advani resigned as opposition leader. Shortly thereafter, however, the BJP had changed its tune. Advani commented that the demolition reflected "an exasperation with the frustrating sluggishness of the judicial process." By blaming the courts, the BJP sought further to discredit an already weakened state for its poor handling of the issue and to deflect attention from the illegality of its own actions.

When the BJP boasted, as it often did prior to December 1992, that it was planning to launch the biggest mass movement in history, its claims appeared to be wildly exaggerated. However it did in fact organize the most significant social movement of the postindependence period, judging by the numbers of people involved, the several-year duration of the movement, and its impact on both the state and civil society. How did the campaign in Ayodhya acquire the attributes of such a powerful social movement?

The Ayodhya campaign provided a striking instance of Hindu nationalists' attempts to broaden the political domain through discursive means. The VHP effectively linked the everyday and the extraordinary, the local and the national, the cultural and the political. For example, prior to the *shilanyas*, a ceremony to lay the foundations of a temple in Ayodhya in November 1989, the VHP oversaw the *ram shila puja*, the manufacture, consecration, and transportation of tens of thousands of bricks from all over the country to Ayodhya. The campaign implied that ordinary people had built the temple from the ground up. Another example was the *ram jyoti* ceremony, in which activists lit the Ram Agni, a specially consecrated torch, in Ayodhya. With this they lit other torches, and fanned out throughout the country, lighting torches along the way. Each newly lit torch symbolized the awakening of a new Ram devotee. Through these and other campaigns, the VHP suggested that people in far-flung regions of the country could become activists in the movement without traveling any distance, spending any money, or incurring any risk. Simply blessing a brick, lighting a torch, placing a saffron flag on their roof tops or a sticker on their doors could signify their commitment.

Politicizing and redefining religious practice constituted another means by which the VHP and BJP extended definitions of the political. Whereas the exaggerated importance that Hindu nationalists accorded to the precise place of Ram's birth was alien to the amorphous character of Hindu observance, the *ram shila puja* and the *ram jyoti* processions better captured its spirit. Many of the symbols that the BJP and VHP employed in the course of the Ayodhya movement drew upon traditional forms of observance but infused them with new meaning. Advani, in his Toyota chariot, assumed the attributes of a mythological hero on his journey to Ayodhya in October 1990. Hindu nationalists transformed the familiar North Indian greeting, "Jai Sita Ram," into the battle cry "Jai Shri Ram." They even made *bindis* imprinted with images of the temple, the lotus, and the trident.

Social movements often convey the aura of greater disinterest than political parties in the material and symbolic rewards of political engagement. Most movement activists are unpaid volunteers who work long hours under difficult conditions. Few of them gain national stature and those who do often maintain their commitments when they achieve renown. To gain the stature of a committed activist amidst the towering examples of Mahatma Gandhi, Jyotirao Phule, and Vinoba Bhave is a major feat.

The BJP depicted its commitment to building a temple at Ayodhya as indicative of its disinterest in power. It also sought to differentiate its conception of nationalism from narrow forms of statism. Govind Acharya juxtaposed Nehruvian nationalism, which centered on the state, with Hindu nationalism, which identifies the nation with its people, religion, and culture.[1] The power of this linguistic turn lies in its extending definitions of the nation beyond a top-down state-centered understanding to comprise a more popular, culturally grounded conception of nationalism. It also lies in its exclusion of Muslims from majoritarian definitions of the nation. When Hindu nationalists spoke of Muslims in the early 1990s, they depicted them as outsiders. They not only characterized the sixteenth-century Muslim emperor Babar, who supposedly destroyed the temple in Ayodhya, as an invader, but even described Bangladeshi Muslim immigrants as "infiltrators."

When Hindu nationalism was most movement-like, it was also most xenophobically anti-Muslim. The BJP sought to foster solidarity among Hindus by both appealing to hope, courage, and selflessness, and to bigotry, hatred, and fear. The notion that Muslims were anti-Indian was a staple of the Hindu nationalist campaign. Indeed one of the reasons that the BJP could elicit such anger at the Muslim emperor Babar's supposed destruction of a temple at Ayodhya was by implying that Muslims who wielded power in contemporary India were similarly anti-Hindu. It constantly decried the Muslim leadership and exaggerated its influence. Its favorite target was Syed Shahabuddin, community leader, co-founder of the Babri Masjid Action Committee, and publisher of the journal *Muslim India*. In numerous UP towns which experienced riots in the early 1990s, the BJP also targeted locally prominent Muslims.

We have already noted the extent to which the *shilanyas*, *ram jyotis*, and Advani's procession to Ayodhya were celebratory, affirmative expressions of community identity. However, each of these ceremonies also fostered violence between Hindus and Muslims. Following the prayer meetings that the VHP held in connection with the brick consecration ceremonies, religious activists goaded the throngs of Hindus who had gathered to engage in violence against Muslims in retaliation for their violence centuries earlier. The *ram jyoti* processions provoked confrontations with the police who tried to prevent them from entering the state and often triggered riots.

For all the festivity that surrounded Advani's procession, this too was an extremely violent event. Agitated by Bajrang Dal propaganda before-

---

[1] Interview with Govind Acharya, New Delhi, February 20, 1991.

hand, people would present Advani with swords, spears, and maces. Pramode Mahajan, the BJP architect of this procession, commented: "If we are to use all the weapons presented to us, we can liberate the Ramjamnabhumi in a day" (*The Organiser*, October 14, 1990). At various points along the way, the procession incited Hindus to attack Muslim homes and shops. Advani's arrest on October 23, the BJP's call for a movement of protest thereafter, and the arrival of Hindu volunteers at Ayodhya on October 30, resulted in violence throughout the country. Between September 1 and November 20, 116 riots occurred in which 564 people died. UP alone experienced twenty-four riots in which 224 people were killed.[2]

The VHP created a youth organization, the Bajrang Dal (literally Army of Hanuman the monkey god), in 1986 with the explicit aim of mobilizing young people to participate in the Ayodhya movement. The Bajrang Dal played a prominent role in the most violent phases of the movement – assaults on the mosque in 1990 and its destruction in 1992, and in riots throughout this period. As with most social movements, which feed on a range of motivations, the young men who joined the ranks of Hindu nationalism were responding to a variety of frustrations, particularly high unemployment and limited prospects for upward mobility, aggravated by the government's decision to implement the Mandal recommendations which restricted upper-caste access to public employment.

In planning the 1990 procession to Ayodhya, Giri Raj Kishore, the joint general secretary of the VHP, carefully charted out highly visible roles for women. He organized two massive women's *satyagrahas*, one of which included children. It placed women at the forefront of the procession of Hindu activists to Ayodhya. "Having women in the forefront creates an emotional response," he noted, adding that officers would be less likely to use force if women were present. After the police fired on the men who broke through the picket lines and climbed atop the mosque, these women questioned their masculinity by presenting them with bangles and asked, "Are you such cowards that you can't even stand up for the *kar sevaks*?"[3]

The BJP also made extensive efforts to draw women into its campaigns. The manner in which it did so was more reminiscent of a movement than a party. In general the BJP did not seek to mobilize

---

[2] Divided We Stand As Ayodhya Sets the Agenda, A Dossier On Mandir–Masjid Conflict, no page given.
[3] Interview with Acharya Giri Raj Kishore, joint general secretary of the VHP, New Delhi, March 19, 1991.

women by appealing to their interests as women or by promising them access to institutional power. It did not even frame its demand for the uniform civil code as a question of women's rights. Women like Uma Bharati and Vijay Raje Scindia, who occupied positions of prominence, did not exert the kind of leadership roles within the party that would have enabled them to shape party policy. The BJP's record of nominating women to run for political office was relatively poor. The BJP was most effective in engaging women's activism through gendered appeals to the motherland in danger and to women's responsibilities as mothers and wives (Basu and Jeffery 1998).

Social movements can be highly effective when they undertake single-issue campaigns. The achievements of the Chipko movement, the Narmada Bachao Andolan, and the farmers' movement are in part a reflection of their singlemindedness in mobilizing around a single set of objectives over a sustained period of time. Political parties, however, cannot afford to be as narrowly focused. Even when the Ayodhya campaign was at its height, party leader Kusabau Thakre admitted that the BJP could not build its identity exclusively around the campaign. "We hope to form a government. We must demonstrate that we would bring about many kinds of changes, not just one."[4] As the 1991 elections approached, the BJP was anxious to broaden its reputation from being a single-issue campaign. Thus the party changed its rallying cry from "Ram" to "Ram aur Roti" (Ram and Bread) and for good measure added *swadeshi* (economic nationalism) to its platform.

However, the BJP also sought to reap electoral dividends from the Ayodhya campaign. The notion that the *babri* mosque stood on the birthplace of Ram, that the BJP was committed to righting a historical injustice by building a temple, and that Muslims who defended the mosque were antinational, did not simply figure in the election speeches of the most militant leaders like Uma Bharati and Sadvi Rithambara, but also those of Sikander Bhakt, Atal Behari Vajpayee, and L.K. Advani.[5] The BJP mobilized thousands of VHP and RSS workers to participate in its campaign. The movement also enabled the BJP to mount an aggressive election campaign in UP, particularly in the western region of the state where it had traditionally been weak. Its efforts bore fruit. The BJP won fifty-one out of eighty-five parliamentary seats and 211 out of 425 legislative assembly seats, enabling it to form a government in UP in 1991.

The BJP combined attributes of a party and a movement but increasingly became more movement than party-like between 1989 and 1992.

---

[4] Interview with Kusabau Thakre, New Delhi, April 3, 1991.
[5] Audio cassette that the BJP produced and sold in preparation for its election campaign.

In 1989 the BJP was still seeking to maintain the aura of a moderate party; a year later, it had withdrawn support from the Janata Dal government and embarked on a literal and metaphoric voyage from which Advani emerged as a leader and the BJP as a social movement. However, even at the height of its movement phase, the BJP continued to assess the implications of electoral trends, state policies, and party relations in determining its future trajectory.

## The centrist party phase (1993–2000)

The BJP hoped to reap the rewards of the Ayodhya campaign after the destruction of the mosque. Its 1993 legislative assembly election manifesto devoted eleven paragraphs to the campaign, which it described as "the biggest mass movement in the history of independent India . . . a symbol and a source of our national solidarity, economic power and social cohesion." However, it was chastened by humiliating electoral setbacks. Public opinion polls conducted after the demolition of the mosque showed that 52 percent of the population disapproved, 39 percent approved, and 8 percent had no opinion. Fifty-two percent of those who were surveyed believed that the BJP had broken the law.[6]

The November 1993 election results were a public referendum on the BJP's militant social movement activities. Significantly, the BJP's losses were greatest in Madhya Pradesh followed by Uttar Pradesh, where its posture was most militant and riots were most numerous. By contrast, the BJP retained power in Rajasthan, where it benefited from the moderate, relatively secular leadership of chief minister Bhairon Singh Shekavat. Support for the BJP continued to dwindle at the 1995 legislative assembly elections. The BJP came to power in only two states, neither of which it had ruled before, as a result of popular discontent with incumbent Janata Dal governments. The BJP–Shiv Sena alliance came to power with a slim majority – just 1 percent over Congress – in Maharashtra, while the BJP came to power with a comfortable two-thirds majority in Gujarat.

Both the 1993 and the 1995 election returns suggest that a violent social movement strategy had ceased to pay off. The BJP took heed. At its national council meeting in Bangalore in June 1993, it projected itself as a responsible political party and highlighted its commitments to liberalizing the economy and ending corruption. It reaffirmed its commitment to a secular state and downplayed the possibility of building a

---

[6] "A Nation Divided," *India Today*, January 15, 1993: 18.

temple in Ayodhya. Two years later, at the Goa conclave, the BJP was seeking to eradicate its anti-Muslim veneer. Party president L.K. Advani asked party members to try and rid Muslims of their "misapprehensions of the BJP."

Tensions between a party and a movement-based approach became increasingly evident. The BJP valued mobilization only as long as it yielded electoral gains. By contrast, the VHP viewed mobilization around Ayodhya as an end in itself. Thus the mobilization it undertook was more confrontational, spontaneous, and open-ended than that of the BJP. Unlike the VHP, the BJP could not countenance the short-term effectiveness of a single-issue campaign. The violence associated with the Ayodhya issue may have mobilized people in the short run, but ultimately backfired. Even if Muslims were the chief victims, Hindus also suffered from political instability, material losses, and threats to their safety. The BJP's response was to broaden its agenda and put Ayodhya on the back burner, whereas the VHP was unwilling to drop the temple issue.

The BJP's retreat from militant social movement tactics may also have been a cost of its expansion. Although the movement's growth initially contributed to the party's growth, at some point this trend shifted. The BJP has experienced what has been termed "congressization" as it has evolved from a narrowly based, disciplined cadre party into a mass party. Expansion has brought about a more disparate, corrupt, unprincipled membership, rendering the party less equipped to play a transformative role. In UP, as in some other states, many of the new entrants have criminal backgrounds and have engaged in lawless behavior. Tensions within the party have also grown as a result of upper-caste members' resentments at the entry of lower castes into the party.

The BJP has also adopted a moderate party-based approach in order to make inroads among the lower castes. Exit polls for the 1996 parliamentary elections showed that although it succeeded in fracturing the OBC vote, only 11 percent of scheduled castes supported the BJP compared to 31 percent who supported Congress, 21 percent who supported the National Front, and 16 percent who supported the Bahujan Samaj Party (BSP).[7] By 1998, although the BJP was still heavily reliant on upper-caste votes, its support among OBCs had increased dramatically. Forty-two percent of OBCs voted for the BJP, making it the largest recipient of OBC votes of any political party.[8]

---

[7] The remaining 14 percent supported state parties and 7 percent supported other parties. "How India Voted," *India Today*, May 11, 1996: 50.
[8] "Post Poll: Who Voted For Whom?" *India Today*, March 16, 1998: 33–34.

Furthermore, the BJP realized that a major handicap to its continued electoral growth concerned its regional confinement to northwestern India. Although it won more seats than any political party in the 1996 parliamentary elections, 74 percent of these seats were in the Hindi heartland. The addition of Gujarat and Maharashtra accounted for 96 percent of the seats it won. The BJP won only 4 percent of seats from southern, eastern and northeastern India. Although it had recorded a significant growth in Andhra Pradesh and West Bengal in 1991, it had declined in these states by 1996. The BJP was unable to mobilize in the south around building a temple, opposing caste-based reservations, and attacking Muslims. In order to make inroads into southern and eastern India, the BJP sought to demonstrate its centrist party attributes. Two years later this strategy bore fruit. In 1996 the BJP had secured only 9 percent of votes in the seven coastal states; by 1998 the BJP and its allies secured 31 percent of the vote.

Overall, Muslims' response to the events surrounding the Ayodhya campaign has checked the further growth of the social movement dimensions of Hindu nationalism. The BJP can only polarize religious communities if it can provoke a militant response from Muslims. However, since 1992 most Muslims have distanced themselves from the opportunistic Muslim leadership and affirmed secular principles. Syed Shahabuddin organized a meeting on July 9, 1993 to discuss the reconstruction of the mosque. But what had been billed as a day-long round table ended within two hours because it met with so little enthusiasm. By 1998, large segments of the Muslim community claimed that if the BJP built the temple, they would not resist. Their priority was to attend to their real needs, particularly better and more extensive educational facilities. Meanwhile they would lend support to lower-caste parties which provided the major opposition to the BJP. Their respect for Mulayam Singh Yadav matched their disdain for Syed Shahabuddin.[9]

## The endurance of movement politics

If, as we have seen, the BJP has adopted the stance of a centrist party on many issues, it is not in its interests to wholly abdicate a movement identity which distinguishes it from other political parties. The BJP is keenly aware of the costs of being assimilated into the political main-

---

[9] Based on interviews conducted by me in Nizamuddin, New Delhi on November 18 and 20, 1997.

stream and has for years sought to avoid doing this without becoming a pariah party. Before and since 1993, the period of relative moderation, the BJP has periodically revived anti-Muslim sentiment to reignite memories of its movement identity.

The BJP has sought to keep the Ayodhya dispute alive. Uma Bharati, minister of state in the BJP government that was formed in 1998, suggested that December 6, the day the mosque was demolished, should be commemorated as a national holiday (Engineer 1997: 325). Lest her views be regarded as aberrant, the ostensibly moderate Atal Behari Vajpayee defended the destruction of the mosque by arguing that it had occurred because Hindus had been outraged by the way political parties were supposedly pandering to Muslims in order to gain their electoral support. In an essay entitled "The Sangh is my Soul," he lauded the regeneration of Hindu India that the demolition entailed and argued that "this was the prime test of the RSS. Earlier Hindus used to bend before an invasion. Not now, this change in Hindu society is worthy of welcome." Far from repudiating Vajpayee's essay, the BJP posted it on a website it had created for the 1998 election campaign.[10] The BJP's 1996 and 1998 election manifestos both reiterated its commitment to building a temple at Ayodhya.

Political parties cannot adopt and shed identities at will. They face pressures by leaders and constituencies to abide by past commitments that make it extremely difficult for them to reinvent themselves entirely. Changes in strategy are more likely to be cyclical than permanent. As a result, to a greater extent than other political parties, the BJP engages in double speak, by seeking to demonstrate simultaneously its moderation and its militancy. A good example is the BJP's revival of a campaign against cow slaughter, this time seeking Muslim support. "If the cow is sacred to Hindus because of religious reasons," Uma Bharati argued at a convention of Muslim youth in Delhi in December 1997, "it is also sacred to Muslims because they drink cow milk."[11]

The BJP's 1998 election manifesto provided an especially striking instance of its attempt to reconcile party and movement identities. On the one hand, the BJP remained committed to the core demands associated with the militant stance that it adopted in 1989. These included building a temple at Ayodhya, abrogating a constitutional provision that provides a special status to Kashmir, introducing a uniform civil code, abolishing the Minority Commission, and banning cow slaughter and beef export. It promised to undertake a comprehensive review of the constitution including the feasibility of a presidential

[10] "The Sangh is my Soul" was first published in *The Organiser* in 1995.
[11] "BJP: Dilli Dur Ast?" *Outlook*, December 15, 1997: 21.

system of government. Its rhetoric was sometimes fiery – India must choose between nationalism and "a foreign hand" – and sometimes inspirational – "The BJP is convinced that Hindutva has enormous potential to regenerate this nation and is committed to facilitating the construction of a magnificent temple at the Ram Janmasthan in Ayodhya."

On the other hand, it shifted back and forth within the same document between rabble-rousing and reason, when, for example, it promised to seek "consensual, legal, constitutional means to facilitate the construction of the Ram Mandir." The election manifesto not only speaks in two voices but also offers two options, of either pursuing these objectives or dropping them if elected! Accordingly, just prior to taking office in March 1998, the BJP and its coalition partners published a national agenda which dropped the issues of the temple, the uniform civil code, and Kashmir's special constitutional status.

The BJP contested the 1999 parliamentary elections as the leader of the National Democratic Alliance (NDA), an umbrella coalition comprising most of its 1998 partners and a few new ones like the DMK. The NDA election manifesto dropped all references to building a temple, the uniform civil code, and article 356. "Whatever is there in the national agenda of governance is our agenda and there is no question of raising those three issues at all," BJP general secretary M. Venkaiah Naidu said while responding to allegations that the BJP had a hidden agenda. This statement was triggered by a reported assertion by Uttar Pradesh chief minister Ram Prakash Gupta that constructing a temple in Ayodhya was part of the BJP agenda.[12]

The BJP's cultivation of the apparently moderate Atal Behari Vajpayee and the militant L.K. Advani are symptomatic of its double speak. Vajpayee as prime minister and Advani as minister for home affairs personify the BJP's attempt to sustain these two different identities as well as the relative priority it assigns to each of them. Just after the BJP government was formed, L.K. Advani argued that the fiftieth anniversary of Indian independence offered a good opportunity to review the functioning of the constitution and propose some reforms. A few days later, Vajpayee assured the opposition that the BJP had no intention of changing the structure of the constitution.[13] However, on February 13, 2000 the Vajpayee government announced the composition of an eleven-member committee to review the constitution within the framework of parliamentary democracy. The double speak continues since reports suggest that Mr. Venkatachaliah consented to head the com-

---

[12] *India Today*, December 27, 1999.
[13] Reuters' news wire service, March 31, 1998.

mittee after being assured that the constitution's "basic features" and "parliamentary system of democracy" would be left untouched.[14]

The BJP knows that polarizing the electorate along Hindu–Muslim lines often pays rich electoral dividends. This was surely one of the central lessons it derived from the 1991 parliamentary elections in which it was the beneficiary of the violence it had instigated in connection with Advani's procession to Ayodhya in October 1990. Other political parties, most notably Congress, have employed communal appeals and violence to gain the support of the majority community. However, the BJP is unique in the extent to which it has precipitated violence with the explicit intention and effect of influencing electoral outcomes. The BJP provoked riots just before the 1991 elections in several Uttar Pradesh towns and cities including Agra, Banaras, and Aligarh; it won a majority of votes in each of these towns and in the state as a whole (Brass 1993: 275). The BJP's share of the vote in Uttar Pradesh went up to 20.08 percent from 11.36 percent in the previous elections. The BJP also came to power in Gujarat and Maharashtra in 1995, following serious incidents of communal violence two years earlier.

One of the major deterrents to the BJP pursuing a centrist path are its ties to the RSS, which is intolerant of political pluralism. This is best illustrated by the RSS's refusal to negotiate with the government or with Muslim groups on the Ayodhya issue. Although differences in the philosophies of the BJP and RSS have grown in recent years in Rajasthan, Madhya Pradesh, Maharashtra, Uttar Pradesh, and Gujarat, the two organizations are unlikely to sever ties. The RSS has found in the BJP a vehicle for influencing political life without incurring the risks of participating directly itself. Given the dismal state of the Congress Party, the BJP provides a preferable ally.

The BJP faces a more difficult decision for a movement identity can be costly. It formed a government that lasted only thirteen days in 1996, for most political parties shunned a party that had ties to the RSS. Even in 1998, the BJP only put together a governing coalition with great difficulty. Although relinquishing its ties to the RSS would make the BJP more acceptable to other parties, the RSS has been vital to the BJP's phenomenal growth since the late 1980s. It has enabled the BJP to assume the character of a social movement which can mobilize on a larger scale than any other political party in India today. Ties to the

---

[14] *India Today*, February 13, 2000. The committee, which is headed by former chief justice Venkatachaliah, will include Law Commission chairman Justice B.P. Jeevan Reddy, Attorney General Soli Sorabjee, former Lok Sabha speaker P.A. Sangma, and eminent newspaper editor C.R. Irani, among others.

Sangh Parivar have also earned the BJP the support of many state functionaries who have longstanding RSS affiliations.

It is also hard to visualize a split between the RSS and the BJP when the BJP's leadership is dominated by men of RSS backgrounds. Approximately 70 percent of BJP officials at the national level and 60 percent at the state level are RSS members. In the BJP's central office, twenty-eight of forty-one BJP officials are of RSS backgrounds.[15] Furthermore, the BJP has become dependent on the RSS to mend the rifts that have surfaced in the party in the states in which it has held power. In November 1996 the RSS directly confronted the problem of growing caste, personality, and organizational divisions within the BJP and decided to monitor it closely.

The 1998 parliamentary elections confirmed the strength of BJP–RSS ties. Even while taking pains to assert the moderate, secular character of the BJP government, Atal Behari Vajpayee praised the RSS for its dedication to the well-being of the country. Not surprisingly, opposition parties claimed that the BJP was being run by "remote control" (Chalmers in Reuters, March 31, 1998). The BJP government's choice of cabinet ministers also revealed the strength of RSS influence. Some of its key appointments included RSS heavyweights like L.K. Advani, minister of home affairs, Murli Manohar Joshi, minister of human resource development, Uma Bharati, his counterpart as minister of state, M.L. Khurana, minister of parliamentary affairs, and Sushma Swaraj, minister of information and broadcasting.

The composition of the Vajpayee cabinet following the victory of the NDA alliance in the 1999 parliamentary elections demonstrates the rift within the BJP between adherents of "party" and "movement" orientations. The key cabinet portfolios of finance, power, external affairs, urban development, and law are held by persons who are not part of the RSS inner circle. The BJP high command axed M.L. Khurana and Sushma Swaraj and shifted Uma Bharati to tourism. Vajpayee and his supporters have increasingly asserted the "party" identity against the "movement" identity that Advani and the RSS are championing. The tussle between these two identities was starkly manifest over the Indian Airlines hijacking crisis in late December 1999. Home Minister Advani claimed that the government had damaged the BJP's image as a nationalist party when it agreed to release three militants in exchange for the hostages.[16] RSS joint general secretary K.S. Sudarshan similarly criticized the Vajpayee government for its "capitulation."

[15] Singh (1996).
[16] Interview with L.K. Advani in *Aaj Tak*, January 11, 2000.

Tensions between the moderates and militants are also evident around the issue of rebuilding the temple in Ayodhya. Party president Kusabau Thakre stated unambiguously, "Abhi hamaari shakti nahin hai. Jab hogi to mandir banega" (loosely translated: "Right now we don't have the strength. When we do, the temple will be built").[17] Similarly, senior BJP leader Sushma Swaraj told reporters in Bhopal in December 1999 that the BJP had not "deserted" Ram and that "if the party ever comes to power on its own, it will not shy away from introducing a Uniform Civil Code, repealing Article 370 of the Constitution and other issues."[18] But when asked by an angry opposition in parliament about these statements, the prime minister was evasive.

Unlike the BJP and even the Shiv Sena, both of which are subject to electoral pressures and constraints, the VHP, which is not, has remained firm on the temple. Shortly after the BJP government was elected, the VHP announced that it would build temples in four sites, one of which was Ayodhya. Its initial budget for the temple construction was 300 million rupees. It planned to construct half the temple within three years, by which time it expected the BJP to enact legislation that would enable it to be completed. The VHP also announced that it had approached the Delhi government with a request for land near the Qutab Minar monument where it planned to construct a large monument depicting "the massacre of Hindus by Muslim and British invaders."

### Conclusion

The BJP's history is characterized by alternating cycles, of militant social movement and moderate political party. What explains this pattern? What are the implications of the vicissitudes of party–movement relations for Indian democracy? Is it likely that these cycles have drawn to an end and that the BJP will succumb to the centripetal forces of Indian democracy? Elsewhere I have addressed certain aspects of the external political environment that influence the BJP's choice of strategy, such as the changing character and attitude of political parties, of the state, and of the Muslim community (Basu 2000). Here my focus is on party–movement dynamics.

The BJP appreciates that at different times a militant social movement and a moderate party-based approach can both be electorally profitable. In the 1967 parliamentary elections, shortly after the Jan Sangh had

---

[17] *India Today,* June 22, 1998.
[18] *India Today,* December 11, 1999.

organized a prolonged agitation demanding that the state should ban cow slaughter, it received 9 percent of the vote, an increase from 6 percent in 1962 and 4 percent in 1957. It paid for its subsequent moderate phase under Vajpayee's leadership in the 1971 elections, when it declined to 7 percent of the vote. The same pattern recurred in the following decade. The BJP received 6.4 percent of the vote in the 1984 elections, following a period of moderation. By 1989, at the start of the Ayodhya campaign, the BJP's share of the national vote increased to 11.4 percent and by the 1991 elections, when the campaign was in full flower, 20.1 percent. However, it was by pursuing a moderate party-based strategy that the BJP increased its share of the vote slightly, to 20.3 percent in the 1996 parliamentary elections and to 25 percent in 1998. What explains this pattern?

The BJP found its relationship to the VHP almost wholly beneficial until 1990 and largely beneficial until 1993. It received an unprecedented 11.7 percent of the vote in UP. A year later it received an extraordinary 31.6 percent of the vote in the UP legislative assembly elections. The benefits the BJP derived from its relationship with the VHP range from the material to the symbolic. The VHP amassed millions of dollars overseas in connection with its temple construction campaign. It channeled large sums into the BJP's election campaign in 1991. Govind Acharya estimated that the BJP employed some 2,000 VHP members to participate in door-to-door campaigning in the 1991 elections.

These concrete benefits were important in themselves but the symbolic capital that the BJP derived from the Ayodhya movement was even more significant. As an elitist political party that was identified with upper-caste and class interests historically, the BJP found in the Ayodhya movement a means of acquiring the attributes of a grassroots movement without fundamentally altering its policies. Drawing women and scheduled castes into both the campaign and the riots that accompanied it appeared to broaden the movement's social base. Associating itself with the VHP's ongoing campaign implied that the BJP's commitment to the issue was not electorally driven.

However, the BJP's gains from a militant social movement approach were relatively short-lived. Once Hindu nationalists destroyed the mosque in Ayodhya, people lost interest in the construction of a temple and the reconstruction of the mosque. After some initial attempts to keep the issue alive, the BJP put it on the back burner. When asked why the BJP had not pursued its promise of building a temple, L.K. Advani responded, "There is less intensity of feeling around the issue now that the structure has been removed."[19] Uma Bharati commented that the campaign had had its desired impact.[20]

Popular support for temple construction may also have diminished as anti-Muslim violence increased. Although riots had accompanied the BJP's first procession to Ayodhya in October 1990, the scale of the violence in Bombay in the aftermath of the demolition dramatically increased. By 1992 the media had become more hostile to the campaign. Thus newspaper photographs and television clips depicted less romanticized images of the movement than they had two years earlier. Whereas earlier reports had dwelt on symbols of Hindu pride, later accounts depicted the destruction of the mosque as symptomatic of the assault on the Muslim community. Whether the BJP was seen as unable to control its supporters or as inciting them, the press and public opinion held it responsible for the violence in and around Ayodhya.

Another possible explanation for the BJP's shift from a movement to a party-based approach is that symbolic politics do not yield sustained electoral gains. Both in the 1991 and the 1993 national elections, the BJP sought to attract votes from some of the same groups it had mobilized around Ayodhya. Govind Acharya acknowledged that it had campaigned particularly intensively among women, youth, and the lower castes.[21] However, its major gains came from the upper castes, who shifted allegiance from Congress to the BJP. The BJP was unable to gain significant support from women and scheduled castes. Their token, symbolic forms of inclusion in the Ayodhya movement did not result in electoral support for the BJP. Once the limitations associated with broadening its constituency through mobilizational and movement politics became evident, the BJP opted to pursue electoral means of doing so.

It is impossible to predict the demise of the social movement phase of Hindu nationalism without considering the likely trajectory of caste and ethnic movements. Hindu nationalism was in part a reaction to the growing political power of the OBCs in UP and other parts of the country. When the government responded to the growth of OBC influence by legislating reservations for them, the BJP took to the streets in protest. However, the very mobilization of the upper castes under the BJP's leadership led to the further politicization of the lower castes and thus the growth of the predominantly Dalit Bahujan Samaj Party and the predominantly Yadav Samajvadi Janata Party. If, as in the past, caste

[19] Interview with L.K. Advani, New Delhi, January 27, 1995.
[20] Interview with Uma Bharati, New Delhi, December 28, 1995.
[21] Interview with Govind Acharya, April 9, 1991.

and ethnic groups continue to mobilize identity-based movements, Hindu nationalism is likely to follow suit.

The literature on relations between political parties and social movements generally concurs that movements are most likely to influence the electoral process, exercise pressure on authorities, and acquire national significance when they form alliances with parties. However, such alliances tend to deradicalize movements (Offe 1985; Hellman 1994; Basu 1992). There is ample evidence that in the case of Hindu nationalism, the party has triumphed over the movement and correspondingly moderation prevails over militancy. At their December 1999 national executive meeting in Chennai, BJP leaders expressed their desire to transform the BJP into a right-of-center party. "India has reached a coalition era and the need is to convert coalitions into a positive force for change," argued BJP general secretary Narendra Mody.[22] The BJP's 1999 electoral campaign accorded prominence to Atul Behari Vajpayee and promised him latitude in reorienting the party. Hardliners have temporarily backed off from their attempt to deny Kashmir its special constitutional status. "Once normalcy is restored and avenues opened for tourism and economic packages, the Article [370] would become a dead letter," claimed party vice president Jana Krishnamurthy, the most likely successor to Kusabau Thakre as party president.[23]

The struggle between party and movement is being played out most dramatically in Gujarat, where the national party has been trying to rein in the more militant state leadership, with notable success. The national leadership has been pressuring a Gujarat state legislative assembly member to withdraw the controversial Gujarat Freedom of Religion Bill (1999), which provides for stringent punishment and trial by special courts when religious conversions which employ force or allurement are found to occur.[24] An even more important issue concerns the Gujarat government's desire to allow government employees to become RSS members. In January 2000 Advani delivered a fiery speech in which he argued that there was no constitutional provision for the center to intervene in the decisions of another state. It was rumored that the RSS had made the question a litmus test of the BJP's relationship with it. However, following a sustained protest by Congress and members of his own coalition two months later, Vajpayee forced the Gujarat government to reimpose the ban on state government employees' participation in the RSS. The Sangh Parivar was generally willing to go along with Vajpayee. "If we want to take a leap forward, we may have to retreat a

[22] *India Today*, December 27, 1999.
[23] *India Today*, February 9, 2000.
[24] *Times of India*, March 6, 2000.

little. It's part of our political strategy," said a Gujarat government minister, speaking as a member of the RSS.[25]

However, even in this broadly moderate phase, the movement dimensions of Hindu nationalism continue to surface, as do tensions between movement and party. Given the growing chasm between the priorities of the BJP in power and the unelected Sangh Parivar, the latter often become active around cultural issues. Two years ago the VHP and RSS launched an attack on Deepa Mehta's film *Fire*, which depicts a lesbian relationship. More recently, VHP and RSS workers stole and set fire to Mehta's most recent film *Earth*, claiming that the film's depiction of widows who were forced into prostitution in the 1930s denigrated Indian culture. Emotions ran so high that a Shiv Sena supporter attempted suicide after pleading that film production should be halted. VHP leader Ashok Singhal exhorted Indian youth to come forward and save Indian culture. Heeding pressure from the Sangh Parivar, the BJP-led state government ordered Mehta to stop the filming in UP.

Similarly, in Kanpur on Valentine's Day, the Bajrang Dal went on a rampage against young boys and girls who it claimed were falling prey to decadent Western ways of expressing love. The VHP announced a *rath yatra* from Somnath to Ayodhya, brushing aside the BJP's pleas to maintain the status quo. The RSS publication *The Organiser* lashed out at Advani for saying that the BJP had given up the contentious issues on its agenda. "If the BJP does not need an agenda, why does it need a majority?" it taunted.[26]

The response of senior VHP leaders to the BJP's decision to demolish a temple in Gujarat further attests to ongoing tensions between movement and party. The Ahmedabad Municipal Corporation (AMC) ordered the demolition of the Uttamnagar temple which was encroaching on municipal roads in Maninagar in Gujarat in February 2000. Whether it did so to demonstrate its commitment to a 1998 policy which opposed such encroachment, as government officials claimed, or to curry the favor of minorities, as movement spokespersons claimed, the BJP incurred the VHP's displeasure. One senior VHP leader stated "mandir chhodi ne millennium apnaviyun" – "How can we trust them when they abandoned the mandir and caught on to the millennium?"[27]

A similar struggle has taken place in UP. The UP legislature passed a bill prohibiting the construction of religious sites in February 2000. A month later VHP president Ashok Singhal announced that construction work on the Ram temple at Ayodhya would begin in four to six months.

[25] *Times of India*, March 9, 2000.
[26] *Times of India*, March 13, 2000.
[27] *Times of India*, February 20, 2000.

Contradicting the official BJP stance that the temple was no longer part of the government's agenda, he said that the VHP's stand on the temple issue had not changed. However, the VHP would build the temple at an alternative site, two kilometers from the disputed site. He did not say whether the temple would subsequently be shifted to a different location.

Another potential fault line between movement and party adherents is over the BJP's economic philosophy, for the RSS remains deeply committed to *swadeshi* while the NDA is committed to economic liberalization. The draft Chennai resolution of December 1999 records a shift in the BJP's stance from *swadeshi* to favoring the speeding-up of reforms in insurance, banking, and other areas of the financial sector, rationalization of subsidies, and cutting government expenditure to help restore fiscal discipline.[28] RSS leaders have responded by asking the Bharatiya Mazdoor Sangh to oppose the "anti-*swadeshi*" policies of the Vajpayee government. The Sangh Parivar also organized a Chintan Baithak to oppose the BJP's economic policies.[29] More ominously, the first act of Sudarshan, the new RSS leader, whose relations with Vajpayee are strained, was to ask Vajpayee to discard his panel of economic advisers and replace them with Gandhian economists whose outlook was compatible with *swadeshi*.

In the short run, the party and movement are likely to work out their differences by making concessions to one another. "A government or a political party has to take its own decisions," Advani stated. "Decision-making cannot be from any outside organization but the Sangh Parivar is always concerned about values and ethics in public life. Therefore, it is legitimate for the Sangh to extend its moral authority on the functioning of a government in which there are *swayamsevaks*."[30] But what are the parameters of such moral authority? So far, this has included getting bureaucrats sacked, preventing particular people from occupying ministerial posts, and influencing cultural and economic policies. The BJP cannot cut its ties to the Sangh Parivar, for it remains dependent on the mobilizing skills of the 4,000 RSS full-timers and the 40,000 *shakhas*. Hence displeasing the RSS has a direct impact on electoral success.

More difficult to gauge, however, is the long-term impact of Hindu nationalism as a social movement. Discourses of majoritarian nationalism, which find many articulations, are unlikely to disappear simply because the BJP's formal positions on the uniform civil code or the

[28] *India Today*, December 27, 1999.
[29] *Times of India*, March 13, 2000.
[30] *India Today*, Swapan Dasgupta, February 2000.

Ayodhya temple have changed. The success or failure of parties can be more easily determined than that of movements. For if movements fail when parties succeed, movements also succeed in ways that parties do not contemplate, comprehend or control.

*Part III*

Social demands and democratic deepening

# 8    The struggle for equality: caste in Indian politics

*Myron Weiner*

## Introduction

More than one hundred years of social reform movements, public pronouncements by political leaders, constitutional declarations, and legislation have undermined the ideological basis of caste in India. No political parties, and no political leaders, no intellectuals support the idea that caste is part of a natural moral order based upon hierarchy and sustained by endogamous consanguinity and rules of commensuality, that caste is occupationally linked and hereditary, that each caste (*jati*) embodies its own code for conduct (*dharma*), and that low-caste membership is the consequence of transgressions in one's previous life. There is no public opposition to the preamble to the constitution of India which calls for "equality of status and of opportunity" or to the constitutional provisions that prohibit discrimination on grounds of religion, race, caste, sex, or place of birth and call for equality of opportunity for all citizens in matters relating to employment or appointment to any office. Indian scholars and social reformers have argued that there is a long history of opposition to the ideology of caste both within and outside the Hindu tradition (Rao 1989: 28). Long before colonial rule, it is said, Buddhism and *Virasaivism* frontally attacked Brahminical supremacy,[1] while the *bhakti* devotional movements undermined the Brahminical emphasis on scriptures, knowledge,

---

Editor's note: Myron Weiner died in 1999, shortly after completing this essay. While other essays in this volume were updated in early 2000, this essay is being published without any change.

[1] Not all Buddhist scholars regard Buddha as a social reformer opposed to caste. The distinguished scholar of Buddhism, Richard Gombrich, writes that Buddha's "concern was to reform individuals and help them to leave society forever, not to reform the world. Life in the world he regarded as suffering, and the problem to which he offered a solution was the otherwise inevitable rebirth into the world. Though it could well be argued that the Buddha made life in the world more worth living, that surely was an unintended consequence of his teaching . . . He never preached against social inequality, only declared its irrelevance to salvation. He neither tried to abolish the caste system nor to do away with slavery" (Gombrich 1988: 30).

and ritual as the only means to salvation. Throughout the nineteenth and the early part of the twentieth centuries religious reform movements not only sought to undermine Brahminism but attacked the ideological foundation of caste. Opposition to caste came from both the highest and the lowest castes. In the nineteenth century the Brahmo Samaj, founded by a Bengali Brahmin, Ram Mohan Roy, rejected caste and the concept of transmigration. In the 1920s a non-Brahmin, anti-Brahmin, anticaste movement, known as the Self-Respect movement (later, the Justice Party), emerged as a major political force in South India. The scheduled caste leader, B.R. Ambedkar, created the Scheduled Caste Federation (later, the Republican Party) which called for the removal of barriers and greater economic and political opportunities for the untouchables. India's nationalist leaders of all political persuasions opposed the caste system and called for the creation of a more egalitarian social order. Even those who defended Hinduism from its Western Christian critics, such as Dayanand Sarasvati the founder of the Arya Samaj in 1875 who called for a return to the Vedas including the belief in the consequence of former deeds (*karma*) and transmigration, did not support caste.

There were some orthodox movements, such as the Sanatan Dharma Sabha and Ram Rajya Parishad, but these had few supporters. Ram Rajya Parishad, founded by Swami Karapatri in 1948, issued an election manifesto in India's first national parliamentary elections in 1952 promising to provide untouchables with "high posts" in the management of the sanitation departments and leather and hides trades – traditional occupations for outcaste Hindus – and called for a return to the "blessed days of Lord Rama's reign," but the party was ignored by the English-language press and the intelligentsia. Though it won two million votes (mostly in Madhya Bharat and in Rajasthan), it subsequently disappeared as an organization (Weiner 1957: 174). The pre-independence Hindu nationalists who wrote of "Hindu rashtra" and "Hindutva" – Madhav Golwalker, Veer D. Savarkar, Keshev Hedgewar, founders and leaders of the Rashtriya Swayamsevak Sangh – did not support the caste system, nor does the contemporary Hindu nationalist party, the Bharatiya Janata Party.

Perhaps no other major society in recent history has known inequalities so gross, so long preserved, or so ideologically well entrenched. In the traditional civilizations of Islam and China, the ideal if not always the practice of equality had an honorable and often commanding place in the culture. But in India the notion that men should remain in the same occupation and station of life as their forefathers was enshrined in religious precepts and social custom. While life was not as immobile as theory prescribed, and from time to time revolts against the dominance of Brahmins and other high castes broke out, the idea of social equality never became as widespread in Hinduism as it did in other great traditions. It was not simply that India has had gross inequalities in material standards, but more profoundly, social relations were marked by indignities: the kissing of one's feet by a beggar and supplicant for a job, the outstretched hands of the groveling poor, the stooped backs of low-caste sweepers.

The principle of equality implied a revolutionary transformation in India. The nationalist elite that took power in 1947 wrote a constitution that contained the full panoply of democratic institutions – parliament and legislatures, elections, universal suffrage, freedom of assembly, freedom of the press, legal rights – all based on the principle of equal political rights. Equality was to be achieved in part through democratic institutions and procedures, particularly universal suffrage without a literacy requirement, equality before the law, legislation banning discrimination, and through the establishment of a system of reservations that would guarantee representation to members of scheduled castes and tribes. Equality was also to be achieved through socialist planning, broadly understood as an activist state that would do what the elite believed the market could not do in a developing country – accelerate investment and growth that would ultimately benefit all social classes. Equality of opportunity, they said, would come through universal and compulsory elementary education and an expanded system of higher education. The nationalist elite did not promise a classless society, but they did offer the promise of a casteless society in which social status would not be based upon hereditary social rankings and individuals would not be denied opportunities because of their birth.

### The rise of caste politics

The revolutionary transformation did not of course take place. Caste as an ideology may be (almost, but not quite) moribund, but as a lived-in social reality it is very much alive. The demise of orthodoxy, right beliefs, has not meant the demise of orthopraxy, right practice. Castes remain endogamous.[2] Lower castes, especially members of scheduled castes, remain badly treated by those of higher castes. But the gap between beliefs and practices is the source of tension and change. The lower castes no longer accept their position in the social hierarchy, no longer assume that their lower economic status and the lack of respect from members of the higher castes are a "given" in their social existence.

[2] In a national survey 72 percent said they would not allow their son or daughter to marry someone from another caste. *India Today International*, August 18, 1997: 34.

But the movement for change is not a struggle to end caste; it is to use caste as an instrument for social change. Caste is not disappearing, nor is "casteism" – the political use of caste – for what is emerging in India is a social and political system which institutionalizes and transforms but does not abolish caste. Thirty-five years ago India's distinguished anthropologist, M.N. Srinivas, presciently wrote that "caste is so tacitly and so completely accepted by all, including those who are most vocal in condemning it, that it is everywhere the unit of social action" (1962: 41).

This paper will address the following questions: (1) To what extent, and why, have the lower castes become incorporated into the political system and significantly increased their political power? (2) How and why has caste conflict intensified, and what is the relationship between caste identities and other identities, including class? (3) Why has the increase in political power of the backward castes and Dalits not resulted in policies and programs to significantly narrow the vast gulf in income, wealth, and economic opportunities that divide classes in India? (4) How has the growth of casteism in politics affected the distribution of power between the central and state governments? In a concluding section we shall speculate as to the future role of caste in Indian politics.

## Political cooptation

The political elite which assumed power in 1947 was drawn from the upper castes: disproportionately Brahmins, Rajputs, Kayasthas, Bhumi-hars, Vaishyas, and other "forward castes." Members of these castes were in every respect privileged. They dominated the colleges and universities, the senior civil services in the state and central governments, and the higher ranks of the military and the police. The key institutions that shaped political power, social status, and economic privilege in India – the nationalist movement, the educational system, the bureau-cracy, and the system of land ownership – were largely in their hands. The senior leaders of all of India's political parties – even those on the left – were recruited from the higher castes, were often educated abroad, and with few exceptions came from families that were well placed.

Several factors mitigated against the perpetuation of political power by the higher castes. One critical factor was the mobilization of the lower castes by the Indian National Congress. Before independence the British warned that independence would mean the subordination of the lower and middle castes to the upper castes who dominated the nationalist movement. E.V. Ramaswami Naicker, leader of the non-Brahmin movement in Madras, and B.R. Ambedkar, national leader of the scheduled castes, were hostile to the nationalists whom they regarded as representing the interests of the upper castes. From the early 1920s onward, Congress set out to win the support of all social strata. The Congress leadership was predominantly high caste, but by the late 1930s many of the presidents of the district and *taluka* Congress committees were drawn from the lower and middle castes. By the 1950s many of these individuals moved into positions of political power in the state governments. In Tamil Nadu, for example, the Brahmin leadership was replaced by Nadars and other lower castes; in Andhra by Reddis and Kammas; in Maharashtra by Marathas. In India's first parliamentary elections in 1951–2, three opposition parties sought support from the lower castes – the Peasants' and Workers' Party in Bombay, the Dravida Kazhagam (DK) in Madras, and the Scheduled Caste Federation – but Congress defeated all three by a strategy of incorporating elites from their would-be supporters.

The capacity of the Congress Party to incorporate members of the middle castes and the scheduled castes – much less so for the other backward castes – was strengthened by intra-party factionalism and rivalries among members of the upper castes. As party leaders from the upper castes competed with one another for positions within the party and for seats in parliament and the legislative assemblies, they set out to broaden their own base by recruiting new members. The result of intraparty factionalism, as well as competition between political parties, was to induce party leaders to mobilize caste leaders at the local level and to create vote banks (Brass 1984–1985; Rudolph and Rudolph 1967). These recruitment efforts brought into the elite structure social groups that were previously excluded from the political process.

The process was a slow one and not uniform throughout India. In UP, for example, the upper-caste Congress leadership won the support of the scheduled castes and the Muslims, but failed to attract the middle castes – notably the Jats – or the backward caste peasantry. Congress was not alone in seeking to mobilize supporters along caste lines. In North India the Praja Socialist Party, following the lead of their strategist and leading theoretician, Ram Manohar Lohia, set out to mobilize the backward castes, while Charan Singh, a Jat, a former Congressman, and an articulate spokesman for the peasant proprietor class, brought large numbers of members of the middle and backward castes into his political party, the Bharatiya Kranti Dal (BKD).

In both UP and Bihar, the opposition parties proved to be particularly skillful in undermining the electoral strength of the Congress Party by building a coalition of the middle and the lower castes, then pulling in large numbers of Muslims alarmed by the growth of the Bharatiya Janata Party. In both states, non-Brahmin, non-upper-caste elites took power, first the Jats, then the Yadavs, and by the latter part of the 1990s, UP had a Dalit chief minister. By the 1990s two new lower-caste political parties, the Samajwadi Party and the Bahujan Samaj Party, were part of the governing coalitions in UP and Bihar (Duncan 1997).

In South India the mobilization of the non-Brahmin castes was earlier than in the north. The story of the rise of the non-Brahmin castes has been told in detail elsewhere (Manor 1989; Washbrook 1989). In neither Karnataka nor in Tamil Nadu were the non-Brahmin movements seeking radical change, but rather aimed to gain greater power in administration and in elected local bodies and state legislatures. In Karnataka the Kaligas and Lingayats became the political base of the ruling Congress Party. Devraj Urs, the paramount Congress leader in Karnataka in the 1970s, broadened the social base of the party by appealing to the more disadvantaged backward castes and scheduled castes.[3] In Tamil Nadu the Dravidian movement was committed to the destruction of the caste system but, in practice, as Washbrook (1989: 207) noted, it used caste as a means of political mobilization and ultimately increased the political importance of caste. Though Congress initially succeeded in gaining the support of non-Brahmin elites, the Dravida Munnetra Kazhagam (DMK), an offshoot of the Dravida Kazhagam, was ultimately able to win control of the state, largely by transforming its anti-Brahmin ideology into an antinorthern Tamil nationalism, a strategy which could be adopted by a regionally based political party but which was obviously not possible for the nationally oriented Congress Party in Tamil Nadu.

Even as the upper-caste leaders of Congress created caste vote banks they spoke out against "casteism." Many Congress leaders imagined an India free from the rancor of communal identities, caste politics, and linguistic fervor, characterized by Nehru as "fissiparous" tendencies. But the democratic system created an incentive for political mobilization along the lines of caste, religion, and language. Indian politics became the arena within which group identities were sharpened, and individuals sought material benefits through group membership. Factions and parties were often based upon these identities, and leaders vied with one another by appealing to these "fissiparous" tendencies. To many educated Indians this has been an unhappy outcome of the democratic process. However, India's messy identity politics proved to be more effective at holding the country together than has been the case in many

---

[3] The Mandal Commission reported that by the mid-1970s 48 percent of all government jobs in Karnataka were reserved for other backward classes (OBCs), in addition to 18 percent for scheduled castes and tribes. In Tamil Nadu the figures were 50 percent and 18 percent respectively (Government of India 1980: 61).

other multiethnic countries, in large part because the competitive democratic system provided mechanisms for the incorporation of groups and elites that had previously been excluded from political power.

### Political mobilization

A second factor in the rising political consciousness and organization of the lower castes was, as noted earlier, the widespread rejection of the ideological foundations of India's hierarchical social order. Once caste lost its moral legitimacy the upper castes no longer had the moral authority and the political will to stand in the way of lower castes who sought greater political power, access to education, and social respect. The deconstruction of the ideology underlying caste politicized the scheduled castes and the other backward castes. With the erosion of the moral basis of caste, the self-imposed barrier to protest by the lower castes, that is, their acceptance of their place in the hierarchy, was also eroded. Some middle and lower castes sought equality with the upper castes through the process of Sanskritization, that is, by emulating the orthopraxy of the higher castes, but, paradoxically, at the same time proclaimed their status as backward castes and demanded greater political power. Activists among the scheduled castes called themselves Dalits, literally "oppressed" or "ground down." They rejected what they regarded as Mahatma Gandhi's paternalistic call for the abolition of untouchability but supported the *varna* system (*varnashram*), and called instead for the mobilization from below of the untouchables. Many Dalits followed Babaseheb Ambedkar's call to leave the Hindu fold and became Buddhists (Zelliot 1991). In the mid-1970s the Dalits launched a series of political campaigns aimed at improving their economic and social status. In 1977 scheduled caste students demanded that Marathwada University in Maharashtra be renamed in honor of Ambedkar, leading to riots by upper-caste students. Two decades later, in mid-1997, Dalits rioted in Mumbai when a statue of Ambedkar was desecrated with a garland of shoes placed around his neck. In 1977, in Belchi, Bihar landlords attacked and killed an untouchable caste leader and burned eight agricultural laborers to death for their campaign for land reform. In Gujarat, caste warfare erupted in 1981 over the reservation of places in medical schools for the scheduled castes. In 1982 the public conversion of a thousand untouchables to Islam in Meenakshipuram district in Tamil Nadu led to a demand by Hindu nationalists that conversions be banned. In the 1989 parliamentary elections, the newly formed Bahujan Samaj Party (BSP), under the Dalit leader, Kanshi Ram, built a coalition of "oppressed" groups, Muslims, scheduled castes, and other backward castes. In 1995 the BSP joined with other parties to form a government in UP, with a Dalit woman, Mayawati, as chief minister. Her tenure was short, but in 1997 Mayawati returned as chief minister in an unusual (and also short-lived) coalition with the Hindu nationalist Bharatiya Janata Party.

A half-century after independence, the chief ministers of most of India's states were non-Brahmins, some from the middle castes, but many drawn from the backward castes. The chief minister of UP was a scheduled caste woman. Members of the Yadav, Kurmi, and other OBCs were prominent figures in the politics of UP and Bihar, India's most populous states. In August 1997, a half-century after independence, India elected K.R. Narayanan, a member of a scheduled caste, as the country's president.

### Caste reservations

A third factor that facilitated the rise to political power of the lower castes was the Indian system of affirmative action known as reservations. The system of reservations was initially put in place by the British over the objection of the nationalist movement, but in time it was embraced by Congress and by virtually all political parties in India. The pre-independence nationalist leadership supported the liberal notion of one man, one vote and no representation along communal lines and opposed the British proposal for communal electorates under which Muslims, Christians, and Sikhs could only vote for candidates of their own community. Congress nationalists, led by Gokhale, ultimately agreed to separate electorates for Muslims, but balked when the British sought to create separate electorates for the scheduled castes. Gandhi was particularly adamant in his opposition and began a threatened death fast that ended in the "Poona Pact" of 1932 which provided for proportional representation for scheduled castes, but not separate electorates. The reservation provision was subsequently incorporated into the Indian constitution, along with a constitutional commitment to ensure more adequate representation of the scheduled castes in government service, though no quota was established (Galanter 1983).

There is a tension between, on the one hand, the goal of a casteless society in which the individual is the unit of public policy and, on the other, the concept of reservations for scheduled castes and tribes with the group as the unit of public policy. This tension is embodied in the Indian constitution. According to article 15, "the state shall not discriminate against any citizens on grounds only of religion, race, caste, sex or place of birth," but article 15(4) modifies article 15 by asserting that "nothing in this article . . . shall prevent the state from making any special provision for the advancement of any socially and educationally backward classes of citizens or for the scheduled castes and the scheduled tribes." Thus, the constitution simultaneously embodies two conflicting notions of equality, one based on individual rights, the other on group rights. Other provisions of the constitution go beyond *enabling* the government to give preferences to specified classes of citizens but *require* that the government give preferences. Article 335 provides for reservations of jobs for scheduled castes and scheduled tribes in the administrative services while other constitutional provisions provide for reservations in parliament and the state assemblies. The provision of other "backward classes" referred to in article 15(4) was not amplified, leaving open two questions: who are the other backward classes and what special provisions or reservations should they be given?

There was a consensus that two groups were so disadvantaged that they ought to be beneficiaries of a system of affirmative action. One was the scheduled castes, comprising about 15.7 percent of the population. The other was the scheduled tribes, 7.7 percent of the population. There are about 400 communities classified by the government as tribes, varying in size, language, social characteristics, and traditional modes of livelihood. They generally live in isolated high regions and in forest areas in the interior of the country or on the frontiers. Tribes were regarded as disadvantaged because they were generally isolated and their isolation was associated with a backward technology and relatively unstratified social structure. The scheduled castes, sometimes called ex-untouchables, harijans, or now Dalits, were disadvantaged because of the long history of discrimination, socially, economically, and politically. Unlike the tribal communities they are found in virtually every part of the country and do not have any distinctive languages. Traditionally they occupied the lowest position in the economic hierarchy, were denied access to many amenities of civil life, bore the stigma of pollution, and were often relegated to settlements outside the villages. Both the scheduled castes and scheduled tribes were given seats in parliament and other elected bodies in proportion to their population and provision was also made for quotas for admission into schools, colleges, and medical and engineering schools and for employment in government services. By and large these provisions were acceptable to most Indians and they were not politically contested.

Though the Indian constitution also contained a provision that special benefits could also be provided to other backward communities, it did not specify who these other communities were or what the benefits might be. The other backward classes (OBCs) or, as they were sometimes designated, the socially and educationally backward classes (SEBCs), were conceived basically in terms of caste. There were various attempts to make a list of OBCs, but before 1979 no such list was prepared, in part because there was a controversy over whether caste membership or the economic standing of the individual should be the basis for determining backwardness. It is also impossible to give population figures for the OBCs because, with the exception of the scheduled castes, caste has not been enumerated in the census since 1931. According to most estimates, the OBCs constitute about half of the Indian population, so that along with the scheduled castes and tribes they form about three-quarters of the country's population. The OBCs are highly internally differentiated in terms of their income, occupation, and education, and for this reason many who supported reservations for the scheduled castes and tribes opposed giving benefits to those who belong to the OBCs.

The reservation provisions were not without controversy. India's left intellectuals and left parties were not advocates of caste-based policies. They argued instead that a more egalitarian social order could be built through property redistribution and the expansion of the public sector. Land reform, they argued, was the key to equality, since caste was sustained by unequal property relations which permitted the upper castes to maintain their social, political, and economic dominance. Some Marxist theorists argued that caste and ethnic identities were epiphenomena created by the ruling classes to prevent the rise of class consciousness. This false consciousness could be overcome by fundamental structural changes in the economic order, and through the efforts of the left to instruct the masses as to what constituted their class interests. The caste system could be smashed, not through an attack against orthodoxy, or ameliorative measures such as reservations, but through changing the mode of production.

The postindependence government was committed to reservations. The government set a quota for scheduled castes and scheduled tribes for all government appointments, including representation in the public sector. Quotas were established for admission into elite educational institutions such as medical schools and the national universities. A national commission was appointed to consider whether reservations should be granted to the "other backward classes." Though the commission recommended reservations in government service and education, the chairman, Kaka Kalelkar, declared his opposition and the recommendations were not acted upon. None the less, several state governments – most notably Karnataka – did extend reservations to other backward classes.

In 1979 the government of India appointed another commission, known after its chairman as the Mandal Commission, to consider the proposal for extending reservations to the OBCs. The Mandal Commission, like its predecessor, defined backward classes in caste rather than class terms, enumerating specific castes as "backward" by virtue of their social as well as their economic status. Given the material benefits from reservations, there was considerable lobbying to be classified as backward since, unlike the socially defined and widely accepted category of untouchables, there was no agreement as to which castes were backward. The commission drew up a list of some 400 castes they classified as "backward," most of whom belonged to the laboring or *shudra varna*. The principles implicitly put forth by the Mandal Commission and previous commissions that recommended reservations for the backward classes were: (1) that caste membership rather than individual class characteristics should determine the beneficiaries; (2) low social ranking in the caste system rather than average per capita income or other economic criteria should be the principal consideration for inclusion on the OBC list; (3) religious and linguistic groups, no matter what their economic condition, should not qualify for inclusion in the backward category; and (4) reservations should be in the public sector, including college admissions, government employment, and, for the scheduled castes and tribes, seats in legislative bodies.

The central premise of the Mandal Commission was that India should proceed from an ideology that rested upon hereditary hierarchy to an ideology that emphasized equality of outcomes – not equality of opportunity. "If a tree is to be judged by its fruits," wrote the commission, "equality of results is obviously the most reliable test of our aspirations and efforts to achieve a just and equitable order. A formidable task under any circumstances, it becomes particularly so in a society which has remained segmented in a finely graded caste hierarchy for centuries" (Government of India 1980).

Though the government approved the recommendations of the Mandal Commission, no action was taken at the time and reservations at the national level remained limited to the scheduled castes and tribes. The central government's policy continued to be one of balancing a commitment to equal rights for all (article 15) with special benefits to some (article 15(4)).

In August 1990, Prime Minister V.P. Singh, then the leader of a fragile coalition non-Congress government in need of solidifying his electoral base, announced that 27 percent of central government positions would be set aside for the other backward classes in addition to the 22 percent set aside for scheduled castes and tribes. The 400 castes enumerated in the Mandal Commission report were to be given reservations. The annual number of jobs in government service to be set aside was small – estimated at 50,000 annually – but the government's announcement triggered large-scale violence across northern India, especially in the universities. Though many of the opponents of reservations did so because they were excluded, there was also a growing sense that a moral injustice was being committed, that equality of opportunity was being eroded, that appointments would be made on the basis of membership in a caste irrespective of whether the individual was economically or socially handicapped, and that the government had extended the benefits for political reasons.

Supporters of reservations argued that since political power resided in India's administrative system it was important that OBCs be given a greater share of administrative positions. The widely held view was that economic benefits were derived from political power; the demand, therefore, was for reservations in the administrative services, not in the private sector, nor for that matter in the military or appointments in colleges and universities. The issue was not simply jobs, but administrative and political power.

Though a comparison between the old Soviet nomenklatura and India's political and administrative elites would not be apt given the openness of India's system of elite recruitment, it should be noted that those who exercise political power in India belong to a highly privileged class. Government officials are given virtually rent-free housing, low-interest loans, privileged access for their children to special government schools, priority seats on planes and trains, the private use of government vehicles, government-financed medical care, and good pensions. In the era of state regulation of the economy officials controlled the allocation of foreign exchange, the distribution of a wide variety of commodities including steel, coal, paper, and fertilizers, and determined what could or could not be imported. There was an elaborate system of patronage jointly controlled by elected politicians and officials that determined who got electric power, tube wells, schools, district colleges, railway stations, irrigation works, roads, bus lines, health centers, and jobs in government. Voters turned to politicians when they needed admission into a government hospital, or admission for their children into a local college. In time the system of patronage grew into what is euphemistically known as "rent-seeking" with the business community paying increasingly larger sums to corrupt government officials and elected politicians. It is no wonder that tens of thousands of politicians sought to get elected to state assemblies and to the national parliament and why jobs in the administrative services were coveted even when the pay scales failed to keep up with inflation and were not commensurate with the pay in the private sector. Ambitious members of the lower castes saw the material benefits of holding office and serving in adminis-tration.[4] If politicians and officials from the higher castes were on the take, why not members of the lower castes?[5] To a very considerable extent the campaign by V.P. Singh and other politicians to increase the number of OBCs in administration and in elected bodies was an offer to share the spoils of office, not a promise of social justice for the poor.

The government's decision to extend reservations from the scheduled castes and tribes to the other backward classes led some supporters of reservations for scheduled castes and tribes to question the entire system of reservations. Opponents of reservations defined the issue as individual merit and achievement versus benefits based upon group membership. Anything less than merit and achievement was morally wrong, they argued, and would, moreover, lead to a deterioration of the public services. Supporters of reservations defined the issue as a matter of social justice for those who were victims of the Brahmin-dominated caste system. Even the left, once advocates of abolishing caste, now regarded the demand by the OBCs for reservations as part of the struggle against oppression and for shifting India's social structure away from hierarchy toward a system of plurality (Kothari 1997: 443).

Though the country was divided, none of the major political parties openly opposed V.P. Singh's reservations policy. It was widely under-stood, however, that the leaders and members of the Bharatiya Janata Party regarded caste reservations for the OBCs as a policy that divided Hindu society and weakened it against its presumed Muslim adversaries. Whether the subsequent Hindu nationalist militancy of the BJP, the RSS, and the Vishva Hindu Parishad in calling for the demolition of the Ayodhya mosque was a political response to V.P. Singh is a matter of conjecture, but political lines were quickly drawn between advocates of "mandal" (community organizations) and advocates of "mandir" (temples).

So many groups within the electorate now benefit from reservations that a policy reversal is politically unlikely. As I have argued elsewhere (1983), there is a political logic to preferential policies that shapes subsequent policy debates and political responses. Once the principle was established that preferences would be given to groups that are

---

[4] As part of the patronage system each of the 540 members of parliament are also allocated Rs. 10 million annually to be used as a discretionary development expenditure in their constituency.

[5] One defense for Laloo Prasad Yadav, chief minister of Bihar arrested on charges of corruption, is that he behaved no differently than high-caste politicians and, therefore, his arrest was an attack against the rising power of the lower castes.

"backward" or "oppressed," the issue then became who qualifies. There are now demands that reservations be extended to women – they already have reservations in local government – and to Muslims. A second question is what should be reserved. Seats to all elected bodies? Jobs in the administrative services? Admissions into engineering and medical schools? Jobs in the public sector? The private sector and the military have been excluded from the reservation system, but there are already demands that both be included. A related question is over which categories of employment in government service should be by quota and whether there should be a quota for promotions as well as for initial appointments. Once a system of group preferences was introduced, leaders of political parties regarded support for preferences as a strategy for winning political support.

By some estimates as many as 75 percent of the male population of India have been granted preferences and the percentage will increase if preferences are extended to all women and to Muslims. The demand by Muslims for reservations and support for their demand from parties eager to win Muslim votes seems likely to be particularly divisive given the emotional baggage associated with the British policy of communal electorates. The proposal to extend reservations to women is also vexing since it raises questions about whether each existing reservations category should have its own quota for women and whether women from the middle and upper castes should be included. Moreover, since India's supreme court has limited reservations to 49 percent of government jobs and university admissions an increase in the number of beneficiaries reduces the benefits for each of the included groups.

Some public figures have proposed that benefits not be given to what they call the "creamy layers." Proponents of a means test argue that the scheduled castes and the OBCs are producing a middle class whose members should not be given preference over the less-educated and poorer members of the middle and upper castes, but a means test is opposed by OBC and scheduled caste legislators and their supporters.

To recapitulate, the political mobilization of the lower castes, their increasing incorporation into the Indian political system, and their rising political power can be attributed to the demise in the ideological legitimacy of caste among the upper castes; the inclusive character of the Indian National Congress as a mass-based political movement; the intrafactional conflicts within the postindependence Congress; the Congress strategy of building vote banks among the scheduled castes and tribes, the Muslims, and the middle and upper castes; the counter-strategy of the non-Congress opposition parties to win support among the other backward castes and to build their own caste-based alliances;

the system of reservations which provided opportunities for access to higher education, administration, and elected bodies to members of the scheduled castes and tribes; and finally the extension of reservations to hundreds of other backward castes.

The increasing political clout of the lower castes should also be seen in the context of an increase in social mobility. The abolition of the zamindari system and land redistribution plus the introduction of the Green Revolution improved the economic position of many lower-caste tenants who gained title to land; the expansion of the system of mass education, though very limited, along with the system of reservations, enabled some individuals to obtain employment which brought them into the middle class. But, as we shall show later, the low public investment in primary and secondary schools, the country's slow economic growth, and the limited expansion of employment opportunities have left large sections of the OBCs, the Dalits, and the tribals among the poorest in Indian society, notwithstanding their rising political power.

### Caste, class, and other identities

The central political struggles in India continue to be over ethnicity and nationalism. For much of this century Indian political passions have centered around the question of who we are, what our collective identities are, and how we establish collective self-esteem. In the broadest sense, the struggles for status by castes, tribes, and linguistic and religious communities are a powerful contemporary form of the quest for equality. Both Marxists and liberals mistakenly believed that the drive for equality could be satisfied solely through the struggle of social classes or through the social mobility efforts of individuals, but in India, as in so many other places in the world, the struggle for equality has been linked with ethnic assertiveness and with new social constructs based upon language, religion, tribe, and caste.

The relationship between caste and class and between both categories and other group identities is a complex one in India's highly stratified and pluralist social system. As all observers of India have noted, Indians have cross-cutting, multiple identities. A member of the Yadav caste may be a landlord, a cultivating peasant proprietor, a tenant, or an agricultural laborer. An untouchable may be Hindu, Christian, Buddhist, Sikh, or Muslim. *Jati* is usually bounded by linguistic region, so castes generally share a linguistic and regional identity. Which identity is politically salient can vary over time. In the 1950s and 1960s, for example, supporters of the linguistic reorganization of states attempted to build regional identities and to minimize caste identities. In the early

1970s Prime Minister Indira Gandhi won popular support and attracted the left with a campaign to eliminate poverty and to emphasize class-based issues. And in the 1990s Hindu nationalists attempted to forge a national identity based on Hindu culture and to play down caste and regional identities.

Politicians pick and choose which identity they want to use as the basis for political and social mobilization. Whichever identity they emphasize, the rhetoric is invariably one of "social justice" and equality. Those who emphasize linguistic identity and other territorially based identities have demanded statehood if it had not already been granted, and called for a more equitable distribution of benefits between the states and the center and among the states. Hindu nationalists have been more concerned with the inequalities between India and the world than the inequalities within India. They believe that national power rests upon a strong military, nuclear weapons, a more resurgent and unified India, a single nationality based upon Hindu culture that overrides the divisiveness of caste, language, and religion and, above all, a strong central government. The left, broadly and loosely defined, continues to argue for the importance of asset redistribution, land reform, a large public sector, control over private capital, and for state control over prices and the distribution of essential commodities.

Which identities are politically salient also varies greatly from one part of India to another. Caste and Hindu nationalism are now particularly salient in the north; linguistic and regional identities loom large in Assam and the smaller states of the northeast; the left has made class a politically salient identity in West Bengal and Kerala. But, as we have noted, at other times caste politics has been a more central issue in Tamil Nadu and caste and Hindu nationalism are now the dominant political conflicts in Maharashtra, a state that was once a bastion for linguistic regionalism. One of the more interesting theoretical issues is what accounts for the changing salience of these different identities, and why identity-based violent conflict is in some places and not others, and at one time and not another.

All the group identity-based movements demand greater equality, but they each have a different conception of what it is that needs to be equalized. For caste-based movements, it is their place in the social hierarchy. Though caste leaders often employ a rhetoric that seems similar to a class-based rhetoric, caste and class are not the same. It might be otherwise if all the members of the same caste engaged in the same traditional occupation, and there were little or no differences in property ownership, education, wealth, and income. But the reality is that castes have become economically more differentiated. Many members of castes classified as OBCs have become economically better off as a consequence of the zamindari abolition legislation which transferred property ownership from the zamindars to peasant proprietors in much of northern India. The Green Revolution also differentially benefited members of the same castes since those with land gained from the introduction of high-yielding varieties and subsidized fertilizers, water, and electricity, while agricultural laborers belonging to the same castes did not reap these benefits. Clashes between untouchables demanding higher wages and OBC cultivators are a regular feature of rural life in Bihar and eastern UP and incidents of rape, the burning of houses, and attacks against untouchable wedding processions have become widespread. But class differences are also developing within the scheduled castes as some individuals reap the benefits of preferential access to education and employment in government service. None the less, caste solidarity overshadows class differences and, as noted earlier, lower-caste leaders have resisted efforts to means test preferential benefits. Lower-caste political leaders have been particularly effective at creating a loyal following – witness the popular appeal of Laloo Prasad Yadav in Bihar, MGR in Tamil Nadu, Kanshi Ram and Mayawati in UP – by symbolic appeals to caste solidarity and opposition to the forward castes. Violent attacks by the higher castes, the desecration of statues of lower-caste leaders, real or imagined insults, and high-caste opposition to reservations, all help lower-caste political leaders blur intracaste class divisions by appeals to caste solidarity. Caste political leaders argue that by organizing along caste lines the entire community will gain material benefits and social respect. Caste, once an instrument for the maintenance of hierarchy, is, paradoxically, seen as the vehicle for egalitarianism between castes, though not within them.

Some scholars and journalists, both of liberal and Marxist persuasions, continue to regard caste and other ethnic identities and antagonisms as surrogates for more material interests and as anomalies in an increasingly globalizing world. They characterize ethnic identities as "social constructions" and as "imagined communities." Identities and ethnic and caste conflicts are seen principally as the product of political entrepreneurs appealing to group identities to enhance their own quest for political power. To these characterizations some postmodernists add the notion that individual conflicts are turned into group conflicts by "master narratives" that induce individuals to interpret (or misinterpret) conflicts in ways that enlarge them, and that these narratives are often imposed upon events by hegemonic actors who dominate the media or the educational system. Though these concepts have considerable relevance and explanatory power, it is striking that they are not used with respect to class identities which are no less socially constructed, no less imagined, and no less instruments of political entrepreneurs. If the language of imagination is used for the one and not for the other perhaps it is to convey the notion that class rests upon material forces and is rational, while ethnic identities are neither. When the language of imagination is used, ethnogenesis is seen as the product of literary figures, poets, and politicians, while class-consciousness is regarded as the product of the means of production and hence has an objective dimension that ethnicity lacks. Many scholars writing about ethnic identities thus dismiss birth in a linguistic, tribal, religious, or caste community as the basis of identity ("primordialism," they note dismissively), as if these attachments carry no weight unless they are subsequently "constructed."

One can argue that both class and ethnic identities are social constructs or alternatively that they both have their basis in some "objective" reality, but one is hard put to distinguish one from the other in this regard. What we can say is that individuals everywhere have class or ethnic group identities or both, that these identities are often fluid and contested, but they do rest on something "real" or at least measurable and observable (e.g., occupation, income, language, religion), that these identities may or may not generate conflict, but are often the basis for political action, and that people unhappy with their lot may express their discontent by organizing themselves (or being organized by others) along any one of these identities.

Caste has been a far more potent form of social identity and political action in India than class, notwithstanding the history of kisan (agricultural and farming) movements and trade unions. India now has a plethora of caste-based educational institutions, caste associations, and caste-based political parties. Indeed, it is the kisan agitations that have proven to be episodic and less institutionalized than caste movements. Caste-based movements are based not only (if at all) on material demands but on demands for respect from others. They thus have a hard edge to them, for unlike other forms of ethnic identity they cannot be based on pride, but must emphasize their antipathy to those castes that fail to grant them respect and often continue to torment them. Of the three meanings of equality – equality of economic condition, equality of opportunity, and equality of social relations – it is the latter that forms the basis of the emotional ties that give caste movements their social cohesion. Well-educated middle-class members of the scheduled castes and scheduled tribes recount their humiliating experiences at the workplace and in private relationships at the hands of members of the higher castes. Major Dalit agitations have been over the desecration of statues of Ambedkar, the right to hold wedding processions in villages, and atrocities perpetrated against women. The need for self-protection and self-respect are powerful forces behind the mobilization of the lowest castes and tribes in India's ranked and hierarchical social order.

### The lower castes and public policy

A half-century after independence India still remains one of the world's most inegalitarian societies. By some estimates 350 million people – nearly the whole population of India in 1947 – remain below the poverty level. Half the adult population is illiterate. Infant mortality rates are among the highest in Asia (the under-five mortality rate is 142 per thousand, compared with 30 in South Korea, 34 in Thailand, 42 in China, 69 in the Philippines, and 97 in Indonesia) and longevity among the lowest. Morbidity rates are high with a variety of endemic diseases that have disappeared elsewhere in Asia. Plague, malaria, and gastro-intestinal diseases are the product of unsafe water, poor sanitation, and inadequate rural health services. The incidence of child labor is among the highest in the world, with half the children dropping out of school by the fifth grade. Women have significantly higher morbidity and mortality rates than men and greater illiteracy (65 percent for women, 36 percent for men), and the incidence of child labor among young girls is high. Human development conditions are particularly egregious in four northern states, Bihar, Rajasthan, UP and Madhya Pradesh.[6] The UNDP report on the Human Development Index reports that India ranks 134th, behind almost all the countries of the Middle East and behind many African countries with lower per capita incomes.

The incorporation into the political system of backward caste elites and members of the scheduled castes has apparently done little to reduce the enormous social and economic disparities that persist in India's hierarchical and inegalitarian social order. That raises the funda-mental question: if there are now so many OBC and scheduled caste bureaucrats and politicians, why is this not reflected in state policies to promote the well-being of their communities? Why have state govern-

---

[6] In 1991 the female literacy rate in these four states was under 30 percent and as low as 20 percent in Rajasthan. The combined population of the four states was 335 million in a total population of 846 million. Eighty-six million were members of the scheduled castes or tribes or 25.6 percent of the population. The southern states with a long history of lower-caste movements – Andhra, Karnataka, and Tamil Nadu – have higher overall adult literacy rates, but even these are low by Asian standards – 44 percent in Andhra, 56 percent in Karnataka, and 63 percent in Tamil Nadu. The highest literacy rate in India is in the state of Kerala (86 percent). Adult literacy in China (1990) was 73 percent, in Indonesia 77 percent, and in Thailand, the Philippines, Korea, Mongolia, and Sri Lanka, 90 percent or higher.

ments given so little attention to the expansion and improvement of primary education, considering the low literacy level of the scheduled castes and tribes? Why has so little attention been given to the plight of low-caste child laborers and why are child labor laws not enforced? Why has public investment in public health, sanitation, and the provision of safe drinking water remained so inadequate? Why has the increase in political power for members of the lower castes done so little to raise these communities?

Before turning to the question of the distribution of public goods, it is first necessary to note that the persistence of poverty in India is in large part a consequence of the country's poor economic performance. Though rising per capita income is no guarantee that poverty will be eliminated or, for that matter, significantly reduced, a low per capita income assuredly means massive poverty. Until recently, India's growth rate was between 3 and 4 percent per annum, with per capita incomes rising at between 1 and 2 percent yearly. The low economic growth meant that employment did not keep pace with population growth, agricultural wages remained low, and opportunities for social mobility among the lower classes were limited. It also meant that resources for investments in public goods – schools, health services, sanitation, drinking water – expanded slowly. Still, it is important to note that elsewhere low-income, low-growth countries have devoted more of their limited resources to public goods that benefit the lower classes than India has, and that within South Asia itself (in Sri Lanka, and the Indian state of Kerala) state and national governments have been more equity-oriented.

Given the very considerable increase in the number of individuals from the scheduled castes and tribes in the higher ranks of the civil service and the role the bureaucracy has played in the distribution of public goods in India, one might have expected to see a significant rise in public expenditure for services that benefit the lower castes. In Karnataka, for example, the percentage of class I employees – the highest rank in the state civil service – belonging to the scheduled castes rose from only 1.9 percent in 1960 to 12.2 percent in 1986 (Jalal 1993: 104). The Karnataka state government has become increasingly responsive to the growing political power and political mobilization of the Dalits. The then chief minister, Devraj Urs, introduced a variety of schemes to benefit the scheduled castes – housing schemes, nutrition programs for children, free legal aid, scholarships, educational concessions, and more money for the Social Welfare Department (ibid.: 102). However, the administration did little to implement these programs. As one scholar reports, "scheduled caste children continued to drop out before completing their schooling, housing loans did not go to the deserving and the allotment of land to the landless and of credit facilities to the marginal farmers was not implemented."

Though there are differences between the states, even in those where the backward castes have moved into administrative and political offices literacy rates remain low, school attendance is low, and child labor – principally children from the scheduled castes and other backward castes – is widespread. Tamil Nadu and Karnataka, states which witnessed the political rise of the lower castes earlier than those of the north, spend no more of their state budgets (measured in rupees per capita) on primary education than do Gujarat and Maharashtra, while Andhra, dominated by the non-Brahmin Telugu Desam, spends less per capita on primary education than most other states. In UP, a Dalit chief minister invested state resources on constructing statues of Ambedkar, but did little to promote primary education. In Bihar, a Yadav chief minister did little for the lower castes, though he appointed fellow Yadavs into positions in the state civil service. The middle classes within the lower castes promoted their own interests and for the rest there was little more than the psychological benefit promised by the Mandal Commission.

This is not to suggest that there are no policies or programs to improve the position of Dalits. Tamil Nadu has a midday school lunch program. Maharashtra has had a food-for-work program. Kerala has near universal primary education. West Bengal has a number of successful rural development schemes. But, with the exception of Kerala, the efforts of states to provide material benefits for the Dalits remain marginal; more to the point Dalit politicians and bureaucrats and Dalit associations and political parties have had little impact on public policies.

Dalit politicians have sought to create a broader rainbow coalition of subordinate groups – particularly with OBCs and Muslims. In both UP and Bihar there have been political alliances between OBC and Dalit-based political parties, but they are handicapped by conflicts between these groups on the ground. OBC peasant landowners and Dalit agricultural laborers collide over agricultural wages and OBCs engage in atrocities against Dalits over their efforts to change their social status.[7] Indeed, even before the abolition of the zamindari system many Yadav tenants served as *lathaits* (musclemen) for upper-caste landlords (Mitra

---

[7] Efforts to build a rainbow coalition of OBCs, Dalits, and Muslims in UP have also floundered because of the conflicts between the Dalit leaders Mayawati and Kanshi Ram and backward class leaders led by Mulayam Singh Yadav. In UP the Bahujan Samaj Party briefly formed a coalition government with the Bharatiya Janata Party (BJP), a party backed by the upper castes and regarded as anathema by the Muslims.

1997: 16). Precisely because many OBCs have improved their social standing they are in no mood to share their new status with the Dalits.

Have the OBCs fared better? The OBCs are better placed than the scheduled castes and tribes in the central and state bureaucracies and in political positions where they can have a major influence on policies and their implementation. Moreover, it has become a widespread practice for newly appointed OBC cabinet members in state government to transfer members of their own castes to senior positions within their own departments and ministries. In UP and Bihar the Yadavs have also substantially increased their power at the level of district administration. None the less, there is no evidence that either in UP or Bihar the lower-income members of the backward castes have materially benefited from the rising political power of their community.

One explanation is that caste leaders of the OBCs do get what *they* want. Though most members of the backward castes are agricultural laborers, tenants, and small landholders, OBC leaders are drawn heavily from among the better-off owner cultivators. The leading OBC parties in UP, for example, demand higher food grain prices and government subsidies for fertilizers, irrigation, pesticides, and electricity. Their leaders seek reservations for their sons to the universities and for employment in the bureaucracy. The material beneficiaries of OBC mobilization in UP are landowning Yadavs, Kurmis, and Koeris whose interests diverge from those of the agricultural laborers from these communities. By emphasizing the importance of caste political solidarity the richer peasants among the OBCs mobilize the poor sections of their castes to further their own class interests.

One other explanation for the low government expenditure on public goods is that the bureaucrats and politicians who set the course of Indian public investment in the first decades after independence had little interest in programs that would benefit the poor. At first this appears to be an unlikely explanation, given the rhetorical emphasis of planners and politicians on poverty-reduction programs and Prime Minister Indira Gandhi's campaign to end poverty. But the fiscal expenditures tell another story. India's expenditure on education was lower than that of many developing countries and a disproportionate share of the education budget was devoted to higher education and providing grants-in-aid to private schools. The country's elites sent their children to private schools and to the virtually tuition-free colleges and universities, while primary public schools were given few resources, schooling was not made compulsory, and drop-out rates were so high that half the children in state-funded schools failed to complete five standards. Neither the central nor state governments paid attention to the enforcement of the weak child labor laws, nor did state and local authorities put significant resources into delivering healthcare services, drinking water, or improved sanitation facilities in rural areas or in the slums that grew up in every urban conglomeration. The massive subsidies introduced by the government – for fertilizers, electricity, irrigation, petrol – benefited the peasants who owned land and the urban middle classes, not the poor.

The peculiar form of socialism introduced by Nehru and the Congress leadership after independence used the rhetoric of redistribution, but it was largely a statist, antibusiness, antimarket set of policies. For many of India's intellectuals, politicians, and bureaucratic planners socialism promised a noncapitalist model of development, a way of achieving economic growth without the exploitation of capitalism. As in so many newly independent countries, nationalists equated imperialism with capitalism and the market. To understand what socialism meant in the Indian context, one might begin with what Nehru wrote in his widely read book, *Discovery of India*, written during the war when he was in jail, and published in 1946.

Political change there must be, but economic change is equally necessary. That change will have to be in the direction of a democratic planned collectivism . . . A democratic collectivism will not mean an abolition of private property, but it will mean the public ownership of the basic and major industries. It will mean the cooperative or collective control of the land. In India especially it will be necessary to have, in addition to the big industries, cooperatively controlled small and village industries. Such a system of democratic collectivism will need careful and continuous planning and adaptation to the changing needs of the people. The aim should be the expansion of the productive capacity of the nation in every possible way, at the same time absorbing all the labor power of the nation in some activity or other and preventing unemployment. As far as possible there should be freedom to choose one's occupation. An equalization of income will not result from all this, but there will be far more equitable sharing and a progressive tendency towards equalization. In any event, the vast differences that exist today will disappear completely, and class distinctions, which are essentially based on differences in income, will begin to fade out.

Nehru regarded Indian socialism not as a Western import but as an expression of India's traditional culture. He wrote:

Such a change would mean an upsetting of the present-day acquisitive society based primarily on the profit motive. The profit motive may still continue to some extent but it will not be the dominating urge, nor will it have the same scope as it has today. It would be absurd to say that the profit motive does not appeal to the average Indian, but it is nevertheless true that there is no such admiration for it in India as there is in the west. The possessor of money may be envied, but he is not particularly respected or admired. Respect and admiration still go to the man or woman who is considered good and wise, and especially those who sacrifice themselves or what they possess for the public good. The Indian outlook, even of the masses, has never approved of the spirit of acquisitiveness (Nehru 1983: 522–523).

In 1955, at the annual meeting of the Congress Party, Nehru moved what is known as the Avadi resolution committing the party to the principle that "planning should take place with a view to the establishment of a socialistic pattern of society where the principal means of production are under social ownership or control" (Nehru 1983). The socialist goal of collectivist agriculture was aborted by opposition from rural leaders but the Congress government and its planners shaped the strategy of industrial development. Though Mrs. Gandhi, who became prime minister in 1966, declared that the abolition of poverty would be the government's goal, the socialist measures she introduced involved the nationalization of the banks, the grain trade, insurance companies, and coal mining rather than measures which directly benefited the poor. The Monopolies and Restrictive Trade Practices Act was passed, the Monopolies and Restrictive Trade Practices Commission was established, controls were placed on the allocation of cement, steel, coal, and electricity to the private sector, and a lengthy list of other bureaucratic controls were placed over the private sector.

If there was any traditional element in Indian socialism it was the antagonism of the Brahmins and other upper castes toward merchants and traders, and when Nehru wrote that the "Indian outlook . . . has never approved of the spirit of acquisitiveness" he was referring to the Brahminical outlook and its antagonistic view of the commercial castes and money-making. The ideology of caste may thus have had a dual effect on India's strategy of development. On the one hand, the upper castes, who dominated the bureaucracy and government, pursued an industrial policy that was antagonistic to the bania castes and the profit motive, and on the other they pursued an educational policy that undervalued the importance of mass education for the shudras and the scheduled castes. Caste as an ideology is no longer significant among India's educated classes and upper castes, but the mentality of caste may have had a deeper hold on the thinking of policymakers than is readily apparent.

Reservations in education and employment proved to be a low-cost strategy for reducing disparities between castes. They were low-cost because they permitted government to pay little attention to primary and secondary school education. Because limited financial resources were spent on mass education, the pool of qualified untouchables and tribals who could have entered the universities and obtained employment on an equal basis remained small.

The creation of a two-tiered educational system – one that is private, but government-funded, with education in English, largely serving the higher castes, and the other that is entirely government-funded with education in vernacular languages serving the lower castes – is now so well established that socially mobile members of the lower castes aspire to get into the private system. OBCs and Dalits who can afford it (including OBC politicians and bureaucrats) send their children to private, English-medium schools. In the past decade there has been a proliferation of low-cost, fee-paying schools not only in the large cities but in the small towns whose students come from families that are themselves barely literate.[8]

The primary public education system throughout much of northern India serves the Dalits badly, and the rise to power in UP of the Bahujan Samaj Party (BSP), a Dalit-based political party, has thus far done little to raise expenditures on primary schools or to improve their quality. Per capita educational expenditures in UP, Bihar, Rajasthan, and Madhya Pradesh remain below the national average. There has actually been a decline in per capita expenditures on education by all state governments and a decline in the absolute number of teachers in primary schools in the early 1990s (Ramachandra et al. 1997: 41). Changes in the caste composition of state governments has not led to increases in public investment in primary education.

What then do the Dalits seek? Dalit college students have formed their own student associations; Dalits in government have formed their own scheduled caste employee associations; and there are now numerous Dalit welfare associations. At the local level Dalit activists – most of whom, it should be noted, are high school and college graduates – are concerned less with getting benefits from the state and changing public policies than they are in promoting the mobilization of the scheduled castes against upper-caste domination. In Bihar they are often engaged in armed conflict with upper-caste-based armed militia, such as the Ranvir Sena, an upper-caste Bhumihar landlord group fighting against farm laborers. Caste-based private armies in Bihar – organized not only by upper-caste Rajputs and Bhumihars, but by Yadavs and Kurmis – attack Dalits who refuse to work during the peak seasons of planting and harvesting. Both upper castes and the upper strata of the backward castes continue to humiliate the Dalits. Dalit marriage processions are

[8] A nationwide survey by Org-Marg commissioned by *India Today* surprisingly reports that 19 percent of the adult population claim to speak English and 31 percent claim to understand English, one indication of the spread of private schools. The same survey reports that 53 percent answered "no" to the question "Is the Government's policy based on caste justified?" Only 35 percent answered "yes." *India Today International*, August 18, 1997: 31–32.

halted. Dalit women are often sexually harassed. Dalit members of the civil service complain that they are not invited to the social functions organized by their upper-caste colleagues and that they are often treated with disdain as untouchables. The cry for "social justice" is as much a demand for respect and equal treatment in ordinary everyday relationships as it is a demand for economic benefits. The Indian experience supports the hypothesis that in highly ranked social systems those who are regarded as in the lower ranks are principally concerned with ending the indignities they have suffered from those of the higher ranks (Horowitz 1985).

### Caste politics and government formation

No single party has been able to win a majority of seats in India's parliamentary elections since 1989. Neither Congress nor the BJP, the country's two largest parties, can form a national government without support from the smaller parties. Since both parties want to prevent the other from dominating the center, each in turn has supported coalitions of the smaller parties, thereby enabling the United Front of some thirteen parties to form a government. A similar pattern exists in several of the states, though in many states the regional parties have had sufficient popular support to form governments on their own without the support of either Congress or the BJP.

All political parties are aware of the need to build electoral support by appealing to particular castes, tribes, and religious communities. In the early postindependence years Congress drew its electoral support from Muslims, scheduled castes and tribes, and from the higher castes. This electoral coalition provided Congress with a majority of seats in parliament and in most of the state assemblies, though Congress rarely won more than 50 percent of the vote. Jan Sangh, the precursor of the Bharatiya Janata Party, drew its support from members of the upper castes, especially Rajputs and the merchant castes, and from Hindu refugees who had fled Pakistan at Partition, too small a constituency to enable the party to break out of single-digit support. The first major break in the lock that Congress had upon Muslims and the scheduled castes came during the Emergency when Mrs. Gandhi and her son Sanjay eliminated slums in the larger urban settlements and campaigned for male vasectomies, two programs that adversely affected these two communities. In most states the non-Congress parties (except for the Jan Sangh) built their electoral support on the middle and shudra castes, that is the OBCs. The Emergency put these parties in a position to broaden their base by appealing to Muslims and to Dalits.

As Dalits defected from Congress, especially in northern India, many were drawn to the Bahujan Samaj Party (BSP), founded by Kanshi Ram, a Dalit who sought to build a party of the "oppressed." The party did well in the parliamentary elections in UP, jumping from 8.7 percent of the vote in 1991 to 20.6 percent in 1996, with nearly two-thirds of its support (63.4 percent) from the scheduled castes and another 16.8 percent from the non-Yadav OBCs. The party had less success in winning the support of Muslim voters (only 4.7 percent of the BSP vote) or the Yadavs. Seventy-three percent of the Yadavs voted for the United Front, the coalition in the forefront of the demand for OBC reservations (Chandra and Parmar 1997).

With the decline of the Congress Party in the south and the inability of the BJP to break into the south on a sufficiently large scale to give it a parliamentary majority, the struggle for control over the national government has centered on UP and Bihar, the two states with the largest share of parliamentary seats. When the Congress Party failed to win a majority of seats in the parliamentary elections of 1989, a National Front coalition government was formed, led by the Janata Dal leader, V.P. Singh, with support from the BJP. V.P. Singh's efforts to strength his electoral base among the OBCs by promising reservations and his opposition to the campaign by Hindu nationalists for constructing a temple to replace the sixteenth-century mosque at Ayodhya led the BJP to withdraw its support. The assassination of Rajiv Gandhi on the eve of the parliamentary elections in 1991 gave Congress enough of an electoral boost to enable it to emerge as the largest single party and P.V. Narasimha Rao, with support from a few smaller parties, formed a minority government. In 1996, for the third consecutive time, no party emerged with a majority and once again a coalition government was formed of regional, caste, socialist, and left parties, with support from the Congress parliamentary party.

Since neither the BJP nor Congress have been able to win a majority of parliamentary seats, the power of the smaller regional parties has increased in the center, particularly since several of them also control state governments. The BSP in UP, the Janata Party in Bihar and in Karnataka, the Telugu Desam in Andhra, the DMK in Tamil Nadu: these and other regional and caste-based parties have been part of the national government. Each of these parties derive their electoral strength from the Dalits, the OBCs, or both. There is hardly a party in India that is not conscious of the need to make appeals to specific castes or groups of castes, coopt caste leaders into positions within the party, and take caste into account in the allocation of seats in parliamentary and state assembly elections. With deregulation, the liberalization of the economy, and higher economic growth rates, we can anticipate that there will be greater economic differentiation within and between castes. As some members of the lower castes have acquired higher levels of education and are able to benefit from educational and employment reservations, class divisions are likely to grow within each of the lower castes, including the Dalits. Social mobility for educated members of the lower castes is likely to increase, particularly in urban areas, while the grosser forms of discrimination are likely to diminish.

Paradoxically, as caste has become somewhat less important in determining individual life chances, caste has become more salient as a political identity, and as an institutionalized element of civil society. There are now caste-based political parties, caste-based educational institutions and hostels, and caste-based housing societies. Caste is institutionalized politically through reservations for scheduled castes and tribes in elected bodies and for all backward castes in government employment and in admissions to educational institutions. The tendency in India is toward institutional structures based upon caste that are not open and inclusive and which therefore nurture distrust and conflict between castes. What are the implications for social order and political development in the coming decades?

The first is that caste conflict is unlikely to subside. It will be intensified at two levels. At the micro level – in India's half-million villages – we can anticipate continued strife between Dalits and the local dominant castes. As Francine Frankel and others have pointed out (Frankel 1978), the Green Revolution combined with the abolition of the zamindari system disrupted the old jagmarti system based on mutual obligations, and put in place a more market-oriented labor market that is conducive to bargaining and protest on the part of agricultural laborers, but which also induces the landowning dominant castes to use their control over the local machinery of the state (particularly the police and the judiciary) to attempt to maintain their dominance. The result, as M.N. Srinivas has argued (Srinivas 1962), is that in place of acceptance within the hierarchy, one sees greater competition and conflict between the castes and a bleeding process of violent conflict and rising distrust. In rural India the lower castes are, to use the American phrase, "uppity" in their efforts to raise their social state through marriage rites and other rituals, and by engaging in protest movements against the local landowners for whom they work. The upper and middle castes and the landowning ranks of the OBCs often respond by forming armed Senas of their own or utilizing the local police and judiciary to beat down the Dalits. In UP and Bihar, and elsewhere in the Hindi belt, violent conflicts at the local level are likely to persist, with clashes between young Dalit militants (their numbers increasing with the high population growth rates that characterize northern India) demanding jobs, higher agricultural wages, land redistribution, and greater social respect, and private armies hired by landowners but recruited from among the OBCs. Some of the most acute conflicts take place not between Dalits and Brahmins and other forward castes, but between Dalits and OBCs and other intermediate castes. The violence is generally sporadic and localized with high levels of violence in only a few areas. But elsewhere relations between castes are likely to be strained and high levels of distrust may well impede the functioning of local governments. The combination of fear and humiliation is a growing force for collective action in many rural areas of North India. Caste cohesion is thus built not upon ethnic pride, but rather on anger toward those who seek to perpetuate their domination. As we have noted, this is one reason why political leaders of the lower caste offer their constituencies measures aimed at providing greater protection against the dominant castes by seeking to gain control over the local constabularies.

The expansion of the power of local governments as prescribed by recent constitutional amendments and subsequent legislation may empower the lower classes and increase the accountability of local health and educational officials who at present shirk their responsibilities. However, it is too soon to pass judgment, especially since the fiscal implications of decentralization have yet to be worked out. Moreover, the maldistribution of wealth at the local level and the persistence of dominant castes locally may make it difficult for the lower castes to exercise political power in ways that result in significant material benefits. Where the dominant castes control the *panchayats*, the Dalits and OBCs may fight back; and where the lower castes are in control, the dominant castes may become disruptive so as to force the intervention of state governments. In some communities the creative tension may result in more responsible and productive local governments; but elsewhere local governments may remain as ineffective as they have been in the past. Political decentralization and the political empowerment of the lower castes – the current formula for the achievement of greater equity in Indian society – may yield few benefits if state and central governments continue to pay as little attention as they have to human resource development policies.

At the macro political level we can anticipate that the issue of reservations will become ever more contentious as a result of economic liberalization. Job reservations remain confined to the public sector since these jobs have been regarded as sinecures, opportunities for corruption, a means of political access, and a source of social status. The Mandal Commission called attention to the symbolic effects of government employment.

In India Government service has always been looked upon as a symbol of prestige and power. By increasing the representation of OBCs in Government service, we give them an immediate feeling of participation in the governance of the country. When a backward class candidate becomes a Collector or a Superintendent of Police, the material benefits accruing from his position are limited to the members of his family only. But the psychological spin off of this phenomenon is tremendous; the entire community of that backward class candidate feels socially elevated. Even when no tangible benefits flow to the community at large, the feeling that now it has its "own man" in the "corridors of Power" acts as a morale booster (Government of India 1980).

Should the Indian economy continue to expand significantly in the next decade, with a contraction of employment in the public sector and an expansion of employment in the private sector, we can anticipate that scheduled caste and OBC leaders will demand reservations in the private sector. So long as such a large proportion of employment was in the public sector, the demand for an extension of reservations was mute, but as the economy and employment expands and there is a fall-off in employment in the public sector, middle-class members of the scheduled castes and tribes and OBCs are likely to raise their voices for a fixed share of job, in the private sector. The result could well be an acute political struggle, this time involving not only the excluded higher castes, but the business community whose involvement in the earlier debates over Mandalization was minimal precisely because they were unaffected.

Reservations remain a source of conflict between those who are included and those who are excluded. Proposals to extend reservations in all elected bodies to women (a constitutional proposal is pending to grant women one-third of seats in parliament and in state legislatures) and to grant educational and job reservations to Muslims are bitterly contested. Any expansion of reservations to new groups – given the decision of the high court that no more than 49 percent of jobs and educational places can be reserved – reduces the reservations for existing beneficiaries. Proposals to apply a means test for reservations and thereby exclude the children of well-educated members of the lower castes is still another contested proposal, regarded by the middle-class members of the lower castes as a wedge issue intended to destroy the solidarity of their communities.

Among the beneficiaries there are likely to be conflicts as well. Among the hundreds of scheduled castes and OBCs there are variations in how well each group is able to take advantage of the opportunities provided through the system of reservations. Some castes invariably do better than others. The competition and tension between the castes has become palpable as the political leaders of each caste take note of who is getting jobs and political offices.

We can thus anticipate two kinds of caste-based political struggles in India. At the village level Dalit agricultural laborer and service classes will continued to be embattled with the local dominant castes as they seek social respect, demand higher wages, and resist the armed efforts of dominant castes to keep them in their place. In the urban areas, the struggle will be between the middle classes of the OBCs and scheduled castes on the one hand, and the middle and upper castes on the other over reservations and their extension. The middle classes among the forward castes will resist reservations, for they increasingly view reservations as an affront to the moral order they seek to create, one based on equality of opportunity not equality of outcome; and they will be resentful at the demand for jobs from middle-class members of the lower castes (the "creamy layers") who want benefits for their children. Each of these middle classes, one drawn from the forward castes, the other from the backward castes, will assert its claims by moral appeals, the one to the principle of merit and equality of opportunity, the other to a history of centuries of victimization and a demand for equality of outcome. To Americans, the story is a familiar one.

Neither of these conflicts, however, is likely to resolve the fundamental contradiction that characterizes the efforts to reduce social hierarchy and economic inequalities in India. A central theme of this paper is that India's democratic system has proven resilient in its capacity to incorporate hitherto excluded elements, and that the lower castes have indeed moved into positions of power in the administrative services, in parliament, and in executive positions. But I have argued that the material benefits to the lower castes have largely gone to their more advanced members, that some castes (Yadavs, for example) have benefited substantially, others hardly at all, and that there are growing class divisions within each of the lower castes as the more successful individuals obtain positions in government while others receive few if any benefits. Those who wield political power among the lower castes have tended to use their positions for self-benefit and to provide symbolic benefits to those who have been left behind. One does not see state government controlled by OBCs and Dalits devote new resources to expand mass education so as to provide greater opportunities for mobility for the poor, or to commit substantial new resources for drinkable water, health services, and sanitation. The resources are available if the state governments ended or reduced the subsidies they now provide for power and irrigation which largely benefit those who are better off. Compared with many lower-income countries India has not adopted policies that governments elsewhere have pursued to benefit the lower classes, notwithstanding India's egalitarian socialist rhetoric and the growing political empowerment of elite members of the lower castes. India's educational system – a poorly funded, badly managed, and educationally inadequate system of publicly financed primary schools for the poor, and a private, higher-quality, often government-aided educational sector for the middle and upper classes and castes – in effect reproduces the old social order based on hierarchy. The system of reservations simply provides a window within which a small section of the lower castes can enter into the middle class; in this fashion, the old *varna* system provides some flexibility, but persists in maintaining the fundamental distinction between those who have access to knowledge and those who do not, between those who use their minds and those who work with their hands.

The low rate of economic growth in India over the last half-century has made it more difficult to improve the well-being of the lower castes. With the introduction of liberal market-oriented policies we can antici-pate a higher rate of economic growth and an expansion of employment opportunities that should provide some benefit for the lower classes. But in the absence of a system of mass education and an adequate healthcare delivery system to rural areas, most members of the lower castes will lack the human capital to enable them to take advantage of whatever opportunities the expanding economy provides. Indeed, the state budgets for mass education have declined in recent years and the pace at which lower-caste children are incorporated into what is in any event a pitiful system of mass education continues to be small. There will continue to be some social mobility across and within castes and the caste-based division of labor will continue to be eroded in some parts of the country, but the overall picture is likely to change only slowly, barring the adoption of new policies in the areas of health and educa-tion. Elsewhere in Asia, notably in China, Taiwan, South Korea, and Indonesia, high economic growth rates combined with substantial state involvement in the expansion of health and educational facilities have meant greater income equality and greater social mobility. But high rates of economic growth in a society marked by sharp disparities in human capital invariably mean a widening of incomes and a reinforce-ment of social hierarchies. There are few signs yet that the Indian government, the center, the states, or local bodies have turned their attention to improving human capital. Unless that is done, India will remain a ranked hierarchical social order, but without the ideological legitimacy and social stability that undergirded the old social order. The familiar phrase rings true for India: the old order has begun to disintegrate, but the new order has not yet risen.

# 9    Sharing the spoils: group equity, development, and democracy

*Pranab Bardhan*

## I

In recent years it has become a well-worn cliché to assert that for four decades or so socialist governments have kept the innate propensities of the Indian people for capitalism and markets in check, and now the opportunity has arisen for letting loose what imaginative journalists have called the "caged tiger." I will not pause here to comment on the widespread confusion between statism (which India had and still has in great measure) and socialism, or between socialist rhetoric and substance. Nor shall I question the existence of the indomitable entrepreneurial spirit and resourcefulness of the people that thrive in all corners of India even against considerable odds. But in this paper I intend to point to a dominant antimarket streak in the collective passion for group equity that rages among the common people in India, which no amount of exorcising of the ghost of British Fabianism or die-hard Stalinism among its intellectual elite will quite eliminate. I venture to claim that a large part of mass political culture in India can be broadly described as equity-centric, and in this respect largely anticapitalist, though not pro-socialist, and that this can considerably complicate matters for both economic growth and democratic governance.

Indian society is, of course, extremely hierarchical in structure and heterogeneous in composition. Both of these aspects fuel the drive for equity in the context of a democratic polity. On the frenzy for equity generated by democracy in a hierarchical society, Alexis de Tocqueville commented[1] more than 160 years back on the basis of his experience of the unequal society of Europe:

Democratic peoples love equality at all times, but in certain periods they carry their passion for equality to the point of madness. This happens when the old, long-threatened social hierarchy is finally destroyed after a final, intestine battle, and the barriers that once separated citizens are finally overturned. Men then

[1] See Tocqueville (1954), vol. II: 103.

hurl themselves upon equality as upon some item of conquered booty and clutch it to them.

I am often reminded of this passage when I see, for example, the frenzy over job reservations and caste quotas in India. This passion for group equity, the aspiration to compensate for centuries of slights and indignities[2] from (and discrimination by) the upper strata, is, however, often unidirectional and asymmetrical, not basically egalitarian. In the infinitely layered social structure of India a group, say the Jats in Uttar Pradesh or the Yadavs in Bihar, can go on clamoring for equity in the sense of parity with upper castes, while not doing much about their customary oppression of the Chamars, who are placed below them in the village society (often taunting them for special government favors bestowed on them and calling them *sarkar ki jamai* or the government's sons-in-law).

I shall consider the economic and political effects of pandering to intergroup equity issues in the context of three kinds of group interaction. The first relates to the standard economic interest groups, the second to caste groups, and the third to collectivities at the regional levels.

## II

In terms of organized economic interest groups India contains a relatively large plurality. Apart from the dominant classes – industrial capitalists and large traders, rich farmers, and white-collar workers and professionals, largely in the public sector – there are sections of unionized manual workers, small traders, and other small propertied groups that are quite vocal in lobbying for their separate economic interests. (All the lobbies, of course, speak in the name of the poor; even the major left parties, which claim particular entitlement to the championship of the poor, essentially act as pressure groups for the relatively affluent farmers, office-workers, and the unionized "labor aristocracy.")

With a weak development of capitalism under the colonial regime, no individual economic group was strong enough to hijack the state after independence. Over time the diverse interest groups, facing the usual

---

[2] See, for example, the interview of Laloo Yadav, the then chief minister of Bihar, by Dalrymple (1997). He asked Laloo about his childhood: "My father was a small farmer," began Laloo scratching his groin. "He looked after the cows and buffalo belonging to the upper castes . . . All my childhood I was beaten and insulted by the landlords . . . Because we were from the Yadav caste we were not entitled even to sit on a chair; they would make us sit on the ground. I remember all that. Now I am in the chair and I want those people to sit on the ground. It is in my mind to teach them a lesson."

collective action problem in large and heterogeneous coalitions for pulling together in their long-run collective interest, worked out short-run particularistic compromises in the form of sharing the spoils of the system to the detriment of aggregate welfare, a kind of "log-rolling" familiar from the history of pork-barrel politics in many democracies. The attendant problems in terms of economic growth are, of course, more acute in a country of India's size and bewildering criss-cross of interest alignments in the dominant coalition.

In catering to their demands a large part of public resources gets frittered away in the form of implicit or explicit subsidies, of galloping amounts of what are called nondevelopment expenditures, and political and administrative mismanagement of public capital. The recent attempts at deregulation and liberalization, while impressive by India's past standards, have not yet succeeded in making big dents in the fiscal deficit, the vast network of subsidies, and the colossal public debt (servicing which takes up a large and increasing part of the budgetary funds, moving inexorably toward an internal debt trap, and keeps the interest rates high, choking private investment). The interest payments of the central government on the public debt as a proportion of GDP rose from about 3 percent in the middle 1980s to 4 percent in 1990-1, and near 5 percent in more recent years. While the fiscal deficit of the central and state governments taken together as a proportion of GDP was more than 10 percent in 1999–2000 (higher than in the early 1990s), a significant part of it is revenue deficit (in a way eating into the public capital formation), which as a proportion of GDP increased from about 4 percent in 1990–1 to near 6 percent in 1998–9, and is likely to go up even more, particularly as the hefty upward revision of wage and salary scales of government employees at all levels following the recommendations (and ignoring those about trimming the size of the bureaucracy) of the Fifth Pay Commission, and its usual chain reactions for other public services at the central and state levels, take full effect. At the mere hint of a strike by central government employees on the issue of pay scale revision, the Government capitulated.[3]

Apart from the mounting expenditure on wages and salaries for the highly organized government and other public-sector employees, the government budget caters to the demands of this and other interest groups in the private sector largely in the form of subsidies. A recent document submitted to the parliament by the Ministry of Finance, *Government Subsidies in India* (May 1997), based on a detailed study by the National Institute of Public Finance and Policy (NIPFP), provides a

---

[3] At the state levels the implementation of the central pay scales and allowances has started imposing large cuts in development expenditure.

fairly comprehensive estimate of the explicit and implicit[4] budget-based subsidies. According to this estimate the budget-based[5] subsidies of the central and state governments taken together amounted to about Rs.1.4 trillion, which is 14.4 percent of GDP (which is about twice the size of the aggregate fiscal deficit) in 1994–5. This study computes subsidies as the excess of providing a service over the recoveries from that service (excluding defense and general administration). If one excludes expenditure items like primary education, public health and sanitation, flood control and drainage, roads and bridges, soil and water conservation, agricultural and various scientific research, and many social welfare schemes, and concentrates on what the study (not quite accurately) calls "non-merit goods and services" (a large part of which goes to the non-poor), the total estimate of budget-based subsidies amounted to Rs. 1.04 trillion, or 10.9 percent of GDP in 1994–5.

The first casualty of a budgetary crunch is usually public investment in long-gestation infrastructure projects (power, ports, roads, irrigation, etc.), or social expenditures for the unorganized poor (particularly basic health and sanitation, primary education, etc.). Expenditure on the social sector (which includes rural development and food subsidies, not all of which go to the poor) of the central and state governments together, after an initial drop in the early 1990s, has risen somewhat to slightly below 8 percent of GDP in more recent years. Capital expenditure of the central and state governments taken together as a proportion of GDP, has, however, declined from about 8 percent in 1990–1 to less than 6 percent in more recent years. In particular, public investment in infrastructure as a proportion of GDP has declined significantly, and the hoped-for private investment to fill the gap has not materialized (largely on account of anticipated political problems of recovery of user fees and tolls, and frequent political interventions in regulatory institutions).

The budgetary problems are severe, particularly at the state level, where the governments, exposed as they are more closely to some of the

[4] This includes, apart from explicit cash subsidies (e.g. on food, fertilizer, and export), interest or credit subsidies (i.e. loans given at below market rates), tax subsidies (e.g. tax exemption of medical expenses, deduction of mortgage interest payment from taxable income, etc.), in-kind subsidies (e.g. provision of free medical services), equity subsidies (investment in equity in state enterprises yielding low dividends), procurement subsidies (say in government purchase of food grains), and regulatory subsidies (administered pricing). The estimate, by its method of computation, includes the effects of cost overruns, wastages, and inefficiencies on capital projects, and thus goes beyond the usual meaning of subsidies.

[5] This estimate excludes an off-budget subsidy like the petroleum subsidy. In view of administered prices lagging far behind world prices, the "oil pool deficit" is large and is expected to grow as world oil prices follow their recent upward climb.

particularistic interest groups, are practically bankrupt in many cases,[6] dependent on gap-filling transfers from the center (which thus generate perverse incentives for fiscal management). In some cases "development grants" for capital projects authorized by the Planning Commission are being used by the states largely to pay salaries to public officials. An increasingly larger share of the central loan to the states is utilized to repay the earlier loans, and the states' aggregate outstanding loan to the center came to nearly Rs. 1.5 trillion by the end of financial year 1996–7. Circumventing the constitutional ceiling on market borrowings by the state government, the state-owned enterprises are issuing bonds with state government guarantees, generating staggeringly large contingent liabilities. In the first half of the fiscal year 1999–2000 the center had already doled out about Rs. 30 billion to eight states as what are called WMA (ways and means advance to tide over excess current expenditure, which is supposed to be a last resort when normal revenue flows and current borrowings are insufficient), with little hope of repayment – the center is now trying to insist on agreements with the states about time-bound fiscal reform measures in return.

In many states water and electricity are provided free or at throwaway prices[7] (as are higher education and urban transport), much below even the operations and maintenance costs of the facilities, not to speak of the capital cost. In 1996–7 the gross electricity subsidy of all the states for the agricultural sector alone exceeded Rs. 138 billion.[8] In the same year the annual commercial losses of the state electricity boards were more than six times what they were in 1985–6, and their combined rate of return is now estimated to be a negative 17.6 percent. The interstate distribution of per capita electricity subsidy indicates that in richer states it is substantially higher than in poorer states.

There is a growing sense in some quarters that bankruptcy and the diminishing transfers from the center will at last make the states wake up to the hard reality and the pressing need for reform. As the states are increasingly asked to fend for themselves and as interstate competition in luring private investment heats up, this game is clearly to the advantage of the infrastructurally already better-off states. What is less clear, however, is how the Indian federal system will resolve the tension between the demands of the better-off states for more competition and

---

[6] In Uttar Pradesh, for example, debt servicing is now more than the total tax revenues of the state.

[7] In a small number of states (like Orissa or Andhra Pradesh) there are some hopeful signs of this changing.

[8] This estimate probably includes part of the regular theft of electricity from transmission by the state electricity boards. In this theft the SEBs are sometimes in collusion with both farmers and industrialists.

those of other states (whom a weaker center can ill afford to ignore politically) for redistributive transfers through constitutional bodies like the Finance Commission or extra-constitutional agencies like the Planning Commission. Can, for example, a shaky coalition government at the center, dependent on crucial numbers of MPs from the infrastructurally weak states like Bihar or Uttar Pradesh or Madhya Pradesh, ignore their redistributive demands to compensate for their losing out in interstate competition for private investment?

The proliferation of government handouts, both at the central and the state levels, is often in the name of intergroup equity: farmers demand and get away with high administered prices of food grains and low administered prices of fertilizers[9] in parity with the benefits of protection for the industrial sector; even the large industrialists facing the cold wind of international competition (either in the product market or that for corporate control in the family-run business houses) clamor for a "level playing field" or relief from competition that is always described as "unfair dumping" or predatory multinational takeover; small industrial firms are protected against competition from larger domestic factories (the number of industrial products "reserved" exclusively for the small-scale sector still exceeds 800, in spite of several years of economic reform); pointing to the tax and other benefits to industrial capital, organized labor has so far successfully resisted major changes in the industrial labor laws which are among the most stringent in the world on the question of labor retrenchment, even in "sick" industries, both in the public and organized private sector, or changes in dysfunctional but customary labor practices like automatic promotion and bonus payment unrelated to worker productivity; and so on.

To readers of my book (1984) describing the intergroup collective action problem in breaking out of the political equilibrium underlying an economic deadlock, all this may sound exasperatingly familiar. But it would be wrong to get the impression that no substantial changes have taken place in the period since the early 1980s, either in terms of policy breakthroughs or in the alignments of the conflicting interest groups. There have been impressive, and in many ways unprecedented, changes in major industrial, trade, tax, financial, and regulatory policies. There have also been some increased diversity, fluidity, and fragmentation in the coalition of dominant interest groups and a discernible change in the mindset of large sections of the elite about the limits of the role of the state. This is not the place to elaborate on these changes, but one should

---

[9] On average nearly half of the fertilizer subsidies are estimated to accrue to the producers/suppliers of fertilizers rather than the farmers.

also guard against exaggerating the extent of shift in the basic political equilibrium.

I see such signs of exaggeration in, for example, an otherwise plausible and incisive analysis of the process of economic reform in Jenkins (1997). He claims that the reforms to date have been quite substantial and that the Indian democratic process has clever, if sometimes clandestine, ways of diffusing resistance to reform. He correctly points out how reformers may enjoy some autonomy in the context of the great malleability and fragmentation in the Indian interest group structure, how accommodations arranged through informal political networks mediate conflicts between winners and losers, and how particular reform measures generate a chain reaction of demand for more reforms from within (especially from newly mobilized interests including those in new areas of opportunities for the old interest groups).

But, as our discussion above of the staggering burden of subsidies and public debt and the continuing fiscal crisis suggests, the changes are as yet not substantial and purposive enough to break the political logjam in the macroeconomy. Financial bankruptcy, particularly at the state level, has persuaded politicians to relax the interventionist regime somewhat and reach a partly false consensus on the need for reforms. But beyond the rhetoric of "second-generation reforms" very little has as yet been achieved in actually breaking the grip of the network of subsidies catering to the dominant interest groups, or taking on the national-level unions of better-off workers (for example, in banking and insurance), or restructuring the management of public-sector companies and installing truly independent regulatory authorities (which involves seriously challenging the dominance of much of the obstructive bureaucracy and the pervasiveness of the nexus with the criminal underworld in pilfering public-sector-produced inputs at all levels of the enterprise hierarchy, or kickbacks from supply contracts or underinvoicing to buyer clients). Jenkins cites cases of some "backdoor reforms" in public-sector companies and in deliberate nonenforcement of existing regulations and labor laws, but it is as yet not clear how such "reform by stealth" can be sustained over the long run.

## III

Just as on crucial matters like subsidies, labor laws, the closing of unviable factories, or public-sector reorganization, no major political party in India is publicly opposed to the demands of the special interests, no political party in India is opposed to the strong movements demanding large caste quotas in public-sector jobs and admission to higher education for the so-called backward castes (long effective in southern India, and now spreading to the north) in addition to those stipulated in the constitution for the scheduled castes and tribes. As the expansion of the public sector over the years created more opportunities for secure jobs and, not infrequently, for the associated extra illicit income if the job is in some regulatory capacity, more and more mobilized groups in the democratic process have started using their low-caste status for staking a claim to the loot. It is a great irony that even as market reform is being heralded as a big change in the Indian economic policy direction, one of the most popular planks in the party platforms is to increasingly carve up the public-sector job market into protected niches, drowning all considerations of efficiency in the name of intergroup equity.

To the extent that special preferential policies for groups are supposed to cope with a historical handicap, their economic rationale is akin to that behind the age-old argument for infant-industry protection in early stages of industrialization. Some disadvantaged groups may need temporary protection against competition so that they can participate in learning by doing and on-the-job skill formation before catching up with the others. Some of the standard arguments *against* infant-industry protection are then equally applicable against job reservation policies. For example, the "infant," once protected, sometimes refuses to grow up; reservations, once adopted, are extremely difficult to reverse. Another argument against infant-industry protection is that even when the goal is justifiable, it may be achieved more efficiently through other policies. For example, a disadvantaged group may be helped by preferential loans, scholarships, job training programs and extension services for its members, instead of job quotas that bar qualified candidates coming from advanced groups (in other words, equality of opportunity may be more justifiable than insistence on equality of outcome). Such indirect policies of helping out backward groups are also less likely to generate political resentment (particularly because in this case the burden may be shared more evenly, whereas in the case of job quotas the redistributive burden falls on a small subset of the people in advanced communities). There are also limits to an infant-industry-type argument when issues of public safety and other vital needs are involved (as, for example, in the cases of medical treatment by unqualified but reserved-quota doctors or bridges built by such engineers). In recent years the minimum qualifications for admission to medical colleges for scheduled caste (or scheduled tribe) candidates in Uttar Pradesh were raised, at the prodding of the supreme court, from 0 percent marks to 35 percent, but the quota remained unfilled; so a scheduled caste chief minister then brought it down to 20 percent.

The search for caste equity has also led to endless fragmentation within the protected castes. In Andhra Pradesh complaints about certain sections of the scheduled caste getting the lion's share of the quota-protected jobs led to demands for a finer categorization of the quotas. The state government in response announced reservations by four categories of scheduled castes, which has in turn led to counter-agitations by the hitherto more successful scheduled castes. A similar problem arose in the recent debate on gender quotas for seats in the parliament: the demands for a 30 percent quota of parliamentary seats for women were undercut by demands for special reservations for backward caste women.

At the regional level also, equity politics has played an important role, often at the expense of economic efficiency. Public investment allocation (and inducements to private-sector investments) in favor of uneconomical plants and unsustainable projects in backward areas has often been supported in the name of regional equity. Many states used to demand their own steel plants, irrespective of the cost; similar demands for the location of public-sector locomotive factories, petroleum refineries, and other industrial enterprises in backward areas, and the railway network to support additional commodity movements, have unproductively absorbed vast amounts of resources. Central government ministers, particularly those belonging to regional parties, now openly discriminate in favor of their own regions, irrespective of efficiency, in matters of investment allocation and project location. Every new minister of railways customarily spends large sums of money to extend the railway network to his own remote constituency, however uneconomical an investment proposition it may be. While there remain severe bottlenecks on the high traffic density routes, MPs of most political parties demand railway lines for their constituency as a show-piece of development. In 1995–6 the losses of the railways on uneconomical branch lines and new lines exceeded Rs. 2.2 billion.

In the 1950s the political system easily acceded to the demand for railway freight equalization for materials across the whole country, making delivery prices of major industrial raw materials (like coal, steel, or cement) more or less equal at different locations. This largely destroyed the locational comparative advantage of the eastern region in processing some of these industrial raw materials available there. Datta-Chaudhuri (1997) illustrates the many inefficiencies of this policy:

The Freight Equalization policy led to the transportation of coal over long distances from the Bengal–Bihar coal fields to industrial locations in western India to serve as a source of industrial energy. Moreover, open-cast collieries with locational advantages did not have any incentive for introducing deep mining. In the regions around the western Himalayas, houses were built with cement and steel transported from faraway places, instead of using forestry products, which could have induced a healthy development of forestry and forestry-based industries in those areas.

This system continued until very recently, contributing to, apart from cost inefficiency all around, the industrial decline in the eastern region; but the political legitimacy of regional equity was so overwhelming that even the politicians in the latter region largely accepted this anti-market dispensation without a great deal of protest.

In the labor market preference for "sons of the soil" has been demanded in some regions from time to time. In the financial capital of India, Mumbai, the Shiv Sena Party union SLS (Sthaniya Lokadhikar Samiti) revived in 1997 an old demand for Maharashtrian preference in government employment: they have demanded that 80 percent of jobs in the clerical grades and 100 percent of class IV jobs should be reserved for Maharashtrians only. In 1995 the then chief minister of Karnataka introduced a policy whereby half of the new jobs in even the private sector were to be filled by people who had been resident in the state for at least the preceding fifteen years. The AGP (Assam Gano Parishad) has now demanded that a fraction of central government posts should be earmarked for the Assamese. And so on.

## IV

Beyond the direct economic consequences of short-run equity politics are the consequences for democratic governance, which in some sense are often more disturbing. The diminishing hold of elite control and the welcome expansion of democracy to reach the lower rungs of the social hierarchy have been associated with a loosening of the earlier administrative protocols and a steady erosion of the institutional insulation of the decision-making process in public administration and economic management. It is now common practice, for example, for a low-caste chief minister in a state to proceed, immediately upon assuming office, to transfer away top civil servants belonging to upper castes and get pliant bureaucrats from his or her own caste. In six months, between March and September 1997, the government of the scheduled caste chief minister of Uttar Pradesh managed to set a record by transferring about 1,400 civil and police officials (thus outshining the none-too-skimpy record of the two "backward caste" chief ministers who preceded her: 521 transfers by one in 1991–2, and 814 transfers by another in 1993–5). Some district magistrates and civil servants of the rank of secretary were transferred and posted as many as four to six times in those six months. In the Indian political culture this is now largely accepted as an inevitable byproduct of group equity. Many members of the supposedly independent civil service now try to curry favor with the politicians to avoid transfers to undesirable jobs and locations. A visit to any state secretariat makes it clear that one of the main activities of a political leader, and one on which a great deal of time and energy is spent (and large sums of money collected), is that of deciding on postings and transfers of officers (apart from prized allotments from the leader's "discretionary quota" of various scarce goods and services). In Madhya Pradesh successive chief ministers have even fixed officer posting and transfer quotas for the members of the legislative assembly, who use this lucrative facility with abandon. Administrative appointments outside the main civil service, like those to the boards of public-sector corporations particularly in state governments, are often used as political sinecures to keep the clamoring factions happy.

There is a certain nonchalance in the rampant corruption among politicians in the newly emergent groups. As Visvanathan (1997) comments, about cases when the scheduled caste politicians come to power nowadays, and are corrupt: "they are often unapologetic; their reply is that the Congress and the upper castes had been corrupt for decades and it is now their turn." Corruption is seen as a collective entitlement in an amoral game of equity politics.

Politicians for many years used to direct managers of public financial institutions to relax their strict criteria in giving out loans to their favored clients. Until very recently political leaders often announced with great fanfare that loans up to a certain amount from those institutions do not have to be paid back. In general there has been widespread presumption among borrowers (both rich and poor) that they can default on these loans with impunity, as the politicians who will have to come back to them for votes cannot afford to let bank officials be too harsh with them. The practice of public-sector banks bailing out "sick" state firms has continued unabated. Not surprisingly, the Indian public banking system has been saddled with massive amounts (estimated to be about Rs. 460 billion in 1998) of what are euphemistically called "nonperforming assets," bringing parts of the system to near bankruptcy. (The situation is now improving, slowly and haltingly, under the recent financial sector reforms.)[10]

One can similarly point to the decay of many public service institu-

---

[10] These include the deregulation of interest rates, more competition in the financial sector, insistence on capital adequacy norms in most public-sector banks, etc. The "nonperforming assets" as a proportion of their total advances has now been brought down to about 14 percent.

tions, sometimes under the pressure of their politically protected employees. Take the case of public hospitals even in a relatively well-administered state like West Bengal. These hospitals are in great disarray, the conditions of medical treatment of patients are often nightmarish, and anyone who can afford private doctors and clinics avoids the public hospitals. There are many reasons for the present conditions and there is enough blame to share on all sides. But one major reason has to do with the fact that the politically powerful (and also strong in numbers) lowest-grade ("class IV") employees have complete job security; so they do not care about doing their duty and they have allowed the basic services of the hospitals to break down with impunity. In fact there are many reports of parts of the public hospitals being taken over by these salaried employees and rented out for their private benefit, of medical supplies and equipment being pilfered, etc. Yet organizing the lowest-paid employees for job security and wage bargaining has been a major priority in labor movements in pursuit of social justice and group equity. Faced with complaints of dereliction of duty these hospital employees regularly point to malfeasance on the part of hospital senior staff (for example, doctors on public salaries indulging in illicit private practice): there is thus equal-opportunity plundering of public resources by all interest groups.

A particularly alarming sign of the politicization of the internal organization of the government in the process of democratic mobilization is indicated by the systematic erosion of the institutional independence of the police and the criminal justice system that is creeping into some states of northern and western India in a way that is familiar from Sicilian politics under the Christian Democrats. (The N.N. Vohra Committee Report a few years back, now shelved, clearly spelled out the nexus between politicians, bureaucrats, the mafia, and even some members of the judiciary.) A significant number of elected politicians in those states are crime bosses or their accomplices. Nearly one in ten candidates who contested the 1996 general elections were facing criminal charges. Recently the Election Commission disclosed that at least forty members of the parliament who were elected that year and 700 members of the state legislative assemblies that year had criminal antecedents. The general pattern has been repeated in the 1998 and 1999 parliamentary elections.

Some of these criminal elements have figured out that once elected on a ruling party ticket they can neutralize the police, who will not press the criminal charges against them with any alacrity. Given their organizational and financial resources the crime bosses have an edge over other politicians in winning elections, and the poor are often dedicated voters for them as they nurse their local constituency assiduously even as they loot from the system in general. Police officers (and even judges) are often rewarded (for example, with plum postings) if they do the elected politicians' bidding. The National Police Commission forcefully pointed out these problems in its eight-volume reports in 1979 and in 1981–2, without making much headway in action taken.

The state of Uttar Pradesh (in terms of population it is one-sixth of India, and as large as the whole of the Russian Federation) may have reached an extreme in these respects, but it is indicative of the general trends in many other states. Many MLAs in the elected legislative assembly of this state are known to have criminal records. More than half of the near-hundred mafia gangs reportedly enjoy the political patronage of one political party or another. Reflecting the political instability of the state, the average tenure of a superintendent of police is only six months (that of a district magistrate, one year). Twenty-five thousand wanted criminals are at large, often with police and political connivance.

Anarchy and plunder are often seen as gambits in a caste struggle. Recently, when the IAS Officers' Association in UP met in an unusually candid gesture to try to select by vote the most corrupt among their own, the officer who was most likely to get the dubious honor resigned from the association and, without refuting the specific charges of corruption, only complained that she was being mistreated because she had married a Yadav. When a chief minister of Bihar, the colorful leader of a "backward caste," was first sought to be interrogated in connection with his possible involvement in a large corruption scandal by the officers of the Central Bureau of Investigation, he threatened to start public agitations against such "mistreatment" of Yadavs by the upper castes, and cited his huge electoral victory in the recent past as a verdict for his innocence in the "court of the people."[11] Nor is this political style confined to the backward fiefdoms of North India. In his analysis of caste violence (between the Kammas and the Kapus) in the coastal Andhra town of Vijayawada, Parthasarathy (1997) shows how the upwardly mobile agricultural caste of Kammas, as they consolidated their position in the towns, imported a rough and rustic political style based on the use of any means, including organized violence, to attain power, in cavalier disregard for the rule of law.[12]

In other words, the unfolding of the logic of populist democracy has

[11] His election results have been much worse since those days of his electoral boast. In general there are some signs now that the electorate gets restive with continued misgovernance.

[12] One hears similar accounts in the recent caste riots in southern Tamil Nadu between the Maravars (a dominant agricultural caste) and the lowly Pallars.

itself become a threat to democratic governance. Kaviraj (1996) has described this as a strange Tocquevillian paradox:

democratic government functioned smoothly in the early years after 1947 precisely because it was not taking place in a democratic society; as democratic society has slowly emerged, with the spread of a real sense of political equality, it has made the functioning of democratic government more difficult.

Some people are not too worried by this and they regard it as part of the initial necessary turmoil of democratic movement forward and group self-assertion. Naipaul (1990), who is fascinated by the "million mutinies" in contemporary India, writes:

When people start moving, the first loyalty, the first identity, is always a rather small one . . . When the oppressed have the power to assert themselves, they will behave badly. It will need a couple of generations of security, and knowledge of institutions, and the knowledge that you can trust institutions – it will take at least a couple of generations before people in that situation begin to behave well.

I wish I could share in this optimistic belief in democratic teleology. The breakdown in democratic governance structures is not easy to repair and there are irreversibilities in institutional decay. Besides, in India's multi-layered social structure, by the time one self-aware group settles down and learns to play by the institutional rules, other newly assertive groups will come up and defy those rules, often in the name of group equity.

## V

We have seen that the political arithmetic of group equity and democratic mobilization, apart from bankrupting the state treasuries and debilitating the government's capacity to invest in necessary social and economic infrastructure, has been eating away the institutional insulation of administrative and economic decision-making at the central and, in particular, at the state levels, with adverse consequences both for development and for governance. In the last five years or so there have, however, been some hopeful signs that some institutions of checks and balances are successfully resisting populist or overpoliticized erosion. Examples are provided by the vigorous way the Election Commission has resisted being run over by politicians and their sharp practices, or how the judiciary has sometimes been active in upholding the rule of law or public interest litigation on matters of citizens' concern, or how some regulatory institutions in the infrastructure sector are trying to resist encroachments by politicians. In some states (Andhra Pradesh being a major example in the 1999 elections) the electorate is even rewarding better governance and not necessarily yielding to parties that pander to them by offering free public goods like water or electricity.

At the level of the local community in the far-flung villages and small towns of India, however, the problem is somewhat different: here it is not so much that of erecting or defending structures of insulation, but more that the top-heavy political regime stifles the development of local-level accountability mechanisms. In most areas elections to local bodies have been infrequent, elected bodies are often suspended or superseded, an entente of local MLAs (or MPs), district and block-level administrators, and contractors, dominates most decision-making on local rural development expenditures, and there is much more concern for accountability upwards (i.e., to the higher-up funding authority) than downwards to the local people. In many parts of India even the recent attempts at devolution of power (following upon the seventy-third and seventy-fourth constitutional amendments) have been partly neutralized by state government officials and politicians hustling to retain their authority (and patronage distribution power) in the local bodies, as has happened quite openly, for example, in Tamil Nadu.

In large parts of North India it is common to observe the serious problem of absenteeism of salaried teachers in village public schools and of doctors in rural public health clinics. The villagers are usually quite aware of the problem but do not have the institutional means of correcting it, as the state-funded teachers and doctors are not answerable to the villagers in the insufficiently decentralized system. Sometimes the school building or the primary health clinic is there only on paper (or abandoned only partly constructed), even though the full amount of money was sanctioned and spent from above. In general, large sums are budgeted and spent every year in the name of the poor, but precious little reaches those who fall outside the active circle of the politics of distributive equity.

In situations of severe social and economic inequality at the local level decentralization can be highly inadequate in helping the poor. It may be easy for the local overlords to capture the local community institutions and the poor may be grievously exposed to their mercies and their malfeasance. Such capture is more difficult at the national level because the local mafia of different regions may partially neutralize one another. Since there are certain overhead costs of organizing resistance groups and lobbies, the poor may sometimes be less organized at the local level than at the national level, where they can pool their organizing capacities. The experience of the *relative* success of decentralization experiments in rural West Bengal over the last two decades suggests that one beneficial byproduct of land reform, underemphasized in the usual cost-benefit analysis of economists, is that such reform, by changing the local political structure in the village, gives more "voice" to the poor, and a stake in the asset base of the local economy induces them to get involved in local self-governing institutions.

Much also depends on how open and visible the political process at the local level is. Large-scale theft and corruption may be more effectively resisted if regular local elections to select representatives to the local bodies are supplemented by nonelectoral mechanisms of accountability, like regular and independent public audits and an institutionalized system of public hearings on items of major public expenditure. In parts of rural West Bengal these public hearings in villages and small towns (apart from the influence of a relatively disciplined ruling party) have helped in restraining decentralized malfeasance. (It is heartening to note that even in backward districts of Rajasthan and Madhya Pradesh a movement under the leadership of the Mazdoor Kisan Shakti Sangathan is growing for the villagers to demand information in public hearings – *jan sunwayi* – on bills, vouchers, and muster rolls on development works.)

In this paper we have emphasized some of the negative political and economic effects of "equity politics." The preceding three paragraphs, however, suggest that if asset distributive policies (like land reforms) and institutions of local accountability take root, there can exist situations in which equity, economic efficiency, and local democracy can coexist, and even become self-reinforcing. In the Indian countryside there now exist some, though as yet all too few, cases of such coexistence; in the vast areas of darkness of this subcontinent there are some flickering points of light.

# 10    Social movement politics in India:
institutions, interests, and identities

*Mary Katzenstein, Smitu Kothari, and Uday Mehta*

In recent years, the coupling of social movement activism with democracy has become almost axiomatic at a global level. Popular movements contributed to the collapse of authoritarianism in the Philippines, in Korea, and in much of Eastern Europe. In Latin America, in countries that have undergone a transition to democracy, social movements have been credited (together with elite forbearance in the face of pressure to quell popular protest) with ushering in democratization and with raising new issues and prompting state institutions to respond to newly articulated needs (Mainwaring 1987: 133; Diamond, Linz, and Lipset 1990; O'Donnell, Schmitter, and Whitehead 1986). The importance of social movements in challenging authoritarianism and in sustaining democratic transitions is well demonstrated.[1]

The significance of social movements under conditions of authoritarianism is broadly captured in the thought that they serve as a venue for sustaining and ultimately expressing popular civic sentiments and interests under circumstances where the prevailing authoritarian political climate does not allow for such forms of expression. They are in this sense collateral channels of popular sovereignty. By way of contrast this explanation sharpens the need to understand the role of such movements under democratic conditions where presumably electoral and other legitimate institutions serve the representative function that social movements often do under authoritarian conditions. In this paper, we ask how social movements are linked to democratic institutions in the case of contemporary India where social activism has been a conspicuous feature of social and political life both prior to and since independence (1947) and where democratic institutions, moreover, are well entrenched.

The theoretical tradition which, broadly speaking, frames this article

The authors are very grateful for suggestions of material and for helpful readings by Amrita Basu, Patrick Heller, Atul Kohli, Karen McGuinness, Raka Ray, Susanne Rudolph, Paul Wallace, and Myron Weiner.
[1] On the more recent studies of social movements in Latin America, see Alvarez et al. 1998; Escobar and Alvarez 1992; Eckstein 1989; Fals Borda 1998.

is the literature on social movements and democracy that has grown out of the historical experience of social movements in the United States and Western Europe.[2] The earliest set of discussions within this literature was set against the backdrop of fascism and the rise of communism, focusing on the immediate postwar period. These studies hypothesized that societal flux (urbanization, modernization) created a rootless population available to mass mobilization. Social movements undermined democracy by stirring sentiments and frustrations that extremist movements captured in their bid for power (Fromm 1941; Hoffer 1951; Kornhauser 1959). A major shift in perspectives developed as social scientists sought to make sense of the social movements of the 1960s and 1970s. This largely American literature recognized grievances to be a persistent rather than exceptional feature of social life, pointing instead to the political conditions (the availability of organizational resources and the existence of political opportunities) under which social discontent was likely to be mobilized (Tilly 1978; McAdam 1982; Tarrow 1994; McAdam, McCarthy, and Zald 1996). Rather than portraying social movements as the expression of societal anomie and undirected frustrations, these studies pictured social movements as enhancing democratic processes by providing unrepresented sectors of the population with alternative channels for political participation. A more recent and still developing conversation suggests that what many democratic countries are now experiencing is the institutionalization of social movement politics and the advent of what Sidney Tarrow and David Meyer call a "social movement society" (Tarrow 1994; Meyer and Tarrow 1998). Social movements, they write, may be becoming part of the conventional repertoire of participation by virtue of three developments. In their words:

First, social protest has moved from being a sporadic, if recurring feature of democratic politics, to become a perpetual element in modern life.

Second, protest behavior is employed with greater frequency, by more diverse constituencies, and is used to represent a wider range of claims than ever before.

Third, professionalization and institutionalization may be changing the major vehicle of contentious claims – the social movement – into an instrument within the realm of conventional politics (Meyer and Tarrow 1998: 4).

---

[2] There is also, of course, a distinguished tradition of political thought in which the well-being of democracies is squarely identified with the existence of secondary civic institutions. Tocqueville's analysis of American democracy with his focus on the New England town meetings and church gatherings is the classic statement of this tradition. It has continued to inspire contemporary reflections on democracy both as a means of representing interests and as a mechanism for facilitating cooperation and cohesion among disparately positioned groups and individuals and finally in creating effective forms of governmental functioning.

This concept of a social movement society which, we will argue, has useful descriptive relevance to India does not challenge the view that social movements are broadly salutary to democracy. But what these three defining aspects of a social movement society leave open to specification is how exactly movements impinge on democratic institutions and define new democratic spaces. It is not self-evident how the professionalization and institutionalization of social movements configure the representational or government functions of democracies. It is sometimes argued in the American case, for example, that interest groups, or rather "special interest groups," distort rather than facilitate the representation function of democratic institutions. Our purpose in this paper is to explore more precisely the relationship between social movements and Indian democracy while drawing on the analytical category of a social movement society because it so clearly captures a current and longstanding aspect of Indian social and political life.

The relationship of democracies to existing social and political forces in society is obviously a complex one. It relates to, apart from gross considerations such as specific constitutional rules,[3] particular distinctions between different branches of government, structures of representation (local, national, bicameral, etc.) and forms of electoral counting (for example, proportional representation vs. winner-takes-all). With respect to India, we offer three propositions which, we argue, describe the relationship of social movements to Indian democracy. These three propositions are the following:

(1) As a general matter, social movements have mobilized both around identity issues and around specific issues, interests, and localities. These different focal orientations have led them to represent their concerns within different institutional environments. Movement activism concerned with the pursuit of particular interests has remained substantially disengaged from electoral politics. Correspondingly, the domain of electoral politics has increasingly become the arena in which issues of identity (in contrast to interests) have come to dominate. Movement activism, most recently the Hindu nationalist movement which is plainly concerned with issues of national and sectarian identity and the earlier identity-focused ethnic, linguistic, and caste or anticaste movements, has largely succeeded with these issues in the electoral arena, whereas movements concerned with the amelioration of poverty or the redress of economic and social problems, when they engage the state, have

---

[3] For a discussion of the effect of social movement organizing on constitutional arrangements, see Jane Jenson (1995).

operated at the national level primarily within the arenas of the bureaucracy and the judiciary.[4]

(2) In terms of effectiveness and focus, issue-based Indian social movements have remained substantially limited to the regions within which they operate. Related to the first proposition is the fact that unlike a number of European and Latin American instances (the German Green Party, the Sandinistas), interest-based social movements have not successfully coalesced to form national electoral movements even when the issues and interests that they represent are national in their relevance. Thus even though social movements are ubiquitous in India and have sometimes formed national networks, they have seldom in the postindependence era come together as organized national electoral forces. Identity movements, by contrast, as evident in the electoral successes of the BJP in the 1990s, have been able to establish themselves as national movements through electoral mobilization.

Interestingly, the regional-based character of much movement activism has not precluded social movement involvement across global networks. In order to accrue power and leverage compensatory to that which movements forgo by their (sometimes self-) exclusion from one or the other arenas of politics, movement activism has increasingly turned to the global arena.[5] Many identity- and interest-based movement organizations have accepted financial help from abroad even as some on principle refuse foreign funding or at least funds from particular sources.

Some movements have been able to use international leverage to shape national and local agendas in India. At the same time global networks combined with financial dependence of many social movement organizations on global institutions result in strong cross-pressures between global and local accountability. This does not mean that global or foreign institutions necessarily set the agenda of interest-based social movements – these relationships are very diverse – but rather that both social movements and global institutions negotiate their interface at least in part in terms of a global discourse.

(3) The institutionalization of both identity- and interest-based activism

---

[4] One significant exception is Kerala, a state where leftist parties have secured electoral power over long periods of time. In Kerala, movements concerned with economic interests and inequalities have engaged at times closely with party/electoral politics.

[5] This tradeoff is not necessarily sought, but with little electoral leverage locally, movements naturally seek out other avenues of influence including ones that engage with international institutions.

located in electoral, bureaucratic, and judicial domains has not precluded the (co)existence of movement politics intent on expanding a discursive space within civil society independent of state politics. Movements whose politics are rooted in a transformative vision of social change often seek to remain at least partly disengaged from the institutions of the state in order to work at the grassroots supporting and creating consciousness change and seeking to reframe public discourse. Movement activists located in this civil society space seek to strengthen the capacities of underrepresented groups through literacy campaigns, workshops, camps, street theater, marches, protests, publications, and films. Much as with "conscientization" activities in Latin America, these processes endeavor to create arenas for popular voices and to provide a space where societal practices as well as government policies that perpetuate inequalities can be identified, critically assessed, and engaged.

In outlining these three propositions, we are all too aware of the way both descriptive and theoretical efforts to capture social movement politics as it is "lived" can be reductive. We seek out general observations here in the spirit of inviting further dialogue between those whose familiarity with movement politics is primarily literature-based and those who have long engaged in movement politics as participants on the ground.

## Defining social movements

In this paper, we take a capacious view of movement politics, understanding social movements as collective action to effect change.[6] This conceptualization of social movements includes activism that *may prioritize a protest agenda or may emphasize, as does much of the NGO sector, development work informed by a deep commitment to grassroots social change.* This broad definition purposefully incorporates groups whose ideological and strategic differences can be stark. As Smitu Kothari writes, movements that are explicitly mobilizational take exception to the NGO label, preferring to be seen as "social action groups" or "political action groups" (Kothari 1993: 134). In his own analysis, Kothari speaks usefully of these groups as "struggle-oriented movements" (ibid.: 143). Philip Eldridge and Nil Ratan make a similar distinction in their study of social activism in Bihar between organizations that "concentrate on conventional programmes of community development – irrigation, drinking water, health centres, agriculture . . . and those whose main

---

[6] This is in broad agreement with Nandita Gandhi and Nandita Shah, relying on M.S.A. Rao, who define movements "as a sustained effort made through collective mobilization, to bring about change based on a pre-determined or emerging ideology" (1993: 23).

efforts center on educating and mobilizing poor people." As they explain, most activists believe in the importance of linking the two but in practice most emphasize one over the other. Eldridge and Ratan note as well that even official policy statements such as the seventh Five-Year Plan (1985–90) support these dual functions in theory. However, "governmental authorities, particularly at the local level tend to look with disfavour at even mild efforts at popular education or mobilization of a kind which increases pressures on officials or local elites" (Eldridge and Ratan 1988, 4–5). In this chapter, we define social movements inclusively, not only because it would be a mistake to ignore the burgeoning NGO sector in any analysis of social activism in India but also because we recognize many service-delivery organizations (some shelters, counseling centers, cooperatives, some rural "developmentalist" organizations) as endeavoring to foster political consciousness and participation even as they may eschew protest activities.

This understanding of social movements also comprises organizations *whose mobilization targets state institutions as well as those that engage with the state.* Social movement activism spans quite divergent views of the state. Some movements, both those that utilize violence (many Naxalite groups) as well as those that adhere to methods of civil disobedience (much of the Narmada Bachao Andolan), explicitly identify the state as a dominant agent of oppression and oppressive policies. Many other activist groups practice a more situationally developed politics. The anti-dowry/anti-bride-burning campaigns of the women's movement were variously directed at the courts when judicial decisions acquitted the clearly guilty or made light of serious crimes but in other situations were simply aimed at creating general social awareness, sometimes by the public shaming of the accused in-laws that attended the protests held outside the house of the accused husband or family. This part critic, part ally relationship to the state has been subtly negotiated by one of the best-known organizations within the women's movement, the Self-Employed Women's Association (SEWA), which, perhaps more typically than atypically, practices a politics of part autonomy from, part engagement with the state. Growing out of a powerful trade union to become a union in its own right of self-employed women workers, SEWA asserted its independence of union ties to the state, insisting that the government recognize the specific needs of poor, self-employed women. But as Bish Sanyal explains, SEWA distributed subsidized credit to poor women that it received from nationalized banks; sold SEWA handicrafts in government-run stores and SEWA-marketed vegetables to government hospitals and prisons. SEWA's campaign for higher piece rates for scrap clothing for members who sold cloth to private merchants was successful, Sanyal notes, because of the support of a state government minister. And Ela Bhatt, the organization's founder, later chaired a governmental commission to explore the problems of self-employed women (Sanyal 1997: 47).

Part of our reason for seeing social movement politics in this broadly encompassing way is to reveal rather than to obscure the diversity of political activism in India.[7] All efforts at typology whether of single movements (the environmental or women's movement) or of social movement activism as a whole reveal the extraordinary range in political ideologies, strategies, locations, and functions of collective action within Indian society.[8]

## The growth and institutionalization of social movement activism

India has been described not only with the well-worn aphorism "the world's largest democracy" but also, no less suggestively, as the "ngo capital of the world" (Kudva 1996: 1). Estimates of nongovernmental organizations in India vary from 10,000 to 100,000 (Kudva 1996: 1).[9]

---

[7] Social movement activism simply "on the left" encompasses a staggering diversity of innovative endeavors which range from subjugated communities and minorities asserting democratic rights to struggles of women to recover their dignity and rights to productive resources; from numerous efforts to nurture plural folk and indigenous traditions of song and theater to alternative networks of decentralized communication; from local actions seeking prohibition of the production, sale, and consumption of alcohol, to collective efforts to ban joint venture licenses to domestic and transnational corporate enterprises; from building democratic producer cooperatives to collective actions against the privatization of profitable public corporations; from campaigns against amniocentesis to regional campaigns against permitting Western drug corporations to patent and penetrate a low-cost and indigenous medicine system; from campaigns against irresponsible and destructive tourism to struggles against "destructive" development projects; from prolonged local agitations against corrupt officials to massive national support to weed out corruption in public life; from initiatives to restore control over local forests to massive collective effort to draft "people's" policies; from people's tribunals to "try" those guilty of human rights and environmental violations to efforts to form joint management systems to conserve and nurture fragile ecosystems; from efforts to educate farmers and workers about the impact of the new trade regime under the World Trade Organization to mass public demonstrations against specific policies of the World Bank; from asserting democratic control over local governments and productive resources to building transnational alliances.

[8] For a discussion of social movements in India and ways of categorizing, see Kothari 1993; Omvedt 1993; Ooomen 1990. For various typologies, *merely* of the women's movement, see Gandhi and Shah 1993, especially 30–32; Kishwar and Vanita 1989; Katzenstein 1989. On the environmental movement, see Guha 1989, 1997; Akula 1995; Khator 1991; Swain 1997; Kothari 2000b.

[9] Kothari (1993: 142) mentions that more than 15,000 groups are listed under the Ministry of Home Affairs-monitored Foreign Contributions (Regulation) Act passed in 1976 and amended in 1984.

The 1989 directory of environmental groups put out in India by the World Wildlife Fund lists 879 NGOs working specifically on environmental issues spread throughout the country.[10] The women's press, Kali For Women, publishes a pocket diary every year listing hundreds of women's organizations across India.[11] The Lokayan directory of NGOs working on gender issues produced for the Coordination Unit and National Alliance for Women lists over 500 entries.[12]

As with social movement organizations, so with protest. Renu Khator remarks with considered understatement: "Protests and demonstrations are not rare events in India: As a matter of fact, the nation ranks among the top ten countries in the reported number of political strikes and anti-regime demonstrations in the world, according to the *World Handbook of Political and Economic Indicators*" (Khator 1991: 156).

Measuring the precise growth of movement organizations is difficult. But most accounts of the women's and environmental movements or the NGO sector point to the 1970s and 1980s as a period of significant growth. For the women's movement, for instance, it was in the late 1970s and 1980s that the campaigns against rape, dowry deaths, and sex selection/amniocentesis gathered momentum (Kumar 1993; Desai 1988; Datar 1993; Omvedt 1993). In the case of environmental activism which as with the women's movement has a very long history in India that predates Independence, the level of media attention intensifies steeply in the late 1970s with the attention to the Silent Valley Hydroelectric Project and the Mathura Oil Refinery protests (Khator 1991: 169). The burgeoning of NGOs also begins in the 1970s. Neema Kudva (1996) describes the evolution of NGOs as moving through five phases. She depicts the third phase (from the late 1960s to the early 1980s) as a period of "phenomenal growth" in which there is a dual emergence of NGOs that are critical of government models of growth and in which there is also the "rise of the technocratic, managerial NGO" (1996: 9). Perhaps the clearest evidence of the growing strength of NGOs was the concern in government circles in this period, as the NGO sector expanded and became financially stronger, that the government should establish a more regularized relationship with the voluntary sector that would enable governmental institutions to more closely monitor the activities of this growing organizational sector. In the early 1980s, with the return of the Indira Gandhi government, NGO activism began to be more closely scrutinized and controlled. In 1981, the government

[10] Environmental Services Group, World Wildlife Fund (India) 1989 as quoted in Swain (1997: 822).
[11] kaliw@de12.vsnl.net.in
[12] Contact: Lokayan: 13 Alipur Road, Delhi 110054. Email: lokayan@vsnl.com.

established the Kudal Commission to investigate alleged corruption among NGOs partly with the apparent intention of clamping down on several NGOs including the Gandhi Peace Foundation and AVARD, which had been critical of the Indira Gandhi government (ibid.: 13). After Indira Gandhi's assassination, during Rajiv Gandhi's term in office, the seventh Five-Year Plan (1985–90) stipulated for the first time that the voluntary sector was a crucial part of the development process and allocated five times the amount of any earlier plan for NGO work.[13]

The institutionalization (routinization, formalization, and professionalization) of movement politics has developed over the last few decades. The existence of organizational directories, documentation centers, organizational histories and newsletters are some of the more overt measures of heightened routines and formalities. Many organizations in the NGO sector now have organizational charters or constitutions and many protest-oriented as well as service-delivery organizations are part of broad multigroup alliances or federations of organizations working on similar or related projects.[14] The increase in salaried workers has also grown with the rise in funds from both the Indian government and abroad.

With this international and state funding, long controversial among sections of movement activists who fear the compromising of organizational autonomy, has also come regulative control by the government

[13] Rajiv Gandhi appointed Bunker Roy, himself the leader of a highly visible NGO in Rajasthan, as adviser to the planning commission. In 1985, Roy proposed a voluntary "code of conduct" (Roy 1985) which precipitated a highly polemical debate among NGOs in part about whether the signing of such a contract constituted cooptation (see "On Voluntarism," *Lokayan Bulletin*, 1985). The government has also used the Society Registration Act of 1860, the Indian Trust Act (1882), the Income Tax Act (1961), and the Foreign Contribution Regulation Act, passed in 1976 and amended in 1985. See Kudva 1996; Gulhati et al. 1995.

[14] Two recent examples are the National Alliance of People's Movements (NAPM) and the National Front for Tribal Self-Rule (NFTSR). The NAPM has a membership of hundreds of movement organizations and was established in 1995 to organize interventions in the economic and political decision-making processes in the country. From the perspective of movements in alliances like the NAPM, top-down, welfarist policies are inadequate solutions to society-wide inequalities. NAPM seeks to identify structural inequalities and lack of rights over productive resources, arguing that there is an economic, political, and moral crisis reflected in what NAPM activists cite as the nearly doubling of inequality in wealth over the past thirty years and the starkly iniquitous sharing of political power. NAPM argues that people must stop being clients and recipients of doles and welfare checks and strive for greater economic and social control over their lives. The NFTSR, formed in 1994, represents tribal movements and communities from across the country and was one of the central actors that spearheaded the national campaign to establish self-rule in tribal areas. These efforts, which included local, regional, and national rallies and civil disobedience, were successful in compelling India's parliament to recommend to the president a constitutional amendment recognizing self-rule in tribal areas (Kothari 2000a; Kothari and Parajuli 1998).

through the monitoring of foreign donations and organizational expenditures.[15] Particularly among NGOs, there has been, as well, an increase in professionalization with an emphasis on training, conferences, reports, and what Kudva calls the rise in technocracy and managerial expertise (1996: 9). The significance of India's social movement society, the proliferation and institutionalization of movement politics cannot be gauged without addressing how such processes have engaged with the institutions of representation and governance.

### Social movements and institutional bifurcation

Different types of social movement activism, we contend, have been institutionalized in different political domains. Political movements are organized around the recognition of identities and have captured (or have been captured by) electoral politics. Movement politics that engage the state are organized around interests that have become institutionalized to some extent within both judicial and bureaucratic realms. Another way of stating this same point is that politics organized around interests do not have the benefit of the kind of popular mobilization that electoral and party politics produce.

India's three most powerful social movements all derive their coherence from identity claims. The movement for linguistic states,[16] the Dalit and backward caste movement and the Hindu nationalist movement are forms of collective action whose mobilization presupposes a given birthright and identity claim. These movements are expressions of identity politics in two senses: first, these movements' representational claims are ascriptive. They seek representation not by anyone who might speak to their issues or on their behalf, but rather by those who are "like them" – who share, as it were, their genealogy. Second, these movements are examples of identity politics in the sense that they seek by electoral recognition and power an answer to the question, "who are we?" These movements are in a sense the successors to the identity agendas of the Congress Party in its nationalist phase. Whereas Congress sought to clarify that those living under the tutelage of British rule were people in their own right, these language, caste, and religious movements are to no small extent also about affirming a sense of self in the face of real or imagined oppression, indignities, and inequalities.

This does not deny the material realities that are often central to the agendas of identity movements. All three movements have pursued

[15] Ibid.
[16] More recent examples of regional identity movements include those of the tribals in central and eastern India (Jharkand), in Assam (Bodoland) or in UP (Uttarkhand).

substantive, concrete goals: the redrawing of state boundaries, the elimination of discrimination and the reservation of jobs and educational preferences, the establishment of a uniform code, the building of a temple, the abolition of special status for Kashmir. But what reveals these movements to be more about identity than interests is the likelihood that any particular issue is likely to be fungible, replaceable by some other issue that does the work of securing recognition for a community's selfhood.[17]

But our point is less that language, caste, and religious movements have often made identity claims than it is that identity claims have captured the business of electoral politics. The proliferation of regional and caste parties that followed the decline of Congress dominance testifies to the importance, so fully evident in the 1998 election, of identity politics within the electoral arena. We are not suggesting, here, that electoral politics is only about identity issues. Clearly popular concerns about stability and corruption have figured in important ways in electoral outcomes. What we are saying is that mobilization around interest politics is weakly represented within the national electoral arena and that, in contrast, the politics of identity has situated itself preeminently within the electoral and party political domain.

This institutional bifurcation of identity and interest-based politics within the electoral and bureaucratic/judicial arenas evolved gradually from the time of independence. In the first months following Partition, the Indian Cooperative Union, a voluntary nongovernmental cooperative, was reinvigorated[18] by a group of young Congress Party socialists. L.C. Jain, one of the organizational founders, recounts how his work as a student in a refugee camp was unsettled by a visitor, Kamaladevi Chattopadhyaya, veteran freedom fighter and socialist leader, who asked him, "What is their [the refugees'] future? How long are they to live in the camps?" A group met the next day, drew up plans for a cooperative project that soon evolved into the Cooperative Union of India (ICU) intent on "a profound value-change in the larger society by a slow permeation, carrying the spirit of democratization, self-reliance, self-governance, mutual assistance and social concern" (Jain and Coelho 1996: 15, 40). Beginning with refugee rehabilitation, the movement turned to rural marketing and production, small industries, handlooms, handicrafts (one of the best-known ICU projects was Delhi's Cottage

---

[17] In this sense it is arguable that the linguistic state movements were more "interest" movements than has been the case for caste and religious movements, in the sense that the agenda of redrawn state boundaries would not have been easily displaced or supplanted by another set of claims.

[18] Amita Baviskar reviews the early days (preindependence) of the cooperative movement and its creation by the colonial state intent on securing a more regularized relationship with small peasant farmers (Jain and Coelho 1996: 52–68).

Industries Emporium), and social welfare. Transformative in its vision, pragmatic in much of its undertakings, at once skeptical of bureaucratic interventionism but dependent on state assistance and regulated by state rules, the ICU was to exemplify much of the action-driven nonidentity social movement politics that was soon to materialize in the nonelectoral sector over India's next decades.[19]

The surge of identity movements soon followed, situated, by contrast, within party politics and the electoral arena. Leftist movements saw in identity politics an opportunity to mobilize politically. Without downplaying the conviction of Communist Party organizers that linguistic reorganization would (as it did) democratize political representation,[20] Selig Harrison is, nevertheless right to suggest that language agitations were seized on by a Communist Party that sought ways to mobilize a popular following and gain political advantage. Harrison offers a dramatic account:

In the newly elected Parliament, the Communist bloc staged walkouts to protest delivery of speeches in Hindi and introduced a motion for "immediate" linguistic reorganization . . . Finally, amid a heightened propaganda barrage throughout the country, the Andhra Communists were able to organize a violent conclusion to the fast unto death for an Andhra State of the Telegu Gandhian disciple Potti Sriramulu in December 1952. The rampant hysteria in Andhra which followed . . . forced the Congress government to concede the Andhra demand gracelessly under the threat of mob destruction which could only encourage other regions to do business with New Delhi in an equally bellicose spirit (Harrison 1960: 284–285).

Already, by the early 1950s, it was clear that identity politics sold well in the electoral arena.

The Indian Cooperative Union and the Communist appeal to linguistic identity politics in the movement for linguistic states were in a sense mere instances in the vast proliferation of social movement politics that surfaced within Indian society even in the early days following

---

[19] The cooperative movement (as distinct from the ICU specifically) borrowed from both a secular Nehruvian vision and Gandhian economic convictions situated between a pragmatic view of state engagement and a principled conviction that cooperation formed by the people should be free of state regulation. Well into the 1960s and beyond, however, the reality was that cooperatives were often enmeshed both in partisan politics and in bureaucracy as state assistance was extended and often stifling regulations were imposed that controlled their operations. More recently, the cooperative movement has sought greater autonomy by delinking itself from governmental oversight and control, succeeding in Andhra Pradesh to secure the passage of the Mutually Aided Cooperative Societies Act (ibid.: 401–402). Significant mobilization is currently working to secure similar legislation at the national level. For a good bibliography on agricultural and credit cooperatives, see ibid.

[20] The linguistic reorganizations and the consequent usage of local languages as the medium of political communication did lead to the decline in English-educated lawyers and urbanites and the rise in legislative representation of local elites (Hardgrave 1968: 60).

independence. We single them out here because they exemplify so vividly the two very different streams of movement activism and their institutionalization in separate arenas of politics.

The separation from the electoral domain of other economic reform movements evolved gradually. The Gandhian-inspired Bhoodan (land gift) movement led by Vinoba Bhave and the reenvisioned Sarvodaya movement led by Jayaprakash Narayan were conceived as extra-political movements, seeking as they did to establish *lokniti* or rule by the people through basic democracy, as distincti from *rajniti*, rule by the state. But by the early 1970s the movement had become involved in electoral politics. Two factions had emerged. Vinoba Bhave and his supporters adhered to a pro-government stand while J.P. Narayan mobilized a massive popular challenge to the Indira Gandhi-ruled Congress Party initially in the states of Gujarat and Bihar and subsequently over significant areas of North India. This mobilization was one of the catalysts of Indira Gandhi's declaration of the Emergency in 1975. The nineteen-month Emergency and the effort by the state to weaken the Sarvodaya movement through the Kudal Commission inquiry into the alleged misuse of funds by the Gandhi Peace Foundation that supported J.P. (Oomen 1990: 199) made the state's hostility to democratic reform movements' efforts to engage in outright electoral challenges amply clear. The two years of authoritarian rule in Delhi were ironically what galvanized the proliferation of much social movement activity but at the same time what may also have steered much of the Gandhian-based democratic reform movements away from further involvement in electoral politics.

The institutionalization of what we have been terming interest politics within the bureaucratic/judicial sectors has become increasingly evident in recent decades with the surge of activism around environmental and gender issues. A point of clarification is in order here: we do not see the environmental/ecology or the women's movement as inherently either issue or identity-based. We understand organizations concerned with ecological preservation in India, for example, to be largely interest-driven, protecting the livelihoods of rural peasants dependent on the forest or villagers who stand to be displaced by dam-precipitated flooding or adults and children whose health is jeopardized by toxic groundwater, etc. But these movements may also impinge on identity issues where villagers see their connection to the land, to a sacred river, or to nature deeply entwined with their sense of self as well as where norms of "ecology versus development" invoke deep-seated questions related to how communities and individuals define their lives. Gender claims can, likewise, be both interest-based and identity-based. We see gender claims in India as being framed more often as interest claims than as identity ones in the sense that issues of women's "difference" are rarely raised by women activists, whereas the language of women's "oppression" is the more widely employed frame, although it is sometimes the case that arguments about reservations for women do at times invoke a justification rooted in an idea about gender difference. Interests and identities are, we should emphasize, almost always braided within any form of political activism. Once again, however, our intent here is not to assert that the politics of a particular group are more identity-based than interest-based or vice versa; rather, what we seek here is to emphasize that electoral politics favors identity claims and bureaucratic/judicial politics the raising of interest-based activism.

Issues raised by environmental/ecology groups and by the women's movement have on occasion been the subject of specific legislative action,[21] but these issues are rarely seen in party politics as significant enough to frame electoral strategies or to mobilize around politically, and rarely are these issues taken so seriously that they come to characterize a party's identity with the voters. In the case of the women's movement, it is striking that as active as political party women have been in challenging discriminatory laws and practices – the CPI-M women's organization, AIDWA, has been, for instance, in the forefront of numerous campaigns, as have the women's organizations of the CPI and socialist left – it is more often on the streets or even in the courts than in the legislatures themselves that women legislators have gained a voice. In one of the most recent chapters of the movement's challenge against chemical contraceptives, for instance, AIDWA itself sought to halt the use of the contraceptive drug Quinachrine not by introducing legislation but by bringing a successful joint writ petition in the courts.[22]

---

[21] Movement activists were important in pressuring for amendments to the Indian penal code, the code of criminal procedure and the Indian Evidence Act as part of rape reform efforts, in the Equal Remuneration Act of 1976, in the passage of the Dowry Prohibition (Amendment) Act of 1984, the Indecent Representation of Women (Prohibition) Act of 1986, the Commission of Sati (Prevention) Bill in 1987, etc. See the chapter on legal campaigns in Gandhi and Shah (1993: 213–272). On the laws passed against pollution, deforestation, and environmental destruction, see Khator (1991: 53–87).

[22] The eighty-first amendment introduced in parliament during the winter session of 1996–7 that would have set aside 30 percent of legislative seats for women did very briefly generate the kind of political debate around gender identity issues that might have made it significant electoral matter, but the proposal was dropped almost immediately when it was opposed by those who argued that quotas for women were unacceptable without assured representation of the other backward classes (OBCs) (Kannabiran and Kannabiran 1997). To the extent that gender or environmental interest issues tend to be taken up by political parties at all, it is in the context of momentary instrumental politics (e.g., when the Shiv Sena used the Enron issue to disparage the Congress Party, turning around subsequently to work out an agreement

When movement activism around issues of gender and ecology engage with the state, they have done so largely in the forum of bureaucratic and judicial politics rather than within the electoral domain. In the case of the women's movement, it is telling that it was by means of a written attack on *the courts* that the mobilization against violence against women was galvanized as a large-scale popular movement.[23] The catalytic event was an open letter sent by four law professors (three from Delhi University) to the supreme court accusing it of unjustly reversing a Bombay high court conviction of two policemen accused of raping a young teenage tribal girl by the name of Mathura. This was followed by organizing campaigns around rape, dowry deaths, battering, sati, sex determination tests, injectable and chemical contraceptives, and other issues of reproductive health. Throughout, when movement organizers have sought to engage institutions of the government, they have worked through ministries (of women's and child welfare, departments of police, departments of rural development, of family planning).[24] The litigation that has emanated from women's rights campaigns has filled court dockets leading to thick tomes analyzing court cases on marriage, divorce, adoption, and property in addition to cases about all aspects of violence against women (Jaising 1996; Kapur and Cossman 1996).

The campaign against parental selection of fetuses and amniocentesis that was taken up in the late 1980s in Maharashtra is revealing for what it says about the weak relationship of interest-based movement politics to the legislative and bureaucratic institutions of government. Different from some of the other issues of the women's movement, legislative reform did feature quite centrally in this campaign. But it is revealing in their description of their political strategizing how inattentive movement activists were to the legislative possibilities. The introduction of a bill in the state legislature proved to be fortuitous, the result of a personal interest taken by a senior civil servant from the Maharashtra secretariat who on his own initiative drafted the bill and urged legislative colleagues to introduce it as a private member's bill. As movement organizers recount, it was when the secretary of the Department of Public Health from the government of Maharashtra indicated that he was willing to get

with Enron that seemed in the end not to depart markedly from the Congress's own initial position).

[23] In the mid-1970s, the coalition of the left had organized a conference in Pune and the CPI-M had organized a conference in Trivandrum on gender. The focus of the discussion was largely work-related. The resolutions did include some on dowry, on Devadasis, and on a common civil code but none, it appears, on rape or other sexuality-related issues (Omvedt 1993: 82).

[24] We will not try to recount in any detail the history of this activism since it has been so well told elsewhere (Gandhi and Shah 1993; Omvedt 1993; Datar 1993; Kumar 1993; Desai 1988).

involved that the legal momentum shifted. After approaching the secretary, D.I. Joseph, at the end of their discussion, he turned to the women activists, commenting: "You may not be knowing it. But you have convinced the right person. Now it is my responsibility to bring about some concrete action on this issue" (Ravindra 1993: 74).

The organizers write:

We took his remarks with a pinch of salt. But our subsequent experience showed that Joseph was indeed seized by the issue. In our country, bureaucrats are virtual rulers. They have tremendous powers . . . As we look back in order to look forward, a mixed picture emerges. It shows our utter ignorance or an ambivalence towards legislative means . . . We did not use the legislature even once after the passing of the bill (ibid.: 74, 97).

Bureaucracies and the courts have been the institutional arena of choice for interest-based women's movement politics; less so, the legislatures. Given the aforementioned account of the women's movement organizing against parental selection of fetuses, it is not surprising that *even* when in 1990 the Maharashtra *legislature* acted to reserve 30 percent of all seats for women in the municipal corporations, councils, *zilla parishads, panchayat samitis* and village *panchayats,* that two prominent movement activists should exclaim, "It was a sudden and surprise announcement. Women's groups and the opposition parties were quite unprepared for it" (Shah and Gandhi 1993: 3).

A similar account could be given of activist politics focusing on ecology. The courts and bureaucracies have long been repositories of considerable power in India and it is not surprising that often highly educated movement activists with the requisite legal and educational skills necessary for exerting leverage in these domains would bring litigation or attempt to negotiate agreements in these arenas. The turn to the courts, moreover, became increasingly compelling in the atmosphere of judicial activism set by several supreme court justices, who in the late 1970s and early 1980s began to allow broadened rules of standing, to make readier use of interim orders, and to encourage the representation of more populist litigants.

Through public interest litigation (PIL) or social action litigation (SAL), momentous judgments were handed down that extended rights to prisoners, bonded laborers, pavement dwellers, rickshaw pullers, construction workers, Adivasis and Dalits.[25] Although this activism did not by any means extend to all levels of the court system, the tenor had

[25] On pavement dwellers, see *Olga Tellis* v. *State of Maharashtra* AIR 1979 SC 1825; on prison conditions, see *Dr. Upendra Baxi* v. *State of Uttar Pradesh* 1981 (3) SCALE 1136; on bonded laborers and the Faridabad stone quarry case, see *Bandhua Mukti Morcha* v. *Union of India and others* AIR 1984 SC 802, etc. For a review of these cases see Baar (1990).

changed as rights claims were increasingly brought to the courts. Time and again – one source cites "4,000 cases regarding environmental pollution pending in various courts in 1991" (Madsen 1997: 256) – ecological activists have sought stay orders to prevent the operation of polluting and hazardous industries, intrusive mining or power projects, or encroachment on natural preserves.[26] No less than other activist groups, the Narmada Bachao Andolan, known for its protest actions and civil disobedience, has, for instance, also submitted numerous petitions in the local courts in Maharashtra and Gujarat, the high court in Gujarat and ultimately in the supreme court itself (Dwivedi 1997).

So broadly suffused are rights-based claims that it is not unusual to find differently affected equality or justice-seeking groups on opposite sides of a courtroom procedure or action campaign. This has been the case, for instance, with the tribal group, the Van Gujjars, who have sought to exercise what they see as their right to livelihood in the face of conservation movements that wish to protect the forests, specifically the Rajaji National Park, from deforestation. NGOs representing both sides have brought their case to ministries at the center and state levels as well as to the courts (Gooch 1997; Madsen 1997).[27]

The constant interaction with ministries and bureaucracy is also a key feature of activism around ecological issues. Forest-based environmental groups, for instance, worked together to contest the national forest policy of 1988 and the circular on joint forest management (JFM) of 1990, not in the halls of the legislatures but in the corridors of ministries and departments (Swain 1997: 822).[28] One account, quite typically, tells

---

[26] For a discussion of public interest litigation and mining, see Madsen (1997).

[27] Another example of this clash of norms occurred with the Sriram case and a follow-up case brought by the advocate M.C. Mehta against the government of Delhi to halt polluting industries in the metropolis. The trade union movement, however, opposed the order because the court as they saw it failed to define protection for the workers thrown out of the industries that were being shut down. The two sides clashed in a difficult 1997 meeting in Delhi that had been called by noted environmentalists to celebrate the closure order against the factories.

[28] Their coalition teamed with other social movements and alliances such as the Jan Vikas Andolan (Movement for People's Development) to draft a people's forest policy and to seek new legislative intervention. Initiatives by numerous groups – the Kashtakari Sanghatana (Organization of Toilers) in the Thane district of Maharashtra, the Tarun Bharat Sangh in the Alwar District of Rajasthan, the Chipko (Hug the Trees) groups in various parts of Uttarkhand in Uttar Pradesh, the Jangal Bachao Manav Bachao (Save the Forest, Save Humanity) groups in the Gadchiroli district of Maharashtra, various forest protection committees in the Kailadevi Sanctuary of Rajasthan, etc. – have lent strength to what is now a nationally visible effort to promote a people's forest policy. Successful efforts at establishing joint forest management have occurred in West Bengal, Orissa, and Gujarat (on Gujarat see Madsen 1993). A similar process has been evident in the mobilization to seek a national legislation defining the rights of those displaced by development projects (Kothari 1996).

of the efforts by one NGO that became involved in this process engaging in forty-nine separate contacts with government officials and bureaucrats in both Gujarat and Delhi (Madsen 1997: 264).

We do not mean to suggest, either in the case of the women's movement or the ecology movement, that engagement with the bureaucracies and with the courts has become a substitute for popular action (demonstrations, street theater, petitions, civil disobedience). What we are observing here is simply that when social movements seek government support, they have done so in India in different institutional arenas depending on whether the issues they address are identity- or issue-based.

This distinction between identity politics operating in the electoral arena and interest politics operating in the bureaucratic/judicial domains does not, of course, perfectly capture every case. Farmers' movements that have pursued an interest politics within the legislative arena fit this framework less neatly, although as a national movement they have fallen short of becoming fully institutionalized electorally and have often (as with the BKU–Jat linkage) relied on identity, particularly caste appeals, when they have been incorporated as political parties into the electoral arena.[29] The land reform movements that have been integral to party agendas in West Bengal and Kerala are also exceptions to the more general rule. Tribal movements that successfully brought identity claims into the legislative domain, securing in 1996 the historic passage of the Provision of the Panchayats (Extension to Scheduled

---

[29] Farmers' movements that have proved the most electorally successful at the state level have done so in part by relying on identity (caste or regional-based) appeals. In her study of "new social movements," Gail Omvedt traces the efforts of the farmers' protests of the 1970s and early 1980s, noting that, in 1980 itself, the movement had come to exercise such popular influence that politicians did "their serious negotiating with the independent peasant organizations" (Omvedt 1993: 112) rather than with the leadership of the leftist parties. But not long thereafter efforts to institutionalize a national farmers' organization faltered as its leaders were unable to superimpose broader interests across the different strong regional and caste-based farmers' movements that made up the national coalition. National-level influence, however, has been sufficient to block efforts, for instance by the Congress Party in 1991, to raise fertilizer prices by 40 percent and the 1993 cross-regional protests against the GATT agreement (an agreement supported by another section of the farmers' movement led by Sharad Joshi in Maharashtra) included a demonstration that drew over 100,000 participants in Bangalore (Lindberg 1997) and demonstrated that regional farmers' movements were capable of impressive national-level coordination. But the strongest expression of farmers' movement politics is at the local level – where, as in western UP and in Punjab, it has been electorally institutionalized in a political party, the BKU. Significantly, however, the BKU has relied heavily not just on its claims to represent the material interests of farmers but also on caste and regional identity appeals – drawing heavily as it does on the Jat populations of the region.

Areas Act 1996),[30] incorporated within their identity protests a strong interest-based antidevelopmentalist agenda.

Such caveats notwithstanding, we maintain that for the most part what has developed is a broad bifurcation of interest and identity movements in different institutional domains. In the chronological narrative that Gail Omvedt sets out in her major study of social movements in India, *Reinventing Revolution,* she argues that the environmental, women's, Dalit, and farmers' movements that emerged in the 1970s represent a new class of social movements. The successors to the union and peasant movements of earlier days, these "new social movements" neither constitute class formations nor do they subscribe to traditional Marxist precepts. The activists of these new movements must instead "reinvent revolution" (Omvedt 1993). Our account of this chronology is somewhat different. We do not see the departure from traditional Marxist precepts as new to the 1970s and more recent movements. The earlier movements of the 1950s and the 1960s – the language, ethnic, and anticaste movements – also invented revolution by fusing identity with interest claims in a manner that stressed their demand to be recognized as Telegu speakers, or Marathi speakers, or as Nadars or Dalit/neo-Buddhists together with some version of populist politics that was sometimes (as in the case of some of the language movements) explicitly Marxist. But what was distinctive about these earlier movements was their linkages to political parties and the electoral process. With the (chronologically) newer movements of the 1970s onwards, it becomes increasingly clear that identity movements have captured the discursive space of electoral politics and that the nonidentity movements that position themselves as advocates of the poor and underprivileged (from action or struggle-oriented groups to the more welfare-delivery forms of NGOs) have carved out institutional spaces for themselves that while seeking changes locally also depend more on channels to the bureaucracy, the courts, or to global institutional fora.

### The regionalism of movement politics and the Hindu nationalist exception

Both identity- and interest-based social movements are for the most part regionally based. That is, the agendas are often shaped by local conditions and by the norms and priorities that the local institutional

---

[30] This recognizes among other rights that every *gram sabha* (village assembly) will have the power to safeguard and preserve the traditions and customs of the people, their cultural identity, community resources, and the customary modes of dispute resolution (Kothari 2000a).

environment supports. Different local conditions (linguistic, economic, political) and the limited administrative and financial capacities of movement organizations make organizing across regions difficult. Broader cultural environs also gives shape to the kinds of movement politics that exist in different regions. As Kudva observes, "the Gandhian movement has had a deeper impact on the voluntary sector in Gujarat, UP, and Bihar, while the Left has been a strong influence in West Bengal and Kerala and parts of Andhra Pradesh and Maharashtra. Similarly the Church has played an important role in some southern states, the northeastern states and in other areas with heavy concentrations of Adivasi and Dalit populations" (1996: 4–5).

Raka Ray makes this argument forcefully in her comparison of women's movements in Bombay and Calcutta. She contends that social movement organizations "inhabit a field" made up of a multiple of organizations whose language and actions frame the organizational terrain. How organizations operate depends on the field within which they are located. Her comparisons lead her to an interesting modification of the widely accepted thesis that women's movements affiliated to leftist organizations are thought to prioritize issues of class and inequality over issues of body politics or violence. Comparing women's movements in Calcutta (a largely Marxist "field") and women's movements in Bombay (a more plural "field"), Ray observes:

First, while autonomous feminist groups in Bombay did indeed consider violence against women a crucial issue, they did not do so in Calcutta, where levels of violence were comparable. Second, autonomous feminist organizations in Calcutta considered important exactly the same issues as did the left wing women's groups – employment and poverty, literacy and ideology – but autonomous feminist groups in Bombay did not do so despite comparable levels of poverty, unemployment and illiteracy. Finally, left wing women's organizations in Bombay adopted the same rhetoric towards violence against women as did Bombay's autonomous feminist groups, a rhetoric that was not reflected in left wing women's organizations in Calcutta. (Ray 1998)

Ray's analysis points to a general observation made in the literature on social movements both in India and more generally – that political opportunities can catalyze or inhibit the emergence of movements and can structure the form that activism takes (Basu 1992; Katzenstein, Mehta, and Thakkar 1997; Tarrow 1994).

It may be interesting to conjecture whether the structure of political opportunities helps to address the question of why Hindu nationalist activists have succeeded in transporting their identity claims into the national electoral arena whereas the environmental movement has not. Why, that is, has the identity politics of the BJP succeeded electorally both regionally and nationally whereas a "green" party has penetrated neither state-level nor national-level electoral arenas despite at least some incipient discussions of such a project?[31] The reasons for this transition from movement to political party of environmental activism in Germany suggests a lens through which this question might be explored in India. This issue in the German context is much debated, but one compelling account suggests that because the claims the Greens advanced in Germany were repudiated by the German courts, the movement had little choice but to turn to the electoral arena (Greve 1987).[32] The application of this argument to India would suggest that the relative ease with which environmental movements have claimed standing in the courts (compared to their German counterpart) goes some way towards explaining why in India ecology activists have not been so pressed to seek to develop an electoral base.[33] Clearly, the question of institutional domains is overdetermined here: Hindu or religious identity as a basis for organizing politically has a longstanding basis in and wider reach among the electorate in India than do the much more recently evident problems of environmental deterioration. Yet if the courts and the bureaucracies were to offer ecological activists no remedial avenues whatsoever, it is worth asking whether activists would not turn more urgently in the direction of party or electoral channels and whether in a city such as Delhi where air quality, for instance, is so severely compromised – a fact no voter can escape – electoral mobilization based on a "green candidacy" around this sort of issue might not carry some weight with voters.

Opportunities figure in another way when it comes to the choice of political domains within which activists seek to operate. Both identity

---

[31] The National Alliance for People's Movement, for instance, met at Wardha in March 1996 where there was some discussion over the need to "positively intervene in the electoral process of the country" (putting up candidates for election or campaigning for those candidates it regarded as sympathetic) (Dwivedi 1997: 34). They met again in 1997 and placed questions before political parties whom they invited to a series of public meetings.

[32] See, however, a set of different arguments summarized in Zirakzadeh (1997).

[33] The inverse cannot be claimed – e.g., that Hindu nationalism has been directed to pursue legislative power because it has been closed out of the courts. The supreme court's receptivity to the BJP's quest for a uniform civil code was evident in their 1985 judgment supporting Shah Bano and in a more recent Allahabad high court ruling declaring the practice of triple *talaq* at a single sitting violative of Muslim law and of the constitution (Kapur and Cossman 1996: 257), and the courts have been reluctant to see the statements of Hindu nationalists such as Bal Thackeray as infringing on the rights of minorities or threatening the civil peace; but in other ways the courts have been less receptive to the Hindu nationalist agenda seeking legal recognition of the Hindu origins of the Ayodhya temple site; nor have the courts supported the petition of a BJP supporter who sought to force stricter censorship of allegedly immoral media portrayals in the *Chole ke Piche* film brouhaha (Kapur and Cossman 1996: 253).

and interest-based social movements in India have made use of the opportunity global networks afford.

Identity movements, no less than interest-based movements, have become immersed in global networks. Movement organizations have used global networks, including the internet and web pages, to secure visibility abroad, to establish themselves as legitimate actors and to promote their interpretation of controversial issues and events.[34] Ethnic and religious movements, such as the VHP or pro-Khalistan organizations have turned to nonresident Indians abroad for financial support. It is widely presumed that the Sikh diaspora in the United States, Canada, and the United Kingdom was a significant source of funds for the early years of the Khalistani movement. Didar Singh Bains, one of the largest peach growers in the US who became president of the World Sikh Organization in 1984 following Operation Bluestar, was reputed to have helped to channel funds to the Khalistan movement but has since returned to mainstream Akali politics.[35] If in recent decades it might be fair to speculate that global networks have sustained more moderate, constitutional forms of interest-based movement politics, it would probably also be worth observing that whatever moderating effects global networks have had on identity movements have not precluded their capacity to draw on the diaspora for support for militant and sometimes violent political activism.

Global institutions have helped directly to galvanize interest-based movement activism. It is striking that in the case of both environmental and women's movement politics, United Nations events were important as early "yeast" giving rise to elite-level consciousness and ultimately movement organizing. In 1971, the United Nations requested that India submit an assessment of the country's environmental status and concerns in preparation for what came to be known as the Stockholm Conference. The committee, headed by B.B. Vohra, reported on the environmental deterioration which they found to be "shocking." The report became the basis for a government-established Committee on Environmental Planning and Coordination (Khator 1991: 55). A parallel situation occurred in the history of the women's movement. Responding to the United Nations' request for a report in preparation for the 1975 International Women's Year, the government of India established a committee that did research on women's issues and submitted a data-

---

[34] A number of different Kashmiri Muslim organizations, for instance, have created web pages providing their own interpretation of Kashmiri history, the transgression, as they see it, of promises for a plebiscite, and the record they would like to see conveyed of human rights abuses in the Valley.

[35] *India Today*, December 22, 1997: 24e. Personal communication, Paul Wallace, March 16, 1998.

filled document that, widely cited in the years to come, became one of the key authoritative sources movement groups could cite as they pressured the government for change. Documenting the stark imbalance in gender ratios, thereby making the differential in female–male infant and adult mortality a matter of the public record, the final 1974 report, *Towards Equality,* was decisive in getting gender issues onto the governmental agenda (Katzenstein 1991–2).

International conferences and workshops also provide occasions for federations of organizations to be formed, as happened in preparation for the 1995 Beijing Women's Conference, and may help to precipitate sometimes intense debate, both before and after, on issues scheduled for discussion in upcoming international conferences, as occurred with the debate over the draft report on a national population policy surrounding the 1994 International Conference on Population and Development held in Cairo.[36]

Movements have made use of international networks in exerting pressure on policymakers at home. The Narmada Andolan is a case in point. Movement agitation received global publicity and was able to exert pressure on policymakers abroad with the support of international networks (the Environmental Defense Fund in Washington, Survival International in London, Friends of the Earth in Tokyo), leading to the withdrawal of Japanese aid and the World Bank's 1992 decision to halt support for the project contingent on the government of India completing a series of studies reassessing the human impact of the project (Kothari 1993; Akula 1995: 144).

This leverage often works both ways. The influx of foreign funds particularly into the NGO sector is sizable but its impact on movement agendas is hard to assess. A 1993 estimate puts international NGO funding of Indian organizations at between $110 and $160 million. This does not include multilateral or bilateral funding that comes from governments or international agencies. One of the largest of the private NGO donor agencies is the German Protestant Church organization (which spends about $20 million a year) with other organizations like the Christian Children's Fund, Oxfam, Save the Children and a handful of others spending in the range of $10 million to $40 million annually (Kudva 1996: 18).

There is no question but that foreign funding is consequential in focusing NGO attention on the bureaucratic arena since it is the bureau-

---

[36] Meetings in preparation for Cairo began in 1993. Many groups individually and together met in consultation, with one group scheduling eighteen meetings. Discussions were often heated with attacks on "family planning wallahs" and "population control" discourse (Ramachandran 1996).

cracy which channels foreign assistance to NGOs. USAID, for instance, has been conducting for the last few years a ten-year $325 million project on reproductive health in the state of UP alone directed by an IAS officer-run umbrella organization that allocates funds to NGOs in the state. The large infusion of foreign funds within the NGO sector inevitably causes tension among NGOs both because of the concern about legitimacy both abroad and at home and because salary differentials between those located in highly professionalized foreign-funded NGO settings, sometimes paying European and American-level salaries, far exceed those of other activist organizations that may be receiving few or no funds.

But the way in which international funding may sway the agenda of local movement organizations is far from clear. It causes groups to frame their requests for funds to satisfy the priorities of the funding agency. With the reframing, for instance, of population control and family planning as "reproductive health," organizations scurried to deploy the appropriate language as they sought to convince donors that their work was worthy of funding (Ramachandran 1996).

But to what extent this means that activist groups undertake tasks they would not have intended to or abandon priorities that they would have otherwise pursued, or to what extent the absence of foreign funds would preclude undertaking some of the documentation and activism that groups are now engaged in, is much debated but, to our knowledge, largely unresearched (Shah and Gandhi 1991: 273–321). Indeed, it is hard to know how to research the counterfactual: if international funding of NGOs were unavailable or refused (much as a number of social movement activists in India have urged), would movement organizations dedicate more resources to the study of and organization around, for instance, inequalities in property and the wide-ranging problems of labor? Does attention to women's rights, to ecological concerns, framed often in the internationally dominant language of the day as "rights discourse," divert attention from concerns about class inequalities, livelihood, and poverty or does it provide at least some means by which these issues can be addressed? What effect do global networks have on "constitutionalizing" protest, diverting it from more spontaneous and possibly violence-prone strategies? Without such funding, would the cross-fertilization of international discourse around gender and environmental rights still occur much as it does now? What is clear is that whether movement activists are nationally or regionally based, the expansion of global networks, the activity of international organizations, and the funding by international NGOs and global diasporas has expanded the nonelectoral space within which both identity and interest-driven movement organizations can seek representation in politics.

### The coexistence of a civic discursive space

Institutionalization of identity and interest movements that engage with the state in electoral, judicial, and bureaucratic domains has not precluded the viability – and importance – of discursive activism in civil society. Writing about Mexico in 1994, Judith Hellman argues that "The most compelling reason to look at popular movements in some light *other* than that of democratization is that, even by the most optimistic reading, this process is not under way in Mexico."

She writes:

We do not need to justify our study of these movements with the claim that they promote institutional responses that reinforce democracy. The formation of new identities, the expansion of civil society, the search for new ways of doing politics, and the mobilization of new sectors of society are all important developments in themselves, and we do not need to see the movements as necessarily fostering the institutionalization of democratic practices in order to legitimate our concern with them (Hellman 1994: 138).[37]

We do not argue that political institutions in India have become less democratic but we echo the importance Hellman accords to the place of social movement activism in civil society. Whether from the "right" or "left," movement activism even when disengaged from the state shapes popular understandings and can foster or transform political identities. For decades, unlinked to the state, the RSS helped to nurture a Hindu identity among broad sections of the Indian populace that is now the well-laid foundation on which the BJP has been able to build electoral power. More recently, many of the movements from the 1970s to the present have sought to create political awareness and to provide unrepresented or impoverished sections of society with conceptual frames through which they can recognize the structural bases of inequality.

Examples of movement efforts to reshape existing beliefs about power relations abound within the women's movement. Mobilizing against violence against women, women's organizations did engage the state – pressuring for legal change and for special police cells and police training to deal with gender violence. But the objective of this mobilization was

---

[37] Hellman argues that Mexico was becoming progressively less democratic as evidenced by the "stolen" 1988 election, the electoral violence and suppression of opposition victories, and the lack of consultation as Mexican leaders liberalized the economy and negotiated the fair-trade deal with the US (Hellman 1994: 138). For a similar emphasis on the importance of movements operating in a "third" civil society space, see Alvarez (1997).

also cultural beliefs and practices themselves which women organizers sought to challenge through marches and demonstrations, street theater, plays, journal stories and personal accounts, songs, and poster exhibitions (Shah and Gandhi 1993: 36–102). Similarly, the organizing in preparation for the 1995 United Nations women's meeting in Beijing was only in part to prepare comments on the government's Country Paper and the Draft Platform of Action. The preparation planned through the Coordination Unit arranged for hundreds of meetings throughout the country which women from all strata of society were invited to attend and in which they were asked to voice their concerns and perspectives on a host of different issues ranging from health to displacement by development projects. The intent was discursive: in part to shape the governmental agenda at Beijing but also to catalyze conversations and networking that might become the basis for a broad transformation in attitudes on a range of gender issues (Women Towards Beijing 1996).

Much of this movement activism walks, as Smitu Kothari has argued, "on two legs." Movement organizers seize opportunities where they exist to influence government policy and at the same time plan programs and strategies that are aimed at transforming the norms and practices throughout society at large. This dual level of political activism was evident in the anti-arrack mobilization of the late 1980s and early 1990s in Andhra Pradesh. The seeds of the campaign were laid in the literacy readers which had been composed to include real-life issues such as stories about the difficulties women and their families suffered from the money wasted and violence spawned by alcoholism and about a protest that had been organized against arrack dealers. Familiar with these stories and with the account of women who had stood up to the arrack dealers and the drinking men, women attending literacy classes initiated organizing campaigns and soon their networking and political actions grew into a powerful mobilization that pressured the then chief minister to (temporarily) ban the sale of liquor.[38] Bridging formal institutions of government and civil society, women's activism has also been directed at efforts to give real meaning to the inclusion of women in the *panchayats* that resulted from the passage of the seventy-third and seventy-fourth constitutional amendments. In strengthening the *panchayat* structure, the amendments included requirements that a third of *panchayat* seats be reserved for women, but much of the promise of this change was often undercut by virtue of the cooptation of wives or daughters whose presence was not intended to provide an independent women's voice.

[38] See the film by Nata Duvurry, *When Women Unite,* on the Andhra campaign that features some of the village women, who participated in the mobilization.

Both through NGOs committed to gender equality objectives and through experimental Mahila Samakhya programs in which feminists have been involved, efforts have been undertaken to create a level of consciousness, self-confidence, and skill among women *panchayat* members that would in the years to come shape the village councils in a more truly democratic fashion (Batliwala 1996; Mohanty 1995).

### Conclusion

Dating back at least to the Nehru Report of 1928, all constitutional plans for India recognized the need for some kind of federal structure. The multivalent diversity of India could only be unified within such a structure. In this as in so much else the constitutional architects of India confronted many of the same challenges and endorsed similar visions as did those in the US. Regular elections, bicameralism at the center, fundamental rights, elected state legislatures, and elected village *panchayats* were all part of this federal vision and its attempt to unify the country without muffling its ineradicable diversity of conditions.

Despite India's long history of organizational activism, few in the 1940s and 1950s imagined that social movements/NGOs, rather than the power of the ballot, would play a critical role in representing the diversity that was such a conspicuous fact of the country's present and preoccupation regarding its future. And yet, as we have argued, it is precisely through the range and dense welter of such movements and organizations that democratic institutions (such as the courts and the bureaucracy) have been able to finetune their responses to the fluidity and diversity of India. It is not that these institutions can be (despite their rhetoric) a substitute for the state, but without the pressures they bring to bear and the issues that they raise at state and local levels, it is clear that the democratic institutions would not be able, in however inadequate a manner, to meet the challenge of India's diversity and shifting conditions. In this, social movement activism has been a largely unacknowledged bulwark against the materialization of the conditions that so often propel authoritarian responses. As the experience in Latin America in the 1960s, 1970s and 1980s suggests, states, when confronted with the frustration of generalized sentiments and hopes which are not addressed or are refracted through subsidiary political institutions, often resort to a blanket authoritarianism. Counterfactually, it appears likely that interest-based social movement activism along with the courts and bureaucracy have played a significant role in safeguarding against such an eventuality in India. It is unlikely that electoral practices alone would have been able to secure a similar outcome.

In contrast to this role that social movement activism has played regarding the fluid diversity of India, electoral and party politics has increasingly become the mainstay for representing and endorsing essentialized identities and institutionalizing them. The picture one gets from the most recent elections and the party platforms that preceded them is less of a diversity of interests and more of a diversity of caste, ethnic, and religious identities. What is new here is not sectarian politics itself. Clearly, the Congress Party by the mid-1960s was never above playing this card. Rather what one is witnessing in the aftermath of the breakup of the Congress canopy is a form of electoral politics in which these identities become the principal means for organizing and negotiating the unity of national political life. What is, however, clear is that social movement activism that represents and allows the state to negotiate a diversity of interests performs a very different democratic function than party and electoral politics. Both of course are concerned with the diversity of India.

In this curious mix may lie the secret to the country's stability and its predicament. Perhaps ironically, especially when considered alongside so much of the third world, India pays a price for its very institutional stability. It is easy to imagine a civil servant from the mid-nineteenth century being perfectly familiar with the broad functioning of India's present institutional structure. Barring the fact of India being a republic and not a colony, the expansion in the number of states and changes in some administrative regulations, there is little in the judicial and administrative structure that has been radically transformed in the last hundred years. In this the Indian experience contrasts sharply with most of Latin America and Africa. But this very stability renders the politics of the country strangely insensitive to changes that cannot easily fit into its extant structure. Hence one observes the peculiar fact of institutions that are unresponsive, inefficient, and corrupt and yet which have a manifest stability to them. Under such conditions these very institutions cannot exhaust the domains within which political life is carried out. For the student of Indian politics this means there has to be sensitivity to the importance of those forms of activity which do not meet the threshold of institutional significance: what we have referred to as a discursive space in which new and transformative meanings are constantly being generated. What this requires is that we weigh the impact of social movement activism against both the benefits *and* the costs of India's much touted political and constitutional stability.

# Bibliography

Aggarwal, J.C. and N.K. Chowdhry, 1998. *Elections in India 1998*. New Delhi: Shipra Publications.

Akbar, M.J., 1985. *India: The Siege Within: Challenges to a Nation's Unity*. Harmondsworth: Penguin.

Akula, Vikram K., 1995. "Grassroots Environmental Activism in India," in Bron Raymond Taylor, ed., *Ecological Resistance Movements: The Global Emergence of Radical and Popular Environmentalism*. Albany: State University of New York Press.

Alvarez, Sonia E., 1997. "Reweaving the Fabric of Collective Action: Social Movements and Challenges to 'Actually Existing Democracy' in Brazil," in Richard G. Fox and Orin Sarn, eds., *Between Resistance and Revolution: Cultural Politics and Social Protest*. New Brunswick: Rutgers University Press.

Alvarez, Sonia E., Evelina Dagnino, and Arturo Escobar, eds., 1998. *Cultures of Politics/Politics of Cultures: Re-visioning Latin American Social Movements*. Boulder, Colo.: Westview Press.

Ambedkar, B.R., 1948. *The Untouchables: Who Were They, and Why They Became Untouchables*. New Delhi: Amrit Book Co.

Amnesty International, 1993. *India: An Unnatural Fate: Disappearances and Impunity in the Indian States of Jammu, Kashmir, and Punjab*. New York: Amnesty International.

Arora, B. and D. Verney, eds., 1995. *Multiple Identities in a Single State*. New Delhi: Konark Publishers.

Asia Watch, 1991. *Punjab in Crisis: Human Rights in India*. Washington, D.C.: Asia Watch.

Austin, G., 1966. *The Indian Constitution: Cornerstone of a Nation*. Oxford: Clarendon Press.

1999. *Working a Democratic Constitution: The Indian Experience*. New Delhi: Oxford University Press.

2000. "Constitution: Ain't Broke, So Why Fix It?" *India Today*, International edition, January 31.

Baar, Carl, 1990. "Social Action Litigation in India: The Operation and Limitations of the World's Most Active Judiciary." *Policy Studies Journal*, 19(1), Fall, 140–150.

Bagchi, Amaresh, 1994. "India's Tax Reform, A Progress Report." *Economic and Political Weekly*, October 22.

Bajpai, Kanti, 1997. "Redefining India's Security." Paper read at an International Institute of Strategic Studies conference, Neemrana.

Ball, T., 1988. *Transforming Political Discourse*. Oxford: Blackwell.

Bardhan, Pranab, 1984. *The Political Economy of Development in India*. Oxford: Blackwell.

Barnett, Marguerite R., 1976. *The Politics of Cultural Nationalism in South India*. Princeton: Princeton University Press.

Basu, Amrita, 1992. *Two Faces of Protest: Contrasting Modes of Women's Activism in India*. Berkeley: University of California Press.

2000. "The Transformation of Hindu Nationalism: Towards a Reappraisal," in Francine R. Frankel, Zoya Hasan, Rajeev Bhargava, and Balveer Arora, eds., *Transforming India: Social and Political Dynamics of Democracy*. New Delhi: Oxford University Press.

Basu, Amrita and Patricia Jeffery, eds., 1998. *Appropriating Gender: Women's Activism and Politicized Religion in South Asia*. New York: Routledge.

Basu, Amrita and Atul Kohli, 1997. "Introduction: Community Conflicts and the State in India." *Journal of Asian Studies*, 56(2), May, 320–324.

Basu, D.D., 1994. *Introduction to the Constitution of India*. New Delhi: Prentice Hall of India.

1999. *Shorter Constitution of India*, twelfth edition. Agra: Wadhwa Law.

Basu, S., 1994. *Jharkhand Movement*. Shimla: Indian Institute of Advanced Study.

Batliwala, Srilatha, 1996. "Transforming of Political Culture: Mahila Samakhya Experience." *Economic and Political Weekly*, May 25.

Baxi, Upendra, 1980. *The Indian Supreme Court and Politics*. Meher Chand Memorial Law Lectures, Lucknow: Eastern Book Company.

1985. *Courage, Craft, and Contention: The Indian Supreme Court in the Eighties*. Bombay: N.M. Tripathi.

Bayly, C.A., 1996. *Empire and Information*. Cambridge: Cambridge University Press.

1998. *Origins of Nationality in South Asia*. Delhi: Oxford University Press.

Beer, S.H., 1993. *To Make a Nation. The Rediscovery of American Federalism*. Cambridge, Mass.: Harvard University Press.

Beiner, R., ed., 1999. *Theorizing Nation*. Albany: State University of New York Press.

Bermeo, Nancy, 1997. "Myths of Moderation: Confrontation and Conflict During Democratic Transitions." *Comparative Politics*, 29(3), April, 305.

Beteillé, André, 1969. *Castes: Old and New. Essays in Social Structure and Social Stratification*. Bombay: Asia Publishing House.

1971. *Caste, Class, and Power: Changing Patterns of Stratification in a Tanjore Village*. Berkeley: University of California Press.

1991. *Society and Politics in India: Essays in a Comparative Perspective*. London School of Economics Monographs on Social Anthropology 63. London: Athlone Press.

Bhabha, Homi, 1994. *The Location of Culture*. London: Routledge.

Bhagwati, Jagdish, 1993. *India in Transition*. Oxford: Clarendon Press.

Bharatiya Janata Party, 1993. *White Paper on Ayodhya and the Ram Temple*. New Delhi: BJP.

Bhattacharya, Harihar, 1997. "Post Colonial Context of Social Capital and Democratic Governance: The Case of West Bengal in India." Unpublished manuscript, Burdwan.

1998. *Micro-Foundations of Bengal Communism*. Delhi: Ajanta.

Bhattacharyya, Dwaipayan, 1993. "Agrarian Reforms and the Politics of the Left." Unpublished Ph.D. dissertation, University of Cambridge.

1996. "Social Capital, Redistributive Reforms, Panchayati Democracy and Norms of Justice in West Bengal." Unpublished paper presented at a conference on Social Capital and Democracy, Toshali Sands, Orissa.

Blomkvist, Hans, ed., 1996. "Democracy and Social Capital in Segmented Societies." Unpublished paper presented at a conference on Social Capital and Democracy, Toshali Sands, Orissa (India).

Bondurant, Joan V., 1958. *Regionalism versus Provincialism: A Study in Problems of Indian National Unity*. Berkeley: University of California Press.

Bose, Sumantra, 1997. *The Challenge of Kashmir: Democracy, Self-Determination and a Just Peace*. New Delhi: Sage.

Braithwaite, Valerie and Margaret Levi, eds., 1998. *Trust and Governance*. New York: Russell Sage Foundation.

Brass, Paul R., 1984–1985. *Caste, Faction and Party in Indian Politics*, vol. I (1984); vol. II (1985). Delhi: Chanakya Publications.

1990. *The Politics of India Since Independence*. Cambridge: Cambridge University Press.

1991. *Ethnicity and Nationalism: Theory and Comparison*. New Delhi and Newbury Park, Calif.: Sage.

1993. *Riots and Pogroms*. Basingstoke: Macmillan.

1997. "National Power and Local Politics in India: A Twenty-Year Perspective," in Partha Chatterjee, ed., *State and Politics in India*. Delhi: Oxford University Press.

Brass, Paul R., ed., 1985. *Ethnic Groups and the State*. Totowa: Barnes and Noble.

Brubaker, C.A., 1998. "Myths and Misconceptions in the Study of Nationalism," in J.A. Hall, ed., *The State of the Nation*. Cambridge: Cambridge University Press.

Byres, T.J., 1988. "A Chicago View of the Indian State: An Oriental Grin Without an Oriental Cat and Political Economy Without Classes." *Journal of Commonwealth and Comparative Politics*, 34(3), November, 246–269.

Center for Monitoring Indian Economy, 1996. *Public Finance in India*. Bombay: Economic Intelligence Service.

Chandra, Bipan et al., 1989. *India's Struggle for Independence*. New Delhi: Penguin.

1999. *India After Independence*. New Delhi: Viking.

Chandra, Kanchan and Chandrika Parmar, 1997. "Party Strategies in the Uttar Pradesh Assembly Elections, 1996." *Economic and Political Weekly*, February 1.

Chatterjee, Partha, 1986a. "The Fruits of Macaulay's Poison Tree," in Asok Mitra, ed., *The Truth Unites*. Calcutta: Subarnarekha.

1986b. *National Thought and the Colonial World: A Derivative Discourse*. London: Zed Books.

1994. "Secularism and Toleration." Economic and Political Weekly, July 9.

1996. *Nationalist Thought and the Colonial World: A Derivative Discourse*. Delhi: Oxford University Press.

Chaudhry, Kiren Aziz, 1997. *The Price of Wealth: Economies and Institutions in the Middle East*. Ithaca: Cornell University Press,.

Chitnis, S., 1990. "Towards a New Social Order," in B.N. Pande, ed., *A Centenary History of the Indian National Congress (1885–1985)*. New Delhi: All India Congress Committee (I).

Copland, I. and J. Richard, eds., 1999. *Federalism: Comparative Perspectives from India and Australia*. New Delhi: Manohar.

Crook, Richard C. and James Manor, 1998. *Democracy and Decentralization in South Asia and West Africa: Participation, Accountability, Performance*. Cambridge: Cambridge University Press.

Dalrymple, W., 1997. "Caste Wars." *Granta*, no. 57, spring.

Dandekar, V.M., 1994. "Role of Economic Planning in India in the 1990s and Beyond." *Economic and Political Weekly*, June 11.

Dasgupta, J., 1970. *Language Conflict and National Development*. Berkeley: University of California Press.

1978. "A Season of Caesars: Emergency Regimes and Development Politics in Asia." *Asian Survey*, 18(4), April.

1981. *Authority, Priority and Human Development*. Delhi: Oxford University Press.

1995. "India: Democratic Becoming and Developmental Transition," in L. Diamond, J.J. Linz and S.M. Lipset, eds., *Politics of Developing Countries*. Boulder, Colo.: Lynne Rienner.

1997. "Community, Authenticity, and Autonomy: Insurgence and Institutional Development in India's Northeast." *Journal of Asian Studies*, 56(2), May, 345.

Dasgupta, S., 1998. "Political Parties: New Chemistry . . . New Equations." *India Today*, July 13.

1999. "Government Formation." *India Today*, international edition, October 18.

Datar, Chhaya, ed., 1993. *The Struggle Against Violence*. Calcutta: Stree.

Datta-Chaudhuri, M., 1997. "Legacies of the Independence Movement to the Political Economy of Independent India." Centre for Development Economics Working Paper 43, April.

Desai, Neera, 1988. *A Decade of Women's Movement in India*. Bombay: Himalaya Publishing House.

Dev, S. Mahendre and Ajit Ranade, 1997. "Poverty and Public Policy," in Kirit S. Parikh, ed., *India Development Report 1997*. Delhi: Oxford University Press.

Diamond, Larry, Juan Linz, and Seymour Martin Lipset, eds., 1990. *Democracy in Developing Countries*. Boulder, Colo.: Lynne Rienner.

Drèze, Jean and Amartya Sen, 1995. *India: Economic Development and Social Opportunity*. New York: Oxford University Press.

Dryzek, John. S., 1996. "From Irrationality to Autonomy: Two Sciences of Institutional Design," in K.E. Soltan and S.I. Elkin, eds., *The Constitution of Good Societies*. University Park: Pennsylvania State University Press.

Dua, Bhagwan, 1979. *Presidential Rule in India*. New Delhi: S. Chand.

1985. "India: Congress Dominance Revisited." Paper presented at the Thirty-Seventh Annual Meeting of the Association for Asian Studies, Philadelphia, March.

Duchachek, I.D., 1991. "Comparative Federalism," in D.J. Elazar, ed., *Constitutional Design and Power-Sharing in the Post-Modern Epoch*. London: University Press of America.

Duncan, Ian, 1997. "New Political Equations in North India: Mayawati, Mulayam, and Government Instability in Uttar Pradesh." *Asian Survey*, 37(10), October.

Dutt, Ramesh Chandra, 1982. *Ramesh Rachanabali* (collected works in Bengali). Calcutta: Sahitya Samsad.

Dwivedi, O.P., 1997. *India's Environmental Policies, Programmes and Stewardship*. Houndmills: Macmillan.

Eckstein, Susan, 1989. *Power and Popular Protest: Latin American Social Movements*. Berkeley: University of California Press.

Elazar, D.J., ed., 1991. *Constitutional Design and Power-Sharing in the Post-Modern Epoch*. London: University Press of America.

Eldridge, Philip and Nil Ratan, 1988. "Voluntary Organisations and Popular Movements in Bihar," *Lokayan Bulletin*, 6(4), 3–44.

Ellis, Joseph J., 1998. *American Sphinx: The Character of Thomas Jefferson*. New York: Vintage Books.

Engineer, Ashgar Ali, 1997. "Communalism and Communal Violence 1996." *Economic and Political Weekly*, February 5.

Environmental Services Group, World Wildlife Fund (India), 1989. *Environmental NGOs in India: A Directory*. New Delhi: The Group.

Eschet-Schwarz, A., 1991. "Can the Swiss Federal Experience Serve as a Model of Federal Integration?" in D.J. Elazar, ed., *Constitutional Design and Power-Sharing in the Post-Modern Epoch*. London: University Press of America.

Escobar, Arturo and Sonia E. Alvarez, 1992. *The Making of Social Movements in Latin America*. Boulder, Colo.: Westview Press.

Fals Borda, Orlando, 1998. *People's Participation: Challenges Ahead*. New York: Apex Press.

Fearon, J.D. and Laitin, D.D., 1996. "Explaining Interethnic Cooperation." *American Political Science Review*, 90(4), December.

Fernandes, Louise, 1995. "Reining in Seshan: The Implications of the Supreme Court Verdict against the CEC." *Sunday*, August 6–12, 32–33.

Flavia, Agnes, 1995. *State, Gender, and the Rhetoric of Law Reform*. Research Center for Women's Studies. Bombay: SNDT Women's University.

Forbes, Geraldine, 1996. *Women in Modern India*. New Cambridge History of India, IV. 2. Cambridge: Cambridge University Press.

Forsyth, Murray, 1989. *Federalism and Nationalism*. Leicester: Leicester University Press.

Franda, M.F., 1968. *West Bengal and the Federalizing Process in India*. Princeton: Princeton University Press.

Frankel, Francine, 1978. *India's Political Economy, 1947–77: The Gradual Revolution*. Princeton: Princeton University Press.

Frankel, Francine and M.S.A. Rao, 1990. *Dominance and State Power in Modern India: Decline of a Social Order*, 2 vols. Oxford: Oxford University Press.

Fraser, Nancy, 1992. "Rethinking the Public Sphere: A Contribution to the Critique of Actually Existing Democracy," in Craig Calhoun, ed., *Habermas and the Public Sphere*. Cambridge, Mass: MIT Press.

Friedman, Thomas L., 1998. "Desperado Democracies: Albania and China and Bonnie and Clyde." *New York Times*, July 14.

Fromm, Erich, 1941. *Escape from Freedom*. New York: Rinehart.

Galanter, Marc, 1983. *Competing Equalities: Law and the Backward Classes in India*. Berkeley: University of California Press.

Gandhi, Nandita and Nandita Shah, 1993. *The Issues at Stake: Theory and Practice in the Contemporary Women's Movement in India*, New Delhi: Kali for Women.

Ganev, Venelin, 1999. "Preying on the State: Political Capitalism After Communism." Ph.D. dissertation, Department of Political Science, University of Chicago.

Ghimire, Yubaraj, 1996. "Free of Strings . . . The Noose Tightens." *Outlook*, March 13.

Ghose, S., 1997, "Redemption on Raisina Hill." *Outlook*, New Delhi, November 3.

Gill, M.S., 1998. "Luncheon Address," in *Conference Report: India's Democracy at Fifty*. Washington: International Forum for Democratic Studies, pp. 24–27.

Gilmour, Ian, 1992. *Riots, Risings and Revolutions: Governance and Violence in Eighteenth Century England*. London: Hutchinson.

Giugni, Marco G., Doug McAdam, and Charles Tilly, 1998. *From Contention to Democracy*. Lanham, Md.: Rowman and Littlefield.

Gombrich, Richard, 1988. *Theravada Buddhism: A Social History from Ancient Benaras to Modern Colombo*. New York: Routledge and Kegan Paul.

Gooch, Pernille, 1997. "Conservation for Whom? Van Gujjars and the Rajaji National Park," in Staffan Lindberg and Arni Sverrisson, eds., *Social Movements in Development: The Challenge of Globalization and Democratization*. New York: St. Martin's Press, pp. 234–252.

Gopal, S., 1976. *Jawaharlal Nehru: A Biography*. vol. 1. New Delhi.

Government of India, 1947–1948. *Constituent Assembly Debates* (CAD), Official Report, New Delhi: Lok Sabha Secretariat Reprint. various volumes.

1955. *Report of the States Reorganization Commission*. New Delhi: Government of India Press.

1956. *Balwantrai Mehta Committee Report*, vol. 1. New Delhi.

1978a. *Report of the Committee on Panchayati Raj Institutions*. New Delhi: Ministry of Agriculture and Irrigation, Department of Rural Development.

1978b. *Shah Commission of Inquiry: Interim Report*, vol. 1. Delhi: Ministry of Home Affairs.

1980. *Report of the Backward Classes Commission*, New Delhi: Government of India.

1988. *Report of the Commission on Center–State Relations* (Sarkaria Commission), 2 vols. New Delhi: Government of India.

1991. *Interim Report of the Tax Reforms*. New Delhi: Ministry of Finance.

1994. *Report of the Tenth Finance Commission.* New Delhi: Government of India.

1997. *Economic Survey.* New Delhi: Government of India.

Government of Karnataka, 1983. *Seminar on Centre–State Relations* (organized by the Economic and Planing Council, Government of Karnataka, in association with the Institute for Social and Economic Change, Bangalore, and the Centre for Policy Research, New Delhi). Bangalore: Government of Karnataka Press.

Government of Tamil Nadu, 1971. *Rajamannar Report on Centre–State Relations.* Madras: Inquiry Committee.

Government of West Bengal, 1978. *Views on Centre–State Relations.* Calcutta: Department of Information and Cultural Affairs.

Govinda Rao, M. and R.J. Chelliah, 1996. *Fiscal Federalism in India.* New Delhi: Indian Council of Social Science Research.

Greve, Michael S., 1987. "Environmentalism and the Rule of Law: Administrative Law and Movement Politics in West Germany and the United States." Ph.D. dissertation submitted to the Department of Government, Cornell University.

Guha, Ramachandram, 1989. *The Unquiet Woods: Ecological Change and Peasant Resistance in the Himalaya.* Berkeley: University of California Press.

1997. "The Environmentalism of the Poor," in Richard G. Fox and Orin Star, *Between Resistance and Revolution: Cultural Politics and Social Protest.* New Brunswick: Rutgers University Press.

Gulhati, Ravi and Kaval Gulhati, with Ajay Mehra and Janaki Rajan, 1995. *Strengthening Voluntary Action in India: Health, Family Planning, the Environment and Women's Development.* New Delhi: Centre for Policy Research and Konark Publishers Pvt. Ltd.

Gupta, Smith, 1996. "It's the Last Resort but it Works." *Sunday Times of India Review,* February 4.

Gurr, Ted Robert, 1971. *Why Men Rebel.* Princeton: Princeton University Press.

Habermas, J., 1989. *The Structural Transformation of the Public Sphere: An Enquiry into a Category of Bourgeois Society.* Cambridge, Mass.: MIT Press.

1993. *Justification and Application.* Cambridge, Mass.: MIT Press.

1998. *Between Facts and Norms.* Cambridge, Mass.: MIT Press.

1999. *The Inclusion of the Other.* Cambridge, Mass.: MIT Press.

Haldar, Mahananda, 1943. *Guruchand Charit.* Khulna: Kalibari.

Hall, J.A., ed., 1998. *The State of the Nation.* Cambridge: Cambridge University Press.

Hamilton, A., J. Jay, and J. Madison, 1941. *The Federalist.* New York: Modern Library.

Hardgrave, Robert L., 1965. *The Dravidian Movement.* Bombay: Popular Prakashan.

1968. *India: Government and Politics in a Developing Nation.* New York: Harcourt, Brace and World.

Harrison, Selig, 1960. *India, The Most Dangerous Decades.* Madras: Oxford University Press.

Hasan, M., ed., 1994. *India's Partition: Process, Strategy and Mobilization.* Delhi: Oxford University Press.

Hasan, Zoya, 1998. "Gender Politics, Legal Reform, and the Muslim Community in India," in Patricia Jeffery and Amrita Basu, eds., *Appropriating Gender: Women's Activism and Politicized Religion in South Asia*. New York: Routledge.

    1999. "Region and Nation in India's Political Transition," in I. Copland and J. Richard., eds., *Federalism: Comparative Perspectives from India and Australia*. New Delhi: Manohar.

Heller, Patrick, 1999. *The Labor of Development: Workers and the Transformation of Capitalism in Kerala, India*. Ithaca: Cornell University Press.

Hellman, Judith Adler, 1994. "Mexican Popular Movements, Clientelism, and the Process of Democratization." *Latin American Perspectives*. Issue 81, 21(2): 124–142.

Hewitt, Vernon, 1995. *Reclaiming the Past: The Search for Political and Cultural Unity in Contemporary Jammu and Kashmir*. London: Portland.

Hipsher, Patricia L., 1998. "Democratic Transitions as Protest Cycles: Social Movement Dynamics in Democratizing Latin America," in David S. Meyer and Sidney Tarrow, eds., *The Social Movement Society: Contentious Politics for a New Century*. New York: Rowman and Littlefield, pp. 153–173.

Hoffer, Eric, 1951. *The True Believer: Thoughts on the Nature of Mass Movements*. New York: Mentor.

Holmes, Stephen, 1997. "What Russia Teaches Us Now: How Weak States Threaten Freedom." *The American Prospect*, no. 33, 30–40.

Horowitz, Donald, 1985. *Ethnic Groups in Conflict*. Berkeley: University of California Press.

Human Rights Watch/Asia 1994. *Dead Silence: The Legacy of Abuses in Punjab*. New York: Human Rights Watch.

Huntington, Samuel P., 1968. *Political Order in Changing Societies*. New Haven, Conn.: Yale University Press.

Indian Law Institute, various dates. *Annual Survey of Indian Law*. New Delhi.

Iyer, S., 1999. "NDA Gives Free Hand to Vajpayee to Recast Government." *Hindustan Times*, New Delhi, October 9.

Jain, L.C. and Karen Coelho, 1996. *In the Wake of Freedom: India's Tryst with Cooperatives*. New Delhi: Concept Publishing House.

Jaising, Indira, 1996. *Justice for Women: Personal Laws, Women's Rights and Law Reform*. Goa: The Other India Press.

Jalal, Rita, 1993. "Preferential Policies and the Movement of the Disadvantaged: The Case of the Scheduled Castes in India." *Ethnic and Racial Studies*, 16(I), January.

Jenkins, R.S., 1997. "Democratic Adjustment: Explaining the Political Sustainability of Economic Reform in India." D. Phil. thesis, University of Sussex.

    2000. *Democratic Politics and Economic Reform in India*. Cambridge: Cambridge University Press.

Jenson, Jane, 1995. "What's in a Name? Nationalist Movements and Public Discourse," in Hank Johnston and Bert Klandermans, eds., *Social Movements and Culture*. Minneapolis: University of Minnesota Press.

Jha, P., 1996. "Which Way Will He Rule?" *Outlook*, May 10.

    1997. "Federal in February?" *Outlook*, New Delhi, March 12.

Forthcoming. "Secularism in the Constituent Assembly Debates, 1946–50." Paper presented at a seminar on the Secular/Communal Question, Institute of Advanced Study, Shimla, May 1997.

Jha, P. and B. Kang, 1996. "The Judiciary Takes Over." *Outlook*, March 6.

Joshi, Barbara R., 1982. *Democracy in Search of Equality: Untouchable Politics and Indian Social Change.* Delhi: Hindustan Publishing Corporation.

Kannabiran, Vasanth and Kalpana Kannabiran, 1995. "Looking at Ourselves: The Women's Movement in Hyderabad," in M. Jacqui Alexander and Chandra Talpade Mohanty, eds., *Feminist Genealogies, Colonial Legacies, Democratic Futures.* New York: Routledge, 259–280.

1997. "From Social Action to Political Action: Women and the 81st Amendment." *Economic and Political Weekly*, February 1.

Kapur, Ratna and Brenda Cossman, 1996. *Subversive Sites: Feminist Engagements with Law in India.* New Delhi: Sage.

Karl, Terry Lynn, 1990. "Dilemmas of Democratization in Latin America." *Comparative Politics*, October.

Karlekar, Malavika, Anuja Agrawal, and Maithili Ganjoo, 1995. *No Safe Spaces: Report of a Workshop on Violence Against Women*, March 27–28. Delhi: Centre for Women's Development.

Katzenstein, Mary, 1979. *Ethnicity and Equality: The Shiv Sena Party and Preferential Policies in Bombay.* Ithaca: Cornell University Press.

1989. "Organizing Against Violence: Strategies of the Indian Women's Movement." *Pacific Affairs*, 62(1), spring, 58–71.

1991–2. "Getting Women's Issues onto the Public Agenda: Body Politics in India." *Samya Shakti* (Journal of the Center for Women in Developing Societies, New Delhi), 6.

Katzenstein, Mary, Uday Mehta and Usha Thakkar, 1997. "The Rebirth of Shiv Sena: The Symbiosis of Discursive and Organizational Power." *Journal of Asian Studies*, 56(2), May, 371–391.

Katzenstein, Peter J., 1998. *Left-Wing Violence and State Response: United States, Germany, Italy and Japan, 1960s–1990s.* Ithaca: Cornell University Press.

Kaviraj, S., 1996. "Democracy and Development in India." Unpublished paper, School of Oriental and African Studies, London.

Keck, Margaret E., 1992. *The Workers' Party and Democrataization in Brazil.* New Haven: Yale University Press.

Khanna, B.S., 1994. *Panchayati Raj in India.* Delhi: Deep and Deep.

Khator, Renu, 1991. *Environment, Development and Politics in India.* Lanham, Md.: University Press of America.

Kishwar, Madhu and Ruth Vanita, 1989. "Indian Women: A Decade of New Ferment," in Marshall M. Bouton and Philip Oldenburg, eds., *Indian Briefing.* Boulder, Colo.: Westview Press.

Kohli, Atul, 1987. *The State and Poverty in India: Politics of Reform.* Cambridge: Cambridge University Press.

1990. *Democracy and Discontent: India's Growing Crisis of Governability.* Cambridge: Cambridge University Press.

1997. "Can Democracies Accommodate Ethnic Nationalism? Rise and Decline of Self-Determination Movements in India." *Journal of Asian Studies*, 56(2), May, 325–44.

Kornhauser, William, 1959. *The Politics of Mass Society.* Glencoe, Ill.: Free Press.

Kothari, Rajni, 1970a. *Caste in Indian Politics.* New Delhi: Orient Longman.

1970b. *Politics in India.* Boston: Little Brown and Company.

1997. "Rise of the Dalits and the Renewed Debate on Caste," in Partha Chatterjee, ed., *States and Politics in India.* New Delhi: Oxford University Press.

Kothari, Smitu, 1993. "Social Movements and the Redefinition of Democracy," in Philip Oldenburg, ed., *India Briefing, 1993.* Boulder, Colo.: Westview Press for the Asia Society.

1996. "Whose Nation? The Displaced as Victims of Development." *Economic and Political Weekly,* June 15.

2000a. "To Be Governed or to Self-Govern." *The Hindu Folio,* July.

2000b. "A Million Mutinies Now: Lesser Known Environmental Movements in India." *Humanscope,* October.

Kothari, Smitu and Pramod Parajuli, 1998. "Struggling for Autonomy: Lessons from Local Governance." *Development,* 14(3).

Kudva, Neema, 1996. "Uneasy Partnerships? Government–NGO Relations in India." Working paper 673, University of California at Berkeley: Institute of Urban and Regional Development.

Kumar, P., 1988. *Studies in Indian Federalism.* New Delhi: Deep and Deep.

Kumar, Radha, 1993. *The History of Doing: An Illustrated Account of Movements for Women's Rights and Feminism in India 1800–1990.* Delhi: Kali for Women.

Kymlicka, W., 1995. *Multicultural Citizenship.* Oxford: Oxford University Press.

1999. "Misunderstanding Nationalism," in R. Beiner, ed., *Theorizing Nationalism.* Albany: State University of New York Press.

Levy, Harold, 1973. "Indian Modernization by Legislation: The Hindu Code Bill." Ph.D. dissertation, Political Science Department, University of Chicago.

Lijphart, Arendt, 1996. "The Puzzle of Indian Democracy: A Consociational Interpretation." *American Political Science Review,* 90(2), 258–268.

Lindberg, Staffan, 1997. "Farmers' Movements and Agricultural Development in India," in Staffan Lindberg and Arni Sverrisson, eds., *Social Movements in Development: The Challenge of Globalization and Democratization.* New York: St. Martin's Press, pp. 101–126.

Linder, S. and Guy Peters, B., 1995. "The Two Traditions of Institutional Designing," in D. Weiner, ed., *Institutional Design.* Boston: Kluwer Academic Publishing.

Loveridge, Patricia, 1994. "Approaches to Change: The All India Democratic Women's Association and a Marxist Approach to the Woman Question in India." *Indian Journal of Gender Studies,* 1(2), July–Dec., 215–243.

Madan, T.N., 1987. "Secularism in Its Place." *Journal of Asian Studies,* 46(4).

1993. "Whither Indian Secularism." *Modern Asian Studies,* 27(3).

Madsen, Stig Toft, 1997. "Between People and the State: NGOs as Troubleshooters and Innovators," in Staffan Lindberg and Arni Sverrisson, eds., *Social Movements in Development: The Challenge of Globalization and Democratization.* New York: St. Martin's Press, pp. 252–275.

Mahalingham, S., 1996. "Matters of Conduct: Election Commission Directives Loom Large." *Frontline,* May 3.

Mahar, Michael J., ed., 1972. *Untouchables in Contemporary India*. Tucson: University of Arizona Press.

Mainwaring, Scott, 1987. "Urban Popular Movements, Identity, and Democratization in Brazil." *Comparative Political Studies*, 20(2), July, 131–159.

Majumdar, Bimanbehari, 1965. *Indian Political Associations and Reform of Legislature, 1818–1917*. Calcutta: Firma K.L. Mukhopadhyray.

Majumdar, B.B. and B.P. Majumdar, 1967. *Congress and Congressmen in the Pre-Gandhian Era, 1885–1917*. Calcutta: Firma K.L. Mukhopadhyay.

Manor, James, 1978. "Where Congress Survived: Five States in the Indian General Election of 1977." *Asian Survey*, August, 785–803.

    1989. "Karnataka: Caste, Class, Dominance and Politics in a Cohesive Society," in Francine R. Frankel and M.S.A. Rao, eds., *Dominance and State Power in Modern India: Decline of a Social Order*. New Delhi: Oxford University Press.

    1990. "How and Why Liberal and Representative Politics Emerged in India." *Political Studies*, 33(1), March.

    1996. "Political Regeneration in India," in D.L. Seth and A. Nandy, eds., *The Multiverse of Democracy: Essays in Honour of Rajni Kothari*. New Delhi, Thousand Oaks and London: Sage, pp. 230–241.

March, J.G., 1997. "Administrative Practice, Organizational Theory, and Political Philosophy." *PS: Political Science and Politics*. 30(4), December.

Markovits, Andrei S. and Philip S. Gorski, 1993. *The German Left: Red, Green and Beyond*. Cambridge: Polity Press.

Marriot, McKim and Ronald B. Inden, 1974. "Caste Systems," in *Encyclopedia Britannica*. Chicago.

Masani, M.R., 1975. *Is J.P. the Answer?* New Delhi: Macmillan.

McAdam, Doug, 1982. *Political Process and the Development of Black Insurgency*. Chicago: University of Chicago Press.

McAdam, Doug, John D. McCarthy, and Mayer N. Zald, 1996. *Comparative Perspectives on Social Movements: Political Opportunities, Mobilizing Structures, and Cultural Framings*. Cambridge: Cambridge University Press.

McLane, J.R., 1977. *Indian Nationalism and the Early Congress*. Princeton: Princeton University Press.

Meyer, David S. and Sidney Tarrow, 1998. *The Social Movement Society: Contentious Politics for a New Century*. Boulder, Colo.: Rowman and Littlefield.

Milne, D., 1993. "Whither Canadian Federalism? Alternative Constitutional Futures," in M. Burgess and A. Gagnon, eds., *Comparative Federalism and Federation*. Toronto: University of Toronto Press.

Mitra, Chandan, 1997. "Unholy Alliances." *Seminar*, no. 454, June.

Mitra, S. and F. Ahmed, 2000. "The Constitution, Review Rift," *India Today*, international edition, February 14.

Mitra, Subrata K., 1990. "Between Transaction and Transcendence: The State and the Institutionalization of Power in India," in Subrata Mitra, ed., *The Post-Colonial State in Asia: Dialectics of Politics and Culture*. Hemel Hempstead: Harvester, pp. 73–99.

    1991. "Room to Manoeuvre in the Middle: Local Elites, Political Action and the State in India." *World Politics*, 43(3).

1999a. *Culture and Rationality.* Delhi: Sage.

1999b. "India," in Gabriel Almond, Richard Dalton, Bingham Powell, and Kaare Strom, eds., *Comparative Politics Today.* New York: Addison Wesley Longman.

1999c. "Effects of Institutional Arrangements on Political Stability in South Asia." *Annual Review of Political Science,* Palo Alto, 2, 405–428.

Mitra, Subrata K. and V.B. Singh, 1999. *Democracy and Social Change in India.* Delhi: Sage.

Mohanty, Bidyut, 1995. "Panchayati Raj, 73rd Constitutional Amendment and Women." *Economic and Political Weekly,* December 30.

Moore, Barrington Jr., 1966. *Social Origins of Dictatorship and Democracy: Lord and Peasant in the Making of the Modern World.* Boston: Beacon Press.

Morris-Jones, W.H., 1992. "Shaping the Post Imperial State: Nehru's Letters to Chief Ministers," in M. Twaddle, ed., *Imperialism, the State and the Third World.* London: British Academic Press.

Mozoomdar, Ajit, 1995. "The Supreme Court and Presidents' Rule," in B. Arora and D. Verney, eds., *Multiple Identities in a Single State.* New Delhi: Konark Publishers.

Mukherjee, N. and D. Bandopadhyay, 1994. "New Horizons for West Bengal Panchayats," in A. Mukherjee, ed., *Decentralisation of Panchayats in the 1990s.* New Delhi: Vikas.

Muralidharan, S. 1998a. "The Task of Elections: A Presidential Intervention Becalms the Atmosphere in the Election Commission as it Prepares to Supervise the World's Biggest Democratic Exercise." *Frontline,* January 9, 4–5, 9–11.

1998b. "Law and Practice: Indian Electoral Law Lags Behind the Growing Vigour of its Democracy." *Frontline,* January 9, 13–16.

1998c. "Who's Afraid of Article 356?" *Frontline,* July 17.

Murphy, W.F., 1993. "Constitutions, Constitutionalism, and Democracy," in D. Greenberg, ed., *Constitutionalism and Democracy.* New York: Oxford University Press.

Naipaul, V.S., 1990. *India: A Million Mutinies Now.* London: Heinemann.

Nandy, Ashish, 1990. "The Politics of Secularism and the Recovery of Religious Tolerance," in Veena Das, ed., *Mirrors of Violence,* Delhi: Oxford University Press.

Nayar, Kuldip and Khushwant Singh, 1984. *Tragedy of Punjab: Operation Bluestar and After.* New Delhi: Vision Books.

Nehru, Jawaharlal, 1960. *A Bunch of Old Letters.* New York: Asian Publishing House.

1983. *The Discovery of India.* New Delhi: Oxford University Press. (First published by Signet Press, Calcutta, 1946.)

Nigam, Aditya, 1986. "India After the 1996 Elections: Nation." *Asian Survey,* 36(29), December, 1157–1169.

Noorani, A.G., (1991). "BJP: Child of RSS and Heir to Hindu Mahasabha." *Mainstream,* July 27.

Noorani, A.G., ed., 1981. *Public Law in India.* New Delhi: Vikas, pp. 293–300.

Nossiter, Tom, 1988. *Marxist State Governments in India.* London: Pinter Press.

O'Donnell, Guillermo, Phillippe C. Schmitter, and Laurence Whitehead, eds.,

1986. *Transitions from Authoritarian Rule*. Baltimore: Johns Hopkins University Press.

Offe, Claus, 1985. *Disorganized Capitalism: Contemporary Transformations of Work and Politics*, ed. John Keane. Cambridge, Mass.: MIT Press.

Omvedt, Gail, 1993. *Reinventing Revolution: New Social Movements and the Socialist Tradition in India*. Armonk, N.Y.: M.E. Sharpe.

1994. *Dalits and the Democratic Revolution*. New Delhi: Sage.

Oomen, T.K., 1990. *Protest and Change: Studies in Social Movements*. New Delhi: Sage.

Ostergaard, Geoffrey, 1985. *Non-Violent Revolution in India*. New Delhi: Gandhi Peace Foundation.

Pal, Bepinchandra, 1905. "Composite Nationalism: The Nationalist View." *New India*, May 27. (Reprinted Pal, 1954. *Swadeshi and Swaraj*. Calcutta: n.p.).

Pandey, Gyanendra, 1991. "In Defense of the Fragment: Writing about Hindu–Muslim Riots in India Today." *Economic and Political Weekly*, annual number.

Panneeselvan, A.S., 1996. "The Small Screen Takes Over." *Outlook*, April 24, 16–17.

Parthasarathy, D., 1997. *Collective Violence in a Provincial City*, New Delhi: Oxford University Press.

Patil, S.H., 1981. *The Congress Party and Princely States*. Bombay: Himalaya.

Pattnaik, R.K. et al., 1994. "Resource Gap of the State Governments: Measurement and Analysis," in *Reserve Bank of India Occasional Papers*, 15(4), December, 315–367.

Potter, David, 1986. *India's Political Administrators: 1919–1983*. Oxford: Clarendon Press.

Pradhan, S. 1998a. "The Great Survivor," *Sunday*, March 8–14.

Prasad, Bimal, 1992. *Jayaprakash Narayan*. New Delhi: Vikas.

Prasad, K. and A. Bahal, 1998. "Trident Missile." *Outlook*, April 6.

Przeworski, Adam, 1986. "Some Problems in the Study of the Transition to Democracy," in Guillermo O'Donnell, Philippe Schmitter, and Laurence Whitehead, eds., *Transitions from Authoritarian Rule*. Baltimore: Johns Hopkins University Press.

Putnam, Robert D., 1993. *Making Democracy Work: Civic Traditions in Modern Italy*. Princeton: Princeton University Press.

Qasim, S.M., 1992. *My Life and Times*. Delhi.

Rajadhyaksha, A. and P. Willemen, eds., 1999, 1995. *Encyclopaedia of Indian Cinema*. New Delhi: Oxford University Press.

Rajkumar, N.V., 1949. *Development of the Congress Constitution*. New Delhi: All India Congress Committee.

Ramachandra, V.K., Vikas Rawal, and Madhura Swaminathan, 1997. "Investment Gaps in Primary Education: A Statewise Study." *Economic and Political Weekly*, January 4–11.

Ramachandran, Vimala, 1996. "NGOs in the Time of Globalization." *Seminar*, November 1, 54–59.

Rani, Sarita, 1995. "What Now? T.N. Sechan Ponders His Future." *Sunday*, August 6–12, 28–35.

1998. "Confused Bureau of Investigation?" *Sunday*, January 4–10, 24–26.

Rao, M.S.A., 1989. "Some Conceptual Issues in the Study of Caste, Class, Ethnicity and Dominance," in Francine Frankel and M.S.A. Rao, eds., *Dominance and State Power in Modern India*. New Delhi: Oxford University Press.

Rao, R.S., 1999. "Federalism and Fiscal Autonomy of States: The Indian Experience," in I. Copland and J. Richard, eds., *Federalism: Comparative Perspectives from India and Australia*. New Delhi: Manohar.

Ratnapala, Sur, 1999. "Federalism as a Response to Ethnic Regionalism," in I. Copland and J. Richard, eds., *Federalism: Comparative Perspectives from India and Australia*. New Delhi: Manohar.

Ravindra, R.P., 1993. "The Campaign Against Sex Determination Tests," in Chhaya Datar, ed., *The Struggle Against Violence*. Calcutta: Stree, pp. 51–99.

Rawls, John (1993). *Political Liberalism*. New York: Columbia University Press.

Ray, Raka, 1998. "Women's Movements and Political Fields: A Comparison of Two Indian Cities." *Social Problems*, March.

Reddy, G. Ram, 1989, "The Politics of Accommodation: Caste, Class and Dominance in Andhra Pradesh," in F.R. Frankel and M.S.A. Rao, eds., *Dominance and State Power in Modern India*, vol. I. Delhi: Oxford University Press.

Reserve Bank of India, 1996. *Report on Currency and Finance, 1995–96*, vols. I and II. Bombay: Reserve Bank of India.

Rorty, R., 1998. *Achieving Our Country*. Cambridge, Mass.: Harvard University Press.

Roy, Bunker, 1985. "For Prime Minister, A Word of Advice." *Mainstream*, March 9.

Rudolph, Lloyd and Susanne Hoeber Rudolph, 1967. *The Modernity of Tradition: Political Development in India*. Chicago: University of Chicago Press.

1987. *In Pursuit of Lakshmi: The Political Economy of the Indian State*. Chicago: University of Chicago Press.

Rudolph, Matthew C.J., 1998. "Making Markets: Financial Organization, Economic Transitions, and the Emergence of the Regulatory State in India and China." Ph.D. proposal, Department of Government, Cornell University.

Saez, Lawrence, 1999. "Rethinking Federalism: Party Realignment and Inter-Governmental Relations in India," Ph.D. dissertation, Department of Political Science, University of Chicago.

Sanyal, Bishwapriya, 1997. "NGOs' Self-Defeating Quest for Autonomy." *Annals of the American Academy of Political and Social Science*, 554, November, 21.

Saran, R., 2000. "State Finances." *India Today*, international edition, February 14.

Sarkar, Lotika, 1995. "Women's Movement and the Legal Process." Occasional paper 24, New Delhi: Centre for Women's Development Studies.

Sarkar, Sumit, 1983. *Modern India 1885–1947*. Delhi: Macmillan India.

1996. "Authenticity, Community, and the Anti-Secularist Critique of Hindutva," in Rajeswari Ghose, ed., *In Quest of a Secular Symbol: Ayodhya and After*. Perth: Curtin University of Technology.

1997. *Writing Social History*. Delhi: Oxford University Press.

Forthcoming. "Secularism, Western and Indian." Paper presented at a seminar on the Secular/Communal Question, Institute of Advanced Study, Shimla, May 1997.

Sarkar, Tanika, 1999. *Words to Win: The Making of Amar Jivan, A Modern Autobiography.* Delhi: Kali for Women.

Sarker, P.C., 1994. "Regional Imbalances in Indian Economy Over Plan Periods." *Economic and Political Weekly,* March 12.

Schofield, Victoria, 1996. *Kashmir in the Crossfire.* London: St. Martin's Press.

Scott, James C., 1985. *Weapons of the Weak: Everyday Forms of Peasant Resistance.* New Haven: Yale University Press.

Sen, A.K., 1996. "Secularism and Its Discontents," in Kaushik Basu and Sanjay Subramanium, eds., *Unravelling the Nation.* Delhi: Penguin India.

1997. "Radical Needs and Moderate Reforms," in J. Dreze and A. Sen., eds., *Indian Development: Selected Regional Perspectives.* Delhi: Oxford University Press.

Sethi, Harsh and Smitu Kothari, 1985. *The Non-Party Political Process: Uncertain Alternatives.* Geneva/Delhi: NRISD/Lokayan.

Shah, Nandita and Nandita Gandhi, 1991. *The Quota Question: Women and Electoral Seats.*

Shiva Rao, B., ed., 1964. *The Framing of India's Constitution: Select Documents* (SD), vols. I, II. Delhi: n.p.

1966. *The Framing of India's Constitution: Select Documents,* vol. I. New Delhi: Oxford University Press.

1968. *The Framing of India's Constitution: A Study.* New Delhi: Indian Institute of Public Administration.

Sider, Gerald M., 1993. *Lumbee Indian Histories: Race, Ethnicity and Indian Identity in the Southern United States.* Cambridge: Cambridge University Press.

Sing, N.K., 1996, "Hindu Divided Family." *India Today,* December 15, 69.

Sirsikar, V.M., 1995. *Politics of Modern Maharashtra.* London: Sangam Books.

Smith, Anthony (1995). *Nations and Nationalism in a Global Era.* Cambridge, Mass.: Polity Press.

de Souza, Peter Ronald, 1998. "The Election Commission and Electoral Reforms in India," in D.D. Khanna, L.L. Mehrotra, and Gert W. Kueck, eds., *Democracy, Diversity, Stability: 50 Years of Indian Independence.* Delhi: Macmillan, pp. 51–52.

Srinivas, M.N., 1962. *Caste in Modern India and Other Essays.* Bombay: Asia Publishing House.

1989. *The Cohesive Role of Sanskritization and Other Essays.* Delhi: Oxford University Press.

Stepan, A., 1999. "Modern Multinational Democracies," in J.A. Hall, *The State of the Nation.* Cambridge: Cambridge University Press.

Subramanian, Narendra, 1999. *Ethnicity and Populist Mobilization: Political Parties, Citizens and Democracy in South India.* Delhi: Oxford University Press.

Swain, Ashok, 1997. "Democratic Consolidation? Environmental Movements, in India." *Asian Survey,* 37, September, 818–832.

Swami, P. and S. Mahalingam, 1998. "The BJP's Bihar Fiasco." *Frontline,* Chennai, October 23.

Sztompka, Piotor, 1999. *Trust: A Sociological Theory.* Cambridge: Cambridge University Press.

Tarrow, Sidney, 1991. *Struggle, Politics and Reform: Collective Action, Social Movements and Cycles of Protest.* Ithaca: Center for International Studies, Cornell University.

1994. *Power in Movement: Collective Action, Social Movements, and Politics.* Cambridge: Cambridge University Press.

1996. "Making Social Science Work Across Space and Time: A Critical Reflection on Putnam's *Making Democracy Work.*" *American Political Science Review,* 90(2), June, 389–398.

Taylor, C., 1999. "Nationalism and Modernity," in R. Beiner, *Theorizing Nation.* Albany: State University of New York Press.

Tilly, Charles, 1975. "Food Supply and Public Order in Modern Europe," in Charles Tilly, ed., *The Formation of Modern States in Western Europe.* Princeton: Princeton University Press, pp. 380–425.

1978. *From Mobilization to Revolution.* Reading, Mass.: Addison-Wesley.

Tocqueville, A. de, 1954 [1835]. *Democracy in America,* vol. II. New York: Vintage.

1990 [1835]. *Democracy in America,* vol. I. New York: Vintage.

Tully, Mark and Satish Jacob, 1985. *Amritsar: Mrs. Gandhi's Last Battle.* London: Jonathan Cape.

Twaddle, M., ed., 1992. *Imperialism, the State, and the Third World.* London: British Academic Press.

Varshney, Ashutosh, 1998. "India Defies the Odds: Why Democracy Survives." *Journal of Democracy,* July, 36–50.

2000. "Is India Becoming More Democratic?" *Journal of Asian Studies,* February.

Venkataraman, R., 1975. *My Presidential Years.* New Delhi: HarperCollins.

Venkatesan, V., 1996. "A Complex Process: The Election Machinery at Work," and "Surprises in Store: Interview with M.S. Gill." *Frontline,* April 19, 29–31.

2000. "A Controversial Review." *Frontline,* Chennai, March 3.

Verghese, B.G., 1997. *India's Northeast Resurgent: Ethnicity, Insurgency, Governance, Development.* Delhi: Konark.

Visvanathan, V., 1997. *Economic and Political Weekly,* September 20.

Walker, B., 1999. "Modernity and Cultural Vulnerability," in R. Beiner, *Theorizing Nation.* Albany: State University of New York Press.

Wallace, Paul, 1995. "Political Violence and Terrorism in India," in Martha Crenshaw, ed., *Terrorism in Context.* University of Pennsylvania State University Press, pp. 352–409.

1997. "Sikh Nationalist Terrorism in India," in Martha Crenshaw and John Pimlott, eds., *Encyclopedia of World Terrorism,* vol. II. New York: M.E. Sharpe, pp. 478–481.

Wallich, C., 1982. *State Finances in India,* vol. I. Washington, D.C.: World Bank.

Washbrook, David A., 1989. "Caste, Class and Dominance in Modern Tamil Nadu: NonBrahmanism, Dravidianism and Tamil Nationalism," in Francine R. Frankel and M.S.A. Rao, eds., *Dominance and State Power in Modern India: Decline of a Social Order.* New Delhi, Oxford University Press.

Weiner, Myron, 1957. *Party Politics in India*. Princeton: Princeton University Press.

1962a. *The Politics of Scarcity: Public Pressure and Political Response in India*. Chicago: University of Chicago Press.

1962b. "Political Parties and Panchayati Raj." *Indian Journal of Public Administration*, 8(4), 623–628. Reprinted 1981 in T.N. Chaturvedi and R.B. Jain, eds., *Panchayati Raj*. Delhi: IIPA, pp. 93–98.

1967. *Party Building in a New Nation: The Indian National Congress*. Chicago: University of Chicago Press.

1983. "The Political Consequences of Preferential Policies: India in Comparative Perspective." *Comparative Politics*, October.

1987. "Empirical Democratic Theory," in Myron Weiner and Ergun Ozbudun, eds., *Competitive Elections in Developing Countries*. Durham, N.C.: Duke University Press.

1989. *The Indian Paradox: Essays in Indian Politics*. New Delhi: Sage.

1991. *The Child and the State in India*. Princeton: Princeton University Press.

Wheare, K. C., 1952. *Federal Government*. New York: Oxford University Press.

Women Towards Beijing: Voices from India, 1995. *Lokayan Bulletin* 12(1/2), July–October.

World Bank, 1995. *India, Recent Economic Development and Prospects*. Washington, D.C.

1996. *India's Five Years of Stabilization and Reform and the Challenges Ahead*. Washington, D.C.

Zaidi, A.M., ed., 1987. *The Muslim School of Congress: The Political Ideas of Muslim Congress Leaders from Mr. Badruddin Tayyabji to Maulana Abul Kalam Azad, 1885–1947*. New Delhi: Indian Institute of Applied Political Research.

Zelliot, Eleanor, 1991. "Dalit: New Perspectives on India's Untouchables," in Philip Oldenburg, ed., *India Briefing*. Boulder, Colo.: Westview, pp. 93–122.

Zirakzadeh, Cyrus Ernesto, 1997. *Social Movements in Politics: A Comparative Study*. New York: Addison Wesley Longman.

# Index